Basic Ship Theory   Volume 2

Basic Ship Theory

K. J. Rawson
R.C.N.C., C.Eng., F.R.I.N.A., Wh.Sch.

E. C. Tupper
B.Sc., R.C.N.C., C.Eng., F.R.I.N.A., Wh.Sch.

2nd. Edition in two volumes
Volume 2
Chapters 10 to 16

Ship Dynamics and Design

Longman   London and New York

LONGMAN GROUP LIMITED

London and New York

Associated companies, branches and representatives throughout the world

Published in the United States of America by
Longman Inc., New York

First published 1968
Second edition 1976 (*in two volumes*)
Second impression 1977

Volume 1 ISBN 0 582 44523 X
Volume 2 ISBN 0 582 44524 8

of 8907336

Set in Times New Roman
and Printed in Hong Kong by Wing King Tong Company Limited

Contents

Volume 1

Hydrostatics and Strength

Preface to Second Edition   vii

Foreword to the First Edition   viii

Introduction   ix

Symbols and nomenclature   xvi

1 Art or Science?   1

2 Some tools   7

3 Flotation and trim   55

4 Stability   93

5 Hazards and protection   146

6 The ship girder   175

7 Structural design and analysis   226

8 Launching and docking   275

9 The ship environment   291

Answers to problems   xxi

Index   xxv

Volume 2 Ship Dynamics and Design

Introduction   ix

Symbols and nomenclature   xiii

10 Powering of ships: general principles   340

Fluid dynamics Components of resistance and propulsion Effective horsepower — Types of resistance — Wave-making resistance — Frictional resistance — Viscous pressure resistance — Air resistance — Appendage resistance — Residuary resistance — The propulsion device — The screw propeller — Special types of propeller — Alternative means of propulsion — Momentum theory applied to the screw propeller — The blade element approach — Cavitation — Singing — Interaction between ship and propeller — Hull efficiency — Overall propulsive efficiency — Ship–model correlation Model testing Resistance tests — Resistance test facilities and techniques — Model determination of hull efficiency elements — Propeller tests in open water — Cavitation tunnel tests Ship trials Speed trials — Experiments at full scale Summary Concluding remarks Problems References

11 Powering of ships: application   383

Presentation of data Resistance data — The Froude 'constant' notation — Taylor notation — Propeller data Power estimation Resistance prediction — Froude method — ITTC ship–model correlation line — Effect of small changes of dimensions — Variation of skin frictional resistance with time out of dock — Calculation of wind resistance — Propeller design — Choice of propeller dimensions — Propeller design diagram — Influence of form on resistance — Reducing wave-making resistance — Triplets — Compatibility of machinery and propeller — Strength of propellers — Effect of speed on endurance Summary Concluding remarks Problems References

12 Seakeeping   424

Seakeeping qualities Ship motions Undamped motion in still water — Damped motion in still water — Approximate period of roll — Motion in regular waves — Presentation of motion data — Motion in irregular seas — Oblique and following seas — Motion in oblique seas — Surge, sway and yaw Speed and power in waves Wetness Slamming Ship stabilization Stabilization systems — Brief descriptions of systems — Comparison of principal systems — Performance of stabilizing systems Experiments and trials Model experiments — Ship trials — Stabilizer trials Theory Influence of form on seakeeping Longitudinal bending in waves Concluding remarks Problems References

13 Manoeuvrability   476

Theory Directional stability or dynamic stability of course — Theory of directional stability — The action of a rudder in turning a ship Measurement of manoeuvrability The turning circle — The zig-zag manoeuvre — The spiral manoeuvre — Standards for manoeuvring and directional stability Rudder forces and torques Rudder force — Centre of pressure position — Calculation of force and torque on non-rectangular rudder Experiments and trials Model experiments concerned with turning and manoeuvring — Model experiments concerned with directional stability — Ship trials Rudder types and systems Types of rudder — Bow rudders and lateral thrust units — Special rudders and manoeuvring devices — Automatic control systems Ship handling Turning at slow speed or when stopped — Interaction between ships when close aboard Stability and control of submarines Experiments and trials Design assessment Modifying dynamic stability derivatives — Efficiency of control surfaces Effect of design parameters on manoeuvring Concluding remarks Problems References

14 Major ship design features 523

Machinery Electrical generation Systems Electrical distribution system — Piping systems — Air conditioning and Ventilation — Fuel systems — Sewage systems and waste disposal — Cathodic protection Equipment Cargo handling — Replenishment of provisions — Boats and davits Weapons The ship–weapon system — Shipfitting problems Accommodation Measurement New tonnage regulations *Problems* References

15 Ship design 564

Requirements Warships — Merchant ships Design studies Preliminary studies — Internal volume — Principal dimensions — Displacement and deadweight — Machinery power — Choice of form — Weather deck layout and profile Design development Contract design — The design spiral — Appearance and layout Detailed design Drawing schedules and procedure charts Support functions Design influence diagrams — Network planning — Dependency diagrams — Work study — Design method — Value engineering In service Reliability — Maintainability — Surveys *Problems* References

16 Special ship types 597

Passenger ships Submarines Hydrofoil craft Ground effect machines Catamarans Aircraft carriers Bulk cargo carriers Fishing vessels Tugs Offshore drilling rigs Yachts References

Answers to problems xviii

Index xx

Introduction

Volume 1 of *Basic Ship Theory* has presented fundamental work on ship shape, static behaviour, hazards and protection and upon ship strength. It has also described in detail the environment in which marine vehicles have to work and the properties of the sea and the air. Now we are in a position to discuss the dynamic behaviour of ships and other vehicles in the complex environment in which they operate and how those surroundings can be controlled to the maximum comfort of vehicle and crew. We can also enter upon the creative activity of ship design.

Familiarity with Volume 1 has been assumed throughout but for convenience, certain conversion factors, preferred values and symbols and nomenclature are repeated here.

Special names have been adopted for some of the derived SI units and these are listed below together with their unit symbols:

Physical quantity	SI unit	Unit symbol
Force	newton	$N = kg\,m/s^2$
Work, energy	joule	$J = N\,m$
Power	watt	$W = J/s$
Electric charge	coulomb	$C = A\,s$
Electric potential	volt	$V = W/A$
Electric capacitance	farad	$F = A\,s/V$
Electric resistance	ohm	$\Omega = V/A$
Frequency	hertz	$Hz = s^{-1}$
Illumination	lux	$lx = lm/m^2$

In the following two tables are listed other derived units and the equivalent values of some UK units respectively:

Physical quantity	SI unit	Unit symbol	
Area	square metre	m^2	
Volume	cubic metre	m^3	
Density	kilogramme per cubic metre	kg/m^3	
Velocity	metre per second	m/s	
Angular velocity	radian per second	rad/s	
Acceleration	metre per second squared	m/s^2	
Angular acceleration	radian per second squared	rad/s^2	
Pressure, Stress	newton per square metre	N/m^2	(Note: N/m^2 is known
Surface tension	newton per metre	N/m	also as a pascal. 10^5
Dynamic viscosity	newton second per metre squared	$N\,s/m^2$	N/m^2 is also known as
Kinematic viscosity	metre squared per second	m^2/s	a bar.)
Thermal conductivity	watt per metre degree Kelvin	$W/(m°K)$	

Quantity	UK unit	Equivalent SI units
Length	1 yd	0·9144 m
	1 ft	0·3048 m
	1 in	0·0254 m
	1 mile	1609·344 m
	1 nautical mile (UK)	1853·18 m
	1 nautical mile (International)	1852 m
Area	1 in^2	645·16 × 10^{-6} m^2
	1 ft^2	0·092903 m^2
	1 yd^2	0·836127 m^2
	1 mile^2	2·58999 × 10^6 m^2
Volume	1 in^3	16·3871 × 10^{-6} m^3
	1 ft^3	0·0283168 m^3
	1 UK gal	0·004546092 m^3
Velocity	1 ft/s	0·3048 m/s
	1 mile/hr	0·44704 m/s; 1·60934 km/hr
	1 knot (UK)	0·51477 m/s; 1·85318 km/hr
	1 knot (International)	0·51444 m/s; 1·852 km/hr
Standard acceleration, g	32·174 ft/s^2	9·80665 m/s^2
Mass	1 lb	0·45359237 kg
	1 ton	1016·05 kg
Mass density	1 lb/in^3	27·6799 × 10^3 kg/m^3
	1 lb/ft^3	16·0185 kg/m^3
Force	1 pdl	0·138255 N
	1 lbf	4·44822 N
Pressure	1 lbf/in^2	6894·76 N/m^2
Stress	1 tonf/in^2	15·4443 × 10^6 N/m^2
Energy	1 ft pdl	0·0421401 J
	1 ft lbf	1·35582 J
	1 cal	4·1868 J
	1 Btu	1055·06 J
Power	1 hp	745·700 W
Temperature	1 Rankine unit	5/9 Kelvin unit
	1 Fahrenheit unit	5/9 Celsius unit

Prefixes to denote multiples and sub-multiples to be affixed to the names of units are:

Factor by which the unit is multiplied	Prefix	Symbol
$1\ 000\ 000\ 000\ 000 = 10^{12}$	tera	T
$1\ 000\ 000\ 000 = 10^{9}$	giga	G
$1\ 000\ 000 = 10^{6}$	mega	M
$1\ 000 = 10^{3}$	kilo	k
$100 = 10^{2}$	hecto	h
$10 = 10^{1}$	deca	da
$0.1 = 10^{-1}$	deci	d
$0.01 = 10^{-2}$	centi	c
$0.001 = 10^{-3}$	milli	m
$0.000\ 001 = 10^{-6}$	micro	μ
$0.000\ 000\ 001 = 10^{-9}$	nano	n
$0.000\ 000\ 000\ 001 = 10^{-12}$	pico	p
$0.000\ 000\ 000\ 000\ 001 = 10^{-15}$	femto	f
$0.000\ 000\ 000\ 000\ 000\ 001 = 10^{-18}$	atto	a

We list, finally, some proposed metric values (values proposed for density of fresh and salt water are based on a temperature of 15°C (59°F).)

Item	Accepted British figure	Direct metric equivalent	Preferred SI value
Gravity, g	32.17 ft/s^2	9.80665 m/s^2	9.807 m/s^2
Mass density salt water	64 lb/ft^3 35 ft^3/ton	1.0252 tonne/m^3 0.9754 m^3/tonne	1.025 tonne/m^3 0.975 m^3/tonne
Mass density fresh water	62.2 lb/ft^3 36 ft^3/ton	0.9964 tonne/m^3 1.0033 m^3/tonne	1.0 tonne/m^3 1.0 m^3/tonne
Young's modulus, E	$13,500$ tonf/in^2	2.0855×10^7 N/cm^2	209 GN/m^2
Atmospheric pressure	14.7 lbf/in^2	$101,353$ N/m^2 10.1353 N/cm^2	10^5 N/m^2 or Pa or 1.0 bar
TPI (salt water) TPM NPM	$\dfrac{A_w}{420}$ tonf/in A_w (ft^2)	$1.025\ A_w$ tonnef/m $10,052\ A_w$ (N/m)	$1.025\ A_w$ tonnef/m $10^4\ A_w$ (N/m)
MCT 1″ (salt water) $\dfrac{\Delta\overline{GM_L}}{12L}$ $\dfrac{\text{tonf ft}}{\text{in}}$		$\dfrac{\Delta\overline{GM_L}}{L}\left(\dfrac{\text{MN m}}{\text{m}}\right)$	$\dfrac{\Delta\overline{GM_L}}{L}\left(\dfrac{\text{MN m}}{\text{m}}\right)$

(Units of tonf and feet)

One metre trim moment
(Δ in MN or $\dfrac{\text{tonnef m}}{\text{m}}$, Δ in tonnef)

Force displacement 1 tonf		1.01605 tonnef 9964.02 N	1.016 tonnef 9964 N
Mass displacement Σ1 ton		1.01605 tonne	1.016 tonne
Weight density: Salt water Fresh water			0.01 MN/m^3 0.0098 MN/m^3
Specific volume: Salt water Fresh water			99.5 m^3/MN 102.0 m^3/MN

Of particular significance to the naval architect are the units used for displacement, density and stress. The force displacement Δ, under the SI scheme must be expressed in terms of newtons. In practice the meganewton (MN) is a more convenient unit and 1 MN is approximately equivalent to 100 tonf (100·44 more exactly). This new unit will eliminate any confusion between the displacement and tonnage of a ship but, to assist students in making the change from one system of units to another, the authors have additionally introduced the tonnef (and, correspondingly, the tonne for mass measurement) as explained more fully in Chapter 3.

Many preferred values are used by naval architects, e.g. 36 for the number of cubic feet in a ton of fresh water, although the precise figure is slightly different. Conversion to the metric system will involve the adoption of new preferred values which are not precisely equivalent to the old. The authors have adopted those shown in the table immediately above.

PROBLEMS

Where actual examination questions have been used acknowledgement is made according to the following list:

RNC   Royal Naval College, Greenwich
RNATE   Formerly R.N. Artificer Training Establishment
AP & S   Attwood, E. L., and Pengelly, H. S. revised by Sims, A. J.,
           Theoretical Naval Architecture Longmans, 1953.
HMDTC   H.M. Dockyard Technical Colleges.

Symbols and Nomenclature

GENERAL

a	linear acceleration
A	area in general
B	breadth in general
D, d	diameter in general
E	energy in general
F	force in general
g	acceleration due to gravity
h	depth or pressure head in general
h_w, ζ_w	height of wave, crest to trough
H	total head, Bernoulli
L	length in general
L_w, λ	wave-length
m	mass
n	rate of revolution
p	pressure intensity
p_v	vapour pressure of water
p_∞	ambient pressure at infinity
P	power in general
q	stagnation pressure
Q	rate of flow
r, R	radius in general
s	length along path
t	time in general
$t°$	temperature in general
T	period of time for a complete cycle
u	reciprocal weight density, specific volume
u, v, w	velocity components in direction of x-, y-, z-axes
U, V	linear velocity
w	weight density
W	weight in general
x, y, z	body axes and Cartesian co-ordinates
	Right-hand system fixed in the body, z-axis vertically down, x-axis forward. Origin at c.g.
x_0, y_0, z_0	fixed axes
	Right-hand orthogonal system nominally fixed in space, z_0-axis vertically down, x_0-axis in the general direction of the initial motion.
α	angular acceleration
γ	specific gravity
Γ	circulation
δ	thickness of boundary layer in general
θ	angle of pitch
μ	coefficient of dynamic viscosity
v	coefficient of kinematic viscosity
ρ	mass density
ϕ	angle of roll, heel or list
χ	angle of yaw
ω	angular velocity or circular frequency
∇	volume in general

GEOMETRY OF SHIP

A_M	midship section area
A_W	waterplane area
A_X	maximum transverse section area
B	beam or moulded breadth
$\overline{BM}$	metacentre above centre of buoyancy
C_B	block coefficient
C_M	midship section coefficient
C_P	longitudinal prismatic coefficient
C_{VP}	vertical prismatic coefficient
C_{WP}	coefficient of fineness of waterplane
D	depth of ship
F	freeboard
$\overline{GM}$	transverse metacentric height
$\overline{GM}_L$	longitudinal metacentric height
I_L	longitudinal moment of inertia of waterplane about CF
I_P	polar moment of inertia
I_T	transverse moment of inertia
L	length of ship—generally between perps
L_{OA}	length overall
L_{PP}	length between perps
L_{WL}	length of waterline in general
S	wetted surface
T	draught
Δ	displacement force
λ	scale ratio—ship/model dimension
∇	displacement volume
Σ	displacement mass

PROPELLER GEOMETRY

A_D	developed blade area
A_E	expanded area
A_O	disc area
A_P	projected blade area
b	span of aerofoil or hydrofoil
c	chord length
d	boss or hub diameter
D	diameter of propeller
f_M	camber
P	propeller pitch in general
R	propeller radius
t	thickness of aerofoil
Z	number of blades of propeller
α	angle of attack
ϕ	pitch angle of screw propeller

RESISTANCE AND PROPULSION

a	resistance augment fraction
C_D	drag coeff.
C_L	lift coeff.
C_T	specific total resistance coeff.
C_W	specific wave-making resistance coeff.
D	drag force
F_n	Froude number
I	idle resistance
J	advance number of propeller
K_Q	torque coeff.
K_T	thrust coeff.
L	lift force

P_D	delivered power at propeller
P_E	effective power
P_I	indicated power
P_S	shaft power
P_T	thrust power
Q	torque
R	resistance in general
R_n	Reynolds' number
R_F	frictional resistance
R_R	residuary resistance
R_T	total resistance
R_W	wave-making resistance
s_A	apparent slip ratio
t	thrust deduction fraction
T	thrust
U	velocity of a fluid
U_∞	velocity of an undisturbed flow
V	speed of ship
V_A	speed of advance of propeller
w	Taylor wake fraction in general
w_F	Froude wake fraction
W_n	Weber number
β	appendage scale effect factor
β	advance angle of a propeller blade section
δ	Taylor's advance coeff.
η	efficiency in general
η_B	propeller efficiency behind ship
η_D	quasi propulsive coefficient
η_H	hull eff.
η_O	propeller eff. in open water
η_R	relative rotative efficiency
σ	cavitation number

SEAKEEPING

c	wave velocity
f	frequency
f_E	frequency of encounter
I_{xx}, I_{yy}, I_{zz}	real moments of inertia
I_{xy}, I_{xz}, I_{yz}	real products of inertia
k	radius of gyration
m_n	spectrum moment where n is an integer
M_L	horizontal wave bending moment
M_T	torsional wave bending moment
M_V	vertical wave bending moment
s	relative vertical motion of bow with respect to wave surface
$S_\zeta(\omega), S_\theta(\omega)$, etc.	one-dimensional spectral density
$S_\zeta(\omega, \mu), S_\theta(\omega, \mu)$, etc.	two-dimensional spectral density
T	wave period
T_E	period of encounter
T_z	natural period in smooth water for heaving
T_θ	natural period in smooth water for pitching
T_ϕ	natural period in smooth water for rolling
$Y_{\theta\zeta}(\omega)$	response amplitude operator—pitch
$Y_{\phi\zeta}(\omega)$	response amplitude operator—roll
$Y_{\chi\zeta}(\omega)$	response amplitude operator—yaw
β	leeway or drift angle
δ_R	rudder angle
ε	phase angle between any two harmonic motions
ζ	instantaneous wave elevation
ζ_A	wave amplitude

ζ_w	wave height, crest to trough
θ	pitch angle
θ_A	pitch amplitude
κ	wave number
ω_E	frequency of encounter
Λ	tuning factor

MANOEUVRABILITY

A_C	area under cut-up
A_R	area of rudder
b	span of hydrofoil
c	chord of hydrofoil
K, M, N	moment components on body relative to body axes
O.	origin of body axes
p, q, r	components of angular velocity relative to body axes
X, Y, Z	force components on body
α	angle of attack
β	drift angle
δ_R	rudder angle
χ	heading angle
ω_C	steady rate of turn

STRENGTH

a	length of plate
b	breadth of plate
C	modulus of rigidity
ε	linear strain
E	modulus of elasticity, Young's modulus
σ	direct stress
σ_y	yield stress
g	acceleration due to gravity
I	planar second moment of area
J	polar second moment of area
j	stress concentration factor
k	radius of gyration
K	bulk modulus
l	length of member
L	length
M	bending moment
M_p	plastic moment
M_{AB}	bending moment at A in member AB
m	mass
P	direct load, externally applied
P_E	Euler collapse load
p	distributed direct load (area distribution), pressure
p'	distributed direct load (line distribution)
τ	shear stress
r	radius
S	internal shear force
s	distance along a curve
T	applied torque
t	thickness, time
U	strain energy
W	weight, external load
y	lever in bending
δ	deflection, permanent set, elemental (when associated with element of breadth, e.g. δb)
ρ	mass density
ν	Poisson's ratio
θ	slope

NOTES

(*a*) A distance between two points is represented by a bar over the letters defining the two points, e.g. $\overline{GM}$ is the distance between G and M.

(*b*) When a quantity is to be expressed in non-dimensional form is it denoted by the use of the prime '. Unless otherwise specified, the non-dimensionalising factor is a function of ρ, L and V, e.g. $m' = m/\frac{1}{2}\rho L^3$, $x' = x/\frac{1}{2}\rho L^2 V^2$, $L' = L/\frac{1}{2}\rho L^3 V^2$.

(*c*) A lower case subscript is used to denote the denominator of a partial derivative, e.g. $Y_u = \partial Y/\partial u$.

(*d*) For derivatives with respect to time the dot notation is used, e.g. $\dot{x} = \mathrm{d}x/\mathrm{d}t$.

10 Powering of ships: general principles

The power required to drive a ship through the water depends upon the resistance offered by the water and air, the efficiency of the propulsion device adopted and the interaction between them. It is because there is an interaction between the two that it is vital to consider the design of the hull and the propulsive device as an integrated system. When the water surface is rough, the problem is complicated by increased resistance and by the propulsive device working in less favourable conditions. Powering in waves is considered in more detail in Chapter 12 and this chapter is devoted to the powering of ships in calm water.

For the merchant ship, the speed required is dictated by the conditions of service. It may have to work on a fixed schedule, e.g. the transatlantic passenger liner, or as one of a fleet of ships maintaining a steady supply of material. It is essential, therefore, that a designer be able to predict accurately the speed a new design will attain. The fuel bill is a significant feature in the operating costs of any ship, so the designer will be anxious to keep the power needed for the operating speed to a minimum.

The speed of a warship is dictated by the operational requirements. An antisubmarine frigate must be sufficiently fast to close with an enemy submarine and destroy it. At the same time, excessive speed and fuel consumption can only be met at the expense of the amount of armament the ship carries.

In all ships, the power needed should be reduced to a minimum consistent with other design requirements. In this way the weight, cost and volume of the machinery and fuel provided are kept to a minimum. It follows, that an accurate knowledge of a design's powering characteristics is of considerable importance and that a fair expenditure of effort is justified in achieving it. Several methods are available to the designer:

(a) use of full-scale data from ships built over a considerable period of years;
(b) use of theoretical analysis;
(c) use of models for predicting full-scale resistance.

Generally speaking, full-scale data is limited in usefulness because of the process of evolution to which ships are subject. To mention two factors, the introduction of welding led to a smoother hull, and ships have tended over the years to become larger. Again, the new ship is often required to go faster so that data from her predecessors cannot be used directly for assessing her maximum power. Clearly, this method is not valid when a new ship type is introduced.

Theory has been used as an aid to more practical methods and continues to develop. It is not yet, however, adequate to provide answers on its own. Its main contribution has been to guide the model experimenter and to provide him with a more rational and scientific background to his work, suggesting profitable lines of investigation and indicating the relative importance of the various design parameters. The interplay of theory and experiment in assessing wave-making resistance is discussed in Ref. 1.

The main tool of the designer has been, and remains, the model with theory acting as a guide and full-scale data providing the all-essential check on the model prediction. The model is relatively cheap and results can be obtained fairly rapidly for a variety of changes to enable the designer to achieve an optimum design.

A very good example of the results obtainable by a judicious blend of theory and model data is provided in Ref. 2. This particular example also illustrates the important part to be played by the modern computer in aiding the naval architect. Basically, a mathematical expression is produced for the resistance of the ship (in this case a trawler type), in terms of various ship parameters such as L/B ratio, C_P, etc. This expression is then used to deduce the required trend on these parameters to minimize resistance and produces a form superior to those currently in use.

These various considerations are developed more fully later but first it is necessary to consider some of the properties of the fluids in which the ship moves. These are fundamental to the prediction of full-scale performance from the model and for any theoretical investigation.

Fluid dynamics

There are two fluids with which the naval architect is concerned, air and water. Unless stated otherwise water is the fluid considered in the following sections. Air resistance is treated as a separate drag force. Models are used extensively and it is necessary to ensure that the flow around the model is 'similar' to that around the ship in order that results may be scaled correctly. Similarity in this sense requires that the model and ship forms be geometrically similar (at least that portion over which the flow occurs), that the streamlines of the fluid flow be geometrically similar in the two cases and that the fluid velocities at corresponding points around the bodies are in a constant ratio.

Water possesses certain physical properties which are of the same order of magnitude for the water in which a model is tested and for that in which the ship moves. These are:

the density, ρ
the surface tension, σ
the viscosity, μ
the vapour pressure, p_V
the ambient pressure, p_∞
the velocity of sound in water, a

The quantitative values of some of these properties are discussed in Chapter 9. Other factors involved are:

a typical length, usually taken as the wetted length L for resistance work, and as the propeller diameter D for propeller design;

velocity, V
propeller revolutions, n
resistance, R
thrust, T
torque, Q
gravitational acceleration, g.

Dimensional analysis provides a guide to the form in which the above quantities may be significant. The pi theorem states that the physical relationship between these quantities can be represented as one between a set of non-dimensional products of the quantities concerned. It also asserts, that the functionally related quantities are independent and that the number of related quantities will be three less (i.e. the number of fundamental units—mass, length, time) than the number of basic quantities.

Applying non-dimensional analysis to the ship powering problem, it can be shown that

$$\frac{R}{\rho V^2 L^2} = F\left\{\frac{VL\rho}{\mu}, \frac{V}{\sqrt{(gL)}}, \frac{V}{a}, \frac{\sigma}{g\rho L^2}, \frac{p_\infty - p_v}{\rho V^2}\right\}$$

$$\frac{T}{\rho n^2 D^4} \text{ and } \frac{Q}{\rho n^2 D^5} = F\left\{\frac{V}{nD}, \frac{VD\rho}{\mu}, \frac{V^2}{gD}, \frac{\sigma}{\rho g L^2}, \frac{p_\infty - p_v}{\rho V^2}\right\}$$

Expressed in another way, it is physically reasonable to suggest that if data can be expressed in terms of parameters that are independent of scale, i.e. non-dimensional parameters, the same values of these data will probably be obtained from experiments at different scales if the parameters are constant. Where the governing parameters cannot be kept constant, data will change in going from the model to full scale. The above are not the only non-dimensional parameters that can be formed but they are those in general use. Each has been given a name as follows:

$\dfrac{R}{\rho V^2 L^2}$ is termed the resistance coefficient

$\dfrac{VD\rho}{\mu}$ or $\dfrac{VL\rho}{\mu}$ is termed the Reynolds' number (the ratio μ/ρ is called the kinematic viscosity and is represented by ν)

$\dfrac{V}{\sqrt{(gD)}}$ or $\dfrac{V}{\sqrt{(gL)}}$ is termed the Froude number

$\dfrac{V}{a}$ is termed the Mach number ⎫ These two quantities are not significant in the context of the present book and are not considered further

$\dfrac{\sigma}{g\rho L^2}$ is termed the Weber number ⎭

$\dfrac{p_\infty - p_v}{\rho V^2}$ is termed the cavitation number

$\dfrac{T}{\rho n^2 D^4} = K_T$ = thrust coefficient

$\dfrac{Q}{\rho n^2 D^5} = K_Q$ = torque coefficient

$\dfrac{V}{nD}$ $= J$ = advance coefficient

Unfortunately, it is not possible to set up model scale experiments in which all the above parameters have the same values as in the full-scale. This is readily seen by considering the Reynolds' and Froude numbers. Since ρ, μ and g are substantially the same for model and ship, it would be necessary for both VL and $V/\sqrt{L}$ to be kept constant. This is physically impossible. By using special liquids instead of water in which to test models, two parameters could be satisfied but not all of them.

Fortunately, certain valid results can be obtained by keeping one parameter constant in the model tests and limiting those tests to certain measurements. For example, model resistance tests are conducted at corresponding Froude number and model propeller cavitation tests at corresponding cavitation number. This means that resistance forces which depend on Reynolds' number will have to be modified in going from model to ship. It will be shown that, had this difficulty of achieving physical similarity not been present, the early experimenters would not have experienced so much difficulty in predicting the resistance of the full-scale ship.

Components of resistance and propulsion

It is necessary to provide a propulsive device to drive the ship through the water. It has been explained, that since the propulsion device interacts on the resistance of the ship the two cannot be treated in isolation. However, as a matter of convenience, the overall problem is considered as the amalgamation of a number of smaller problems. The actual divisions are largely arbitrary but are well established. In the following, it is assumed that the propulsive device is a propeller.

If the naked hull of the ship could be driven through the water by some device which in no way interacted with the hull or water, it would experience a total resistance R_T which would be the summation of several types of resistance as is explained later. The differentiation between types of resistance is necessary because they scale differently in going from model to full-scale. The product of R_T and the ship's speed V defines a horsepower which is known as the *effective horsepower* (e.h.p.). The e.h.p. can be regarded as the useful work done in propelling the ship.

The power actually delivered to the shafts for propelling a ship is the *shaft horsepower* (s.h.p.). The ratio between the s.h.p. and e.h.p. is a measure of the overall propulsive efficiency achieved and is termed the *propulsive coefficient*

(PC). The propulsive coefficient arises partly from the efficiency of the propeller, and partly from the interaction of propeller and hull. In addition, it has to be modified to make model and full-scale data compatible.

Following on from the above, four basic components of the powering problem suggest themselves:

(*a*) e.h.p., or the hull resistance
(*b*) the propeller
(*c*) hull/propeller interaction
(*d*) ship/model correlation.

EFFECTIVE HORSEPOWER (E.H.P.)

One horsepower is the rate of performing 33,000 ft lbf of work per minute, or 550 ft lbf of work per second. In metric units, 1 h.p. is equal to 745·7 W (J/s). As far as propelling the ship through the water is concerned, the 'useful' or 'effective' work is that done in overcoming the resistance of the ship by its speed of advance. The resistance concerned is conventionally taken to be that of the 'naked' hull, i.e. without any appendages. This leads to the following definition:

The *effective horsepower* of a ship is the product of the resistance of the naked hull and the speed of the hull. It is usually denoted, even in mathematical equations, by the initial letters e.h.p. Therefore,

e.h.p. $= R_T \times V$

A corresponding definition can be evolved using the resistance of the hull including that of appendages and this is conventionally denoted by e.h.p.´

The ratio of e.h.p.´ to e.h.p. is known as the *Appendage Coefficient*, i.e.

$$\text{Appendage coefficient} = \frac{\text{e.h.p.´}}{\text{e.h.p.}}$$

EXAMPLE 1. At 825 ft/min the tow rope pull of a naked hull is 8000 lbf. Find the effective horsepower of the hull at this speed.

Solution:

$$\text{e.h.p.} = 825 \text{ ft/min} \times 8000 \text{ lbf} \times \frac{1 \text{ h.p.}}{33,000 \text{ ft lbf/min}} = 200$$

EXAMPLE 2. A 6000 tonnef destroyer develops a total horsepower of 60,000 at 30 knots. Assuming that the e.h.p. is 50 per cent of this total power, calculate the resistance of its naked hull.

Solution:

e.h.p. $= \frac{1}{2} \times 60,000 = 30,000$ h.p. $= 22·37 \times 10^6$ W

Therefore $22·37 \times 10^6$ W $=$ (Resistance) newtons $\times \left(\dfrac{30 \times 1852}{3600} \right)$ m/s

i.e.

Resistance $= 1·449 \times 10^6$ newtons

TYPES OF RESISTANCE

The classical theory of hydrodynamics has shown that a body deeply immersed in fluid of zero viscosity experiences no resistance. No matter how the streamlines may be deflected as they pass the body, they return to their undisturbed state a long way downstream of the body (see Fig. 10.1) and the resultant force on the body is zero. There are pressure variations in the fluid as the streamlines are deflected and particle velocities change. In this respect, Bernoulli's theorem is obeyed, i.e. increased velocities are associated with pressure reductions. Thus, the body can be acted upon by forces of considerable magnitude but they all act so as to cancel each other out.

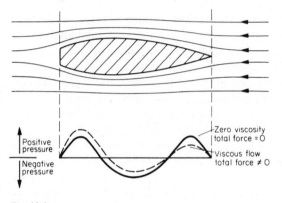

Fig. 10.1

In a practical case the fluid is viscous and a deeply immersed body would suffer a frictional drag. In addition, when the body approaches a free surface, the pressure variations around the body can manifest themselves as elevations or depressions of the water surface. That is to say, waves are formed on the surface. This process upsets the balance of pressures acting on the body which results in a drag force. The magnitude of the drag force is related to the energy of the wave system created.

The total resistance of a ship moving on a calm water surface has several components. They are: wave-making resistance; skin frictional resistance; viscous pressure resistance; air resistance; appendage resistance.

Each component can now be studied separately provided it is remembered that each will have some interaction with the others.

WAVE-MAKING RESISTANCE

It is common experience, that a body moving across an otherwise undisturbed water surface produces a wave system. This system arises from the pressure field around the body and the energy possessed by it must be derived from the body. As far as the body is concerned the transfer of energy will manifest itself as a force opposing the forward motion. This force is termed the *wave-making resistance*.

A submerged body also experiences a drag due to the formation of waves on the free surface, the magnitude of this drag reducing with increasing depth of submergence until it becomes negligible at deep submergence. This typically occurs at depths equal to approximately half the length of the body. An exception to this general rule can occur with submarines at sea if they are moving close to the interface between two layers of water of different density. In this case, a wave system is produced at the interface resulting in a drag on the submarine.

A gravity wave, length λ, in deep water moves with a velocity C defined by

$$C^2 = \frac{g\lambda}{2\pi}$$

Because the wave pattern moves with the ship, C must be equal to the ship velocity V and λ being a length measurement can, for dimensional analysis, be represented as proportional to the ship length L for a given speed.

Thus it is seen that of the non-dimensional parameters deduced earlier it is V^2/gL or $V/\sqrt{(gL)}$ which is significant in the study of wave-making resistance. As stated in the section on fluid dynamics, the quantity $V/\sqrt{(gL)}$ is usually designated the *Froude number*. In many cases, the simpler parameter $V/\sqrt{L}$ is used for plotting results but the plot is no longer non-dimensional.

Hydrodynamically, the ship can be regarded as a moving pressure field. Kelvin considered mathematically the simplified case of a moving pressure point and showed that the resulting wave pattern is built up of two systems. One system is a divergent wave system and the other a system of waves with crests more or less normal to the path of the pressure point. Both systems travel forward with the speed of the pressure point. (Fig. 10.2.)

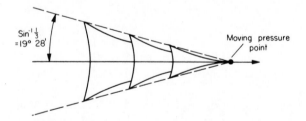

$\text{Sin}^{-1}\frac{1}{3}$
$= 19°\ 28'$

Moving pressure point

Fig. 10.2 Wave system associated with moving pressure point

The wave system associated with a ship is more complicated. To a first approximation, however, the ship can be considered as composed of a moving pressure field sited near the bow and a moving suction field near the stern. The bow produces a wave pattern similar to that produced by Kelvin's pressure point with a crest at the bow. The stern on the other hand produces a wave system with a trough at the stern.

If the line of maximum height of crests of the divergent system is at α, then the wave crests at these positions subtend an angle of approximately 2α to the ship middle line as in Fig. 10.3.

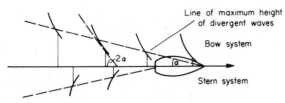

Fig. 10.3 Ship wave pattern

The two transverse wave systems, i.e. at bow and stern, have a wave-length of $2\pi V^2/g$. The transverse waves increase in width as the divergent waves spread out. The total energy content per wave is constant, so that their height falls progressively with increasing distance from the ship.

In general, both divergent systems will be detectable although the stern system is usually much weaker than that from the bow. Normally, the stern transverse system cannot be detected as only the resultant of the two systems is visible astern of the ship.

In some ships, the wave pattern may be made even more complex by the generation of other wave systems by local discontinuities in the ship's form.

Since at most speeds both the bow and stern systems are present aft of the ship, there is an interaction between the two transverse wave systems. If the systems are so phased that the crests are coincident, the resulting system will have increased wave height, and consequently greater energy content. If the crest of one system coincides with the trough of the other the resulting wave height and energy content will be less. The wave-making resistance, depending as it does on the energy content of the overall wave system, varies therefore with speed and also effective length between the bow and stern pressure systems. Again, the parameters V and L are important.

Reference 3 studied the effect on resistance of the length of the ship by towing models with the same endings but with varying lengths of parallel middle body. The results are in line with what could be expected from the above general reasoning.

The distance between bow and stern pressure systems is typically $0 \cdot 9L$. The condition that crests or troughs of the bow system should coincide with the first trough of the stern system is therefore

$$\frac{V^2}{0 \cdot 9L} = \frac{g}{N\pi}$$

For $N = 1, 3, 5, 7$, etc., the troughs will coincide and for $N = 2, 4, 6$, etc., the crests from the bow system coincides with the trough from the after system as in Fig. 10.4.

If there were no interaction between the bow and stern wave systems, the resistance would increase steadily with speed as shown in Fig. 10.5 ('Without interaction' curve). Because interaction occurs at speeds discussed above, the actual resistance curve will oscillate about the curve as indicated.

A 'hump' occurs when N is an odd integer and a 'hollow' when N is an even integer. It is to be expected that the most pronounced hump will be at $N = 1$,

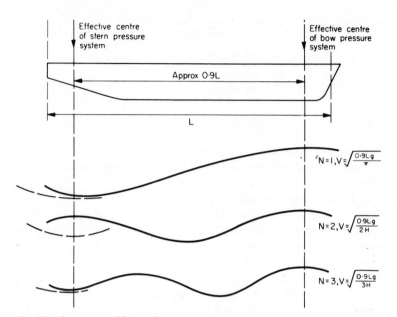

Fig. 10.4 *Interaction of bow and stern wave systems*

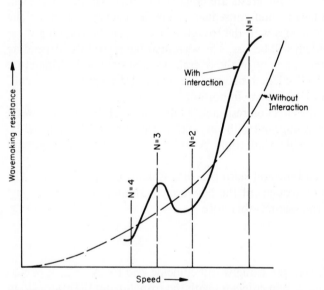

Fig. 10.5 *'Humps' and 'hollows' in wave-making resistance curves*

because the speed is highest for this condition and this hump is usually referred to as the *main hump*. The hump associated with $N = 3$ is often called the *prismatic hump* as its influence is greatly affected by the prismatic coefficient of the form considered.

Since the Froude number $F_n = V/\sqrt{(gL)}$, the values of F_n corresponding to the humps and hollows are shown in Table 10.1.

Table 10.1

N	F_n
1	$\sqrt{\left(\dfrac{0{\cdot}9}{\pi}\right)} = 0{\cdot}54$
2	$\sqrt{\left(\dfrac{0{\cdot}9}{2\pi}\right)} = 0{\cdot}38$
3	$\sqrt{\left(\dfrac{0{\cdot}9}{3\pi}\right)} = 0{\cdot}31$
4	$\sqrt{\left(\dfrac{0{\cdot}9}{4\pi}\right)} = 0{\cdot}27$

Clearly, a designer would not deliberately produce a ship whose normal service speed was at a 'hump' position. Rather he would aim to operate in a 'hollow', although other considerations may be overriding in deciding on the length of the ship.

FRICTIONAL RESISTANCE

The water through which a ship moves has viscosity which is a property of all practical fluids. It was shown earlier, that when viscosity is involved the conditions for dynamic similarity are geometrically similar boundaries and constancy of Reynolds' number.

When a body moves through a fluid which is otherwise at rest, a thin layer of fluid adheres to the surface of the body and has no velocity relative to the body. At some distance from the body the fluid remains at rest.

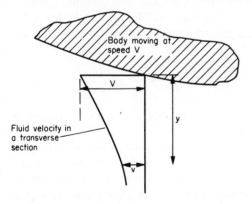

Fig. 10.6 The boundary layer

The variation of velocity of the fluid is rapid close to the body (Fig. 10.6) but reduces with increasing distance from the body. The region in which there is a rapid change in velocity is termed the *boundary layer*.

The definition of boundary layer thickness is to some extent arbitrary since in theory it extends to infinity. It is common practice to define the thickness as the distance from the surface of the body at which the velocity of the fluid is 1 per cent of the body velocity.

Due to the velocity gradient across the boundary layer, the fluid is in shear and the body experiences a resistance which is termed the *frictional resistance*. If the fluid velocity is v at distance y from the body the shear stress in the fluid is given by

$$\tau = \mu \frac{dv}{dy}$$

This applies to the case of *laminar flow* in which each fluid particle follows its own streamline path with no mass transfer between adjacent fluid layers. The shear in this case is due solely to molecular action. Laminar flow conditions are only likely to apply at relatively low Reynolds' numbers. At higher Reynolds' numbers the steady flow pattern breaks down and is replaced by a more confused pattern which is termed *turbulent flow*. The value of R_n at which this breakdown in flow occurs is termed the critical Reynolds' number, and its actual value depends upon the smoothness of the surface and the initial turbulence present in the fluid. For a smooth flat plate, breakdown occurs at a Reynolds' number between 3×10^5 and 10^6. In turbulent flow, the concept of a boundary layer still applies but in this case, besides the molecular friction force, there is an interaction due to the momentum transfer of fluid masses between adjacent layers. The exact mechanism of the turbulent boundary layer is incompletely understood, but it follows that the velocity distribution curve at Fig. 10.6 can represent only a mean velocity curve.

The *transition* from laminar to turbulent flow is essentially one of stability. At low Reynolds' numbers, disturbances die out and the flow is stable. At a certain *critical* value of Reynolds' number, the laminar flow becomes unstable and the slightest disturbance will cause turbulence. The critical R_n for a flat surface is a function of l the distance from the leading edge. Ahead of a point defined by l as follows:

$$(R_n) \text{ critical} = \frac{Vl}{v}$$

the flow is laminar. At distance l transition begins and after a certain *transition region*, turbulence is fully established.

For a flat surface, the critical Reynolds' number is approximately 10^6. For a curved surface, the pressure gradient along the surface has a marked influence on transition. Transition is delayed in regions of decreasing pressure, i.e. regions of increasing velocity. Use is made of this fact in certain aerodynamic low drag forms such as the 'laminar flow' wing. The gain arising from retaining laminar flow is shown by the fact that a flat plate suffers seven times the resistance in all turbulent as opposed to all laminar flow.

The thickness of the turbulent boundary layer is given approximately by

$$\frac{\delta x}{L} = 0.37 \, (R_L)^{-\frac{1}{5}}$$

where L is the distance from the leading edge and R_L is the corresponding Reynolds' number. For example, at 15 m/s, with L = 150 m, δ_τ is about 0·75 m.

Even in turbulent flow, the fluid particles adjacent to the body's surface are at rest relative to the body. It follows that there exists a *laminar sub-layer* although in practice this is extremely thin. It is nevertheless of importance in that a body appears smooth if surface roughness does not protrude through this sub-layer. Such a body is said to be *hydraulically smooth* and a plot of drag against Reynolds' number would be as shown by the basic curve in Fig. 10.7.

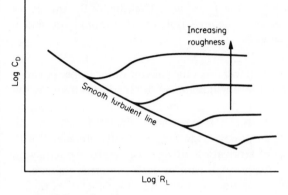

Fig. 10.7 Effect of roughness

For a rough surface, resistance follows the smooth curve as Reynolds' number is increased until a certain value and it then breaks away and eventually becomes horizontal, i.e. the drag coefficient becomes independent of R_n and drag varies as the square of the velocity. The rougher the surface the smaller the value of R_n at which the breakaway occurs.

Owing to the increase in boundary layer thickness, the ratio of roughness (i.e. effective granularity of surface) to the boundary layer thickness decreases along the length of a surface. For this reason, protrusions from a hull of a given size have less effect on resistance at the after end of a ship than they do forward.

For all practical purposes, the complete boundary layer of a ship at sea can be regarded as turbulent. In a model in a towing tank, a portion may be laminar but the extent of this is sensitive to external conditions and it can vary considerably in a given model. Because of the difference in resistance associated with the two types of boundary layer, this phenomenon has led to inconsistent model test data in the past and this has caused most ship tanks to artificially stimulate turbulent flow conditions to ensure reproducible conditions. A number of devices are used to stimulate turbulence but that now most commonly used is a row of studs a short distance from the bow of the model.

For convenience, the frictional resistance of a ship is usually divided into two components. The first component is that resistance which would be experienced by a 'flat plate' of equivalent surface area. The second component is the increased frictional resistance occasioned by the actual form of the ship and this component is known as the *frictional form resistance*.

VISCOUS PRESSURE RESISTANCE

Total ship resistance comprises the fore-and-aft component of all pressures normal to the hull. That part of the pressure resistance which manifests itself as waves has already been discussed; the remainder of the pressure resistance is due to viscous effects which inhibit that build-up of pressure around the after end of the ship predicted for a perfect fluid. Because this viscous pressure resistance is affected by the form of the ship it is known as form drag or form resistance. Pressure energy lost to the sea is thus seen as waves and as eddies or vortices. Examination of the energy dissipated in the wake and in the waves may enable some of the resistance due to form to be calculated. That due to the transfer of energy between wave and wake is sometimes isolated for examination and is called wave breaking resistance.

AIR RESISTANCE

Air is a fluid, as is water, and as such will resist the passage of the upper portions of the ship through it. This resistance will comprise both frictional and eddy-making components.

In an artist's impression of a ship it is possible to depict a very smooth streamlined above water form. In practice, the weight penalty associated with such fairing and the difficulties of fabrication are not justified by the reduction in air resistance or by the relatively small gain in usable internal volume. In practice, therefore, air flowing over the superstructure meets a series of discontinuities which cause separation, i.e. streamlines break down and eddies are formed. As expected, air resistance like water eddy resistance will vary as V^2.

At full speed in conditions of no wind, it is probable that the air resistance will be some 2–4 per cent of the total water resistance. Should the ship be moving into a head wind of the same speed as the ship, the relative wind speed will be doubled and the air resistance quadrupled. Thus, clearly, in severe weather conditions such as in a full gale the air resistance can contribute materially to slowing down the ship.

APPENDAGE RESISTANCE

The discussion up to this point has been concerned mainly with the resistance of the naked hull, i.e. without appendages. Typical appendages are rudders, shaft brackets or bossings, stabilizers, bilge keels, docking keels. Each appendage has its own typical length, which is much smaller than the ship length, and accordingly is running at its own Reynolds' number. Each appendage, therefore, has a resistance which would scale differently to full-size if run at model size, although obeying the same scaling laws.

To include appendages in a normal resistance model would, therefore, upset the scaling of the hull resistance. It is for this reason that models are run naked, and the resulting total ship resistance must be modified by adding in estimates of the resistance due to each full-scale appendage.

The resistance of the appendages may be estimated from formulae based on previous experience or by running models both with and without appendages and scaling the difference to full-scale using different scaling laws from those used for the hull proper. Fortunately, appendage resistances are usually small (of the order of 10 per cent of that of the hull) so that errors in their assessment are not likely to be critical. It is usual to assume that the appendage resistance varies as V^2, so that the contribution to the non-dimensional resistance coefficient is constant.

RESIDUARY RESISTANCE

In addition to the above resistances, the ship in service generally has her resistance to ahead motion increased by the presence of waves and spray generated by the wind. In rough weather, this effect can be of considerable magnitude and often causes a significant fall off in speed. This is discussed in Chapter 12.

For the practical evaluation of ship resistance for normal ship forms, it is usual to group wave-making resistance, form resistance, eddy resistance and frictional form resistance into one force termed *residuary resistance*. This concept is not theoretically correct, but, in practice, provides a sufficiently accurate answer.

Thus the total resistance is given by

$$R_T = R_R + R_F$$

where R_R = residuary resistance, and R_F = frictional resistance of an equivalent flat plate.

Having examined how the resistance of a ship arises, it is necessary to examine the effects of the propulsion device and how consideration of the two cannot be separated. In returning to the evaluation of ship resistance in the next chapter, the resistance will then be considered as the summation of the frictional and residuary resistances.

THE PROPULSION DEVICE

The force needed to propel the ship must be obtained from a reaction against the air, water or land, e.g. by causing a stream of air or water to move in the opposite direction. The sailing ship uses air reaction. Devices acting on water are the paddle wheel, oar and screw propeller. Reaction on land is used by the punt pole or the horse towing a barge.

For general applications, the land reaction is not available and the naval architect must make use of water or air. The force acting on the ship arises from the rate of change of momentum induced in the fluid.

Consider a stream of fluid, density ρ, caused to move with velocity V in a 'tube' of cross-sectional area A. Then the mass of fluid passing any section per second $= \rho A V$ and the momentum of this fluid $= mV = \rho A V^2$. Since fluid is initially at rest the rate of change of momentum $= \rho A V^2$.

In a specific application, the force required is governed by the speed desired and the resistance of the ship. Since the force produced is directly proportional to the mass density of the fluid used, it is reasonable to use the more massive of the two fluids available, i.e. water. If air were used, then either the cross-sectional area of the jet must be large or the velocity must be high.

This explains why most ships employ a system by which water is caused to move aft relative to the ship. A variety of means is available for producing this stream of water aft, but by far the most commonly used is the screw propeller and this is dealt with first.

THE SCREW PROPELLER

Basically, the screw propeller may be regarded as part of a helicoidal surface which, on being rotated, 'screws' its way through the water driving water aft and the ship forward. Some propellers have adjustable blades—they are called *controllable pitch propellers*—but by far the greater majority of propellers have fixed blades. The ones we are concerned with here are *fixed pitch propellers*.

Propellers can be designed to turn in either direction in producing an ahead thrust. If they turn clockwise when viewed from aft, they are said to be *right-handed;* if anti-clockwise, they are said to be *left-handed*. In a twin screw ship, the starboard propeller is normally right-handed and the port propeller left-handed, i.e. they turn as in Fig. 10.8. They are said to be outward turning and this reduces cavitation which is discussed later.

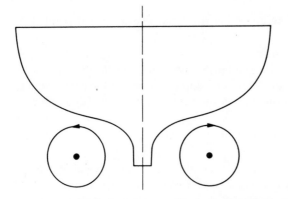

Fig. 10.8 Usual handing of propellers in a twin screw ship. Ship view from aft

Considering each blade of the propeller, the *face* is the surface seen when viewed from aft, i.e. it is the driving surface when producing an ahead thrust. The other surface of the blade is called the *back*. The *leading edge* of the blade is that edge which thrusts through the water when producing ahead thrust and the other edge is termed the *trailing edge*.

Other things being equal, the thrust developed by a propeller varies directly with the surface area, ignoring the boss itself. This area can be described in a number of ways. The *developed blade area* of the propeller is the sum of the face area of all the blades. The *projected area* is the projection of the blades on to a plane normal to the propeller axis, i.e. the shaft axis. The *disc area* is the area of a circle passing through the tips of the blades and normal to the propeller axis.

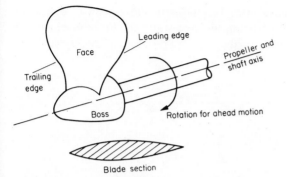

Fig. 10.9 The propeller blade

In non-dimensional work, the *blade area ratio* (BAR) is now generally used. This is the ratio of the developed blade area to the disc area, i.e.

$$\text{BAR} = \frac{A_D}{A_0} = \frac{4A_D}{\pi D^2}, \ A_D \text{ obtained by drawing}$$

If the variation of helical chord length with radius is known, then the true blade area can be obtained analytically by integration. This is known as the *expanded area* and the *expanded area ratio* is defined by

$$\text{EAR} = \frac{4A_E}{\pi D^2}$$

In some earlier work, the concept of a *disc area ratio* (DAR) was employed in which the developed area was increased to allow for the boss. Froude proposed a boss allowance of 25 per cent of the developed area but Gawn used $12\frac{1}{2}$ per cent.

A true helicoidal surface is generated by a line rotated about an axis normal to itself and advancing in the direction of this axis at constant speed. The distance the line advances in making one complete revolution is termed the *pitch*. For simple propellers, the pitch is the same at all points on the face of the blade. This is the *face pitch* of the propeller and the ratio of this to the propeller diameter is the *face pitch ratio*

i.e. face pitch ratio $= \dfrac{P}{D}$

The distance advanced by a propeller during one revolution when delivering no thrust is termed the *analysis pitch*. In practice, this is rather greater than the geometrical pitch of the propeller. When developing thrust, the propeller advance per revolution is less than the analysis pitch. The difference is termed the *slip*. That is,

slip = analysis pitch − advance per revolution

The ratio of the slip to the analysis pitch is correctly called the *slip ratio s*, but by common usage is often referred to simply as slip.

Most modern propellers have pitch varying with radius and to define the geometry of the propeller the variation must be specified. For convenience, a nominal pitch is often quoted which is the pitch at a radius of 0·7 times maximum radius.

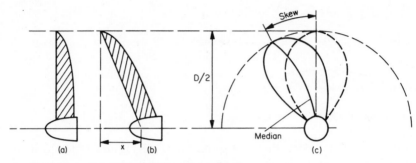

Fig. 10.10 Blade thickness ratio, rake and skew back

The projected shape of a propeller blade is generally symmetrical about a radial line called the median. Some propellers have what is known as *skew back* and this is when the median is curved back, relative to the direction of rotation of the propeller, as shown in Fig. 10.10(*c*). Skew back is defined by the circumferential displacement of the tip of the blade. It is of some advantage when the propeller is working in a flow with a pronounced circumferential variation, as not all the blade is affected at the same time and variations in thrust and torque are smoothed out.

For some applications the blade face is not normal to the propeller axis. In such a case, e.g. Fig. 10.10 (*b*), the blade is said to be *raked*. It may be raked either forward or aft, but generally the latter to increase the clearance between the blade tip and the hull. Referring to the figure

Rake ratio $= x/D$

The blade section shape at any radius is the shape of the intersection between the blade and a co-axial cylinder when the cylindrical surface has been rolled

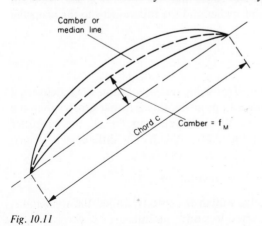

Fig. 10.11

out flat. The *median* or *camber line* is the line through the mid-thickness of the blade. The *camber* is the maximum distance separating the median line and the straight line, the chord c, joining the leading and trailing edges.

Camber is normally expressed as the *camber ratio*, where

camber ratio $= f_M/c$

Similarly the *thickness ratio* of the section is t/c where t is the maximum thickness of the section. In most modern propellers, the thickness varies non-linearly with radius. The *thickness distribution* must be specified for complete definition of the propeller geometry.

SPECIAL TYPES OF PROPELLER

The bulk of this section is devoted to the screw propeller which is by far the most common form of propulsion device. Now consider briefly other types of propeller:

(*a*) *Controllable pitch propeller*

It will be realized that it is necessary to ensure that the machinery can always develop enough torque to turn the propeller at the revolutions appropriate to the power being developed. This is not always possible with a propeller with fixed blades, and to meet such cases propellers can be used in which the blades can be rotated about axes normal to the driving shaft. By turning the blades the thrust and torque can be varied whilst maintaining constant shaft revolutions. Indeed, if the blade rotation is large enough the propeller can be made to produce an astern thrust while still rotating in the same direction. Here, then, is another possible reason for using this type of propeller—a reversing gear box is not needed. In addition, manoeuvring can be more rapid as the blade angle can be varied more rapidly than can the shaft revolutions. To produce the maximum acceleration or deceleration there will be an optimum rate of change of blade angle.

Another suitable application of the CP propeller is to ships which must operate efficiently at two quite different loading conditions, e.g. the tug when towing or running free, the trawler when trawling or when on passage to or from the fishing grounds.

Limitations of the CP propeller include the power that can be satisfactorily transmitted (installations for more than 25,000 s.h.p. are uncommon), the complication of the mechanisms controlling the blade angle and the limitation of BAR to about 0·8 which affects the cavitation performance. The control mechanism must pass down the shaft and into the boss. The boss is enlarged to take this gear and to house the bearings for the blades. This increased boss size slightly reduces the maximum efficiency obtainable. The blade sections at the root are governed by the rotation on the boss and are poor for cavitation.

(*b*) *The vertical axis propeller*

This propeller consists basically of a horizontal disc rotating about a vertical axis. Projecting vertically down from this disc are a number of spade-like blades and these feather as they and the disc rotate. By varying the sequence in which the blades feather a thrust can be produced in any desired direction.

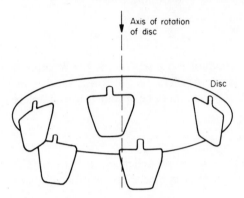

Fig. 10.12 *Vertical axis type propeller*

An obvious advantage of such a propeller is that it confers good manoeuvrability on any ship so fitted. This is touched upon in Chapter 13. With most conventional machinery units, the drive shaft is horizontal and to drive the horizontal disc it is necessary to introduce a bevel gear with consequential limitations on the maximum power that can be transmitted.

(c) Ducted propellers

A typical arrangement is sketched in Fig. 10.13. Improvements over the conventional propeller performance arise from the enlargement of the tail race and the thrust that can be produced by suitable shaping of the duct to offset the drag of the shroud and its supports. Most applications have been made in ships with heavily loaded propellers, e.g. tugs, but the range of use is increasing.

Other advantages of the shroud are that it protects the propeller from physical damage and acts as a cloak masking the propeller noise. It is used in canal and river craft to reduce erosion of the bottom and banks due to the action of the screw race.

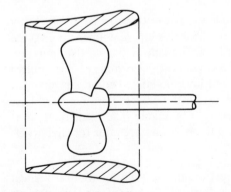

Fig. 10.13 *Shrouded propeller*

Reference 4 gives data for various types of propeller based on open-water tests and Fig. 10.14 is reproduced from that reference. It indicates the type of propeller which will give the best efficiency for a given type of ship. Efficiency is not always the only factor to be considered, of course, in choosing the propulsion device.

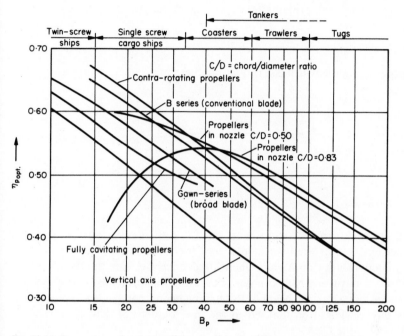

Fig. 10.14 Comparison of optimum efficiency values for different types of propulsion

ALTERNATIVE MEANS OF PROPULSION

These can only be touched upon very briefly, and the following list is by no means exhaustive:

(a) Hydraulic or jet propulsion

If water is drawn into the ship and then thrust out at the stern by means of a pump then the ship can be regarded as jet propelled.

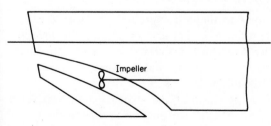

Fig. 10.15 Jet propulsion

Since the pump or impeller is basically a propeller, the overall efficiency of such a system is lower than the corresponding screw propeller, i.e. of diameter equal to the jet orifice diameter, because of the resistance to flow of water through the duct in the ship. It is attractive, however, where it is desirable to have no moving parts outside the envelope of the main hull. This is the case of craft operating in very shallow water and a very successful class of boat has been designed using this principle for operating on shallow rivers in New Zealand and other countries.

(b) Paddle wheels

In essence, the paddle wheel is a ring of paddles rotating about an athwartship horizontal axis.

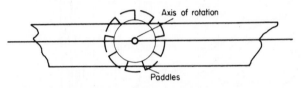

Fig. 10.16 Paddle wheel

In the simplest form, the paddles are fixed but greater efficiency is obtained by feathering them as the blades enter and leave the water. They can confer good manoeuvrability on a ship when fitted on either side amidships and a recent class of naval tug has been designed using this principle. For operation in narrow waters, the large beam of this arrangement may be unacceptable and this was the consideration that led to the development of the 'stern wheeler' on the rivers of the USA.

(c) Wind

The study of wind acting upon sails is a study in itself. In its simplest form, the wind may be regarded as producing a normal force on a sail due to the wind component normal to the mean plane of the sail. In more complete studies the sail, when stretched under the action of the wind, is regarded as an aerofoil section developing lift and drag as would a solid body. (See Chapter 16.)

It is now proposed to return to a more detailed consideration of the principles of the screw propeller.

MOMENTUM THEORY APPLIED TO A SCREW PROPELLER

It was shown above, that the force available for propelling a ship could be related to the momentum in the screw race. Let us now develop this idea in a little more detail. The propeller will cause water to accelerate from some distance ahead of the propeller disc and, because water is virtually incompressible, the flow of water through the disc will be as in Fig. 10.17.

Let A_1 and A_2 be points sufficiently ahead of and abaft the actual propeller disc so that the pressure at these points is effectively that in the free field. Due to the contraction of the screw race, the velocity will increase as shown and

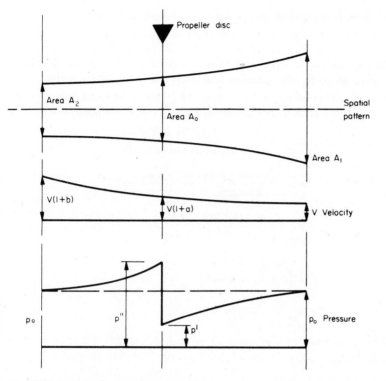

Fig. 10.17 Spatial, velocity and pressure patterns

pressure will decrease between A_1 and the disc, suffer a jump at the disc and then decrease again between the disc and A_2. Now

thrust on propeller $= T = A_0 (p'' - p')$

and applying Bernoulli's principle to both sides of the disc,

$$p_0 + \rho \frac{V^2}{2} = p' + \rho \frac{V^2}{2}(1+a)^2$$

$$p_0 + \rho \frac{V^2}{2}(1+b)^2 = p'' + \rho \frac{V^2}{2}(1+a)^2$$

Subtracting

$$p'' - p' = \rho \frac{V^2}{2}(1+b)^2 - \rho \frac{V^2}{2}$$

Hence

$$T = \frac{\rho}{2} A_0 V^2 (2b + b^2)$$

But, also, thrust = rate of increase of axial momentum

$$\therefore \quad T = \rho A_0 V(1+a)bV = \rho A_0 V^2 (1+a)b$$

Comparing these two expressions for thrust, it is seen that

$$a = b/2$$

That is to say, half the velocity increase experienced in the screw race is caused by the suction created by the propeller and takes place before the water enters the propeller disc. This factor of increase, a, is known as the *axial inflow factor*. This factor controls the propeller efficiency that can be obtained since

$$
\begin{aligned}
\text{Propeller efficiency} &= \frac{\text{useful work done by propeller}}{\text{power absorbed by the propeller}} \\[2mm]
&= \frac{\text{thrust} \times \text{propeller speed}}{\text{overall change in kinetic energy}} \\[2mm]
&= \frac{\rho A_0 V^2 2a(1+a)V}{\frac{1}{2}\rho A_0 V(1+a)V^2[(1+2a)^2-1]} \\[2mm]
&= \frac{2\rho A_0 V^3 a(1+a)}{\frac{1}{2}\rho A_0 V^3(1+a)(4a^2+4a)} \\[2mm]
&= \frac{1}{1+a}
\end{aligned}
$$

This shows that even in the ideal case, high propeller efficiency is only possible with a small inflow factor, i.e. with a large diameter propeller.

THE BLADE ELEMENT APPROACH

The momentum theory is useful in indicating the influence of the propeller on the water ahead of its own disc, and in demonstrating that even theoretically there is a limit to the efficiency which can be achieved. It is not, however, of direct value in assessing the torque and thrust developed in a propeller of a particular geometry.

One approach is to consider each blade of the propeller as made up of a series of annular elements such as the shaded portion in Fig. 10.18 which represents that portion of the blade between radii r and $r+\delta r$. If the propeller is turning at n r.p.m., then the element will have a tangential velocity of $2\pi rn$ besides a velocity of advance V_1 relative to the water. The element, which can be regarded

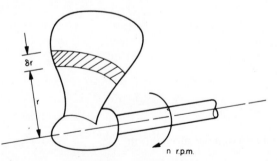

Fig. 10.18 Annular element of propeller blade

as a short length of aerofoil section, will experience a relative water velocity as shown in Fig. 10.19.

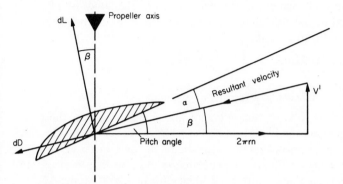

Fig. 10.19 Water flow relative to blade element

It will be seen that the blade element is at an angle α, to the resultant velocity. This angle is known as the *angle of attack*. To explain what happens now, it is necessary to introduce the concept of a *vortex*. In a potential vortex, fluid circulates about an axis, the circumferential velocity of any fluid particle being inversely proportional to its distance from the axis. The strength of the vortex is defined by the *circulation* Γ. If the blade element were in an inviscid fluid, the potential flow pattern around it would be as in Fig. 10.20(*a*). In a real fluid, the very high velocities at the sharp trailing edge produce an unstable situation in the viscous fluid due to shear stresses. The potential flow pattern breaks down and a stable flow pattern is established as in Fig. 10.20(*c*). This consists of the original uniform flow with a superimposed vortex (Fig. 10.20(*b*)) having the foil as a core. The strength of the circulation depends upon the shape of the section and its angle of attack.

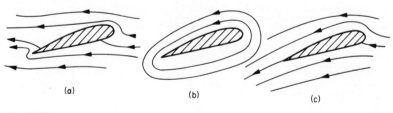

(a)   (b)   (c)

Fig. 10.20

If, in an inviscid fluid, a circulation of this same strength could somehow be established, the blade element would be acted on by a lift force normal to the resultant velocity and the force would be proportional to the circulation. In a real fluid, the viscosity which gives rise to the circulation also introduces a small drag force whilst having little influence on the lift.

In Fig. 10.19, the lift and drag acting on the blade element are shown as d*L* and d*D* respectively. As already stated, the circulation depends upon the shape of the section and the angle of attack. A number of so-called aerofoil sections are available which produce high lift for small drag. If one of these sections is being used, its characteristics will be available from standard tests. Hence, the lift and drag on each element of the blade can be calculated. By resolving parallel and normal to the propeller axis, the contributions of the element to the overall thrust and torque of the propeller are

$$dT = dL \cos \beta - dD \sin \beta$$

and,

$$dQ = (dL \sin \beta + dD \cos \beta) \times (\text{radius of element})$$

By repeating this process for each element and integrating over the blade, the thrust and torque on each blade and hence of the propeller can be obtained. Account can be taken of propellers in which the pitch angle varies with radius, but a really comprehensive theory of propellers must also take into account the interference between blades, and the tendency for pressures on the face and back of the blade to be equalized by flow around the tip of the blade.

These advanced theories, often referred to as Vortex Theory Design, are used more and more to design propellers either individually, or to indicate lines of development for methodical series. They are beyond the scope of this book.

So far, the propeller has been considered to be in open water in uniform flow and it has been assumed that the flow is similar in the model and full-scale propeller. In actual ship applications, these conditions are fundamentally affected by two factors which are considered in more detail below. They are:

(*a*) the propeller behind the ship is not in open water and its performance will be affected by interactions between the hull and propeller;
(*b*) the flow can break down around the propeller, a phenomenon known as cavitation. When this occurs, the law of similarity no longer applies.

CAVITATION

The thrust and torque of the propeller depend upon the lift and drag characteristics of the blade sections. The lift on the section is produced partly from the suction on the back of the blade and partly from positive pressure on the face. In this context, suction and positive pressure are relative to the free field pressure at the blade. A typical pressure distribution is shown in Fig. 10.21.

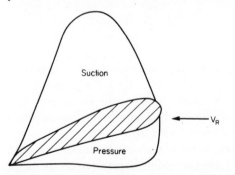

Fig. 10.21 Pressure distribution over an aerofoil section

As the pressure on the back falls lower and lower, with increasing propeller r.p.m., say, the absolute pressure will eventually become low enough for the water to vaporize and local cavities form. This phenomenon is known as *cavitation*. Since the water cannot accept lower pressures, the lift cannot increase as rapidly and the presence of cavitation manifests itself, therefore, as a fall off in thrust and torque compared with what would otherwise have been obtained. Radial variation of pitch can improve cavitation performance and need have little effect on propeller efficiency. The pressure at which cavitation occurs depends upon temperature, the amount of dissolved air or other gases present and the surface tension. Without gases in solution, the pressure might typically be of the order $\frac{1}{2}$ p.s.i. for fresh water and the presence of air can increase this to about $1\frac{1}{2}$ p.s.i. The first cavitation to occur is usually that in the tip vortex—the *tip vortex cavitation*—arising from the low pressure in the core of the vortex. The vortex itself is formed by the rolling-up of the various trailing vortices shed by the blade which is a necessary corollary to the circulation around the blade which produces the lift force. As σ, the cavitation number, is reduced, the cavitation spreads across the back of the blade giving the appearance of a sheet or surface of separation. This is known as *sheet cavitation*.

Other forms of cavitation are *bubble cavitation* which usually occurs at the thick root sections of the blades and is particularly susceptible to local irregularities in the blade surface. Unfortunately, the bubbles formed in a region of low pressure can be swept away into regions of high pressure where they collapse. This can lead to intense local pressures which may cause pitting or erosion of the propeller blades. Such pitting not only produces a weaker propeller but also increases the surface irregularities of the blades. *Face cavitation* can occur when the blade sections are working at very small or negative angles of incidence which can arise when a propeller operates in a varying velocity field. An undesirable aspect of cavitation in warships is the noise associated with the cavitation bubbles and their collapse. This can betray the ship's presence to an enemy and can attract homing weapons.

A special situation arises in propellers running at high r.p.m., as might be the case in a high speed motor boat. In these circumstances, it is impossible to eliminate cavitation but reasonable efficiency can be obtained by using a propeller designed to have the back completely covered by cavitation; although the lift generated by the back is limited by the vapour pressure, the torque component due to skin friction on the back of the blade is eliminated. Such a propeller is known as a *super-cavitating* propeller. It is no use at speeds lower than 40 – 50 knots.

SINGING

Before the onset of cavitation, the blades of a propeller may emit a high-pitched note. This singing, as it is termed, is due to the elastic vibration of the material excited by the resonant shedding of non-cavitating eddies from the trailing edge of the blades. Heavy camber appears to be conducive to singing. Cures can be effected by changing the shape of the trailing edge or increased damping of the blade.

INTERACTION BETWEEN THE SHIP AND PROPELLER

The interaction manifests itself in the following ways:

(a) the hull carries with it a certain mass of water as was pointed out in considering the boundary layer. This means that the average velocity of water
relative to the propeller disc is no longer equal to the velocity of advance
of the propeller relative to still water;
(b) the water velocity will vary in both magnitude and direction across the
propeller disc and the performance of the propeller will differ from that in
open water even allowing for the difference in average velocity;
(c) the propeller causes variation in local pressures in the water and these will
react upon the hull, leading to an effective increase in resistance.

Let us proceed to consider each of these effects in more detail.

The difference between the ship speed and the speed of the water relative to
the ship is termed the *wake*. The wake is the combination of the boundary layer
associated with skin friction, the flow velocities occasioned by the streamlined
form of the ship and the orbital velocities of the waves created by the ship.
If the water is moving in the same direction as the ship, the wake is said to be
positive. If the ship speed is V and the average velocity of the water relative
to the hull at the propeller position is V_1, then:

Wake $= V - V_1$

To non-dimensionalize this relation, the wake can be divided by either
V_1 or V. The former was proposed by Froude and the latter by Taylor leading
to two wake factors as follows:

Froude wake factor $= w_F = (V - V_1)/V_1$

Taylor wake factor $= w = (V - V_1)/V$

Clearly, these are merely different ways of expressing the same phenomenon.

Apart from this *average* flow of water relative to the hull there will be variations in velocity over the propeller disc. As the hull is approached more closely,
the water moves less fast relative to the ship. Apart from this general effect of
the hull there will be local perturbations due to the shaft, shaft bossings or
shaft brackets and other appendages. Due to the fact that the water must
'close-in' around the stern the flow through the propeller disc will not be
everywhere the same and will not, in general, be parallel to the shaft line. These
effects are combined and expressed as a *relative rotative efficiency* (RRE) which
is defined as

$$\text{RRE} = \eta_R = \frac{\text{efficiency of propeller behind the ship}}{\text{efficiency of propeller in open water at speed } V_1}$$

Finally, there is the influence on the hull of pressure variations induced by
the propeller action. As far as the propeller is concerned it has to produce a
thrust T which is greater than the resistance R of the hull without propeller.

As with the wake, there are two ways of expressing this physical phenomenon. It can be considered as an *augment of resistance, a,* where

$$a = \frac{T-R}{R}$$

or, it can be regarded as a *thrust deduction factor, t,* where

$$t = \frac{T-R}{T}$$

HULL EFFICIENCY

The thrust horsepower (t.h.p.), developed by the propeller is given by the product of T and V_1. On the other hand, the effective horsepower is given by the product RV.

Now

$$\text{t.h.p.} = TV_1 = R(1+a)\frac{V}{1+w_F} = \frac{RV(1+a)}{1+w_F} = RV(1+a)(1-w) = RV\frac{(1-w)}{(1-t)}$$

therefore

$$\frac{\text{e.h.p.}}{\text{t.h.p.}} = \frac{1+w_F}{1+a} \text{ or } \frac{1-t}{1-w}$$

This ratio is known as the *hull efficiency* and seldom differs very greatly from unity.

To complete the picture of the propeller acting behind the ship, the concept of relative rotative efficiency must be added in. The three factors, augment, wake and RRE are referred to collectively as the *hull efficiency elements.* Augment and wake are functions of Reynolds' number but variation between ship and model is ignored and the error so introduced is taken account of by the trials factors.

OVERALL PROPULSIVE EFFICIENCY

The shaft horsepower (s.h.p.) is the power needed to propel the complete ship. The ratio between the e.h.p. and s.h.p. is a measure of the overall propulsive efficiency achieved and is termed the *propulsive coefficient* (PC)

$$PC = \frac{\text{e.h.p.}}{\text{s.h.p.}}$$

The overall efficiency can be regarded as the cumulative effect of a number of factors. Consider the following in addition to e.h.p. and s.h.p.

e.h.p.′ = power to tow hull complete with appendages,
t.h.p. = thrust horsepower developed by propellers = TV_1,
d.h.p. = power delivered to propellers when propelling the ship,
d.h.p.′ = power delivered to propellers when developing a thrust T in open water at a speed V_1.

Now the propulsive coefficient can be defined as:

$$PC = \frac{\text{e.h.p.}}{\text{s.h.p.}} = \frac{\text{e.h.p.}}{\text{e.h.p.}'} \times \frac{\text{e.h.p.}'}{\text{t.h.p.}} \times \frac{\text{t.h.p.}}{\text{d.h.p.}'} \times \frac{\text{d.h.p.}'}{\text{d.h.p.}} \times \frac{\text{d.h.p.}}{\text{s.h.p.}}$$

where

$$\frac{\text{e.h.p.}}{\text{e.h.p.}'} = \frac{1}{\text{appendage coefficient}}$$

$$\frac{\text{e.h.p.}'}{\text{t.h.p.}} = \text{hull efficiency, } \eta_H$$

$$\frac{\text{t.h.p.}}{\text{d.h.p.}'} = \text{propeller efficiency } \eta_0 \text{ in open water at speed } V_1$$

$$\frac{\text{d.h.p.}'}{\text{d.h.p.}} = \text{relative rotative efficiency, } \eta_R$$

$$\frac{\text{d.h.p.}}{\text{s.h.p.}} = \text{shaft transmission efficiency}$$

That is

$$PC = \left[\frac{\eta_H \times \eta_0 \times \eta_R}{\text{appendage coefficient}} \right] \times \text{transmission efficiency}$$

Reference 5 recommends that the transmission efficiency be taken as 0·97 for ships with machinery amidships and 0·98 for ships with machinery aft.

The quantity in the brackets is known as the *quasi-propulsive coefficient* (QPC), η_D, and can be obtained from model results. There is some error in applying this to the full-scale ship and to allow for this and transmission efficiency and any differences between the ship and model test conditions, e.g. wind, waves, cavitation, use is made by the MOD (Navy) of a *QPC factor* which is defined as

$$\text{QPC factor} = \frac{\text{PC from ship trial}}{\text{QPC from model}}$$

The value to be assigned to the QPC factor when estimating power requirements for a new design is usually determined from results of a similar ship.

The National Physical Laboratory (Ref. 5) uses a *load factor* instead of the QPC factor, where

$$\text{load factor} = 1 + x = \frac{\text{transmission efficiency}}{(\text{QPC factor})(\text{appendage coefficient})}$$

In the NPL analysis, the *overload fraction* x is intended to allow for the basic shell roughness, fouling, weather conditions and depends on ship length and type. It is recommended that whatever value of x is used in estimates a standard power estimate should also be made with a load factor of unity, i.e.

with x = zero, and an appendage scale-effect factor $\beta = 1$, i.e. assuming appendage resistance scales directly from the model to the ship.

SHIP–MODEL CORRELATION

The conduct of a ship speed trial is dealt with later together with the analysis by which the ship's actual speed is deduced. This demonstrates whether the ship meets its specification but does not tell the designer much about the soundness of his prediction method. If the specified speed is not reached it. may be that he wrongly estimated the ship's resistance or hull efficiency elements, the propeller design may have been incorrect or the machinery may not have developed the intended power. A much more comprehensive analysis of the trials data is required by the designer to assist him with later designs. Even if the speed prediction was acceptable, it is still possible that several errors in assessing various factors cancelled each other out.

The analysis method used must depend upon the design methods to be checked. Froude developed the following method using 'circular' functions defined as below:

$$\textcircled{E} = \frac{1000\,(\text{e.h.p.})}{\Delta^{\frac{2}{3}} V^3}, \quad \text{using naked model e.h.p.}$$

$$\textcircled{E}_A = \frac{1000\,(\text{h.p.})_A}{\Delta^{\frac{2}{3}} V^3}, \quad \text{where } (\text{h.p.})_A = \text{horsepower to tow the appendages}$$

$$\textcircled{E}_{WP} = \frac{1000\,(\text{h.p.})_{WP}}{\Delta^{\frac{2}{3}} V^3}, \quad \text{where } (\text{h.p.})_{WP} = \text{horsepower to overcome windage and fouling under trials conditions}$$

$$\textcircled{E}_T = \textcircled{E} + \textcircled{E}_A + \textcircled{E}_{WP}$$

N.B. If the speed trial is carried out under good conditions, $\textcircled{E}_{WP}$ should be negligible.

$$\textcircled{T}_M = \frac{1000\,(\text{t.h.p.})}{\Delta^{\frac{2}{3}} V^3} = \textcircled{E}_T (1+a)(1-w)$$

$$\textcircled{T}_R = \frac{H \times 1000}{\Delta^{\frac{2}{3}} V^3} = H\,\textcircled{T}_M / \text{t.h.p.}$$

where

$\quad H$ = thrust horsepower from open water propeller data using the trial r.p.m. and speed and the model wake

$$\textcircled{D} = \frac{1000\,(\text{d.h.p.})}{\Delta^{\frac{2}{3}} V^3}$$

$$\textcircled{I} = \frac{1000\,(\text{s.h.p.})}{\Delta^{\frac{2}{3}} V^3}$$

Each of the above parameters is calculated for each run and plotted to a base of speed. The propulsive coefficient, equal to $\textcircled{E}/\textcircled{I}$, is also plotted with the

QPC factor which is the ratio of the PC from the ship trial to the QPC from model tests.

If the predictions from model experiments were exact the QPC factor would equal the shaft transmission efficiency, and:

$$\textcircled{T}_R = \textcircled{T}_M$$

In general, this relationship is not precise as $\textcircled{$T$}_R$ includes some scale effects including those due to cavitation on the ship propeller.

Thus, both the QPCF and the ratio $\textcircled{$T$}_R/\textcircled{$T$}_M$ show the essential differences between the model and full-scale data. In a new design the designer uses these quantities, deduced from previous trials, to assist in scaling from the model to the ship. He would make allowance for any differences in the two designs such as different appendage coefficients.

Model testing

RESISTANCE TESTS

Many great men attempted to use models or to show how they could be used to predict full-scale behaviour, including Bouguer, Tiedemann, Newton, Chapman, Euler and Beaufoy, but it was not until the time of William Froude that full-scale prediction became a practical proposition.

It was William Froude who postulated the idea of splitting the total resistance into the residuary resistance and the frictional resistance of the equivalent flat plate. He also argued that air resistance and the effects of rough water could be treated separately. By studying the wave patterns created by geometrically similar forms at different speeds, Froude found that the patterns appeared identical, geometrically, when the models were moving at speeds proportional to the square root of their lengths. This speed is termed the *corresponding speed,* and this is merely another way of expressing constancy of Froude number. He also noted that the curves of resistance against speed were generally similar if the resistance per unit displacement was plotted for corresponding speeds. Proceeding further, he found that by subtracting from the total resistance an allowance for the frictional resistance, determined from flat plates, the agreement was very good indeed.

This led to *Froude's law of comparison* which may be stated as:

If two geometrically similar forms are run at corresponding speeds (i.e. speeds proportional to the square root of their linear dimensions), then their residuary resistances per unit of displacement are the same.

Thus the essentials are available for predicting the resistance of the full-scale ship from a model. The steps as used by Froude are still used today, refinements being restricted to detail rather than principle. For each particular value of the ship speed:

(*a*) measure the resistance of a geometrically similar model at its corresponding speed, (*b*) estimate the skin friction resistance from data derived from experiments on flat plates,

(*c*) subtract the skin friction resistance from the total resistance to obtain the residuary resistance,

(*d*) multiply the model residuary resistance by the ratio of the ship to model displacements to obtain the ship residuary resistance,

(*e*) add the skin friction resistance estimated for the ship to obtain the total ship resistance.

It should be noted that any error in estimating frictional resistance applies both to the model and ship. Thus, only the effect on the difference of the two is significant.

It is now possible to see why earlier attempts to correlate the total resistance of ship and model failed. Two models with identical resistances could only represent ships with identical resistances if the ratios of their residuary and skin friction resistance were the same. In general, this could not be true unless the forms were themselves the same. Indeed, if model A had less total resistance than model B it did not even follow that ship A would be less resistive than ship B. Thus, even the qualitative comparisons made between models, used so frequently even today in many branches of naval architecture, may be invalid.

RESISTANCE TEST FACILITIES AND TECHNIQUES

With the aid of a grant from the Admiralty, Froude constructed the world's first model tank at Torquay in 1871 where R. E. Froude continued his father's work on the latter's death in 1879. The work of the Froudes proved so useful that, when the lease on the Torquay site expired in 1885, a grant was made to erect another at Haslar in 1887. This was the beginning of the Admiralty Experiment Works (AEW) which has grown over the years and has always remained one of the world's leading establishments in this field.

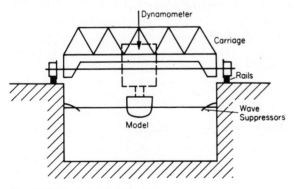

Fig. 10.22 Typical ship tank section

Modern ship tanks for measuring model resistance are fundamentally the same as the first tank made by Froude. Such a facility is essentially a long tank, of approximately rectangular cross-section, spanned by a carriage which tows the model along the tank. Improvements have been made over the years in respect of the methods of propelling the carriage, in the constancy of speed maintained by the carriage and in the dynamometers used to record the model resistance.

In a typical run, the carriage is accelerated up to the required speed, resistance records and measurement of hull sinkage and trim are taken during a period of constant speed and then the carriage is decelerated. With increasing ship lengths and service speeds, there has arisen a demand for longer and longer tanks to cope with the longer acceleration and deceleration runs.

Several very interesting features of model test procedures are described in Ref. 6 and arise from the very methodical and painstaking approach used by W. and R. E. Froude. As early as 1880, R. E. Froude was aware of unexplained variations in the resistance measured in repeat experiments on a given model. He suspected currents set up in the tank by the passage of the model and variations in skin friction resistance due to temperature changes. Methodical investigation into the first of these two features led to the adoption at AEW of small propeller type logs to record the speed of the model relative to the water. Investigation of the temperature effect led Froude to postulate that a 3 per cent decrease in skin resistance for every 10°F rise in temperature could be adopted as a fair working allowance and linked this with a standard temperature of 55°F.

In the temperature experiments, R. E. Froude used the model of HMS *Iris*, a 300 ft, 3700 tonf despatch vessel, as a 'standard' model to be tested at various times throughout the year. Final proof that, even after correcting for tank currents and temperature, significant variations in resistance were occurring, came in tests on the *Iris* model in the tank at Haslar to correlate with those previously run at Torquay. This led to the application of a so-called *Iris correction* obtained by running the standard model at frequent intervals and applying a correcting factor to the resistance of a new model depending on the variation of the *Iris* resistance from its standard value. Generally, the *Iris* correction varies between 1 and 6 per cent, but during abnormal periods, commonly referred to as 'storms', the correction can be more than 10 per cent. The cause of the storms is now believed to be due to the presence in the water of substances having long chain molecules (Ref. 7). The concept of a standard model has since been adopted by other ship tanks.

MODEL DETERMINATION OF HULL EFFICIENCY ELEMENTS

Experiments must be carried out with the hull and propeller correctly combined as illustrated in Fig. 10.23.

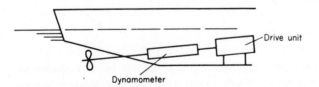

Fig. 10.23 Experimental technique

With the model at the correct speed, corresponding to that of the ship under study, a series of runs is made over a range of propeller r.p.m. straddling the self-propulsion point of the model. Model speed and resistance are recorded together with the thrust, torque and r.p.m. of the propeller. Results are plotted to a base of propeller r.p.m., as shown for thrust in Fig. 10.24, to find the model self-propulsion point.

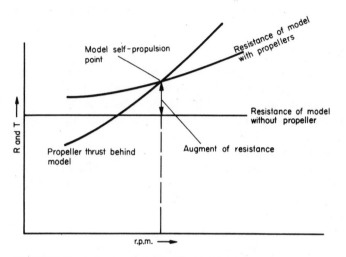

Fig. 10.24 Determination of model self-propulsion point

The model propeller then has its thrust and torque measured in open water at a speed of advance estimated to be that of the flow through the propeller when behind the hull, i.e. making allowance for the wake. By comparing this curve with that obtained in the combined experiment, the correct speed for the propeller in open water can be calculated. The difference between the model speed in the combined experiment and the corrected open water speed is the *wake*. The relative rotative efficiency follows as the ratio between the torques measured in the open water and combined experiments at self-propulsion r.p.m. The *augment of resistance* is obtained as illustrated in Fig. 10.24.

It should be noted that, although the propeller used in these experiments is made as closely representative of the ship propeller as possible, at least the first estimate of its geometry, the scale is too small to enable the thrust and torque figures to be used directly. Instead, the hull efficiency elements calculated as above are used with either methodical series data or specific cavitation tunnel measurements in order to produce the propeller design.

PROPELLER TESTS IN OPEN WATER

It is important that the designer has data available on which to base selection of the geometric properties of a propeller and to determine likely propeller efficiency. Such data is obtained from methodical series testing of model propellers in open water. (Refs. 8 and 9.) Such testing eliminates the effects of cavitation and the actual flow of water into a propeller behind a particular ship form, and makes comparisons of different propellers possible on a consistent basis.

The tests are carried out in a ship tank with the propeller mounted forward of a streamlined casing containing the drive shaft. The propeller is driven by an electric motor on the carriage. Thrust, torque, propeller r.p.m. and carriage speed are recorded and from these K_T, K_Q, J and η can be calculated. Usually runs are carried out at constant r.p.m. with different speeds of advance for each run.

CAVITATION TUNNEL TESTS

It is impossible to run a model propeller in open water so that all the non-dimensional factors are kept at the same values as in the ship. In particular, it is difficult to scale pressure because the atmospheric pressure is the same for ship and model and scaling the depth of the propeller below the surface does not provide an adequate answer. If cavitation is important, the pressure of air above the water must be reduced artificially and this is the reason for using *cavitation tunnels* to study propeller performance. Such a tunnel is shown diagrammatically in Fig. 10.25, and is usually provided with means for reducing the air content of the water to improve viewing.

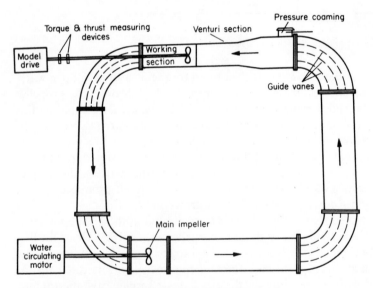

Fig. 10.25 *Diagrammatic arrangement of a cavitation tunnel*

In practice, experiments are usually run under the following conditions:

(*a*) the water speed is made as high as possible to keep Reynolds' number high to avoid serious scaling of skin friction;

(*b*) the model propeller is selected to have as large a diameter as is compatible with the tunnel size (tunnel wall effects must be avoided);

(c) model is run at the correct *J* value. This fixes the rate of propeller revolutions;

(d) the pressure in the tunnel is lowered to produce the correct cavitation number at the propeller axis.

Since the propeller revolutions are the most easily adjusted variable, it is usual to set the tunnel water speed, adjust the tunnel pressure to give the correct cavitation number and then vary the propeller r.p.m. systematically to cause a variation in the advance coefficient. The whole series can then be repeated for other *σ* values.

The tunnel shown in Fig. 10.25 is a fairly simple one and suffers from the fact that it is difficult to simulate the actual flow conditions at the after end of the ship. In some cases, attempts to reproduce this have been made using specially designed grids to control the local flow conditions. Also, the flow is from right to left in the working section so that the drive shaft on the model propeller is aft of the disc rather than forward of it as is the case for the ship. In big tunnels, both objections can be overcome by modelling the after end of the hull complete inside the tunnel and driving the propeller from inside this model hull.

In spite of these limitations, tunnels have produced useful information on cavitation and the various forms it can take.

Ship trials

SPEED TRIALS

When a ship has been completed, speed trials are carried out to confirm that the ship has met its specification as regards design speed. Such trials also provide useful data to help the designer in producing subsequent designs.

The trials are carried out over a 'measured mile' which is a precisely known distance although it need not be precisely a nautical mile. The distance is marked clearly by prominently marked posts set up on land. A typical arrangement is illustrated in Fig. 10.26.

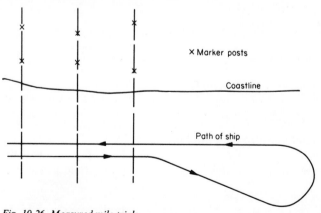

Fig. 10.26 Measured mile trials

(*Note: Drawing not to scale. A straight approach run of about 3 miles is used.*)

The ship approaches on a course normal to the lines joining corresponding pairs of 'mile' posts and sufficiently far off shore to ensure adequate depth of water to eliminate the effect of depth of water on resistance. The time to traverse the measured distance is accurately noted together with shaft thrust, torque and revolutions. A fine day with little wind and calm seas is chosen. To reduce its effect upon resistance the use of the rudder is kept to a minimum during the run. At the end of the run the rudder is put over to a moderate angle and the ship is taken round in a large sweep, as illustrated, to provide adequate run-up for the next pass to ensure that the ship has stopped accelerating by the time it passes the first pair of posts.

The trial is carried out for a range of powers up to the maximum the machinery can generate. At each power, several runs are made in each direction to enable. the effect of any tide to be eliminated. If the runs are made at regular time intervals, it is adequate to take a mean of means, i.e. by meaning each consecutive pair of speeds, taking means of consecutive pairs of results so obtained and so on. The process is illustrated by the following example in which the mean speed is 15 knots.

EXAMPLE 3. A ship on a measured mile course records the speeds of 14·82, 15·22, 14·80, 15·20, 14·78 and 15·18 knots for six consecutive runs at regular time intervals. Calculate the mean speed.

Solution:

Measured Speeds (knots)	Means				
	First	Second	Third	Fourth	Fifth
14·82					
	15·02				
15·22		15·015			
	15·01		15·010		
14·80		15·005		15·005	
	15·00		15·000		15·00
15·20		14·995		14·995	
	14·99		14·990		
14·78		14·985			
	14·98				
15·18					

Mean ship speed = 15·00 knots.

If runs are not carried out at regular time intervals, it is necessary to assume that the tide varies with time according to a mathematical equation such as

$$\text{Speed of tide} = v = a + a_1 t + a_2 t^2$$

where t is the time measured from the initial run made.

It is then assumed that the speed without tide would be V, say, and that the readings obtained represent $V + v$ where v is the value appropriate to the time the run was made.

EXAMPLE 4. A ship on a measured mile course records the speeds of 15·22, 14·82, 15·20 and 14·80 at times of 1200, 1300, 1430 and 1530 hours. Calculate the speed of the ship and the equation governing the variation of the tidal current with time.

Solution: It is convenient to take the times at $t = 0$, $t = 1$, $t = 2.5$, $t = 3.5$, i.e. measuring in hours from the time of the initial run. Then, assuming that the ship speed is V and the tide is given by $v = a_0 + a_1 t + a_2 t^2$, we can write

at 1200 hrs; $15.22 = V + a_0$
at 1300 hrs; $14.82 = V - a_0 - a_1 - a_2$
at 1430 hrs; $15.20 = V + a_0 + 2.5a_1 + 6.25a_2$
at 1530 hrs; $14.80 = V - a_0 - 3.5a_1 - 12.25a_2$

Solving these equations,

$V = 15.01$ knots
$v = (0.21 - 0.028t + 0.008t^2)$ knots, t in hours

The difference in sign in alternate equations merely denotes that the tide is with or against the ship. Clearly, the tide is with the ship when it records its higher speeds but this is not significant to the mathematics since, if the wrong assumption is made, the tidal equation will lead to a negative tide.

EXPERIMENTS AT FULL SCALE

Ship trials over a measured distance in calm water can confirm, or otherwise, the accuracy of the prediction of ship speed for a given power. They cannot, however, prove that the fundamental arguments underlying these estimates are valid. In particular, they cannot prove that the estimation of e.h.p. was accurate because the influence of the ship propulsion system is always present.

William Froude realized this and with Admiralty assistance carried out full-scale resistance measurements on HMS *Greyhound* in 1874 as described in Ref. 10. More recently, full-scale resistance trials were carried out using the *Lucy Ashton* (Ref. 11) and HMS *Penelope* (Ref. 14).

In the earlier trials, the screw sloop *Greyhound* was towed from an outrigger fitted to HMS *Active*, a vessel of about 3100 tonf displacement. This method (Fig. 10.27) was adopted to avoid, as far as possible, any interference between the towing and the towed ship. Trials were carried out with the *Greyhound* at three displacements and covered a speed range of 3–12½ knots. Some trials were with and some without bilge keels. For some runs the tow rope was slipped and the deceleration of the ship noted.

William Froude concluded that the experiments:

. . . substantially verify the law of comparison which has been propounded by me as governing the relation between the resistance of ships and their models.

In the BSRA trials the problems associated with towing a vessel were overcome by fitting the ship with four jet engines mounted high on the ship and outboard of the main hull to avoid the jet efflux impinging either on the hull or on the water in the immediate vicinity of the hull. Accurate measurement of thrust, totalling just over 6 tonf from the four engines, was achieved by using hydraulic load measuring capsules. Speeds were measured over measured mile distances and Ref. 11 provides an interesting account of the special measures taken to ensure accurate results and also to measure the surface roughness of the hull.

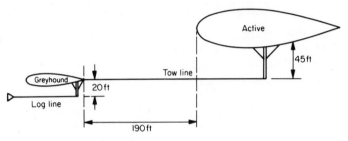

Fig. 10.27 Greyhound *experiments*

Resistance tests were made over a speed range of 5–15 knots with a clean naked hull with first a red oxide paint surface and then a bituminous aluminium paint. Each trial was repeated for sharp seams of plating and with the seams faired off with a plastic composition. Additional trials were run to study the effect of dummy twin-screw bossings, with twin-screw 'A' brackets and shafts and with a hull surface which had been allowed to foul for about a month.

The main purpose of the trial was to compare the various methods available for scaling model resistance to full-scale. The results indicated that Froude's law of comparison is valid for the scaling-up of wave-making resistance, but that the usual assumption that the skin friction of models and ships is the same as that of the corresponding plane surface of the same length and wetted surface is not strictly correct. Fortunately, the error is not very important in in practical calculations. The results also indicate that over the range of models tested, the interference between the skin-frictional and wave-making resistance is not significant.

The results of the trials proved that full-scale ship resistance is sensitive to small roughnesses. For instance, the bituminous aluminium paint, which was the smoother of the two surface finishes, gave about $3\frac{1}{2}$ per cent less total resistance which was estimated to be equivalent to about 5 per cent of the skin frictional resistance. Fairing the seams gave about a 3 per cent reduction in total resistance. The effect of 40 days fouling on the bituminous aluminium painted hull was to increase the skin frictional resistance by about 5 per cent, i.e. about $\frac{1}{8}$th of one per cent per day.

Trials in HMS *Penelope* (Ref. 14) were conducted by the Admiralty Experiment Works while the ship was operating as a special trials ship. *Penelope* was towed by another frigate using a mile-long nylon rope. Although the main purpose of the trial was to measure radiated noise from, and vibration in, a dead ship, the opportunity was taken to measure resistance and wake pattern of *Penelope* in calm water and in waves. For this purpose both propellers were removed and a pitot rake fitted to one shaft. Propulsion data were recorded in the towing ship also. Propulsion data for *Penelope* were obtained from separate measured mile trials with three different sets of propellers fitted.

Correlation of ship and model data showed the resistance of *Penelope* to be some 14 per cent higher than predicted over the range 12–13 knots but indicated no significant wake scale effects. The hull roughness, using the BSRA wall roughness gauge was found to be about 0·3 mm mean apparent amplitude per 50 mm. The mean apparent amplitude per 50 mm is the standard parameter used in the UK to represent the average hull roughness. The propulsion results showed that thrust, torque and efficiency of the ship's propellers were higher than predicted by model tests.

Reference 14 includes details of the methods used to record the various parameters during the trials and discusses the recording accuracies.

Summary

In studying the powering of ships, it is essential that the hull and propulsion device be considered together. The shaft horsepower required to drive a ship at a given speed can be derived from a series of model tests and calculations. The basic elements in the assessment of the shaft horsepower have been established and are summarized in Fig. 10.28.

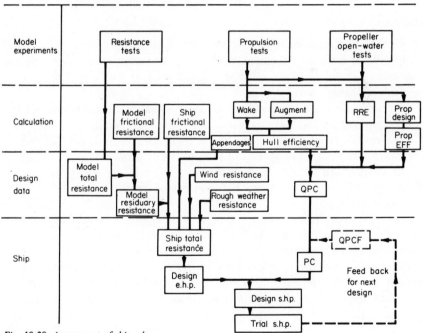

Fig. 10.28 Assessment of ship s.h.p.

It remains to show how model data is presented and the necessary calculations carried out. This is done in the next chapter.

380 Basic ship theory

Concluding remarks

Basic elements of the resistance and propulsion of ships have been presented here. There remain many areas which have been much further developed, for which there is no room in a book of this sort. For example, considerable work has been done on the nature of the wake of a ship in the vicinity of a propeller so that the interaction between hull and propeller may be better understood and allowed for. This has resulted in wake-adapted propellers in which the pitch varies with the radius and these are now quite common. The ducted propeller has become more common following development of a theory and a better understanding of the interference between the boundary layer on the inside of the duct and the tips of the propeller blades.

New facilities at ship model basins include devices for suppressing waves—and the effects of Froude Number—by a solid air/surface interface around a ship model in a closed circulating water channel. This permits a better representation of Reynolds' number for the ship, although correspondence of Reynolds' number for ship, propeller and appendages remains a problem. From all facilities in model basins, direct digital recording of results has also become common, to be recalled from the computer and manipulated in accordance with prescribed programs.

These and many other important advances make it even more important to understand the general principles which this chapter has outlined.

Problems

1. A 50 MN displacement ship, length 120 m, is to be represented by a model 3 m long. What is the displacement of the model? At what speed must it be run to represent a speed of 20 knots in the ship and what is the ratio of the ship to model e.h.p. at this speed?

2. Show how wave-making resistance at a given speed is affected by varying the length of parallel middle body, entrance angle and run remaining unchanged.

On the resistance curve for a ship length 70 m with 20 m of parallel middle body, one hump occurs at a speed of 14 knots and an adjacent one at $\sqrt{\frac{3}{2}}$ times this. At what speed would the main hump occur? If the length of parallel middle body is increased 15 m, at what sequence of speeds will humps occur on the resistance curve? (RNC)

3. How are waves created when a typical warship form passes through the water? With the aid of sketches describe a typical ship wave pattern and explain what effect 'shoulders' on the curve of areas would have on this pattern. Draw a typical resistance curve for a ship indicating the main features of its characteristic shape and explaining why humps and hollows occur. Derive the expressions from which the position of these humps and hollows may be determined and, hence, determine the speeds at which the two most prominent humps occur for a ship of effective wave-length 99 m. (HMDTC)

4. Sketch and describe a typical ship wave pattern. What is meant by interference between wave systems? Show, with the use of diagrams, why humps and hollows occur in the curve of wave-making resistance against $V/\sqrt{L}$, giving approximate values of $V/\sqrt{L}$ at which the humps and hollows occur.

A destroyer, length 122 m, is observed to be steaming at high speed. The first trough of the bow wave system is seen to coincide with the stern trough. Estimate the speed of the destroyer assuming that the wave system distance is 0·9*L*.   (HMDTC)

5. A ship at full speed has an e.h.p. naked of 7×10^6 W. The appendage coefficient is 1·15, the hull efficiency 0·98, the propeller efficiency 0·69, the RRE 0·99 and the QPCF 0·90. Calculate the propulsive coefficient, the quasi-propulsive coefficient and the s.h.p. required.

6. A 50 MN displacement ship 100 m long, is towed in the naked condition on a long tow rope at a speed of 20 knots. The force in the tow rope is 1 MN. Find the e.h.p. for the ship. Deduce the s.h.p. for a geometrically similar ship 120 m long at 20 knots assuming that s.h.p. in this speed region is proportional to the cube of the speed and that:

appendage coefficient	1·20
hull efficiency	0·97
propeller efficiency	0·72
RRE	1·00
QPCF	0·95

7. Describe how speed trials are conducted, listing the items recorded. What factors would you consider important when choosing a site for a new measured mile course?

Full-power trials of a new frigate involved five passes over the measured mile, each pass being followed by one in the opposite direction. The times of the start of each run and the speeds attained are as quoted in the table:

Time of start	1045	1103	1127	1227	1245
Speed of run (knots)	27·59	28·66	27·64	28·60	27·69

Making suitable adjustments to the time intervals and assuming the tide speed is given by $v = a + bt + ct^2 + dt^3$, determine the true speed of the ship.

      (HMDTC)

8. List the measurements which are made, during sea trials, on each run over the measured mile, explaining briefly how each measurement is made.

The following data were obtained during progressive speed trials on a merchant ship. Assuming that the tidal velocity may be expressed in the form $v = a + bt + ct^2$, calculate the true speed at each power.

Run no.	Direction	Time of day	Recorded speed (knots)	r.p.m.	s.h.p.
1	N	0830	10·35 ⎫	83	1155
2	S	0900	9·60 ⎭		
3	N	0930	12·52 ⎫	102	2040
4	S	1000	11·70 ⎭		
5	N	1130	14·30 ⎫	126	3250
6	S	1200	13·96 ⎭		

      (HMDTC)

9. A vessel on successive runs on the measured mile obtains the following speeds in knots:

27·592, 28·841, 27·965, 28·943, 27·777, 28·426

Calculate (i) ordinary average speed, (ii) mean of means of six runs, (iii) mean of means of first four runs, (iv) mean of means of second four runs, (v) mean of means of last four runs.   (AP & S)

10. Assuming that the speed runs reported in the last question were obtained as a result of runs at intervals of one hour, deduce the true speed of the ship assuming that the tide is governed by an equation

$$v = a + bt + ct^2 + dt^3 + et^4$$

Determine the values of the coefficients in this equation.

11. A propeller 3 m in diameter moves ahead at 15 knots in 'open' sea water. If the propeller race has a 3 knots increase in speed, approximate by the axial momentum theory to the thrust developed.   (AP & S)

12. The propellers of a twin-screwed ship operate in a wake of 2 knots, the ship moving ahead at 21 knots. The e.h.p. naked is 6000, the appendage coefficient is 1·12. If the thrust developed by each propeller is 26·5 tonf, calculate (a) the t.h.p. of each propeller, (b) the hull efficiency, (c) the augment of resistance factor.   (AP & S)

References

1. Weinblum, Georg. P. Practical applications of wave resistance theory. *SNAME*, Northern California Section, April, 1955.
2. Doust, D. J. Optimised trawler forms. *TNECI*, Vol. 79, 1962–3.
3. Froude, William On experiments upon the effect produced on the wave-making resistance of ships by length of parallel middle body. *TINA*, 1877.
4. Van Manen, J. D. The choice of the propeller. *Marine Technology*, April, 1966.
5. *Standard procedure for resistance and propulsion experiments with ship models.* National Physical Laboratory Ship Division Report No. 10.
6. Newton, R. N. Standard model technique at Admiralty Experiment Works, Haslar. *TRINA*, 1960.
7. Barnaby, K. C. and Dorey, A. L. A towing tank storm. *TRINA*, 1965.
8. Gawn, R. W. L. Effect of pitch and blade width on propeller performance. *TINA*, 1953. (Paper actually presented at Rome in 1952.)
9. Troost, L. Open water test series with modern propeller forms. *TNECI*, 1950–1.
10. Froude, W. On experiments with HMS *Greyhound*. *TINA*, 1874.
11. Denny, Sir Maurice E. BSRA resistance experiments on the *Lucy Ashton*, Part 1; Full-scale measurements. *TINA*, 1951.
12. Conn, J. F. C., Lackenby, H. and Walker, W. B. BSRA resistance experiments on the *Lucy Ashton*, Part II; The ship-model correlation for the naked hull condition. *TINA*, 1953.
13. Hadler, J. B. and Cheng, H. M. Analysis of experimental wake data in way of propeller plane of single- and twin-screw ship models. *TSNAME*, 1965.
14. Canham, H. J. S. Resistance, propulsion and wake tests with HMS *Penelope*. *TRINA*, 1974.
15. Massey, B. S. *Mechanics of fluids.* Van Norstrand, 1975.
16. Isherwood, R. M. Wind resistance of merchant ships. *TRINA*, 1973.

11 Powering of ships: application

Presentation of data

Any method of data presentation should bring out clearly the effect of the parameters concerned on the resistance of the ship. A non-dimensional form of plotting is desirable but further than this it is difficult to generalize. The best plot for a designer may not be the best for research. The best form of plotting may depend upon whether data is being processed by hand calculating machines. An interesting discussion of this subject is given in Ref. 1.

RESISTANCE DATA

The Froude 'constant' notation

The Ministry of Defence uses the so-called 'constant' notation described in Ref. 2. The method of presentation is truly non-dimensional, although appearing a little strange at first to those used to the more common forms of non-dimensional presentation used in general engineering.

As the characteristic unit of length, Froude used the cube root of the volume of displacement and denoted this by U. To define the ship geometry he used the following

$$\textcircled{M} = \text{length constant} = \frac{\text{wetted length}}{U}$$

$$\textcircled{B} = \text{breadth constant} = \frac{\text{wetted breadth}}{U}$$

$$\textcircled{D} = \text{draught constant} = \frac{\text{draught at largest section}}{U}$$

$$\textcircled{S} = \text{wetted surface constant} = \frac{\text{wetted surface area}}{U^2}$$

$$\textcircled{A} = \text{section area constant} = \frac{\text{section area}}{U^2}$$

As performance parameters he used relationships between speed and displacement and speed and length

$$\textcircled{K} = \frac{\text{speed of ship}}{\text{speed of wave of length } U/2} = V\left(\frac{4\pi}{gU}\right)^{\frac{1}{2}}$$

$$\text{\textcircled{L}} = \frac{\text{speed of ship}}{\text{speed of wave of length } L/2} = V\left(\frac{4\pi}{gL}\right)^{\frac{1}{2}}$$

And as a resistance constant

$$\text{\textcircled{C}} = \frac{1000 \times \text{resistance}}{\Delta\text{\textcircled{K}}^2}$$

In verbal discussions, $\text{\textcircled{M}}$ is referred to as 'circular M', $\text{\textcircled{B}}$ as 'circular B', and so on.

The resistance used in calculating $\text{\textcircled{C}}$ can be the total, residuary or frictional resistance and these can be denoted by $\text{\textcircled{C}}_T$, $\text{\textcircled{C}}_R$ and $\text{\textcircled{C}}_F$ respectively.

Standard expressions can be derived for each constant as in Table 11.1. In this form they are dimensional.

Table 11.1

Froude 'constant' notation (sea water).

Parameter	Symbol	Expression	
		British units (tonf, ft, knots)	Metric units (tonne, m, knots)
Characteristic length	U	$3\cdot271\Delta^{\frac{1}{3}}$	$0\cdot992\,\Sigma^{\frac{1}{3}}$
Length	$\text{\textcircled{M}}$	$0\cdot3057L/\Delta^{\frac{1}{3}}$	$1\cdot0083\,L/\Sigma^{\frac{1}{3}}$
Breadth	$\text{\textcircled{B}}$	$0\cdot3057B/\Delta^{\frac{1}{3}}$	$1\cdot0083\,B/\Sigma^{\frac{1}{3}}$
Draught	$\text{\textcircled{D}}$	$0\cdot3057T/\Delta^{\frac{1}{3}}$	$1\cdot0083\,T/\Sigma^{\frac{1}{3}}$
Wetted surface	$\text{\textcircled{S}}$	$0\cdot0935S/\Delta^{\frac{2}{3}}$	$1\cdot0167\,S/\Sigma^{\frac{2}{3}}$
Section area	$\text{\textcircled{A}}$	$0\cdot0935A/\Delta^{\frac{2}{3}}$	$1\cdot0167\,A/\Sigma^{\frac{2}{3}}$
Speed	$\text{\textcircled{K}}$	$0\cdot5834V/\Delta^{\frac{1}{6}}$	$0\cdot5848\,V/\Sigma^{\frac{1}{6}}$
	$\text{\textcircled{L}}$	$1\cdot055V/\sqrt{L}$	$0\cdot5824\,V/\sqrt{L}$
Resistance	$\text{\textcircled{C}}$	$\dfrac{427\cdot1 \text{ e.h.p.}}{\Delta^{\frac{2}{3}}V^3}$	$\dfrac{579\cdot7\,P_E}{\Sigma^{\frac{2}{3}}\,V^3}$

Note: The U.K. nautical mile, 6080 ft (1853·18 m) is greater than the international nautical mile which is 1852 m. P_E is the power in kW and Σ is the mass displacement.

For comparison of design data, the results from model tests carried out at the Admiralty Experiment Works are plotted in the form of $\text{\textcircled{C}}$–$\text{\textcircled{K}}$ curves with the data corrected to represent a 16 ft model. Separate curves are drawn for each displacement value at which the model is run. (Fig. 11.1.) Superimposed on the plots are curves showing the skin friction correction in passing from the 16 ft model to ships of various length.

This plotting is included in the *Elements of Form Diagram* which is the standard method of summarizing the important information on ship's form and resistance. The principal dimensions and form coefficients are given in tabular form. The curve of areas, waterline and midship section for the design displacement are plotted non-dimensionally by dividing length dimensions by U and areas by U^2. To facilitate comparison of forms, the curves are drawn on a common base length and the ordinates of the curve of areas adjusted to keep the area under the curve unchanged.

The data from a large selection of models is assembled as plots of $\text{\textcircled{C}}$ against $\text{\textcircled{M}}$ for a range of $\text{\textcircled{K}}$ values. Generally, displacement and length are fairly well established by other design considerations so that for a given speed $\text{\textcircled{M}}$ and $\text{\textcircled{K}}$

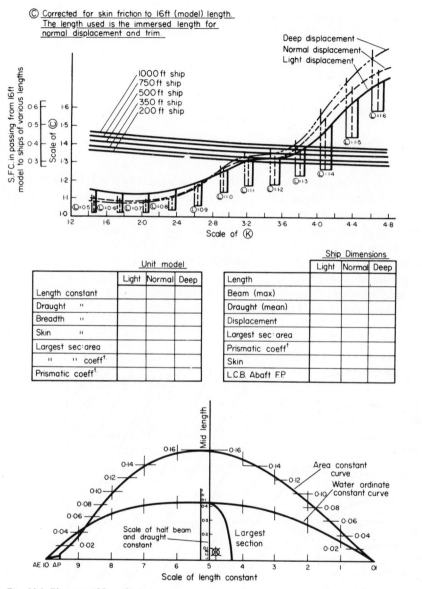

Fig. 11.1 *Elements of form diagram*

are known. The best form of those already tested can be selected and the data for this form provides the first approximation to the resistance of the new design.

Taylor's method

Taylor (Ref. 3) expressed resistance, both frictional and residuary, in lbf per tonf of displacement (i.e. R/Δ). For similar models at corresponding speeds such quantities are constant for resistances following Froude's law of comparison. They are compared on the basis of the following parameters:

$$\text{Speed coefficient} = \frac{V}{\sqrt{L}}, \quad V \text{ in knots, } L \text{ in ft}$$

$$\text{Displacement/length ratio} = \frac{\Delta}{(L/100)^3}, \quad \Delta \text{ in tonf}$$

Prismatic coefficient
Beam/draught ratio

Taylor chose the displacement/length ratio as a quantity which is independent of displacement for similar ships. Length is used in the denominator as being the linear dimension having most influence on resistance. In this expression, Δ is in tonf of salt water whether ship or model is under consideration.

Unfortunately, this type of presentation is not truly non-dimensional and care must be taken with units in applying Taylor's data.

Nonetheless, the Taylor data is still extensively used for determining the effect on resistance of variation in form. Some typical curves taken from Ref. 3 are reproduced as Figs. 11.2 and 11.3.

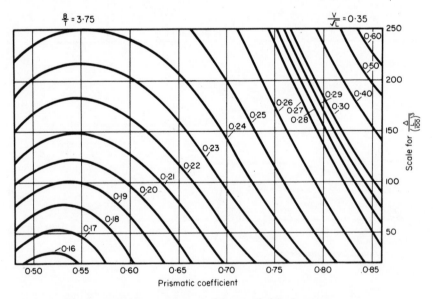

Fig. 11.2 Contours of residuary resistance in lbf per tonf of displacement

Taylor studied the influence of bow shape on resistance by considering the slope of the curve of sectional areas at the bow. This slope is expressed by a quantity t obtained as follows. Draw the tangent at the bow to the curve of sectional areas. This will cut the vertical at the centre of length, intercepting it

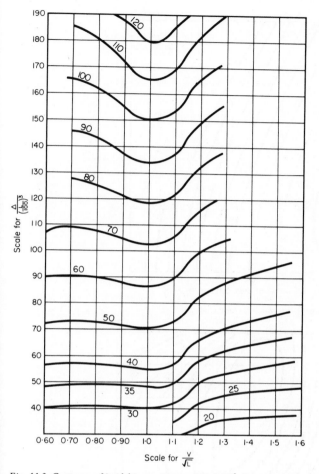

Fig. 11.3 Contours of (midship section area)/(L/100)² for minimum residuary resistance

on a certain ordinate. Then t is the ratio between this ordinate and the ordinate of the sectional area curve at the centre of length (Fig. 11.4).

Taylor suggested that the wetted surface area of vessel could be obtained from the formula:

$$S = C(\Delta L)^{\frac{1}{2}}$$

where C is defined by Fig. 11.5.

Statistical analysis

A statistical analysis of resistance data for destroyers and frigates, sponsored by AEW, Haslar, used regression equations for $\textcircled{C}$ for a 16 ft model in the form:

$$\textcircled{C} = b_0 + b_1 x_1 + b_2 x_2 + \cdots + b_n x_n$$

The first nine terms of the right-hand side of these equations represented form parameters as follows:

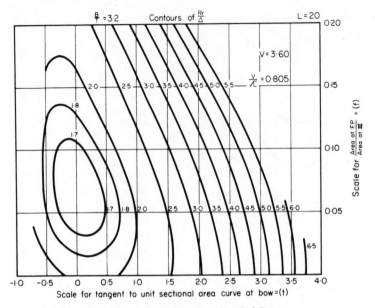

Fig. 11.4 *Variation of resistance with tangent value (Ref. 3)*

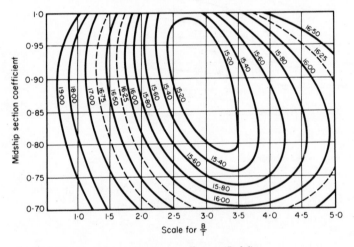

Fig. 11.5 *Contours of wetted surface coefficients (Ref. 3)*

$x_1 = \overline{F_{WL}G}/L_{WL}$, where $\overline{F_{WL}G}$ is the horizontal distance of the c.g. from the fore end of the static waterline.

x_2 = half angle of entrance.

$x_3 = B/T$

x_4 = (max. transverse sectional area below WL)/BT

x_5 = transom area as a percentage of the max. section area

x_6 = (distance of ACU from FE of static waterline)/L_{WL}

$x_7 = \text{(M)}$

x_8 = prismatic coefficient

The remaining terms represented various combinations of these basic variates, i.e. they represented non-linear terms. The best fit was obtained with the more complex equations containing the non-linear terms. This is to be expected but it does not follow that the complex equations give better predictions for a new design. As an example, Table 11.2 gives the b coefficients for the simpler equations for four $\textcircled{K}$ values.

Table 11.2

Coefficient	$\textcircled{K}$			
	1·8	3·2	4·6	6·0
b_0	0·1032/01	0·3269/01	0·7393/01	0·4589/01
b_1	0·2798/00	−0·2364/01	−0·5395/01	−0·2332/01
b_2	0·6697/−02	0·1531/−01	−0·1972/−02	−0·6813/−02
b_3	0·3620/−01	0·8618/−01	0·1225/00	0·7545/−01
b_4	−0·4145/00	−0·1035/01	−0·5765/00	−0·1309/00
b_5	0·5635/−02	0·7369/−03	0·1501/−01	0·1200/−01
b_6	−0·1618/00	0·1293/00	0·6622/00	0·1280/00
b_7	0·5690/−01	−0·1536/00	−0·3577/00	−0·1669/00
b_8	−0·3060/00	0·1384/01	−0·5878/00	−0·6869/00

Note: The 'b' coefficients are given in exponential form, i.e. 0·1032/01 represents 1·032; −0·4145/00 represents −0·4145; 0·1200/−01 represents 0·01200, etc.

This method of analysis is a very powerful one and will be increasingly used in this and other fields. At this stage of development, however, the method must be treated with care. The parameters used are those which are thought to be most significant. Experience may show that other parameters are more suitable. So far $\textcircled{M}$ has proved the most significant and a useful relationship is:

$$\textcircled{C} = a + b/\textcircled{M} + c\textcircled{M}^2$$

In general it is not possible to vary one parameter without some consequential change in others. This may explain why the simple equations above indicate that an increase in transom area is always bad. This is not in accord with common experience and illustrates the danger of attributing any particular physical significance to the sign and magnitude of the regression coefficients. The interaction between various parameters also influences the extent to which optimization can be achieved. Values obtained from a mathematical optimization process may not be achievable in one form and in any case do not uniquely define the ship form. The regression equations should only be applied to forms of the same general type as those used to derive the equations.

PROPELLER DATA

In Chapter 10, dimensional analysis led to the derivation of three basic coefficients, viz.:

$$K_T = \frac{T}{\rho n^2 D^4} = \text{thrust coefficient}$$

$$K_Q = \frac{Q}{\rho n^2 D^5} = \text{torque coefficient}$$

$$J = \frac{V}{nD} = \text{advance coefficient}$$

In these coefficients, the product nD is a measure of the rotative speed of the propeller.

The other basic parameter is the propeller efficiency η which is given by

$$\eta = \frac{\text{useful output}}{\text{input}}$$

$$= \frac{TV}{Q \times 2\pi n} = \frac{K_T}{K_Q} \frac{J}{2\pi}$$

For a given advance coefficient, it is only necessary to define two of the factors K_T, K_Q and η as the third follows from the above relationship. The two usually quoted are K_T and η. It was pointed out in Chapter 10 that a propeller designer makes considerable use of the results of methodical model series representing the propeller in open water. Such series are reported in Refs. 4 and 5. Reference 4 presents results for 3-bladed propellers only. For preliminary design, these results can be used for 4- or 5-bladed propellers within an error of about 5 per cent. Reference 5 quotes results for 2-, 3-, 4- and 5-bladed propellers. A typical plot is reproduced from Ref. 4 in Fig. 11.6. Similar plots are available for a range of blade area ratios.

In most design problems, the speed of advance and the power P_D to be absorbed are known. In addition, the propeller r.p.m. are also often fixed by considerations of gear ratios and vibration. Diagrams such as that in Fig. 11.6 can be used to obtain, by interpolation, the propeller diameter for maximum efficiency. This process is described later. Another type of presentation can, however, be adopted to simplify this common type of problem.

This is a plot of B_p against δ where

$$B_p = \frac{nP_D^{\frac{1}{2}}}{V^{2\cdot5}} = 33\cdot08 \left(\frac{K_Q}{J^5}\right)^{\frac{1}{2}}$$

$$\delta = \frac{nD}{V} = \frac{101\cdot27}{J}$$

where n is in r.p.m., P_D is in horsepower, V is in knots, and D is in feet. If D is in metres,

$$\delta = 3\cdot2808 \frac{nD}{V}$$

Such a plot is presented in Fig. 11.7 taken from Ref. 6 and similar plots are given in Ref. 5.

For given values of n, P_D and V, B_p is fixed, and by drawing a vertical ordinate at this value on the figure the maximum obtainable η and corresponding

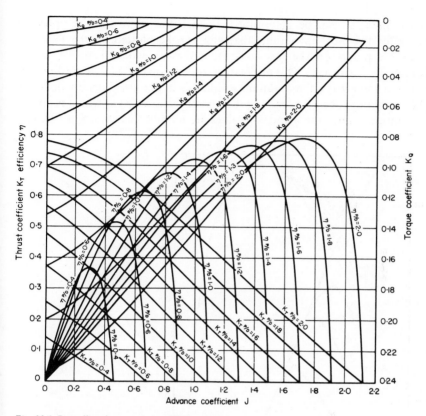

Fig. 11.6 *Propeller characteristics*, BAR = 0·65

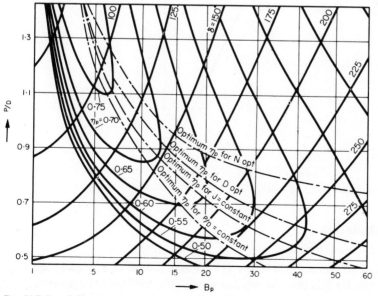

Fig. 11.7 $B_p - \delta$ *diagrams*

propeller diameter can be determined. In fact, the curve for the optimum efficiency for the most favourable diameter can be plotted on the figure. It connects the points on the $\eta =$ constant curves at which these curves are vertical, i.e. $B_p =$ constant. This line is shown dotted on Fig. 11.7. If the diameter is limited in some ways, the optimum within this limitation is readily deduced.

When cavitation occurs, as may be the case of a ship at sea or with a propeller in a cavitation tunnel, the η and K_T values are modified as shown in Fig. 11.8 (Ref. 7).

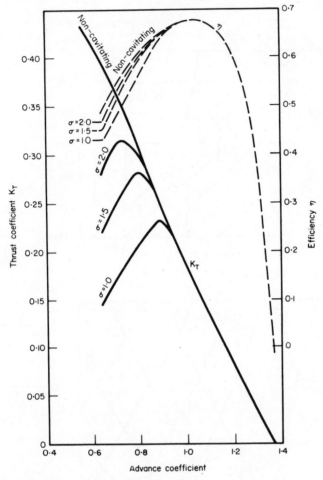

Fig. 11.8 *Effect of cavitation on K_T and η*

Power estimation

RESISTANCE PREDICTION

Froude's law of comparison is the key to most forms of extrapolation from model to ship. By this law, the residuary resistance per unit of displacement is the same for model and ship at corresponding speeds. It remains then necessary to know how the frictional resistance varies with Reynolds' number to enable a plot such as Fig. 11.9 to be produced. Let AA' represent the variation of total resistance of the model with Reynolds' number. Then, provided the skin friction line is a correct one, $\overline{A_1A_2}$ and $\overline{A_2A_3}$ are the residuary and skin friction components at a Reynolds' number $(R_n)_m$. By Froude's law of comparison, if $(R_n)_s$ is the corresponding ship R_n, $\overline{A_1A_2}$ will be equal to $\overline{B_1B_2}$. Thus, the total ship resistance curve can be obtained by drawing curves through points on the model curve parallel to the skin friction line to intersect vertical lines through the R_n values appropriate to the corresponding speeds.

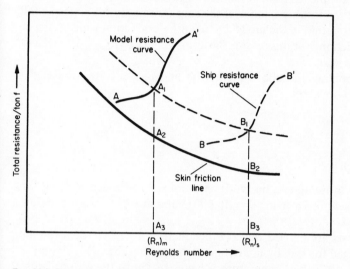

Fig. 11.9 Extrapolation from model to full-scale resistance

Clearly, the accuracy of prediction of such a method is dependent on the accuracy of the curve defining the variation of skin friction resistance with Reynolds' number. Not unnaturally, several curves have been proposed over the years each having its particular advocates. Two methods are of particular importance and these are now considered. The ship resistance prediction resulting from the different skin friction curves are but marginally different.

Froude method

Using the 'constant' notation:

$$\textcircled{C}_F = \frac{1000 \, (\text{frictional resistance})}{\Delta \textcircled{K}^2}$$

$$= \frac{1000}{\rho g U^3} \times \frac{fSV^{1 \cdot 825}}{4\pi V^2/gU}$$

$$= O.\textcircled{S}\textcircled{L}^{-0 \cdot 175}$$

where

$$O = \frac{1000f}{4\pi\rho(gL/4\pi)^{0.0875}} = \text{'Circular } O\text{'}$$

Since for both model and ship

$$ⓒ_T = ⓒ_R + ⓒ_F$$

$$[ⓒ_T]_{\text{ship}} = [ⓒ_T]_{\text{model}} - [O_m - O_s]ⓈⒹ^{-0.175}$$

where O_m and O_s are the 'circular O' values for model and ship respectively.

In other words, the total resistance of the ship expressed non-dimensionally can be obtained from that of the model by making a correction which is dependent on the skin friction. For this reason, the term $(O_m - O_s)ⓈⒹ^{-0.175}$ is known as the *skin friction correction*.

To assist in applying the above method O and f values are tabulated in Tables 11.3 and 11.4 where:

$$\text{Frictional resistance} = fSV^{1.825}$$

and

$$ⓒ_F = O . ⓈⒹ^{-0.175}$$

The values are those agreed by the International Conference of Ship Tank Superintendents held in Paris in 1935 (Ref. 8). Values of $L^{-0.175}$ are tabulated in Table 11.5.

If the model tests are carried out at other than 59°F (15°C), then the data have to be corrected for this by increasing or decreasing the $ⓒ_F$ value by 2·4 per cent for every 10°F the temperature is below or above this value. Thus, if the experiments are conducted at a temperature of t_1°F

$$[ⓒ_F]_{\text{model}} = [1 + 0.0024(59 - t_1)]O_mⓈⒹ^{-0.175}$$

The wetted surface area used in determining Ⓢ is taken as the mean wetted girth of sections multiplied by the length on the waterline. It is therefore less than the true wetted surface area as the inclination of the surface to the middle-line plane of the ship is ignored.

In the Ministry of Defence, it is usual to calculate the appendage resistance. This can introduce an error and this is allowed for in the QPC factor which is deduced from ship trials. The National Physical Laboratory introduce a scaling factor β by which the model appendage resistance can be multiplied, although they recommend that the value of β should generally be taken as unity. (Ref. 9.)

In the absence of firmer data for a ship, the value of Ⓢ can be obtained by applying the Haslar formula:

$$Ⓢ = 3.4 + \frac{Ⓜ}{2.06}$$

or the Taylor formula already given (p. 387).

Table 11.3

O and f values. R. E. Froude's frictional data. Values at standard temperature =
15°C = 59°F (British Units), f related to S in ft², V in knots, R in lbf.

Length (ft)	O	f	Length (ft)	O	f
5	0·15485	0·012585	35	0·10282	0·009908
6	0·1493	0·012345	40	0·10043	0·009791
7	0·1448	0·012128	45	0·09839	0·009691
8	0·1409	0·011932	50	0·09664	0·009607
9	0·13734	0·011751	60	0·0938	0·009475
10	0·13409	0·011579	70	0·09164	0·009382
11	0·1312	0·011425	80	0·08987	0·009309
12	0·12858	0·011282	90	0·0884	0·009252
13	0·1262	0·011151	100	0·08716	0·009207
14	0·12406	0·011033	120	0·08511	0·009135
15	0·1221	0·010925	140	0·08351	0·009085
16	0·12035	0·010829	160	0·08219	0·009046
17	0·11875	0·010742	180	0·08108	0·009016
18	0·11727	0·010661	200	0·08012	0·008992
19	0·1160	0·010596	250	0·07814	0·008943
20	0·1147	0·010524	300	0·07655	0·008902
21	0·1136	0·010468	350	0·07523	0·008867
22	0·11255	0·010413	400	0·07406	0·008832
23	0·11155	0·010361	450	0·07305	0·008802
24	0·1106	0·010311	500	0·07217	0·008776
25	0·10976	0·010269	550	0·07136	0·008750
26	0·1089	0·010224	600	0·07062	0·008726
27	0·1081	0·010182	700	0·06931	0·008680
28	0·1073	0·010139	800	0·06818	0·008639
29	0·1066	0·010103	900	0·06724	0·008608
30	0·1059	0·010068	1000	0·06636	0·008574
			1100	0·06561	0·008548
			1200	0·06493	0·008524

The ITTC 1957 model–ship correlation line

The Froude method is not used universally. Clearly, it is desirable to have a single line accepted by all practitioners which can be accepted as a standard. Much effort has been devoted over the years to trying to reach agreement on such a standard line as the volumes of the Royal Institution of Naval Architects bear eloquent witness. One way of studying the relative merits of different formulations is to carry out tests on a series of models of various sizes so that a range of Reynolds' numbers is covered. By presenting all the results in a single plotting such as Fig. 11.9, the shape of the skin friction line is determined by passing curves through points on each model curve at corresponding Reynolds' numbers. The results from the six models of the *Lucy Ashton* were plotted to compare with each of the above lines (Ref. 10) together with the full-scale data.

Successive International Towing Tank Conferences studied this problem and in 1957, in Madrid, agreed to a standard line. This ITTC line is defined by

$$C_F = \frac{0.075}{(\log R_n - 2)^2} = \frac{R_F}{\frac{1}{2}\rho S V^2}$$

Table 11.4
f values. R. E. Froude's skin friction constants (Metric units)

Length (m)	f	Length (m)	f	Length (m)	f
2	1·966	11	1·589	40	1·464
2·5	1·913	12	1·577	45	1·459
3	1·867	13	1·566	50	1·454
3·5	1·826	14	1·556	60	1·447
4	1·791	15	1·547	70	1·441
4·5	1·761	16	1·539	80	1·437
5	1·736	17	1·532	90	1·432
5·5	1·715	18	1·526	100	1·428
6	1·696	19	1·520	120	1·421
6·5	1·681	20	1·515	140	1·415
7	1·667	22	1·506	160	1·410
7·5	1·654	24	1·499	180	1·404
8	1·643	26	1·492	200	1·399
8·5	1·632	28	1·487	250	1·389
9	1·622	30	1·482	300	1·380
9·5	1·613	35	1·472	350	1·373
10	1·604				

f in metric units $= f$ (Imperial units) $\times$ 160·9.

$$R_F = fSV^{1·825}$$

R_F = Frictional resistance, N
S = wetted surface, m^2
V = speed, m/s
L = waterline length, m

f in metric units $= f$ in Imperial units $\times$ 47·87 when V is in knots.

Table 11.5
Value of $(L)^{-0·175}$

(L)	$(L)^{-0·175}$	(L)	$(L)^{-0·175}$	(L)	$(L)^{-0·175}$
0·00	∞	1·00	1·0000	2·00	0·8858
0·05	1·6892	1·05	0·9915	2·05	0·8819
0·10	1·4962	1·10	0·9835	2·10	0·8782
0·15	1·3937	1·15	0·9758	2·15	0·8746
0·20	1·3253	1·20	0·9686	2·20	0·8711
0·25	1·2746	1·25	0·9617	2·25	0·8677
0·30	1·2345	1·30	0·9551	2·30	0·8644
0·35	1·2017	1·35	0·9488	2·35	0·8611
0·40	1·1739	1·40	0·9428	2·40	0·8580
0·45	1·1500	1·45	0·9370	2·45	0·8549
0·50	1·1290	1·50	0·9315	2·50	0·8518
0·55	1·1103	1·55	0·9262	2·55	0·8489
0·60	1·0935	1·60	0·9210	2·60	0·8460
0·65	1·0783	1·65	0·9161	2·65	0·8432
0·70	1·0644	1.70	0·9113	2·70	0·8404
0·75	1·0516	1·75	0·9067	2·75	0·8378
0·80	1·0398	1·80	0·9023	2·80	0·8351
0·85	1·0288	1·85	0·8979	2·85	0·8325
0·90	1·0186	1·90	0·8938	2·90	0·8300
0·95	1·0090	1·95	0·8897	2·95	0·8275
				3·00	0·8251

Values of C_F for various values of R_n are given in Table 11.6. A full set of values is presented in Ref. 11.

The term 'correlation line' was used quite deliberately in recognition of the fact that the extrapolation from model to ship is not governed only by variation in skin friction.

Table 11.6
Coefficients for ITTC 1957 model–ship correlation line. Coefficients must be multiplied by 10^{-3}

Reynolds' number	$10^5 \times$	$10^6 \times$	$10^7 \times$	$10^8 \times$	$10^9 \times$	$10^{10} \times$
1·0	8·333	4·688	3·000	2·083	1·531	1·172
1·5	7·435	4·301	2·799	1·966	1·456	1·122
2·0	6·883	4·054	2·669	1·889	1·407	1·088
2·5	6·496	3·878	2·574	1·832	1·370	1·063
3·0	6·203	3·742	2·500	1·788	1·342	1·044
3·5	5·971	3·632	2·440	1·751	1·318	1·027
4·0	5·780	3·541	2·390	1·721	1·298	1·014
4·5	5·620	3·464	2·347	1·694	1·280	1·002
5·0	5·482	3·397	2·309	1·671	1·265	0·991
5·5	5·361	3·338	2·276	1·651	1·252	0·982
6·0	5·254	3·285	2·246	1·632	1·240	0·973
6·5	5·159	3·238	2·220	1·616	1·229	0·966
7·0	5·073	3·195	2·195	1·601	1·219	0·959
7·5	4·995	3·156	2·173	1·587	1·209	0·952
8·0	4·923	3·120	2·152	1·574	1·201	0·946
8·5	4·857	3·087	2·133	1·562	1·193	0·941
9·0	4·797	3·056	2·115	1·551	1·185	0·935
9·5	4·740	3·027	2·099	1·540	1·178	0·931

EFFECT OF SMALL CHANGES OF DIMENSIONS

Froude's formula for frictional resistance may be written

$$R_F = f\Delta^{\frac{2}{3}} V^{1 \cdot 825}$$

For geometrically similar ships at corresponding speeds

$$V \propto L^{\frac{1}{2}}; \quad \Delta \propto L^3$$

Hence

$$R_F \propto fL^{2 \cdot 9125}$$

By Froude's law of comparison the residuary resistance varies as L^3. Hence, for small changes in dimensions no large error is introduced if it is assumed that the total resistance varies in the same way, i.e.

$$R_T \propto L^3$$

Variation in residuary resistance with size and speed

At a given speed for any condition, the residuary resistance will vary with displacement and speed as follows:

$$R_R = K\Delta^m V^{n-1}$$

The power then varies as $\Delta^m V^n$. For a geometrically similar form at corresponding speed

$$R'_R = K(\Delta')^m(V')^{n-1}$$

But by Froude's law of comparison

$$\frac{R_R}{R'_R} = \frac{\Delta}{\Delta'}$$

and

$$\frac{V}{V'} = \left(\frac{L}{L'}\right)^{\frac{1}{2}} = \left(\frac{\Delta}{\Delta'}\right)^{\frac{1}{6}}$$

Hence

$$\frac{\Delta}{\Delta'} = \left(\frac{\Delta}{\Delta'}\right)^m \left(\frac{\Delta}{\Delta'}\right)^{(n-1)/6}$$

i.e.

$$m + \frac{n-1}{6} = 1$$

$$6m + n = 7$$

The value of n can be deduced from the slope of the $\textcircled{C}$–$\textcircled{K}$ curve as follows:

$$\textcircled{K} \propto V \quad \text{and} \quad \textcircled{C} \propto \frac{R}{\textcircled{K}^2}$$

Hence

$$\textcircled{C} = \text{Const.} \frac{V^{n-1}}{\textcircled{K}^2} = \text{Const.} \, \textcircled{K}^{n-3}$$

Differentiating,

$$\frac{\partial \textcircled{C}}{\partial \textcircled{K}} = (n-3) \, \text{Const.} \, \textcircled{K}^{n-4}$$

Eliminating the constant in these equations

$$\frac{\partial \textcircled{C}}{\partial \textcircled{K}} = (n-3)\frac{\textcircled{C}}{\textcircled{K}}$$

Hence

$$n = 3 + \frac{\textcircled{K}}{\textcircled{C}} \cdot \frac{\partial \textcircled{C}}{\partial \textcircled{K}}$$

The value of m follows from

$$m = \frac{7-n}{6}$$

VARIATION OF SKIN FRICTIONAL RESISTANCE WITH TIME OUT OF DOCK

When a ship enters the water having been freshly cleaned and painted her resistance is a minimum. With the passage of time, seaweed and barnacles attach themselves to the surface so presenting a rougher surface to the passage of water. This roughening of the surface leads to an increase in the skin frictional resistance. It is to be expected that the amount of fouling as it is called will depend upon the area in which the ship is operating and the time spent at sea compared with the time at rest in harbour.

As a standard, it is usual within the Navy Department of the Ministry of Defence to assume that the increase in skin frictional resistance is a quarter of one per cent per day. To represent an average operating condition the Navy Department considers a ship to be in the 'deep and dirty' state which means at the deep displacement and six months out of dock. In this condition:

$$\text{Increase in } \textcircled{C}_F = \delta\textcircled{C}_F = \frac{365}{200} \times 0.25\textcircled{C}_F = 0.456\textcircled{C}_F$$

Other authorities assume a standard percentage of the available power, e.g. 20 per cent, is used up in overcoming the increased resistance due to fouling and also in overcoming the extra resistance due to running through waves. Whether the 20 per cent overall factor, or percentage per day applied to skin friction only, is the more severe case depends upon the size and speed of the ship. They are, however, generally comparable.

EXAMPLE 1. The $\textcircled{C}$-$\textcircled{K}$ curve for a 16 ft model of a ship 570 ft long and 11,500 tonf displacement, corrected to standard temperature, is defined by the following table:

$\textcircled{K}$	2·2	2·3	2·4	2·5	2·6	2·7	2·8
$\textcircled{C}$	1·130	1·130	1·132	1·138	1·140	1·141	1·150

$\textcircled{K}$	2·9	3·0	3·1	3·2	3·3	3·4
$\textcircled{C}$	1·153	1·156	1·172	1·193	1·236	1·283

Deduce a plot of e.h.p. against speed for the clean condition assuming that $\textcircled{S}$ is given by the Haslar formula with a multiplying factor of 1·03. Also, calculate the e.h.p. for the ship 6 months out of dock assuming that the skin frictional resistance increases by $\frac{1}{4}$ per cent per day out of dock.

Solution: From the formulae quoted in the text the following relationships can be deduced.

$$\textcircled{K} = 0.5834\frac{V}{\Delta^{\frac{1}{6}}}$$

Hence, in this case, $V = 8 \cdot 144 \text{(K)}$ where V is in knots

$$\text{(L)} = 1 \cdot 055 \frac{V}{\sqrt{L}} = \frac{1 \cdot 055}{\sqrt{570}} V$$

$$U^3 = 11{,}500 \times 35 = 402{,}500 \text{ ft}^3$$

Hence $U = 73 \cdot 83$ ft.

$$\text{(M)} = \frac{L}{U} = \frac{570}{73 \cdot 83} = 7 \cdot 72$$

$$\text{(S)} = 1 \cdot 03 \left[3 \cdot 4 + \frac{\text{(M)}}{2 \cdot 06} \right] = 7 \cdot 205$$

$$\text{(C)}_F = O \text{(S)(L)}^{-0 \cdot 175}$$

where, for $L = 570$, $O = 0 \cdot 0711$

$$\therefore \quad \text{(C)}_F = 0 \cdot 0711 \times 7 \cdot 205 \times \text{(L)}^{-0 \cdot 175}$$

$$= 0 \cdot 512 \text{(L)}^{-0 \cdot 175}$$

For the 16 ft model, $O = 0 \cdot 1204$

and

$$\text{(C)}_F = 0 \cdot 867 \text{(L)}^{-0 \cdot 175}$$

The reduction to be applied to the model (C) to obtain the ship (C) is $0 \cdot 355$ $\text{(L)}^{-0 \cdot 175}$.

This is the skin friction correction, SFC.

$$\delta \text{(C)}_F \text{ for the ship in the dirty condition} = 0 \cdot 456 \text{(C)}_F$$

$$= 0 \cdot 233 \text{(L)}^{-0 \cdot 175}$$

Table 11.7
Froude analysis

(K)	V (knots)	(C)	SFC	Clean ship		(L)	$\text{(L)}^{-0 \cdot 175} \delta \text{(C)}_F$	Dirty ship	
				(C)	e.h.p.			(C)	e.h.p.
2·2	17·9	1·130	0·371	0·759	5200	0·79	1·042	0·243	1·002	6770
2·3	18·7	1.130	0·368	0·762	5950	0·83	1·033	0·241	1·003	7810
2·4	19·5	1·132	0·366	0·766	6800	0·86	1·027	0·239	1·005	8890
2·5	20·4	1·138	0·363	0·775	7850	0·90	1·019	0·237	1·012	10,200
2·6	21·2	1·140	0·361	0·779	8800	0·94	1·011	0·236	1·015	11,500
2·7	22·0	1·141	0·357	0·784	10,040	0·97	1·005	0·234	1·018	13,000
2·8	22·9	1.150	0·354	0·796	11,400	1·01	0·998	0·232	1·028	14,700
2·9	23·7	1·153	0·351	0·802	12,800	1·05	0·992	0·231	1·033	16,500
3·0	24·4	1·156	0·349	0·807	14,050	1·08	0·987	0·230	1·037	18,000
3·1	25·2	1·172	0·347	0·825	15,750	1·11	0·982	0·229	1·054	20,150
3·2	26·1	1·193	0·345	0·848	18,000	1·15	0·976	0·227	1·075	22,800
3·3	26·9	1·235	0·343	0·892	20,800	1·19	0·970	0·226	1·118	26,000
3·4	27·7	1·283	0·341	0·942	24,000	1·22	0·966	0·225	1·167	29,600

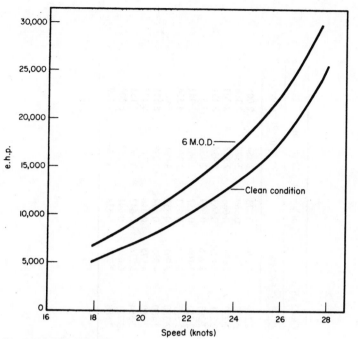

Fig. 11.10 Plot of results

$$\text{e.h.p.} = \frac{\Delta^{\frac{2}{3}}}{427\cdot1}\,C_T V^3 = 1\cdot193\,C_T V^3 \text{ in this case}$$

Table 11.7 can now be constructed and the e.h.p./speed curves plotted as in Fig. 11.10.

EXAMPLE 2. Data for a model 5 m long of a ship 178 m long and 11,700 tonne displacement, corrected to standard temperature, is defined by the following table.

$R_n \times 10^{-6}$	6·600	6·894	7·188	7·522	7·817	8·111	8·445
$C_T \times 10^3$	3·944	3·944	3·951	3·972	3·979	3·982	4·014

$R_n \times 10^6$	8·740	8·995	9·295	9·624	9·918	10·213
$C_T \times 10^3$	4·024	4·034	4·090	4·164	4·310	4·478

Deduce a plot, power against speed for the clean and dirty conditions assuming that the wetted surface area is 3650 m².

Solution: The data having been presented in the form of C_T against R_n, the 1957 ITTC analysis is applied

$$\text{Reynolds' Number, } R_n = \frac{VL}{\nu}$$

Table 11.8
1957 ITTC analysis

$(R_n)_{model}$ × 10^6	$(R_n)_{ship}$ × 10^9	V Ship (m/s)	C_F × 10^{-3} Model	C_F × 10^{-3} Ship	SFC × 10^{-3}	C_T × 10^{-3} Model	Clean ship C_T × 10^{-3}	Clean ship MW	δC_F × 10^{-3}	Dirty ship C_T × 10^{-3}	Dirty ship MW
6·600	1·344	8·97	3·229	1·476	1·753	3·944	2·191	1·534	0·673	2·864	2·005
6·894	1·404	9·37	3·204	1·468	1·736	3·944	2·208	1·817	0·669	2·877	2·368
7·188	1·464	9·77	3·180	1·461	1·719	3·951	2·232	2·082	0·666	2·898	2·704
7·522	1·532	10·22	3·154	1·453	1·701	3·972	2·271	2·423	0·663	2·934	3·131
7·817	1·592	10·63	3·132	1·446	1·686	3·979	2·293	2·736	0·659	2·952	3·557
8·111	1·652	11·03	3·112	1·440	1·672	3·982	2·310	3·100	0·657	2·967	3·982
8·445	1·720	11·48	3·090	1·433	1·657	4·014	2·357	3·566	0·653	3·010	4·554
8·740	1·780	11·88	3·071	1·427	1·644	4·024	2·380	3·991	0·651	3·031	5·082
8·995	1·832	12·23	3·056	1·422	1·634	4·034	2·400	4·390	0·648	3·048	5·575
9·295	1·893	12·63	3·038	1·417	1·621	4·090	2·469	4·975	0·646	3·115	6·277
9·624	1·960	13·08	3·020	1·410	1·610	4·164	2·554	5·716	0·643	3·197	7·155
9·918	2·020	13·46	3·004	1·405	1·599	4·310	2·711	6·639	0·641	3·352	8·209
10·213	2·080	13·88	2·990	1·400	1·590	4·478	2·888	7·723	0·638	3·526	9·429

The standard values (i.e. at 15°C) for v are

$v = 1 \cdot 139 \times 10^{-6}$ m²/s for fresh water

$v = 1 \cdot 188 \times 10^{-6}$ m²/s for sea water

If V is the speed of the ship, the corresponding speed for the 5 m model is $V \sqrt{(5/178)}$. Hence for the ship

$$R_n = \frac{1 \cdot 139}{1 \cdot 188} \left(\frac{178}{5}\right)^{\frac{3}{2}} (R_n)_{\text{model}}$$

$$= 203 \cdot 7 (R_n)_{\text{model}}$$

The ship speed

$$1 \cdot 188 \times 10^{-6} \, R_n/L = 6 \cdot 674 \times 10^{-9} \, (R_n)_{\text{ship}} \text{ m/s.}$$

The C_T values for the model have to be corrected for the skin friction difference in going from model to ship. This correction is the difference between the ordinates of the ITTC line at the Reynolds' numbers appropriate to the model and the ship. Hence, the total resistance C_T can be deduced for the ship. Since

$$C_T = \frac{\text{resistance}}{\frac{1}{2}\rho S V^2}$$

power $= R \times V = \frac{1}{2}\rho S V^3 C_T = 1 \cdot 872 V^3 C_T$ **MW**, V in m/s.

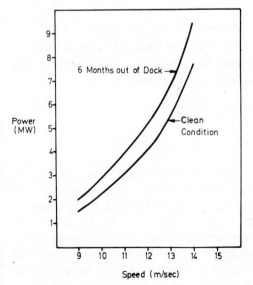

Fig. 11.11 Plot of results

404   *Basic ship theory*

The increase in resistance in the dirty condition is given by

$\delta C_F = 0.456 C_F$ using the ship value

The calculation can now be completed in tabular form as shown in Table 11.8. The results are plotted in Fig. 11.11.

CALCULATION OF WIND RESISTANCE

Reference 12 presents results of wind tunnel tests carried out at the National Physical Laboratory on merchant ship forms. As is to be expected the fair above water portion of the main hull experiences less resistance force per unit area than the superstructure. In fact, the resistance per unit of projected area is only about 30 per cent of that of the superstructures. It was found that the resistance offered by the ship could be represented by the equation

$$\text{Resistance} = KBV^2 \, \text{lbf}$$

where B = projected area onto a transverse plane of the superstructure plus 30 per cent of the projected area of the above water hull (ft^2), V = relative wind speed (knots), and K is a coefficient depending on the ship type and the angle of the relative wind to the middle-line of the ship.

It was found that K was fairly constant for angles up to about 15 degrees off the bow and was a maximum for an angle of about 30 degrees off the bow. Typically, K varied from about 0.0004 to 0.004.

If B is in m^2 and V in knots then, approximately,

$$\text{Resistance} = 48\,KBV^2 \, \text{newtons}$$

More recent work carried out at the National Physical Laboratory is reported in Ref. 13. One useful parameter for comparing results given in that reference is the *ahead resistance coefficient* (ARC) defined by

$$\text{ARC} = \frac{\text{fore and aft component of wind resistance}}{\frac{1}{2} \rho V_R^2 A_T}$$

In the case of a tanker, the ARC values were reasonably steady for relative winds from ahead to 50 degrees off the bow, the value varying from 0.7 in the light condition to about 0.85 in the loaded condition. Corresponding values for winds up to 40 degrees off the stern were -0.6 and -0.7. Variation with relative wind direction between 50 degrees off the bow and 40 degrees off the stern was approximately linear. Two cargo ships exhibited similar trends but the values of the ARC were about 0.1 lower. The same ARC values apply in the metric system provided consistent units are used.

The results include the effect of the velocity gradient existing in atmospheric winds. (See Chapter 9.) They represent the force experienced by a ship of the size tested (tanker 556 ft, cargo ships 488 ft and passenger liner 804 ft, length overall). Smaller ships will have a greater percentage of their area in the lower regions of the gradient and will suffer proportionately less force. The force can be assumed to vary as the square of the velocity. If the results are to be used to deduce the air resistance experienced by a ship moving ahead with no wind then there is no velocity gradient and the forces deduced must be increased by 25 per cent in the light condition and 40 per cent in the deep load condition for the tanker and cargo ships. The increase for a passenger ship is about 21 per cent.

Reference 14 presents data from wind tunnel tests carried out in Japan to help assess the size of mooring rope and the amount of cable veer required by large ships in a strong wind. The problem has acquired greater urgency recently due to the increase in ship size and the limitations of available anchorages.

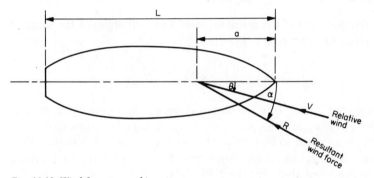

Fig. 11.12 Wind forces on a ship

In Ref. 14, the resultant wind force R is given by

$$R = \tfrac{1}{2}\rho C_r V^2 (A \cos^2 \theta + B \sin^2 \theta), \text{ newtons}$$

where ρ = atmospheric density (kgf m^{-4} s^2) = 0·123 approx., A = frontal projection area (m^2), B = lateral projection area (m^2), and V = relative wind speed (m/s).

Based on results for a number of ships, it is suggested that C_r values are given by the following relationships:

Cargo ship: $C_r = 1·325 - 0·05 \cos 2\theta - 0·35 \cos 4\theta - 0·175 \cos 6\theta$
Passenger ship: $C_r = 1·142 - 0·142 \cos 2\theta - 0·367 \cos 4\theta - 0·133 \cos 6\theta$
Oil tanker: $C_r = 1·20 - 0·083 \cos 2\theta - 0·25 \cos 4\theta - 0·117 \cos 6\theta$

Approximate values of A and B are given by

$$A = B^2[X_A - 0·00475 \, dr]. \text{ In this case, } B = \text{beam}$$
$$B = L^2[X_B - 0·0006 \, dr]$$

where dr = percentage the actual draught is of the fully-loaded draught and values of X_A and X_B are approximately given in Table 11.9.

Table 11.9
Values of X_A and X_B

Ship type	X_A	X_B
3 Island cargo-ship	1·43	0·1195
Cargo-ship with stern machinery	1·225	0·110
Oil tanker	1·095	0·099
Passenger ship	1·455	0·156

The distance aft from the bow at which the resultant wind force acts, expressed as a percentage of ship length, varies uniformly with wind directions between 20° and 160° off the bow and is given by

$$\frac{a}{L} = 0.291 + 0.0023\theta, \qquad \theta \text{ in degrees}$$

Generally, the direction of the resultant wind force, though not the same as the wind direction, changes with it as follows:

$$\alpha = \left\{ 1 - 0.15\left(1 - \frac{\theta}{90}\right) - 0.80\left(1 - \frac{\theta}{90}\right)^3 \right\} \times 90$$

The data reported in Ref. 14 were obtained from measurements on models floating on water. They are therefore subject to a certain unspecified wind gradient. If this is assumed to be comparable to that occurring in nature, then the air resistance force acting on the ship when moving ahead in calm air must be increased as proposed above for the NPL data.

PROPELLER DESIGN

It is only possible in this book to outline the main factors to be considered by the propeller designer. They are:

(a) Shaft revolutions. Apart from the direct influence on propeller efficiency the choice of shaft r.p.m. depends upon the gearing available, critical whirling speeds of shafts and avoidance of the fundamental frequencies of hull vibration;

(b) Number of blades which influences vibration (Fig. 11.13) and cavitation.

(c) Propeller diameter and hence clearance between propeller tips and the hull which has a marked effect on vibration;

(d) Blade area. The greater the blade area for a given thrust the less likely is cavitation;

(e) Boss diameter. Dictated mainly by strength considerations;

(f) Geometry of the blades, e.g. pitch, camber;

(g) The wake in which the propeller is to operate.

The choice of the principal propeller dimensions is an easier problem and is considered below.

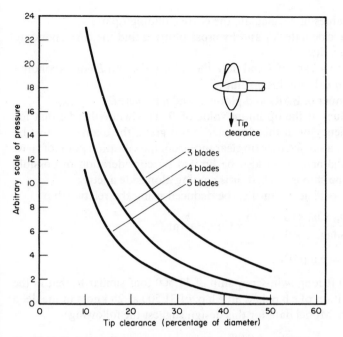

Fig. 11.13 Variation of harmonic pressure with tip clearance. (Ref. 15)

CHOICE OF PROPELLER DIMENSIONS

The propeller dimensions are found using methodical series propeller data. This is adequate if the propeller is to be similar in geometry to those forming the methodical series. If it is to differ in some significant way, the dimensions are first approximated to by using the series data and then adjusted as a result of special tests on the propeller so obtained.

It is assumed that the designer has information on e.h.p., hull efficiency, wake, QPC factor and $\textcircled{T}_R/\textcircled{T}_M$ as a result of model experiments and previous ship trials. The speed will be stated in the requirements for the ship. The steps in the design process are now:

(a) t.h.p. in open water $= TV_1 = $ t.h.p. $\times \dfrac{\textcircled{T}_R}{\textcircled{T}_M}$

   from which thrust T can be deduced;

(b) the designer assesses an allowable pressure on the blades if serious cavitation effects are to be avoided. In the absence of other data, it is recommended that a figure of 0·75 tonf/ft² (80 kN/m²) be used. From this, the blade area to provide the thrust T, and hence BAR can be obtained in terms of the diameter of the propeller;

(c) for values of BAR, for which methodical series data are available, deduce the propeller diameter D. We can now illustrate the method to be used by reference to Fig. 11.6 for a BAR of 0·65. The procedure has to be repeated for each BAR under consideration;

(*d*) for a series of values of J, calculate the corresponding r.p.m., n;
(*e*) for each n value calculate K_T and by cross plotting find the corresponding P/D ratio and η value;
(*f*) plot n, P and η to a base of J and note the values of n and P corresponding to the maximum η. Note this η value;
(*g*) repeat for a number of BARs and plot n, P and η to base D;
(*h*) read off the values at the optimum value of D. This will either be that for maximum efficiency or, if this diameter is too great, the diameter must be restricted to give a satisfactory tip clearance from the vibration point of view. The propeller diameter may also be limited by consideration of possible damage when the ship is docked or is coming alongside a jetty;
(*i*) the propulsive coefficient can then be deduced using the relationship

$$PC = \left[\frac{\eta_H \times \eta_0 \times \eta_R}{\text{appendage coefficient}} \right] \times QPC \text{ factor}$$

(*j*) calculate s.h.p. = e.h.p./PC.

EXAMPLE 3. A 570 ft long twin-screw ship of 11,500 tonf similar to that in the example for calculation of e.h.p. had an e.h.p. of 31,500 at 28 knots in the deep and dirty condition. Model data for this design suggest the following:

Hull efficiency   = 0·98
Relative rotative efficiency = 1·00
Wake   = 10 per cent
Appendage coefficient   = 1·06

Trial data from a similar ship suggest that with a pressure coefficient of 0·75 tonf/ft², the QPC factor is 0·92 and $(T)_R/(T)_M$ is 1·04.

Determine the dimensions and revolutions of the propeller to give maximum efficiency assuming that the maximum diameter from the point of view of docking is 14 ft. Calculate also the propulsive coefficient at 28 knots and horsepower required at this speed.

Solution: Following the procedure outlined above

e.h.p. per screw = 15,750

$$\text{t.h.p. per screw} = \frac{\text{e.h.p.}'}{\text{HE}} \times \frac{(T)_R}{(T)_M} = \frac{15,750}{0·98} \times 1·04 \times 1·06 = 17,680$$

$$V_1 = \frac{28}{1·10} = 25·45 \text{ knots}$$

Since t.h.p. = (thrust) $\times V_1$

$$\text{Thrust per screw}: \frac{17,680}{25·45} \times \frac{550}{2240} \times \frac{3600}{6080} \text{ tonf} = 0·1454 \times \frac{17,680}{25·45} = 101 \text{ tonf}$$

Area of blades to restrict pressure loading to 0·75 tonf/ft²

$$= \frac{101}{0·75} = 135 \text{ ft}^2$$

Hence

$$BAR = \frac{4A_D}{\pi D^2} = \frac{135 \times 4}{\pi D^2} = \frac{172}{D^2}$$

The BARs for which data are presented in Rêf. 4 are 0·2, 0·35, 0·5, 0·65, 0·80, 0·95 and 1·1. Corresponding values of D are: 29·33, 22·16, 18·55, 16·27, 14·66, 13·46, 12·51 ft.

Because of the limitation imposed on the propeller diameter, we need only consider the last three values of BAR the value 0·80 being used merely to define the trends.

$$J = \frac{V_1}{nD} = \frac{25\cdot45}{nD} \times \frac{6080}{60} = 101\cdot3 \times \frac{25\cdot45}{nD} \text{ for } n \text{ in r.p.m.}$$

Hence

$$n = \frac{2578}{DJ} \text{ r.p.m.}$$

Table 11.10 can now be constructed.

For each value of D and n, K_T can be calculated from

$$K_T = \frac{T}{(\rho/g)n^2D^4} = \frac{101 \times 2240}{\frac{64}{32}n^2D^4} = \frac{113,120}{n^2D^4} \quad n \text{ in r.p.s.}$$

The calculation can be simplified somewhat by introducing in this expression for K_T the relationship

$$J = \frac{V_1}{nD}$$

$$K_T = \frac{113,120}{(V_1)^2} \frac{(J)^2(D)^2}{D^4} = \frac{113,120J^2}{V_1^2D^2}$$

$$= \frac{113,120}{(25\cdot45)^2} \times \frac{(3600)^2}{(6080)^2} \frac{J^2}{D^2}$$

$$= 39\cdot17 \times \frac{1}{D^2} \quad \text{for } J = 0\cdot8$$

$$= 61\cdot21 \times \frac{1}{D^2} \quad \text{for } J = 1\cdot0$$

$$= 88\cdot14 \times \frac{1}{D^2} \quad \text{for } J = 1\cdot2$$

By cross plotting the data presented in Ref. 4, the values of P/D and η can be obtained for each value of K_T, J and BAR. In order to obtain a reliable value of η, it is recommended that a line be drawn parallel to the base line at the appropriate K_T value, noting the J value appropriate to each P/D and the

Table 11.10
Propeller calculation

BAR	D	$\dfrac{2579}{D}$	J	n	K_T	P/D	η	Values for η_{max}			
								n	P/D	η	P
0·80	14·66	175·9	0·8	219·9	0·183	1·11	0·658				
			1·0	175·9	0·286	1·50	0·665	200	1·24	0·676	18·2
			1·2	146·6	0·410	1·96	0·638				
0·95	13·46	191·6	0·8	239·5	0·217	1·15	0·648				
			1·0	191·6	0·338	1·56	0·640	228	1·24	0·650	16·7
			1·2	159·7	0·487	2·03	0·610				
1·1	12·51	206·2	0·8	257·8	0·250	1·16	0·615				
			1·0	206·2	0·392	1·59	0·610	247	1·24	0·624	15·5
			1·2	171·8	0·563	2·06	0·585				

corresponding η. Plotting η against P/D the η value required can be obtained knowing P/D.

Now by plotting for each BAR the values of n, P/D and η to a base of J the values of P/D (and hence P) and n corresponding to maximum η can be read off. These results together with the η value are now plotted to a base of D.

In this case, the limitation on propeller diameter is the overriding factor, since efficiency is still increasing as the diameter exceeds the 14 ft value. Corresponding to the 14 ft diameter

$$\eta = 0.66$$

$$n = 217 \text{ r.p.m.}$$

$$P = 17.1 \text{ ft}$$

$$\text{BAR} = \frac{172}{D^2} = \frac{172}{(14)^2} = 0.878$$

Now

$$\text{Propulsive coefficient} = \text{PC} = \left[\frac{\eta_H \times \eta_0 \times \eta_R}{\text{appendage coeff}}\right] \times \text{QPC factor}$$

$$= \left[\frac{0.98 \times 0.66 \times 1.00}{1.06}\right]0.92 = 0.562$$

$$\text{Shaft horsepower} = \frac{31,500}{\text{PC}} = \frac{31,500}{0.562} = 56,000$$

This is the power which must be developed by the machinery.

PROPELLER DESIGN DIAGRAM

The example above shows that the amount of work involved in designing this one propeller is fairly lengthy, particularly when it is realized that the various cross-plottings necessary in the solution have not been reproduced.

A shorter analysis is possible if use is made of a 3-bladed propeller design diagram based on the 20 in. propeller data published in Ref. 4. This diagram,

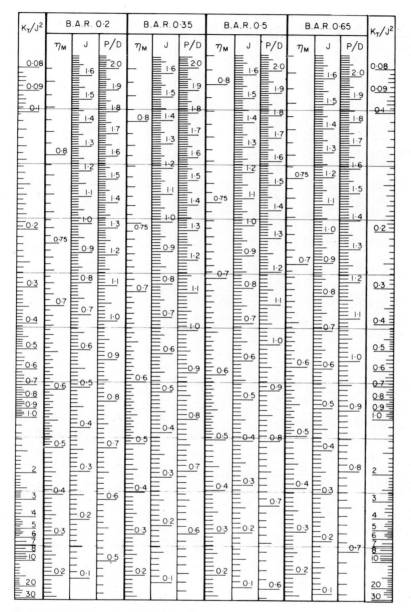

Fig. 11.14 *Preliminary propeller design diagram*

developed by the Admiralty Experiment Works is reproduced as Fig. 11.14. It makes use of the parameter K_T/J^2 which depends only on thrust, propeller diameter and speed of advance, since:

$$\frac{K_T}{J^2} = \frac{T}{\rho n^2 D^4} \bigg/ \frac{V_1^2}{n^2 D^2} = \frac{T}{\rho D^2 V_1^2}$$

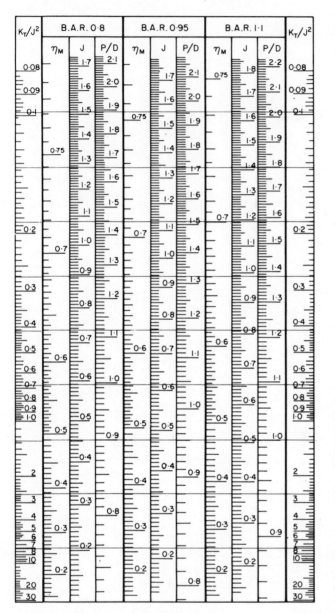

Diagram gives the maximum propeller efficiency, η_M, obtainable for any known value of K_T/J^2 with corresponding values of advance coefficient J and face pitch ratio P/D

$$\frac{K_T}{J^2} = \frac{395 \cdot 1 \, T}{D^2 V_1^2} = \frac{57 \cdot 44 \, \text{t.h.p.}}{D^2 V_1^3}$$

$$J = \frac{101 \cdot 3 \, V_1}{nD}$$

where:
T = thrust in tonf ⎫
D and P are in ft ⎬ In salt
n is in r.p.m. water
V_1 is in knots ⎭

Fig. 11.14 *Preliminary propeller design diagram*

Thus one unknown, n, has been removed. By calculating the value of K_T/J^2 and drawing a line across the diagram at this level the values of maximum efficiency, J, and P/D can be read off directly at the appropriate BAR value.

EXAMPLE 4. Use the propeller design diagram to design the propeller in the previous example.

Solution: In the previous example, it was shown that values of D corresponding to BARs of 0·80, 0·95 and 1·1 were 14·66, 13·46 and 12·51 ft. Other data calculated in that example were:

Thrust per screw = 101 tonf

$$V_1 = \frac{28}{1·10} = 25·45 \text{ knots}$$

Hence

$$\frac{K_T}{J^2} = \frac{T}{\rho D^2 V_1^2}$$

$$= \frac{101 \times 2240}{\frac{64}{32}(D^2)(25·45)^2} \times \frac{(3600)^2}{(6080)^2} = \frac{61·21}{D^2}$$

A table can now be constructed as in Table 11.11.

Table 11.11
Calculation for worked example using propeller design diagram

BAR	0·80	0·95	1·1
D, ft	14·66	13·46	12·51
$\dfrac{K_T}{J^2}$	0·286	0·338	0·392
η_m	0·676	0·650	0·624
J	0·872	0·842	0·830
P/D	1·24	1·237	1·239
P	18·18	16·65	15·50
DJ	12·78	11·33	10·38
r.p.m.	202	228	248

In Table 11.11, the values of η_m, J and P/D are read directly from the propeller design diagram.

The propeller revolutions, n, can be obtained from

$$n = \frac{V_1 \times 101·3}{DJ} = \frac{2578}{DJ}$$

Values of p, n and η_m can be plotted against diameter as before, showing that it is the limit on diameter at 14 ft which is the governing factor and giving a propeller of the following characteristics

$D = 14$ ft,   PC for ship = 0·565

$P = 17·1$ ft,   s.h.p. = 56,000

$n = 217$,   BAR = 0·878

$\eta = 0·664$,

INFLUENCE OF FORM ON RESISTANCE

It must be made clear that there is no absolute in terms of an optimum form. The designer has many things to consider besides the powering of his ship, e.g. ability to fit machinery, magazines, etc., seakeeping, manoeuvrability and so on. Even from the point of view of powering, one form may be superior to another at one displacement and over one speed range but inferior at other displacements or speed ranges.

Again, the situation is complicated by the fact that, in general, one parameter cannot be varied without affecting others. For example, to increase length, keeping form coefficients and beam constant, will change displacement and draught. Thus the following comments can be regarded as being valid only in a general qualitative way. Wherever possible, reference should be made to methodical series tests.

Wetted length

If a designer has freedom of choice of length, keeping displacement sensibly constant, he will choose a short form for slow speed ships and a long, slender form for high speed ships. This is because an increase in length increases the wetted surface area and hence the skin frictional resistance. At low speed this will more than offset any reduction in wave-making resistance, but for high speeds the possible reduction in wave-making resistance will be all important. Nevertheless, the variation of wave-making resistance with length does not obey a simple law as was explained in Chapter 10. Because of the interference between bow and stern wave systems, there will be optimum bands of length with intermediate lengths being relatively poor.

Prismatic coefficient

This coefficient has little influence on the skin frictional resistance but can have a marked effect on residuary resistance. If possible, reference should be made to methodical series data from models similar to the design under development. Broadly, however, the optimum C_P value increases with increasing $V/\sqrt{L}$ value. (Fig. 11.15.) Since the influence of the prismatic coefficient is mainly related to the residuary resistance, it is not critical for low speed ships. In such ships, the

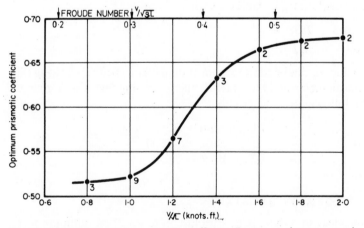

Fig. 11.15 *Curve of optimum prismatic coefficient. Figures on the curve are the approximate percentage increases in resistance for ± 0.05 change from the optimum* C_P.

choice of C_P value is much more likely to be governed by the cargo carrying capacity.

Curve of areas

It is essential that this should be a fair curve with no sudden changes of curvature. Apart from this it is difficult and perhaps dangerous to generalize. Reference 16 shows how very small changes in the curve of areas can produce really large changes in the residuary resistance.

Cross-sectional shapes

Generally, these are not critical but, if other ship requirements permit, U-shaped sections are to be preferred to V-shaped sections forward. This arises principally from the fact that more volume is removed from the vicinity of the waterplane and the wave-making resistance is accordingly reduced. V-shaped sections are used aft for vessels operating at high Froude number.

Centre of buoyancy position

The CB should vary from a few per cent of the length forward of amidships for slow ships to about 10 per cent of the length aft for fast ships.

REDUCING WAVE-MAKING RESISTANCE

Since, physically, wave-making resistance arises from a disturbance of the free surface, it is reasonable to expect that a lower resistance will result from concentrating displacement remote from the waterplane. That is to say, U sections are less resistful than V sections. Other generalizations are dangerous, e.g. in Ref. 16 (Figs. 9 and 10), results for two forms with the same prismatic coefficient and apparently very similar curves of area show that, for one the wave-making resistance is double that of the other for $F_n = 0.23$ with substantial differences for F_n is the range 0.22 to 0.31.

Weinblum states that theory has been able to explain why apparently small form changes can lead to large variations in wave-making resistance. It is for this reason that theory can often guide the model experimenter in his search for a better form. It should be emphasized, however, that there is no universal 'optimum' ship form giving minimum resistance at all speeds but rather a best form for a given Froude number.

It has been demonstrated that significant decreases in wave-making resistance occur when the bow and stern wave systems are out of phase. It is therefore reasonable to enquire whether a reduction can be obtained by artificially creating a wave system to interact with the ship system. In fact, this is the principle of the bulbous bow. Depending on its size, a bulb produces a wave system with crests and troughs in positions governed by the fore and aft position of the bulb relative to the bow. Unfortunately, this again can only produce a reduction in resistance over a limited range of F_n and then only at the expense of resistance at other speeds. Where a ship operates for a large percentage of its time at one speed as, for instance, is usually the case for most merchant ships, such a device can be of great benefit and is becoming more extensively used.

TRIPLETS

In the early stages of ship design it is often useful to quantify the effects on speed or power of small variations in hull shape. Beam, for example, may have to be increased to achieve acceptable stability. Mathematically, the variation of power with length, beam and draught can be expressed in terms of performance coefficients α, β and γ as

$$\frac{\partial P_E}{P_E} = \alpha\frac{\partial L}{L} + \beta\frac{\partial B}{B} + \gamma\frac{\partial T}{T}$$

The values of the performance coefficients are obtained from tests with three models (triplets), two of which have been distorted by about 10 per cent from the parent form in length and beam respectively.

COMPATIBILITY OF MACHINERY AND PROPELLER

Having the geometry of the propeller for the full-power condition, it follows that the thrust and torque variations with shaft revolutions are fully determined. To be satisfactory, the machinery must always be able to develop these torques at the various revolutions, otherwise the machinery will 'lock-up', i.e. as speed is increased the machinery will arrive at a point where its power output is prematurely limited by the torque demanded by the propeller.

If there is no other solution available, it may be possible to solve the problem by fitting a controllable pitch propeller.

STRENGTH OF PROPELLERS

Calculations of propeller strength must take account of the torque and bending moments acting at the blade roots. Stress levels accepted must be such that the propeller will last the life of the ship and must allow for the cyclic variations in loads due to the wake and the increased forces due to ship motions and manoeuvring. Reference 17 presents a simplified design theory.

EFFECT OF SPEED ON ENDURANCE

The rate of fuel consumption depends upon:

(a) the efficiency of the machinery at various power outputs. This feature is to some extent within the control of the machinery designer, e.g. he can design for optimum efficiency at full power, at cruising power or at some intermediate figure in order to balance the two;

(b) the power needed to supply the domestic loads of the ship such as lighting, galleys, air-conditioning, etc. This load is often referred to as the 'hotel' load and is independent of the forward speed of the ship.

The hotel load in a modern ship, particularly a passenger ship, can absorb a large proportion of the power generated at low speed. For this reason, the economical speed has tended to increase in recent years. The economic speed is a complicated thing to calculate but factors to be considered are: the fuel bill for covering a given distance at various speeds; the wages bill for the crew; the number of round voyages possible per year; special considerations depending on the payload of the ship, e.g. for a passenger ship a speedier passage may entice passengers away from the airlines. On the other hand, if the journey is between say Southampton and New York there is no attraction in arriving in one of the ports at midnight—if a faster journey is not feasible then the speed might as well be reduced.

In the following example, the influence of speed on the fuel bill is calculated for a typical steam ship of 35,000 s.h.p.

EXAMPLE 5. The s.h.p. speed curve for a given ship with a total installed power of 35,000 s.h.p., is as shown in Fig. 11.16 and the specific fuel consumption for various percentages of full power are as shown in Fig. 11.17. Calculate the endurance for 1000 tonf of fuel over a range of speeds and the weight of fuel required for 1000 miles endurance.

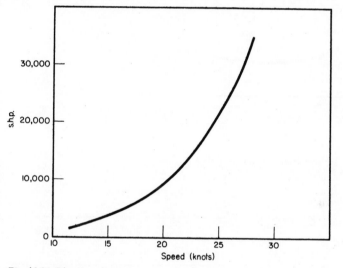

Fig. 11.16 *S.h.p./speed curve*

Solution: At a speed of V knots, the distance travelled in 1 hr is V nautical miles. To travel 1000 miles takes $1000/V$ hr.

If the fuel consumption is S lbf per shaft horsepower hour, the fuel required for 1000 miles at speed V is

$$\frac{S}{2240} \times (\text{s.h.p.}) \times \frac{1000}{V} \text{ tonf}$$

Conversely, the number of hours steaming possible on 1000 tonf of fuel is given by

$$\text{No. of hours} = \frac{1000 \times 2240}{S(\text{s.h.p.})}$$

$$\text{Distance travelled} = \frac{1000 \times 2240}{S(\text{s.h.p.})V} \text{ miles}$$

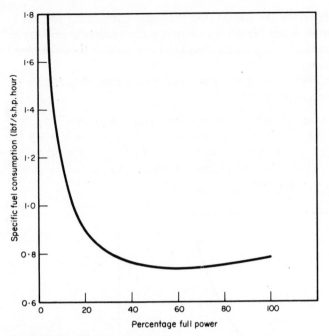

Fig. 11.17 *Specific fuel consumption*

A table can now be constructed as in Table 11.12.

Table 11.12
Calculation of endurance

V (knots)	s.h.p. (from Fig. 11.16)	% full power	SFC (lbf/s.h.p. hr)	tonf of fuel per 1000 miles	Endurance for 1000 tonf fuel
12	1900	5·4	1·75	124	8100
14	3000	8·6	1·34	128	7800
16	4400	12·6	1·10	135	7400
18	6400	18·3	0·93	147	6800
20	9200	26·3	0·80	164	6100
22	13,000	37·1	0·78	206	4900
24	18,200	52·0	0·75	255	3900
26	25,000	71·4	0·75	323	3100
28	35,000	100	0·78	435	2300

It will be seen that there is not a lot of penalty in increasing the cruising or endurance speed from 12 to 16 knots. Indeed, economically, the lower salary bill would probably compensate for the increased fuel bill and the ship is a sounder economic proposition because of its increased mileage in a year.

Summary

The methods of presentation and calculation presented enable the general principles established in Chapter 10 to be applied to the calculation of the shaft horsepower required to propel a new design at the required speed. Allowance can be made for air resistance and for hull fouling as a result of marine growth which increases with time out of dock. As part of the process, a suitable design of screw propeller is obtained from methodical series data.

Concluding remarks

This is, of course, only a beginning. While it enables a suitable design of hull and propeller to be effected, it does not describe many of the refinements to the process. These the student must pursue for himself through the transactions of the learned societies.

There are, perhaps, two areas where such refinements may make a substantial improvement to the ship. The first is in boundary layer control. In particular, the smoothness of ship's hull over its whole life may permit higher fuel economy or devices for delaying breakaway may be developed. Long chain molecule additives such as polyethelene oxide to the water can reduce skin friction by 30 per cent and if means can be found to recover them, could represent a major advance. The second area where the practitioner may be dissatisfied is in the selection of a standard propeller. There are now theories available, based upon the representation of the lifting surfaces of the blades by surfaces of vortices which give theoretical lift and drag. While they are not yet fully developed, they do indicate a much wider choice for the designer. They depend much upon the wake of the ship and its distribution at the propeller disc so that a good deal of attention is now being given to wake survey and prediction.

Similarly, theoretical prediction of wave resistance from the assumption of potential flow is now possible also and has been found remarkably accurate.

Problems

1. A ship of 50 MN displacement is driven at a speed of 12 knots. A ship of 65 MN of similar form is being designed. At what speed of the larger ship should its performance be compared with the 50 MN ship?   (AP & S)
2. A ship of length 64·6 m, 6·02 m beam, 1·98 m draught, wetted surface 369 m^2 and displacement 4·26 MN has a resistance of 35 kN at 15·8 knots.

Deduce the dimensions and effective power of a ship of similar form 233 m long at the corresponding speed.
3. With the definitions of $\textcircled{C}$ and C_T given in the text show that

$$C_T = \frac{8\pi}{1000} \frac{\textcircled{C}}{\textcircled{S}}$$

4. A 5 m model of a 180 m long ship is towed in a ship tank at a speed of 1·2 m/sec. The towing pull is 11·77 newtons. Assuming that 60 per cent of the resistance force is due to skin friction, calculate the corresponding speed for the ship in knots and the e.h.p. at this speed assuming a wetted surface area of 3600 m^2 in the ship.

5. A destroyer 320 ft × 1450 tonf has a full speed of 35 knots with clean bottom. The ⓒ value of a 16 ft model of the same form is 1·75 at the corresponding speed. Estimate the proportion of the ship resistance at full speed attributable to skin friction using
(1) Froude analysis
(2) ITTC ship-model correlation line.   (RNC)
NOTE: Use Question 3 to change ⓒ to C_T.
6. A model of a vessel, 400 ft × 65 ft × 24 ft draught, of 8560 tonf displacement, is run, and the curve of e.h.p. on a base of speed of ship is 3250, 4035, 5020, 6195 and 7660 e.h.p. for 16, 17, 18, 19 and 20 knots respectively. Make an estimate of the e.h.p. of a ship of 16,000 tonf, of similar form, for speeds of 20 and 21 knots and give the dimensions of the new ship.   (AP & S)
7. The data below relates to the 16 ft model of a ship 395 ft long, 4000 tonf displacement. Assuming ⓢ = 7·15 and a propulsive coefficient of 0·57 plot the s.h.p.–speed curve for the ship when 6 months out of dock. Assume that the skin frictional resistance increases by $\frac{1}{4}$ of a per cent per day out of dock.
What speed is likely in this condition with 40,000 s.h.p?

ⓚ	1·6	2·0	2·5	3·0	3·5	4·0	4·5
ⓒ	1·150	1·176	1·245	1·418	1·500	1·770	2·085

8. The following data relates to a 16 ft model of a ship 640 ft long and 14,225 tonf displacement.

ⓚ	1·2	1·5	2·0	2·3	2·5	3·0	3·1	3·2	3·3	3·4
ⓒ	1·205	1·170	1·145	1·145	1·155	1·160	1·170	1·181	1·210	1·253

Compute and plot the s.h.p.–speed curve for the ship 6 months out of dock assuming ⓢ = 7·40, and a propulsive coefficient of 0·55.
What power is required for 20 and 28 knots?
A ship of 6000 tonf displacement is required to have a maximum speed of 25 knots. The total e.h.p. including appendages is 15,000. Other data are:

Hull efficiency	= 1·0
Mean wake	= 1·4 per cent
Relative rotative efficiency	= 0·98
Quasi-propulsive coefficient factor	= 0·88
Pressure coefficient	= 0·7 tonf/ft^2

Use the propeller design diagram to find the propeller diameter and s.h.p. required for shaft revolutions of 200 r.p.m. Calculate the efficiency, pitch and r.p.m. of a 13 ft diameter propeller.
10. A propeller is found by calculation to have a K_T/J^2 value of 0·2225 when developing a t.h.p. of 5000 at a speed of advance through the water of 25 knots. What is the diameter of the propeller?
Use the propeller design diagram to find the maximum efficiency possible and the corresponding pitch.

11. What is *cavitation* and what is its effect on torque, thrust and efficiency of a propeller? Explain why experiments on models to determine the effects of cavitation cannot be carried out in an open ship tank.

A 4 m propeller has been designed for a destroyer to give a top speed of 30 knots at 250 r.p.m. It is desired to run a 50 cm model of the propeller in a cavitation tunnel at a water speed of 6 m/s. At what water pressure and r.p.m. must the model propeller be run, to simulate ship conditions? C.L. of propeller below surface = 4 m. Atmospheric pressure = 10^5 N/m², water vapour pressure = 1700 N/m². Froude wake factor = −0·01. (HMDTC)

12. Estimate the r.p.m. and expected thrust and torque of a model propeller, 9 in. in diameter, fitted behind an 18 ft model of a ship 450 ft long. The model is to be run in fresh water. The following data are available for the ship, (in salt water, 35 ft³/tonf):

shaft r.p.m.	= 110
ship speed	= 15·6 knots
Froude wake factor	= 0·47
d.h.p.	= 6400
t.h.p.	= 3980 (HMDTC)

13. What is meant by the terms quasi-propulsive coefficient and quasi-propulsive coefficient factor? Explain how these quantities are obtained from model experiments and full-scale trials.

The following results were obtained from experiments on a 5 m model of a new design of frigate: Length 130 m, displacement 3600 tonnef,

Ship Ⓒ at 27 knots	= 1·59
Hull efficiency	= 0·95
Relative rotative efficiency	= 0·98
Openwater screw efficiency	= 0·69
Appendage coefficient	= 1·07

On trials, the frigate achieved a speed of 27 knots at a measured shaft power of 22 MW. Calculate the quasi-propulsive coefficient and the quasi-propulsive coefficient factor. (HMDTC)

14. Assuming that the curve of K_T against J is a straight line over the working range, show that, for a given speed of advance, the thrust (T) developed by a propeller varies with its r.p.m. (N) in the following manner:

$$T = AN^2 - BN$$

where A and B are constants for a given propeller and speed of advance.

For a particular 20 in. model propeller, running at 550 ft/min, the constants have the following values: $A = 17$; $B = 65$, when N is measured in hundreds of r.p.m., and T is measured in lbf.

Calculate the thrust of a geometrically similar propeller of 10 ft diameter at 200 r.p.m. and a speed of advance of 12 knots in sea water. (HMDTC)

15. Resistance experiments are to be run on a 20 ft model of a new warship design. Estimate the model resistance in lbf at a speed corresponding to the ship's full speed, given the following design information:

Length, 580 ft; displacement, 11,200 tonf; estimated s.h.p. at full speed of 30 knots, 74,000; estimated propulsive coefficient, 0·54; wetted surface, 38,000 ft².

Use the ITTC line to calculate skin frictional resistance for model and ship; applying a roughness correction of 0·0004 for the ship only.

The appropriate kinematic viscosities are:

fresh water, $1·3234 \times 10^{-5}$ ft²/s
salt water, $1·1979 \times 10^{-5}$ ft²/s   (HMDTC)

16. Describe, briefly, the three main causes of 'wake' when considering a ship moving through the water.

How is the hull efficiency related to wake and augment?

The thrust–r.p.m. curve for a model propeller, run in open water at an advance speed of 2·5 m/s, is given by the equation:

$$T = 53 N^2 - 225 N.$$

where T is in newtons, N is in hundreds of r.p.m.

This curve coincides with the 'behind thrust' curve for the propeller-ship model combination when run at a speed of advance of 2·8 m/s.

The augmented resistance can be approximated to the straight line:

$$T = 45 N - 145$$

and the model hull resistance, when towed without the propellers and at a speed of 2·8 m/s is 51 newtons.

Determine the propeller revolutions for model self propulsion and hence find the wake, augment and hull efficiency for the propeller-ship combination.
                                                                      (HMDTC)

17. Describe the methods by which the hull efficiency elements may be deduced from model experiments.

Why can good comparisons be made between various sizes of propellers by only maintaining the advance coefficient constant, when running deeply submerged in open water?

The results of tests on a 30 cm diameter propeller run at 500 r.p.m. are shown below.

What will be the maximum efficiency obtainable for this propeller, and the appropriate speed of advance?

J	0	0·2	0·4	0·6	0·8	1·0	1·2
K_T	0·715	0·62	0·50	0·37	0·25	0·14	0·03
K_Q	0·13	0·114	0·094	0·072	0·05	0·032	0·014

                                                                      (HMDTC)

18. Very briefly, describe methods by which hull-efficiency elements may be determined from model experiments.

After towing a model, it is deduced that the e.h.p. required to move the ship's hull and appendages at a speed of 28 knots would be 24,000 of which 39 per cent would be due to skin friction. Skin friction for the model would account for 43·5 per cent of the total resistance.

Experiments were then conducted with the model and propellers combined at a model speed of 8 ft/s which corresponds to the required ship's speed. At self-propulsion the shaft speed was 14·0 rev/s and thrust and torque provided were 7·35 lbf and 0·97 lbf ft respectively. Open water experiments with the same propellers gave the same thrust and revs when advancing at 7·65 ft/s. Determine the augment and wake fractions and the propeller efficiency behind the ship.

Hence, assuming RRE and appendage coefficient to be both 1·0, deduce the s.h.p. required for 28 knots and a QPC factor of 0·94. (HMDTC)

19. A new design has a displacement of 115 MN and length 174 m. Corresponding values of $\textcircled{C}$ and $\textcircled{K}$ for a 4·88 m model are:

$\textcircled{K}$	2·2	2·3	2·4	2·5	2·6	2·7	2·8
$\textcircled{C}$	1·130	1·130	1·132	1·138	1·140	1·141	1·150
$\textcircled{K}$	2·9	3·0	3·1	3·2	3·3	3·4	
$\textcircled{C}$	1·153	1·156	1·172	1·193	1·235	1·283	

Assuming $\textcircled{S}$ = 7·205 and a propulsive coefficient of 0·55, plot the curve of power (MW) against speed for the clean ship. Assuming that the skin frictional resistance increases by $\frac{1}{4}$ per cent per day out of dock, plot the corresponding curve for the ship 6 months out of dock.

Assuming 33·56 MW installed power, calculate the maximum speeds (*a*) in the clean condition and (*b*) 6 months out of dock.

References

1. Telfer, E. V. The design presentation of ship model resistance data. *TNECI*, Vol. 79, 1962-3.
2. Froude, R. E. On the 'constant' system of notation of results of experiments on models used at the Admiralty Experiment Works. *TINA*, 1888.
3. Taylor, D. W. *The speed and power of ships*. United States Government Printing Office, Washington, 1943. Gertler, M. A re-analysis. *DTMB Rept 806, 1954*.
4. Gawn, R. W. L. Effect of pitch and blade width on propeller performance. *TINA*, 1953.
5. Troost, L. Open water test series with modern propeller forms. *TNECI*, 1950–1.
6. Van Manen, J. D. The choice of the propeller, *Marine Technology*. April, 1966.
7. Gawn, R. W. L. and Burrill, L. C. Effect of cavitation on the performance of a series of 16 in. model propellers. *TINA*, 1957.
8. *Congrès International Des Directeurs de Bassins*. Paris, 1935.
9. *Standard procedure for resistance and propulsion experiments with ship models*. National Physical Laboratory Ship Division Report No. 10, February, 1960.
10. Conn, J. F. C., Lackenby, H. and Walker, W. P. BSRA resistance experiments on the *Lucy Ashton*, Part II; The ship-model correlation for the naked hull condition. *TINA*, 1953.
11. Hadler, J. B. *Coefficients for International Towing Tank Conference 1957 Model-Ship Correlation Line*. DTMB Report 1185, April, 1958.
12. Hughes, G. Model experiments on the wind resistance of ships. *TINA*, 1930.
13. Shearer, K. D. A. and Lynn, W. M. Wind tunnel tests on models of merchant ships. *TNECI*, Vol. 76, 1959–60.
14. Iwai, A. and Yajima, S. *Wind forces acting on ship moored*. Lecture to the 26th Meeting of the Nautical Institute of Japan, October, 1961.
15. Ramsay, J. W. Aspects of ship vibration induced by twin propellers. *TINA*, 1956.
16. Weinblum, Georg. P. Practical applications of wave resistance theory. *SNAME*, Northern California Section, April, 1955.
17. Conolly, J. E. *Strength of propellers. TRINA*, 1961.
18. Gadd, G. E. Wave resistance calculations by Guilloton's method. *TRINA*, 1973.
19. Lackenby, H. and Parker, M. N. The BSRA methodical series—an overall presentation, etc. *TRINA*, 1966.
20. Hughes, G. and Cutland, R. S. *Viscous and wave components of ship model resistance*. Published by National Physical Laboratory, 1973.
21. van Manen, J. D. *Fundamentals of ship resistance and propulsion, Pt B*. Netherlands Ship Model Basin, 1969.

12 Seakeeping

Seakeeping qualities

The general term seaworthiness must embrace all those aspects of a ship design which affect its ability to remain at sea in all conditions and to carry out its specified duty. It should, therefore, include consideration of strength, stability and endurance, besides those factors more directly influenced by waves. In this chapter, the term seakeeping is used to cover these more limited features, i.e. motions, speed and power in waves, wetness and slamming.

The relative importance of these various aspects of performance in waves varies from design to design depending upon what the operators require of the ship, but the following general comments are applicable to most ships.

Motions

Excessive amplitudes of motion are undesirable even if only from the point of view of crew and passenger comfort. This may be a very significant factor in passenger liner operation. In warships, most weapon systems require their line of sight to remain fixed in space and to this end each system is provided with its own stabilizing system. Large motion amplitudes increase the power demands of such systems and may restrict the safe arcs of fire.

The phase relationships between various motions are also important. Generally, the phasing between motions is such as to lead to a point of minimum vertical movement about two-thirds of the length of the ship from the bow. In a passenger liner, this area would be used for the more important accommodation spaces. If it is desirable to reduce the vertical movement at a given point, then this can be achieved if the phasing can be changed, e.g. in an aircraft carrier the vertical movement of the after end of the flight deck is usually the limiting factor in aircraft operation. Such actions must inevitably lead to increased movement at some other point. In the aircraft carrier, increased movement of the bow would result and if the process were taken to extremes the catapulting of aircraft could become hazardous.

Speed and power in waves

When moving through waves the resistance experienced by a ship is increased and, in general, high winds mean increased air resistance. These factors cause the ship speed to be reduced for a given power output, the reduction being aggravated by the less favourable conditions in which the propeller is working. Other unpleasant features of operating in waves such as motions, slamming and wetness are generally eased by a reduction in speed so that an additional speed reduction may be made voluntarily.

Wetness

When the relative movement of the bow and local wave surface becomes too great, water is shipped over the forecastle. At an earlier stage, spray is driven over the forward portion of the ship by the wind. Both conditions are undesirable and can be lessened by increasing freeboard.

Slamming

Under some conditions, the pressures exerted by the water on a ship's hull become very large and slamming occurs. Slamming is characterized by a sudden change in the vertical acceleration of the ship followed by a vibration of the ship girder in its natural frequency. The conditions leading to slamming are high relative velocity between ship and water, shallow draught and small rise of floor. The area between 10 and 25 per cent of the length from the bow is the area most likely to suffer high pressures and to sustain damage.

Importance of good seakeeping

It is impossible to ascribe a single quantitative index to the importance of seakeeping. In a competitive world, a comfortable ship will attract more passengers than a ship with a bad reputation. A ship with less power augment in waves will be able to maintain tighter schedules or will have a lower fuel bill. In extreme cases, the seakeeping qualities of a ship may determine its ability to make a given voyage at all.

Good seakeeping is clearly desirable, but the difficulty lies in determining how far other design features must, or should, be compromised to improve seakeeping. This will depend upon each particular design, but it is essential that the designer has some means of judging the expected performance. It is to a discussion of such means that the later sections of this chapter are devoted. Theory, model experiment and ship trial all have a part to play. Because of the random nature of the sea surface in which the ship operates, considerable use is made of the principles of statistical analysis.

Having improved the performance as much as possible by general design changes, certain aspects of seakeeping can be further controlled by fitting anti-roll stabilizers. Such devices can be fitted when the ship is in service, e.g. the *Queen Elizabeth* was so fitted some years after completion to improve passenger comfort and to reduce the bill for broken crockery. Fuel economy is, these days, probably more important than equipment damage.

Ship routing

Since the ship behaviour depends upon the wave conditions it meets, it is reasonable to question whether overall performance can be improved by avoiding the more severe waves. This possibility has been successfully pursued by some authorities. Data from weather ships are used to predict the speed loss in various ocean areas and to compute the optimum route. In this way, significant savings have been made in voyage times, e.g. of the order of 10–15 hours for the Atlantic crossing.

Having considered the general problem of seakeeping, it is possible to con-sider each aspect in more detail. Whilst it is convenient to consider each separ-ately, it is essential to remember that they all interact one on the other.

Ship motions

It was seen in Chapter 4, that a floating body has six degrees of freedom. To completely define the ship motion it is necessary to consider movements in all these modes as illustrated in Fig. 12.1. The motions are defined as movements of the centre of gravity of the ship and rotations about a set of orthogonal axes through the c.g. These are space axes moving with the mean forward speed of the ship but otherwise fixed in space.

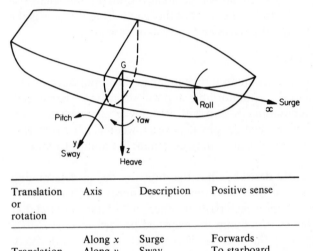

Translation or rotation	Axis	Description	Positive sense
Translation	Along x	Surge	Forwards
	Along y	Sway	To starboard
	Along z	Heave	Downwards
Rotation	About x	Roll	Starboard side down
	About y	Pitch	Bow up
	About z	Yaw	Bow to starboard

Fig. 12.1 Ship motions

It will be noted that roll and pitch are the dynamic equivalents of heel and trim. Translations along the x- and y-axis and rotation about the z-axis lead to no residual force or moment, provided displacement remains constant, as the ship is in neutral equilibrium. For the other translation and rotations, movement is opposed by a force or moment provided the ship is stable in that mode. The magnitude of the opposition increases with increasing displacement from the equilibrium position, the variation being linear for small disturbances. This is the characteristic of a simple spring system. Thus, it is to be expected that the equation governing the motion of a ship in still water, which is subject to a disturbance in the roll, pitch or heave modes, will be similar to that govern-ing the motion of a mass on a spring. This is indeed the case, and for the un-damped case the ship is said to move with simple harmonic motion.

Disturbances in the yaw, surge and sway modes will not lead to such an oscillatory motion and these motions, when the ship is in a seaway, exhibit a different character to roll, pitch and heave. These are considered separately and it is the oscillatory motions which are dealt with in the next few sections. It is convenient to consider the motion which would follow a disturbance in still water, both without and with damping, before proceeding to the more realistic case of motions in waves.

UNDAMPED MOTION IN STILL WATER

It is assumed that the ship is floating freely in still water when it is suddenly disturbed. The motion following the removal of the disturbing force or moment is now studied for the three oscillatory motions.

Rolling

Let ϕ be the inclination of the ship to the vertical at any instant. The moment, acting on a stable ship, will be in a sense such as to decrease ϕ. For small values of ϕ,

$$\text{moment} = -\Delta\overline{GM}_T\phi$$

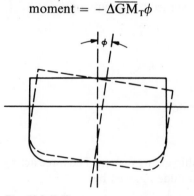

Fig. 12.2 Rolling

Applying Newton's laws of motion

   moment = (moment of inertia about 0x)(angular acceleration)

i.e.

$$-\Delta\overline{GM}_T\phi = +\frac{\Delta}{g}k_{xx}^2\frac{d^2\phi}{dt^2}$$

i.e.

$$\frac{d^2\phi}{dt^2}+\left(g\frac{\overline{GM}_T}{k_{xx}^2}\right)\phi = 0$$

This is the differential equation denoting simple harmonic motion with period T_ϕ where

$$T_\phi = 2\pi\left(\frac{k_{xx}^2}{g\overline{GM}_T}\right)^{\frac{1}{2}} = \frac{2\pi k_{xx}}{(g\overline{GM})^{\frac{1}{2}}}$$

It will be noted that the period of roll is independent of ϕ and that this will hold as long as the approximation $\overline{GZ} = \overline{GM}\phi$ applies, i.e. typically up to ± 10 degrees. Such rolling is termed *isochronous*.

In practice, not only the ship is accelerated, but also some of the surrounding water, so that k_{xx} must be increased to allow for this. To a first order, this effect is not changed for varying period of motion, depending on the geometry of the ship.

Hence

$$T_\phi \propto \frac{1}{(\overline{GM}_T)^{\frac{1}{2}}}$$

Thus the greater is $\overline{GM}_T$, i.e. the more stable the ship, the shorter the period and the more rapid the motion. A ship with a short period is said to be 'stiff'— compare the stiff spring—and one with a long period is said to be 'tender'. Most people find a long period roll less unpleasant than a short period roll.

Pitching

This is analogous to roll and the motion is governed by the equation

$$\frac{d^2\theta}{dt^2} + \left(\frac{g\overline{GM}_L}{k_{yy}^2}\right)\theta = 0$$

and the period of the motion is

$$T_\theta = \frac{2\pi k_{yy}}{(g\overline{GM}_L)^{\frac{1}{2}}} \text{ for very small angles of pitch.}$$

Heaving

Let z be the downward displacement of the ship at any instant. The force acting on the ship tends to reduce z and has a magnitude F_z given by

$$F_z = -\frac{A_W z}{u}$$

where u is the reciprocal weight density of the water.

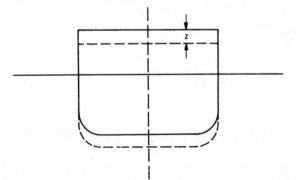

Fig. 12.3 Heaving

Hence, the heaving motion is governed by the equation

$$\frac{\Delta}{g}\frac{d^2z}{dt^2} = -\frac{A_w z}{u}$$

or

$$\frac{d^2z}{dt^2} + \frac{gA_w}{u\Delta}z = 0$$

from which

$$period = 2\pi\left(\frac{u\Delta}{gA_w}\right)^{\frac{1}{2}}.$$

In practice, Δ must be augmented to allow for the water which moves with the ship.

DAMPED MOTION IN STILL WATER

Now consider what happens when the motion is damped. It is adequate to illustrate the effect of damping on the rolling motion.

Only the simplest case of damping is considered, namely, that in which the damping moment varies linearly with the angular velocity. It opposes the motion since energy is always absorbed.

Allowing for the entrained water the equation for rolling in still water becomes

$$\frac{\Delta}{g}k_{xx}^2(1+\sigma_{xx})\ddot{\phi} + B\dot{\phi} + \Delta\overline{GM}_T\phi = 0$$

where,

$$\frac{\Delta k_{xx}^2}{g}\sigma_{xx} = \text{augment of rolling inertia of ship due to entrained water}$$

$$B = \text{damping constant.}$$

This can be likened to the standard differential equation

$$\ddot{\phi} + 2k\omega_0\dot{\phi} + \omega_0^2\phi = 0$$

where

$$\omega_0^2 = \frac{g\overline{GM}_T}{k_{xx}^2(1+\sigma_{xx})} \quad \text{and} \quad k = \frac{Bg}{2\omega_0\Delta k_{xx}^2(1+\sigma_{xx})}$$

which in turn defines the effective period T_ϕ of the motion as

$$T_\phi = \frac{2\pi}{\omega_0}(1-k^2)^{-\frac{1}{2}} = 2\pi k_{xx}\left(\frac{1+\sigma_{xx}}{g\overline{GM}_T}\right)^{\frac{1}{2}}(1-k^2)^{-\frac{1}{2}}$$

When the damping is not proportional to the angular velocity the differential equation is no longer capable of exact solution.

APPROXIMATE PERIOD OF ROLL

Of the various ship motions the roll period is likely to vary most from design to design and, because of the much greater amplitudes possible, it is often the most significant. Various approximate formulae have been suggested for calculating the period of roll and the following are taken from Ref. 1 which assumes that

$$T_\phi = 2\pi \frac{K}{(g\overline{GM_T})^{\frac{1}{2}}}$$

Suggested values of K for merchant ships and warships are given by the respective expressions:

MERCHANT SHIPS:

$$\left(\frac{K}{B}\right)^2 = F\left[C_B C_u + 1 \cdot 10 C_u (1 - C_B)\left(\frac{H}{T} - 2 \cdot 20\right) + \frac{H^2}{B^2}\right]$$

where

C_u = upper deck area coeff. $= \dfrac{1}{LB}$ (deck area)

H = effective depth of ship $= D + A/L_{pp}$

A = projected lateral area of erections and deck

L_{pp} = L.B.P.

T = mean moulded draught

F = constant = 0·125 for passenger and cargo ship,

   = 0·133 for oil tankers,

   = 0·177 for whalers.

WARSHIPS:

$$\left(\frac{K}{B}\right)^2 = F\left[C_B C_u + 1 \cdot 10\, C_e (1 - C_B)\left(\frac{H_n}{T} - 2 \cdot 20\right) + \frac{H_n^2}{B_u^2}\right]$$

where

B_u = max. breadth under water;

C_e = exposed deck area coeff.;

$H_n = D + A_n/L_{pp}$;

D = depth from top of keel to upper deck;

A_n = sum of the projected lateral areas of forecastle, under bridge and gun;

F = constant ranging from 0·172 for small warships to 0·177 for large warships.

MOTION IN REGULAR WAVES

In Chapter 9, it is explained that the irregular wave systems met at sea can be regarded as made up of a large number of regular components. A ship's motion record will exhibit a similar irregularity and it can be regarded as the summation of the ship responses to all the individual wave components. Theoretically, this super-position procedure is valid only for those sea states for which the linear theory of motions is applicable, i.e. for moderate sea states. It has been demonstrated by several authorities, however, that provided the basic data is derived from relatively mild regular components, the technique can be applied, with sufficient accuracy for most engineering purposes, to more extreme conditions. Thus, the basic element in ship motions is the response of the ship to a regular train of waves. For mathematical convenience, the wave is assumed to have a sinusoidal profile. The characteristics of such a system were dealt with in Chapter 9.

In the simple approach, it is necessary to assume that the pressure distribution within the wave system is unaffected by the presence of the ship. This is one of the assumptions made by William Froude in his study of ship rolling and is commonly known as 'Froude's Hypothesis'.

Rolling in a beam sea

The equation for rolling in still water is modified by introducing a forcing function on the right-hand side of the equation. This could be obtained by calculating the hydrodynamic pressure acting on each element of the hull and integrating over the complete wetted surface.

The resultant force acting on a particle in the surface of a wave must be normal to the wave surface. Provided the wave-length is long compared with the beam of the ship, it is reasonable to assume that the ship is acted on by a resultant force normal to an 'effective wave surface' which takes into account all the sub-surfaces interacting with the ship. Froude used this idea and further assumed that the 'effective wave slope' was that of the sub-surface passing through the centre of buoyancy of the ship.

With this assumption it can be shown that, approximately, the equation of motion for undamped rolling motion in beam seas becomes

$$\frac{\Delta}{g}k_{xx}^2(1+\sigma_{xx})\ddot{\phi}+\Delta\overline{GM}_T(\phi-\phi')=0$$

where $\phi' = \alpha \sin \omega t$; α = maximum slope of the surface wave; ω = frequency of the surface wave.

If ϕ_0 and ω_0 are the amplitude and frequency of unresisted rolling in still water, the solution to this equation takes the form

$$\phi = \phi_0 \sin(\omega_0 t + \beta) + \frac{\omega_0^2 \alpha}{\omega_0^2 - \omega^2}\sin \omega t$$

The first term is the free oscillation in still water and the second is a forced oscillation in the period of the wave train.

The amplitude of the forced oscillation is

$$\frac{\omega_0^2 \alpha}{\omega_0^2 - \omega^2}$$

When the period of the wave system is less than the natural period of the ship ($\omega > \omega_0$), the amplitude is negative which means that the ship rolls into the wave (Fig. 12.4(a)). When the period of the wave is greater than the natural period of the ship, the amplitude is positive and the ship rolls with the wave (Fig. 12.4(b)). For very long waves, i.e. ω very small, the amplitude tends to α and the ship remains approximately normal to the wave surface. When the frequencies of the wave and ship are close the amplitude of the forced oscillation becomes very large.

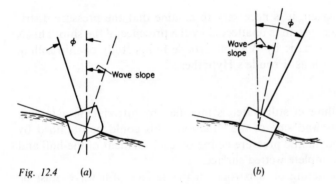

Fig. 12.4   (a)   (b)

The general equation for rolling in waves can be written as:

$$\ddot{\phi} + 2k\omega_0\dot{\phi} + \omega_0^2\phi = \omega_0^2\alpha \cos \omega t$$

The solution to this differential equation is

$$\phi = \mu\alpha \cos(\omega t - \varepsilon)$$

where

$$\tan \varepsilon = \frac{2k\Lambda}{1 - \Lambda^2}$$

Λ = *tuning factor* = ω/ω_0; μ = *magnification factor* = $1/\{(1-\Lambda^2)^2 + 4k^2\Lambda^2\}^{\frac{1}{2}}$.

Plots of the phase angle ε and magnification factor are presented in Fig. 12.5. It will be appreciated that these expressions are similar to those met with in the study of vibrations.

The effect of damping is to cause the free oscillation to die out in time and to modify the amplitude of the forced oscillation. In an ideal regular sea, the ship would oscillate after a while only in the period of the waves. In practice, the maximum forced roll amplitudes occur close to the natural frequency of the ship, leading to a ship at sea rolling predominantly at frequencies close to its natural frequency.

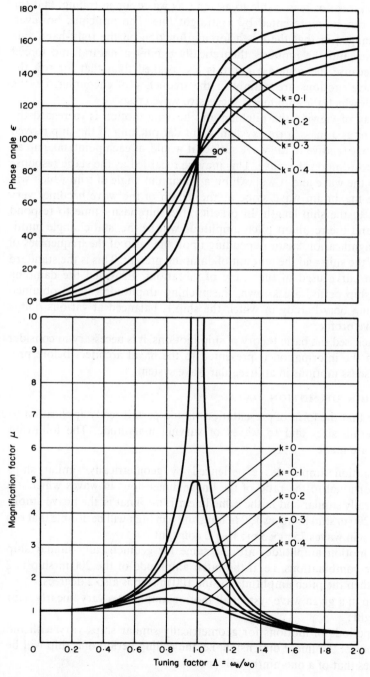

Fig. 12.5 Phase angle and magnification factor

Pitching and heaving in waves

In this case, attention is focused on head seas. In view of the relative lengths of ship and wave, it is not reasonable to assume, as was done in rolling, that the wave surface can be represented by a straight line. The principle, however, remains unchanged in that there is a forcing function on the right-hand side of the equation and the motions theoretically exhibit a natural and forced oscillation. Because the response curve is less peaked than that for roll the pitch and heave motions are mainly in the frequency of encounter, i.e. the frequency with which the ship meets successive wave crests.

Another way of viewing the pitching and heaving motion is to regard the ship/sea system as a mass/spring system. Consider pitching. If the ship moved extremely slowly relative to the wave surface it would, at each point, take up an equilibrium position on the wave. This may be regarded as the static response of the ship to the wave and it will exhibit a maximum angle of trim which will approach the maximum wave slope as the length of the wave becomes very large relative to the ship length. In practice, the ship hasn't time to respond in this way, and the resultant pitch amplitude will be the 'static' angle multiplied by a magnification factor depending upon the ratio of the frequencies of the wave and the ship and the amount of damping present. This is the standard magnification curve used in the study of vibrations. Provided the damping and natural ship period are known, the pitching amplitude can be obtained from a drawing board study in which the ship is balanced at various points along the wave profile.

Having discussed the basic theory of ship motions, it is necessary to consider in what form the information is presented to the naval architect before proceeding to discuss motions in an irregular wave system.

PRESENTATION OF MOTION DATA

It is desirable that the form of presentation should permit ready application to ships of differing sizes and to waves of varying magnitude. The following assumptions are made:

(a) Linear motion amplitudes experienced by geometrically similar ships are proportional to the ratio of the linear dimensions in waves which are geometrically similar and in the same linear ratio. That is, the heave amplitude of a 200 m ship in waves 150 m long and 6 m high will be double that of a 100 m ship in waves 75 m × 3 m; $V/\sqrt{L}$ constant

(b) Angular motion amplitudes are the same for geometrically similar ship and wave combinations, i.e. if the pitch amplitude of the 200 m ship is 2 degrees, then the pitch amplitude for the 100 m ship is also 2 degrees;

(c) For a ship in a given wave system all motion amplitudes vary linearly with wave height;

(d) Natural periods of motions for geometrically similar ships vary with the square root of the linear dimension, i.e. the rolling period of a ship will be three times that of a one-ninth scale model.

These assumptions follow from the mathematical analysis already outlined.

A quite common plot for motions in regular waves, is the amplitude, expressed non-dimensionally, to a base of wave-length to ship length ratio for a series of $V/\sqrt{L}$ values. The ordinates of the curve are referred to as *response amplitude operators*. (See Fig. 12.6.)

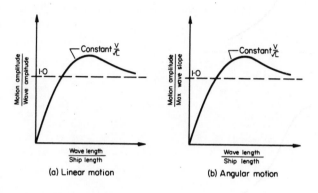

Fig. 12.6 Non-dimensional plotting

This system of plotting is non-dimensional, but a slight complication arises with angular motions when using wave spectra which are in terms of wave height. Also, in applying spectral analysis methods, the response amplitude operators are required at various frequencies of encounter. Since wave height and slope are directly proportional (see Chapter 9) and since ship speed and wave-length determine frequency of encounter as is discussed later, the data can be presented as in Fig. 12.7, using the natural frequency of the motion to non-dimensionalize the abscissa. There is now no need to differentiate between linear and angular motions. Curves are required for a range of $V/\sqrt{L}$ values.

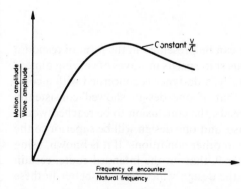
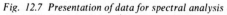

Fig. 12.7 Presentation of data for spectral analysis

Some typical response curves are reproduced in Fig. 12.8.

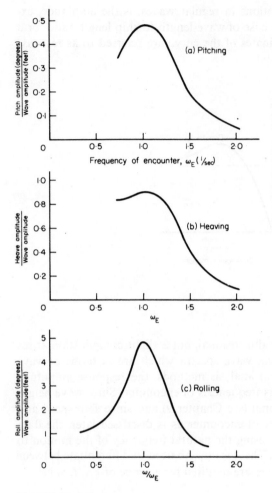

Fig. 12.8 Typical response curves

MOTION IN IRREGULAR SEAS

It has been seen, that the motion data can be presented in the form of response amplitude operators (RAO), for various ship speeds in waves of varying dimension relative to the ship length. Generally, a designer is concerned with a comparison of two or more designs so that, if one design showed consistently lower RAOs in all waves and at all speeds, the conclusion to be reached would be clear cut. This is not usually the case, and one design will be superior to the other in some conditions and inferior in other conditions. If it is known, using data such as that presented in Chapter 9, that on the intended route, certain waves are most likely to be met then the design which behaves better in these particular waves would be chosen.

Of more general application is the use of the concept of wave spectra. It was shown in Chapter 9 that, provided phase relationships are not critical, the apparently iregular sea surface can be represented mathematically by a spectrum of the type

$$S(\omega)(\zeta) = \frac{A}{\omega^5} e - \frac{B}{\omega^4}$$

where ω = circular frequency in radians per second, ζ = wave height.

A and B are constants which can be expressed in terms of the characteristic wave period and/or the significant wave height.

This is the spectrum as it would be deduced by analysing the record of surface elevation taken at a fixed point. A moving ship responds to the waves as it experiences them and allowance must be made for the frequency of encounter as opposed to the absolute frequency of each component wave.

Consider a point P (Fig. 12.9) moving along a straight path at velocity V at ψ to the direction of advance of a sinusoidal wave system of period T and velocity C. Let T_E be the period of encounter of P with the waves.

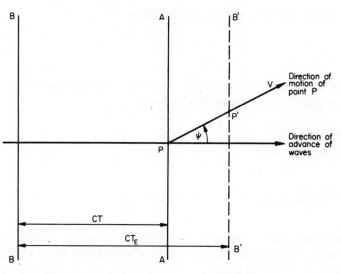

Fig. 12.9 Period of encounter

If P is on wave crest AA at time $t = 0$, then after T_E seconds, the next wave crest moves to B'B' and P moves to P'. Hence

$$CT_E = CT + VT_E \cos \psi$$

i.e.

$$T_E = \frac{T}{1 - (V/C)\cos\psi}$$

and

$$\omega_E = \frac{2\pi}{T_E} = \omega\left(1 - \frac{V}{C}\cos\psi\right)$$

$$= \omega\left(1 - \frac{\omega V}{g}\cos\psi\right)$$

Thus the abscissae of the 'encounter' energy spectrum can be obtained by multiplying those for the 'absolute' spectrum by $[1 - (\omega V/g)\cos\psi]$.

The area under the spectrum remains unchanged if the influence of the presence of the ship on the waves is ignored. Hence

$$S(\omega_E)\,d\omega_E = S(\omega)\,d\omega$$

i.e.

$$S(\omega_E) = S(\omega)\frac{d\omega}{d\omega_E} = \frac{S(\omega)}{1 - (2\omega V/g)\cos\psi}$$

and the ordinates of the spectrum must be multiplied by

$$\frac{1}{1 - (2\omega V/g)\cos\psi}$$

In the case where the ship is moving directly into the wave system $\psi = 180°$ and $\cos\psi = -1$ so that the multiplying factors become

$$\left(1 + \frac{\omega V}{g}\right) \quad \text{for abscissae}$$

and

$$\left(1 + \frac{2\omega V}{g}\right)^{-1} \quad \text{for ordinates.}$$

The effect of ship speed on the shape of the wave spectrum is illustrated in Fig. 12.10 which shows a spectrum appropriate to a wind speed of 30 knots and ship speeds of 0, 10, 20 and 30 knots.

To illustrate the procedure for obtaining the motion spectra, consider one speed for the ship and assume that the encounter spectrum for that speed is as shown in Fig. 12.11(a). Also, assume that the amplitude response operators for heave of the ship, at that same speed, are as shown in Fig. 12.11(b). The ordinate of the wave energy spectrum is proportional to the square of the amplitude of the component waves. Hence, to derive the energy spectrum for the heave motion as shown in Fig. 12.11(c), the following relationship is used

$$S_z(\omega_E) = [Y_{z\zeta}(\omega_E)]^2 S_\zeta(\omega_E)$$

i.e.

$$RC = (RB)^2(RA)$$

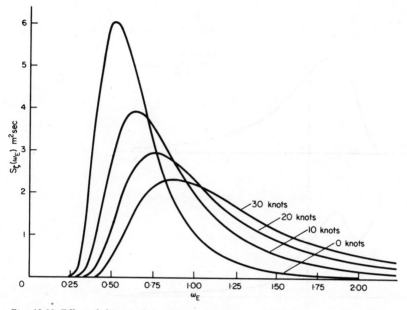

Fig. 12.10 Effect of ship speed on encounter spectrum

If the area under the motion energy spectrum is obtained by integration, the significant heave amplitude, etc., can be deduced by using the same multiplying factors as those given in Chapter 9 for waves.

For example, if m_0 is the area under the roll spectrum

average roll amplitude = $1.25\sqrt{m_0}$

significant roll amplitude = $2\sqrt{m_0}$

average amplitude of $\frac{1}{10}$ highest rolls = $2.55\sqrt{m_0}$.

Any of these quantities, or the area under the spectrum, can be used to compare designs at the chosen speed. The lower the figure the better the design and the single numeral represents the overall response of the ship at that speed in that wave system. The process can be repeated for other speeds and other spectra. Reference 2 demonstrates that the actual wave spectrum chosen is not critical provided the comparison is made at constant significant wave height and not constant wind speed.

EXAMPLE 1: A sea spectrum for the North Atlantic is defined by the following table, $S_\zeta(\omega)$ being in m^2 s.

ω	0·3	0·4	0·5	0·6	0·7	0·8	0·9	1·0	1·1	1·2
$S_\zeta(\omega)$	0·20	2·00	4·05	4·30	3·40	2·30	1·50	1·00	0·70	0·50

Calculate the encounter spectra for a ship heading directly into the wave system at speeds of 10, 20 and 28 knots.

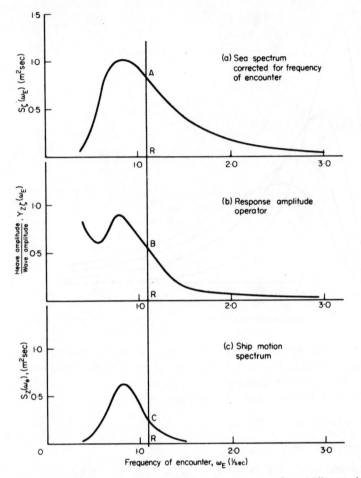

Fig. 12.11 Energy spectra and response of a ship in an irregular sea (illustrated for heave)

Assuming that the heave response of a ship, 175 m in length, is defined by Fig. 12.12 deduce the heave spectra for the three speeds and hence the probability curves for the motion.

Solution: It has been shown for the wave spectra, that

$$\omega_E = \omega\left(1+\frac{\omega V}{g}\right)$$

For 10 knots;

$$V = 10 \times \frac{1852}{3600} = 5\cdot14 \text{ m/s} \quad g = 9\cdot807 \text{ m/s}^2 \quad \therefore \quad \omega_E = \omega(1+0\cdot525\omega)$$

similarly for 20 and 28 knots ω_E is equal to $\omega\,(1+1\cdot05\omega)$ and $\omega\,(1+1\cdot47\omega)$ respectively.

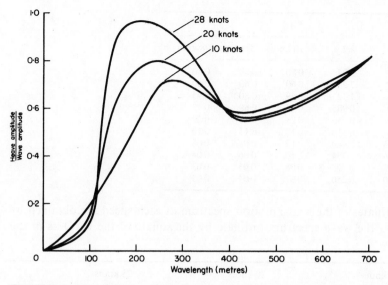

Fig. 12.12

Figure 12.12 is used by calculating the wave-length appropriate to each ω value. λ and λ/L are tabulated below with the response amplitude operators from Fig. 12.12. Since curves show response at each speed the RAO s apply to the appropriate ω_E.

It has also been shown that ordinates of the spectrum must be multiplied by

$$\left(1+\frac{2\omega V}{g}\right)^{-1} = (1+1{\cdot}05\omega)^{-1} \text{ for 10 knots}$$
$$(1+2{\cdot}10\omega)^{-1} \text{ for 20 knots}$$
$$(1+2{\cdot}94\omega)^{-1} \text{ for 28 knots}$$

The calculations can be carried out in tabular fashion as below for 10 knots and repeated for 20 knots and 28 knots.

ω	$1+0{\cdot}525\omega$	ω_E	$S_\zeta(\omega)$	$1+1{\cdot}05\omega$	$S_\zeta(\omega_E)$
0·3	1·158	0·347	0·20	1·315	0·15
0·4	1·210	0·484	2·00	1·420	1·41
0·5	1·263	0·632	4·05	1·525	2·65
0·6	1·315	0·789	4·30	1·630	2·64
0·7	1·368	0·958	3·40	1·735	1·96
0·8	1·420	1·136	2·30	1·840	1·25
0·9	1·473	1·326	1·50	1·945	0·77
1·0	1·525	1·525	1·00	2·050	0·49
1·1	1·578	1·736	0·70	2·155	0·32
1·2	1·630	1·956	0·50	2·260	0·22

ω	λ (m)	λ/L	RAO		
			10 knots	20 knots	28 knots
0·3	689	3·97	0·80	0·80	0·80
0·4	387	2·23	0·60	0·60	0·60
0·5	247	1·42	0·69	0·80	0·95
0·6	171	0·985	0·44	0·69	0·93
0·7	126	0·730	0·28	0·40	0·29
0·8	96·6	0·556	0·18	0·15	0·10
0·9	76·5	0·440	0·12	0·08	0·05
1·0	61·6	0·354	0·10	0·06	0·04
1·1	51·2	0·295	0·08	0·05	0·03
1·2	43·0	0·250	0·07	0·04	0·03

The ordinates of the heave motion spectrum at each speed are obtained by multiplying the wave spectrum ordinate by the square of the RAO as in the table below:

ω	10 knots			20 knots			28 knots		
	$S_\zeta(\omega_E)$	RAO	$S_Z(\omega_E)$	$S_\zeta(\omega_E)$	RAO	$S_Z(\omega_E)$	$S_\zeta(\omega_E)$	RAO	$S_Z(\omega_E)$
0·3	0·15	0·80	0·098	0·12	0·80	0·079	0·11	0·80	0·068
0·4	1·41	0·60	0·508	1·09	0·60	0·392	0·92	0·60	0·330
0·5	2·65	0·69	1·262	1·98	0·80	1·270	1·64	0·95	1·480
0·6	2·64	0·44	0·511	1·91	0·69	0·910	1·56	0·93	1·350
0·7	1·96	0·28	0·153	1·38	0·40	0·207	1·11	0·29	0·093
0·8	1·25	0·18	0·041	0·86	0·15	0·019	0·69	0·10	0·007
0·9	0·77	0·12	0·011	0·52	0·08	0·003	0·41	0·05	0·001
1·0	0·49	0·10	0·005	0·32	0·06	0·001	0·25	0·04	—
1·1	0·32	0·08	—	0·21	0·05	—	0·17	0·03	—
1·2	0·22	0·07	—	0·14	0·04	—	0·11	0·03	—

The heave spectra can now be plotted as in Fig. 12.13 and the areas under each obtained to give m_0. Values of m_0 so deduced are

10 knots: $m_0 = 0·37$ and $\sqrt{(2m_0)} = 0·86$
20 knots: $m_0 = 0·62$ and $\sqrt{(2m_0)} = 1·11$
28 knots: $m_0 = 0·72$ and $\sqrt{(2m_0)} = 1·20$

The probability that at a random instant of time the heave exceeds some value z is given by $P(z) = 1 - \mathrm{erf}(z/\sqrt{(2m_0)})$. The error function, erf, is obtained from standard mathematical tables.

OBLIQUE AND FOLLOWING SEAS
When waves are abaft the beam, long fast waves overtaking the ship can have the same frequency of encounter as short slow waves which are being overtaken. Thus a spectrum based on encounter frequency is not directly usable for ship motion prediction when waves coming from abaft the beam are present. In such cases it is convenient to convert the wave spectrum to a wave length base. It is then unchanged by changes in ship speed or heading, the effects of which will be

catered for by the appropriate response operators.

$$\lambda = \frac{2\pi g}{\omega^2}, \quad \frac{d\lambda}{d\omega} = -\frac{4\pi}{\omega^3} g$$

and for constant spectral area $S(\omega)d\omega = S(\lambda)d\lambda$

Hence the single parameter ITTC spectrum becomes

$$S(\lambda)(\zeta) = S(\omega)\frac{d\omega}{d\lambda} = \frac{\omega^3}{4\pi g} \frac{A}{\omega^5} \exp(-B/\omega^4)$$

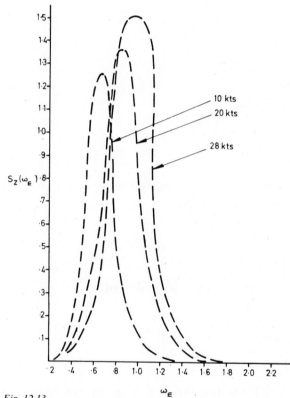

Fig. 12.13

The probability curve for 10 knots is calculated in the table below and is plotted together with those for 20 and 28 knots in Fig. 12.14.

	10 knots	$\sqrt{(2m_0)} = 0\cdot86$					
z	$z/\sqrt{(2m_0)}$	$\text{erf}\dfrac{z}{\sqrt{(2m_0)}}$	$P(z)$	z	$z/\sqrt{(2m_0)}$	$\text{erf}\dfrac{z}{\sqrt{(2m_0)}}$	$P(z)$
0	0	0	1·000	1·50	1·744	0·986	0·014
0·25	0·291	0·319	0·681	1·75	2·035	0·996	0·004
0·5	0·581	0·596	0·404	2·00	2·326	0·999	0·001
0·75	0·872	0·783	0·217	2·25	2·616	0·9998	0·0002
1·00	1·163	0·900	0·100	2·50	2·907	0·99996	0·00004
1·25	1·453	0·960	0·040				

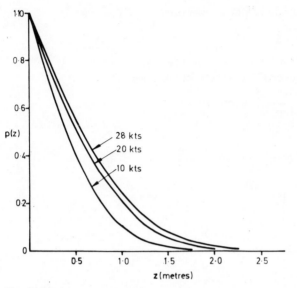

Fig. 12.14

This figure shows that the probability of exceeding a heave of 1 m is 10 per cent at 10 knots and 23·9 per cent at 28 knots.

In metric units,
$$S(\lambda)(\zeta) = \frac{0\cdot103}{10^3}\lambda \exp\left[-\frac{0\cdot82}{10^3}\left(\frac{\lambda}{\zeta_{\frac{1}{3}}}\right)^2\right]$$

Similarly, a spectrum based on wave slope can be derived as
$$S(\lambda)(\alpha) = \frac{13\cdot35}{\lambda} \exp\left[-\frac{0\cdot82}{10^3}\left(\frac{\lambda}{\zeta_{\frac{1}{3}}}\right)^2\right]$$

where α = wave slope in degrees.

MOTION IN OBLIQUE SEAS

The procedure outlined above for finding the motion spectra can be applied for the ship at any heading provided the appropriate encounter spectrum is used and the response amplitude operators are available for that heading. For many years, the model motion data available to the naval architect were restricted to that in head seas with limited results for following seas. The extra data becoming available from new facilities are discussed more fully later, but much existing data suffers from this limitation.

In a regular wave system, as the ship's course is changed from directly into the waves, two effects are introduced, viz.: −

(a) the effective length of the wave is increased and the effective steepness is decreased. Referring to Fig. 12.9 the effective length is increased in the ratio $1/\cos\psi$ and the steepness decreased in proportion to $\cos\psi$;

(b) the frequency of encounter with the waves is decreased as already illustrated.

An approximation to motions in an oblique wave system can be obtained by testing in head seas with the height kept constant but length increased to $\lambda/\cos\psi$ and with the model speed adjusted to give the correct frequency of encounter. This is a reasonable procedure but it is only approximate and data from model tests in oblique seas should be used when available. (Ref. 3.)

SURGE, SWAY AND YAW

As already explained, these motions exhibit a different character from that of roll, pitch and heave. They are not subject to the same theoretical treatment as these oscillatory motions but a few general comments are appropriate.

Surge

At constant power in still water a ship will move at constant speed. When it meets waves there will be a mean reduction in speed due to the added resistance and changed operating conditions for the propeller. The speed is no longer constant and the term surge or surge velocity is used to define the variation in speed about the new mean value. Two main effects are present. First, there is the orbital motion of the wave particles which tends to increase the speed of the ship in the direction of the waves at a crest and decrease it in a trough. In a regular wave system, this speed variation would be cyclic in the period of encounter with the waves. In an irregular sea, the height and hence the resistance of successive waves varies giving rise to a more irregular speed variation. This is superimposed upon the orbital effect which is itself irregular in this case.

The surge experienced by a vessel of length 146·15 m is shown in Fig. 12.15 which is taken from Ref. 4.

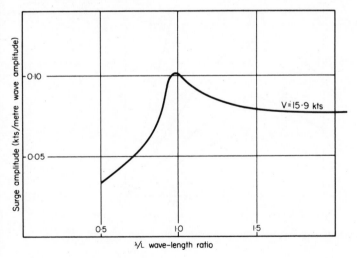

Fig. 12.15 Surging in head sea

The maximum response occurs in waves approximately equal in length to the ship. In waves of this length and 5 m high, the speed oscillation is about ±0·25 knots. The effect varies approximately linearly with speed.

Sway

When the wave system is other than immediately ahead or astern of the ship, there will be transverse forces arising from similar sources to those causing the surging motion. In a regular sea, these would lead to a regular motion in the period of encounter with the waves but, in general, they lead to an irregular athwartships motion about a mean sideways drift. This variation about the mean is termed sway. It is also influenced by the transverse forces acting on the rudder and hull due to actions to counteract yaw which is next considered.

Yaw

When the wave system is at an angle to the line of advance of the ship the transverse forces acting will introduce moments tending to yaw the ship. Corrective action by the rudder introduces additional moments and the resultant moments cause an irregular variation in ship's heading about its mean heading. This variation is termed yawing. In a regular sea with an automatic rudder control system, the motion would exhibit a regular period depending on the period of encounter and the characteristics of the control equation. (See Chapter 13.) In general, however, the motion is quite irregular.

Some of the difficulty of maintaining course in rough weather is indicated in Fig. 12.16 which is taken from Ref. 4 for a ship of 146 m.

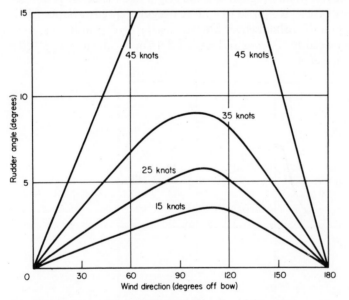

Fig. 12.16 Rudder angles for different wind speeds and directions

Speed and power in waves

As a wave system becomes more severe, the power needed to drive the ship through it at a given speed increases. The difference arises mainly from the increased resistance experienced by the hull and appendages, but the overall propulsive efficiency also changes due to the changed conditions in which the propeller operates. If the propulsion machinery is already producing full power, it follows that there must be an enforced reduction in speed. Past a certain severity of waves, the motions of the ship or slamming may become so violent that the captain may decide to reduce speed below that possible with the power available. This is a voluntary speed reduction and might be expected to be made in merchant ships of fairly full form at Beaufort numbers of 6 or more. The speed reduction lessens as the predominant wave direction changes from directly ahead to the beam (Fig. 12.17.)

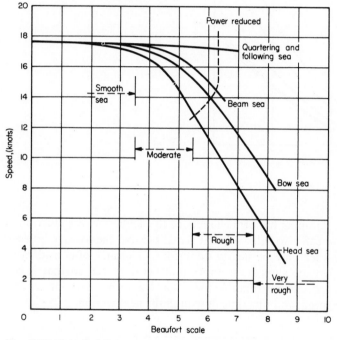

Fig. 12.17 (from Ref. 5)

Figure 12.18 (from Ref. 6) shows how the power required for various speeds increases with increasing sea state as represented by the Beaufort number. The figure applies to a wave system 10 degrees off the bow and to a ship 150 m long with a longitudinal radius of gyration equal to 22 per cent of the length. Decreasing the longitudinal moment of inertia decreases the additional power required and also results in drier decks forward.

Figure 12.19 shows the reduction in speed which occurs at constant power (7830 hp) for the ship in the same conditions and shows the significance of varying the longitudinal radius of gyration. The effect of the variation is less significant in large ships than in small. It is associated with a reduction in natural pitching period.

Other ship design features conducive to maintaining higher speed in rough weather are a low displacement–length ratio, i.e. $\Delta/(L/100)^3$, and fine form

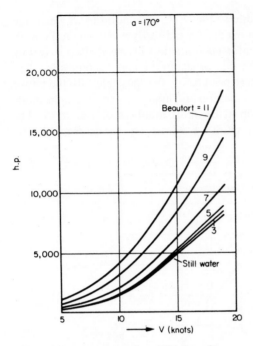

Fig. 12.18 Power in waves for a 150 m long ship

forward. Increased damping by form changes or the deliberate introduction of a large bulbous bow can also help. When it is realized that the passage times of ships in rough weather may be nearly doubled, it is clearly of considerable importance to design the ship, both above and below water, so that it can maintain as high a speed as possible. Wetness is a significant factor influencing the need to reduce speed, and this is dealt with in the next section.

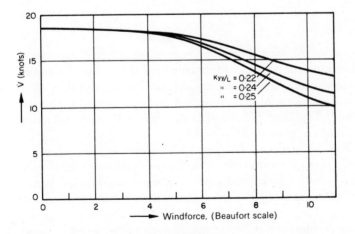

Fig. 12.19 Variation in speed at constant power

Wetness

By wetness is meant the shipping of spray or green seas over the ship and, unless otherwise qualified, refers to wetness at the bow. It has already been mentioned, that wetness is a significant factor in determining the speed a ship can maintain in waves. Two methods of assessing wetness of a ship in the design stages are available, viz.:

(i) By calculating the relative vertical movement of the bow and wave surface. When the increase in draught exceeds the freeboard available at the bow it is assumed that the ship will be wet;
(ii) By running a model of the ship in regular waves and noting in which combinations of wave-length and height the model is wet and assuming that the ship will behave in a similar manner.

The first method is not pursued here because the computation of vertical movement is beyond the scope of this book. It is the preferred method if the required data is available in the form of response amplitude operators for the movement of the bow. It can be noted, however, that wetness depends upon the wave, heave and pitch amplitudes and the phase relationships existing between them. It also depends directly upon the freeboard available. The greater the freeboard the drier the ship.

The second method has been used by the Ministry of Defence (Ref. 7). It was found, that contours for wet and very wet conditions could be plotted as in Fig. 12.20. These contours are applicable to fine warship forms ranging in prismatic coefficient from 0·57 to 0·62, and give confidence in predicting wetness for a new design of the same general type.

The waves in the immediate vicinity of the ship are due to the superimposing of waves generated by the motion of the ship on the general wave system. The ship's bow wave system has a crest some way aft of the bow, and it has been found that the freeboard at a point 15 per cent of the ship length from the bow is more significant than the freeboard right forward.

The degree of wetness present is difficult to define. In practice, it is influenced by the wind strength and direction because of the possibility of spray from the tops of breaking waves being blown over the ship. In this section, definitions are used as follows:

Dry: The resultant wave surface is below the level of the forecastle at all points along its length.

Wet: The wave surface reaches above the level of the forecastle but green seas are not actually shipped.

Very wet: Green seas break over the forecastle, i.e. a solid mass of water passes over the forecastle.

In order to ensure as wide an application as possible, the contours in Fig. 12.20 are plotted non-dimensionally using the following parameters:

$$\textcircled{F} = \frac{\text{Wave height}}{\text{Equivalent freeboard}} \times \frac{\text{Ship's length (WL)}}{\text{Wave-length}}$$

$$\textcircled{T} = \frac{\text{Period of encounter}}{\text{Undamped natural period of pitching in air}}$$

$$= \frac{T_E}{2\pi(k_{yy}^2/g\overline{GM}_L)^{\frac{1}{2}}} = \frac{\lambda/(C+V)}{2\pi(k_{yy}^2/g\overline{GM}_L)^{\frac{1}{2}}}$$

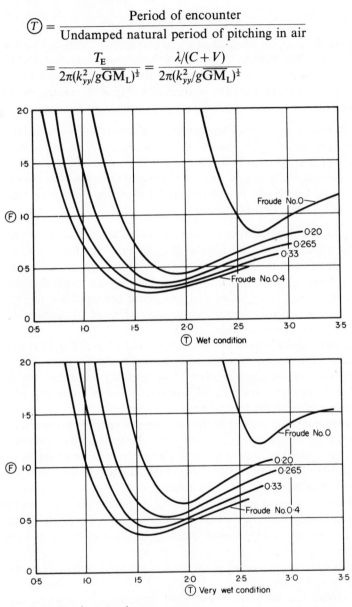

Fig. 12.20 *Non-dimensional wetness contours*

The term equivalent freeboard is introduced to take account of knuckles which can increase the effective freeboard, as described in Ref. 7.

Once the principal dimensions of the new design are determined the wetness at a given speed, i.e. Froude number, can be calculated as follows:

(a) Use Fig. 12.20 to determine wet and very wet contours appropriate to the selected Froude number.

(*b*) Calculate the value of $\textcircled{T}$ for the range of wave-lengths covered by the wave data given in Table 9.11 and Fig. 9.19 (see Volume 1).

(*c*) For each $\textcircled{T}$ value obtain the corresponding $\textcircled{F}$ value appropriate to both contours.

(*d*) From the $\textcircled{F}$ values deduce the wave height which will cause the ship to become wet and very wet.

(*e*) From the wave data deduce the numbers of days in the year that waves of these heights and length are likely to occur.

(*f*) Summate to find the total number of days in the year the ship is likely to be wet or very wet.

The method is illustrated in the worked example which follows. Many approximations are involved but the method is useful for comparing the relative wetness of two designs.

Apart from trying to reduce the incidence of wetness the naval architect should design the decks forward so that water clears from them quickly. He must avoid placing equipments forward which can be easily damaged by green seas or which have a considerably increased maintenance load when subject to salt water spray. A bulwark can be fitted to increase freeboard provided it does not trap water on the deck. The sizes of freeing ports required in bulwarks are laid down by the Board of Trade in the Merchant Shipping (Loadline) Regulations for the UK and by other national authorities following IMCO recommendations.

EXAMPLE 2. A ship, length 390 ft, has a freeboard of 23 ft at 15 per cent of the length from the bow. The natural period of pitching in air is assessed at 3·06 s. Calculate the percentage of the year for which the design is likely to prove wet and very wet.

Solution: For convenience use the contours from Fig. 12.20 for Froude numbers of 0·265, 0·33 and 0·40 which, in this case, correspond to speeds of 17·65, 22·1 and 26·6 knots. If data for a specific speed, say 20 knots, had been required it would have been necessary to find the corresponding contours from Fig. 12.20 by interpolation.

The computation is now best carried out in tabular form as illustrated below for a speed of $V = 17\!\cdot\!65$ knots, i.e. 29·8 ft/s.

For each wave-length, for which data are given in Fig. 9.19, the wave velocity is calculated. The waves less than 275 ft have been ignored as being likely to have little influence on a ship of this size. The period of encounter is obtained by dividing the wave-length by the sum of the wave and ship velocities. Then

$$\textcircled{T} = \frac{\text{Period of encounter}}{\text{Period of pitching in air}}$$

The value of $\textcircled{F}$ appropriate to this value of $\textcircled{T}$ is read from both the wet and very wet contours of Fig. 12.20. The wave height follows from:

$$\text{Wave height} = \textcircled{F} \times \frac{\text{Freeboard} \times \text{wave-length}}{\text{Ship length}}$$

The ship is likely to be wet or very wet when this wave height is exceeded. The number of days during the year that this is likely to happen is shown in Fig. 9.19. The total number of days in the year is obtained by summation and this total can then be expressed as a percentage of the year.

			Very wet				Wet		
λ (ft)	C, wave velocity (ft/s)	V+C (ft/s)	(T)	(F)	Wave height (ft)	Days/year	(F)	Wave height (ft)	Days/ year
275	37·5	67·3	1·34	0·94	15·3	0·5	0·62	10·1	2·0
325	40·8	70·6	1·50	0·64	12·3	3·0	0·43	8·2	9·0
375	43·8	73·6	1·67	0·56	12·4	5·2	0·36	8·0	13·0
425	46·6	76·4	1·82	0·55	13·8	6·2	0·36	9·0	14·0
475	49·3	79·1	1·96	0·57	16·0	5·1	0·38	10·6	14·5
525	51·9	81·7	2·10	0·64	19·6	2·9	0·42	13·0	13·0
575	54·3	84·1	2·23	0·69	23·4	1·4	0·47	16·0	10·0
625	56·6	86·4	2·37	0·76	28·1	0·4	0·51	18·8	7·8
675	58·8	88·6	2·49	0·81	32·2	0·3	0·55	21·9	5·0
725	60·9	90·7	2·61	0·86	36·8	0·3	0·59	25·3	2·2
775	63·0	92·8	2·73	0·90	41·1	0·1	0·63	28·8	2·2
825	65·0	94·8	2·85	0·94	45·8	0·1	0·66	32·2	2·1
875	66·9	96·7	2·96	0·97	49·8	—	0·68	35·1	2·9
925	68·8	98·6	3·06	0·99	54·0	—	0·70	38·2	2·5
975	70·7	100·5	3·16	1·01	58·1	—	0·72	41·5	2·0
1025	72·5	102·3	3·27	1·03	62·0	—	0·74	44·5	1·0
1075	74·2	104·0	3·37	1·04	66·0	—	0·75	47·6	0·3
1125	75·9	105·7	3·47	1·05	70·0	—	0·76	50·5	—
1175	77·6	107·4	3·58	1·06	73·5	—	0·77	53·4	—

Total of days   25·5   103·5

Percentage of year   7·0   28·4

The calculation is repeated for the other two speeds. The results of this are:

	Very wet		Wet	
Ship speed	Days/year	Percentage of year	Days/year	Percentage of year
22·1 knots = 37·4 ft/s	55·4	15·2	169·4	46·5
26·6 knots = 45·0 ft/s	101·7	27·8	225·4	61

A plot of these data can now be produced to a base of speed if desired.

These results must be used with caution. The analysis assumes that the ship is heading directly into the waves. The operator, in practice, can considerably reduce wetness by changing course or reducing speed. It must also be appreciated that the ship will not be wet continuously during each day indicated by the table. It is recommended that the data be used to compare a new design with previous ships. If the incidence of wetness appears less than in a previous successful design the new design should be satisfactory.

Slamming

Slamming is a high frequency transient vibratory response of a ship's hull to wave impact. It occurs at irregular intervals. Each blow causes the ship to shudder and is followed by a vibration of the ship's structure. The impact may be large enough to cause physical damage to the ship, the most vulnerable area being between 10 and 25 per cent of the ship's length from the bow. It is the possibility of this damage occurring that causes an experienced captain to reduce speed when his ship begins to slam badly. This always leads to reduced severity of slamming. Lightly loaded cargo ships are particularly liable to slam and the enforced speed reduction may be as much as 40 per cent. Slamming is likely to occur when:

(a) the relative velocity between the ship's outer bottom and the water is large. This will normally be when the downward velocity of the bow is greatest and, thus, when the ship is in a near level attitude;
(b) the bow has emerged from, and is re-entering, the water with a significant length of the bottom roughly parallel to the local water surface;
(c) the bottom has a low rise of floor forward increasing the extent of ship's bottom parallel with the local water surface.

The slamming impact lasts for about 1/30 s and does not perceptibly modify the downward movement of the bow. It can be detected as a disturbance in the acceleration record and by the ensuing vibration which can last for about 30 s. Slamming pressures as high as $7 \times 10^5 \text{ N/m}^2$ (approximately 100 p.s.i.) have been recorded in low speed ships. Pressures in high speed ships are generally less because of their finer form forward. The pressure can be shown to be proportional to the square of the relative velocity of impact and inversely proportional to the square of the tangent of the angle of deadrise. This is based on analyses of the similar problem of a seaplane landing.

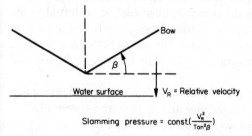

Slamming pressure $= \text{const.}(\frac{V_R^2}{\text{Tan}^2\beta})$

Fig. 12.21 Slamming pressure

When β is very small, the pressures obtained would become infinite on the above simple analysis. In practice, pressures are limited by the elastic response of the ship structure. The peak pressure moves higher in the ship section as the bow immersion increases.

If, in a given case, the conditions for high pressure apply over a limited area, the blow is local and may result only in local plate deformation. If the pressure acts over a larger area, the overall force acting on the ship is able to excite vibrations of the main ship girder. Since the duration of this vibration, typically of the order of 30 s, is long compared with the stress cycle induced by the main wave, the stress record will be as in Fig. 12.22 assuming the slam occurs at time T_0. The primary ship girder stresses may be increased by as much as 30 per cent.

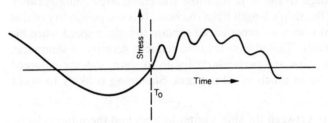

Fig. 12.22 Slamming vibration superimposed on principal stress cycle

Ship stabilization

There is a limit to the extent to which amplitudes of motion can be reduced in conventional ship forms by changes in the basic hull shape. Fortunately, considerable reductions in roll amplitudes are possible by other means, roll being usually the most objectionable of the motions as regards comfort. In principle, the methods used to stabilize against roll can be used to stabilize against pitch but, in general, the forces or powers involved are too great to justify their use.

STABILIZATION SYSTEMS

These fall naturally under two main headings:

(a) *Passive systems*

In these systems, no separate source of power is required and no special control system. Such systems use the motion itself to create moments opposing or damping the motion. Some, such as the common bilge keel, are external to the main hull and with such systems there is an added resistance to ahead motion which has to be overcome by the main engines. The added resistance is offset, partially at least, by a reduction in resistance of the main hull due to the reduced roll amplitude.

Other passive systems, such as the passive anti-roll tanks, are fitted internally. In such cases, there is no augment of resistance arising from the system itself.

The principal passive systems (discussed presently) fitted are:

Bilge keels (and docking keels if fitted)
Fixed fins
Passive tank system
Passive moving weight system.

(b) *Active systems*

In these systems, the moment opposing roll is produced by moving masses or control surfaces by means of power. They also employ a control system which senses the rolling motion and so decides the magnitude of the correcting moment required. As with the passive systems, the active systems may be internal or external to the main hull.

The principal active systems fitted are:

Active fins
Active tank system
Active moving weight
Gyroscope.

BRIEF DESCRIPTIONS OF SYSTEMS

The essential requirement of any system is that the system should always generate a moment opposing the rolling moment.

(a) Active fins

A sensitive gyro system senses the rolling motion of the ship and sends signals to the actuating system which, in turn, causes the fins to move in a direction such as to cause forces opposing the roll. The actuating gear is usually electro-hydraulic. The fins which may be capable of retraction into the hull, or may

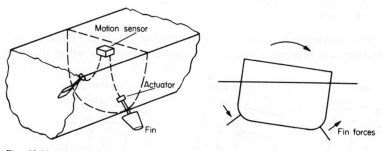

Fig. 12.23 Active fin system

always protrude from it, are placed about the turn of bilge in order to secure maximum leverage for the forces acting upon them. The fins are usually of the balanced spade type, but may incorporate a flap on the trailing edge to increase the lift force generated.

The capacity of a fin system is usually expressed in terms of the steady angle of heel it can cause with the ship moving ahead in still water at a given speed. Since the force on a fin varies in proportion to the square of the ship speed, whereas the $\overline{GZ}$ curve for the ship is, to a first order, independent of speed, it follows that a fin system will be more effective the higher the speed. Broadly speaking, a fin system is not likely to be very effective at speeds below about 10 knots.

(b) Active weights

This may take a number of forms, but the principle is illustrated by the scheme shown in Fig. 12.24. If the weight W is attached to a rotating arm of radius R

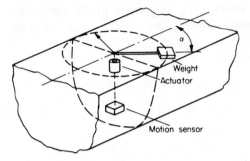

Fig. 12.24 Active weight system

then, when the arm is at an angle α to the centre line of the ship and on the higher side,

Righting moment $= WR \sin \alpha$

Such a system has the advantage, over the fin system, that its effectiveness is independent of speed. It involves greater weight and power, however, and for these reasons is not often fitted.

(c) *Active tank systems*

Again, a variety of systems is available as illustrated in Fig. 12.25. The essential, common, features are two tanks, one on each side of the ship, in which the level

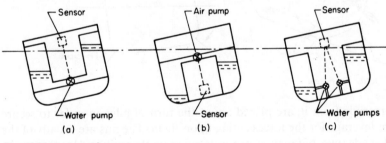

Fig. 12.25 Active tank systems

of water can be controlled in accord with the dictates of the sensing system. In scheme (a), water is pumped from one tank to the other so as to keep the greater quantity in the higher tank. In scheme (b), the water level is controlled indirectly by means of air pressure above the water in each tank, the tanks being open to the sea at the bottom. Scheme (b) has the advantage of requiring less power than scheme (a). In scheme (c), each tank has its own pump but otherwise is similar to scheme (a).

(d) *Gyroscope*

All active stabilizing systems depend upon gyroscopes as part of their control system. If the gyroscope is massive enough, use can be made of the torque it generates when precessed to stabilize the ship. Such systems are not commonly fitted because of their large space and weight demands.

(e) Bilge keels

Bilge keels are so simple and easy to fit that very few ships are not so fitted. They typically extend over the middle half to two-thirds of the ship's length at the turn of bilge. Compared with a ship not fitted, bilge keels can produce a reduction of roll amplitude of 35 per cent or more. They are usually carefully aligned with the flow around the hull in calm water so as to reduce their resistance to ahead motion. Unfortunately, when the ship rolls the bilge keels are no longer in line with the flow of water and can lead to significant increases in resistance. For this reason, some large ships may be fitted with a tank stabilizing system and dispense with bilge keels.

(f) Fixed fins

These are similar in action to bilge keels except that they are shorter and extend further from the ship's side. An advantage claimed for them is that, by careful shaping of their cross-section, the lift generated at a given ahead speed can be increased compared with the drag they suffer. A disadvantage is that, projecting further from the hull, they are more susceptible to damage. They are generally less effective at low speed.

(g) Passive tank system

It is possible to use the roll of the ship itself to cause the water in the tanks to move in such a way as to oppose the motion. Starting from rest with water level in the two tanks, if the ship rolls to starboard water flows from port to starboard until the maximum angle of roll is reached. As the ship now tries to recover, the water will try to return but will nevertheless lag and the moment due to the water will oppose the roll velocity. Also, if the resistance of the duct is high the water will not be able to return before the ship is rolling to port, i.e. the level of water in the tanks can be made to lag the roll motion. By carefully adjusting the resistance of the duct the system can be 'tuned' to give maximum stabilizing effect. This will be when the phase lag is 90 degrees.

One limitation of such a scheme is that the system can only be 'tuned' to one frequency. This is chosen as the natural period of roll because it is at this period that the really large angles of roll can be built up. At other frequencies the passive tank system may actually lead to an increase in roll angle above the 'unstabilized' value, but this is not usually serious because the roll angles are small anyway. A more sophisticated system is one in which the resistance in the duct can be varied to suit the frequency of the exciting waves. In this way roll damping is achieved in all wave lengths.

(h) Passive moving weight system

This is similar in principle to the passive tank system but is generally less effective for a given weight of system.

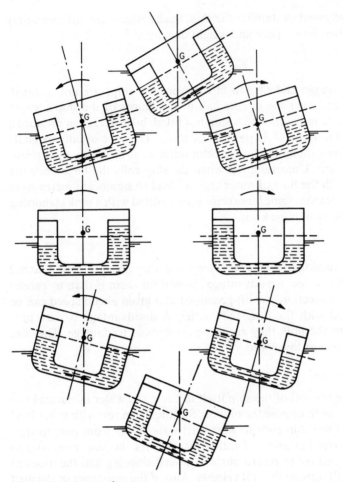

Fig. 12.26 Passive tank system

COMPARISON OF PRINCIPAL SYSTEMS

Ship stabilizing systems are reviewed in Ref. 8. The most commonly fitted, apart from bilge keels, are the active fin and passive tank systems. Table 12.1 compares systems and is taken from Ref. 8.

PERFORMANCE OF STABILIZING SYSTEMS

The methods of predicting the performance of a given stabilizer system in reducing motion amplitudes in irregular seas are beyond the scope of this book. A common method of specifying a system's performance is the roll amplitude it can induce in calm water, and this is more readily calculated.

When the ship rolls freely in still water, the amplitude of each successive swing decreases by an amount depending on the energy absorbed in each roll. At the end of each roll the ship is momentarily still and all its energy is stored as potential energy. If ϕ_1 is the roll angle, the potential energy is $\frac{1}{2}\Delta\overline{GM}\phi_1^2$.

Table 12.1
Comparison of stabilizer systems. (*Figures are for normal installations*)

Type	Activated fin	Passive tank	Active tank	Massive gyro (active)	Moving weight (active)	Moving weight (passive)	Bilge keel	Fixed fin
Percentage roll reduction	90 %	60–70 %	No data	45 %	No data	No data	35 %	No data
Whether effective at very low speeds	No	Yes	Yes	Yes	Yes	Yes	Yes	No
Reduction in deadweight	1 % of displacement	1–4 % of displacement	Comparable with passive tank	2 % of displacement	Comparable with passive tank		Negligible	
Any reduction in statical stability	No	Yes	Yes*	No	Yes*	Yes	No	No
Any increase in ship's resistance	When in operation	No	No	No	No	No	Slight	Slight
Auxiliary power requirement	Small	Nil	Large	Large	Large	Nil	Nil	Nil
Space occupied in hull	Moderate generally less than tanks	Moderate	Moderate	Large	Moderate	Less than tanks	Nil	Nil
Continuous athwartships space	No	Generally	Yes	No	Yes	Yes	No	No
Whether vulnerable to damage	Not when retracted	No	No	No	No	No	Yes	Very
First cost	High	Moderate	Probably high†	Very high	Probably high†	Probably high†	Low	Moderate†
Maintenance	Normal mechanical	Low	Normal mechanical	Probably high	Normal mechanical	Normal mechanical	Often high	Probably high

* There is an effective reduction in statical stability, since allowance must be made for the possibility of the system stalling with the weight all on one side.
† These systems have not been developed beyond the experimental stage and the cost comparison is based on general consideration.

If, on the next roll, the amplitude is ϕ_2 then the energy lost is

$$\tfrac{1}{2}\Delta\overline{GM}(\phi_1^2 - \phi_2^2) = \Delta\overline{GM}\left(\frac{\phi_1 + \phi_2}{2}\right)(\phi_1 - \phi_2) = \Delta\overline{GM}\phi\,\delta\phi$$

where ϕ = mean amplitude of roll.

The reduction in amplitude, $\delta\phi$, is called the *decrement* and in the limit is equal to the slope of the curve of amplitude against number of swings at the mean amplitude concerned. That is,

$$\delta\phi = \left(-\frac{d\phi}{dn}\right)_{\phi}$$

This means that when stabilizers are rolling a ship to a steady amplitude ϕ, the energy lost to damping per swing is

$$\Delta\,\overline{GM}\phi\left(\frac{d\phi}{dn}\right)_{\phi}$$

and this is the energy that must be provided by the stabilizers.

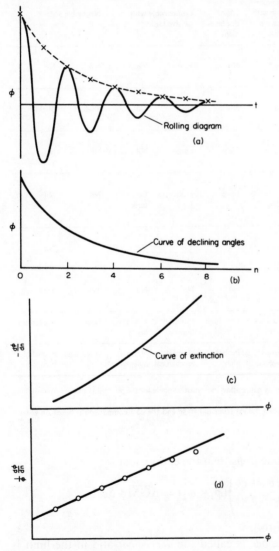

Fig. 12.27 Decrement curve

The value of $d\phi/dn$ can be derived from model or full-scale experiments by noting successive amplitudes of roll as roll is allowed to die out naturally in otherwise still water. These amplitudes are plotted to base n(i.e. the number of swings) and the slope measured at various points to give values of $-d\phi/dn$ at various values of ϕ. (See Fig. 12.27(a), (b) and (c)).

In most cases, it is adequate to assume that $d\phi/dn$ is defined by a second order equation. That is

$$-\frac{d\phi}{dn} = a\phi + b\phi^2$$

or

$$-\frac{1}{\phi}\frac{d\phi}{dn} = a + b\phi$$

By plotting $(1/\phi)\,d\phi/dn$ against ϕ as in Fig. 12.27(d), a straight line can be drawn through the experimental results to give values of a and b.

Instantaneous transfer of weight

Considering forcing a roll by moving weight, the maximum amplitude of roll would be built up if the weight could be transferred instantaneously from the depressed to the elevated side at the end of each swing as shown in Fig. 12.28.

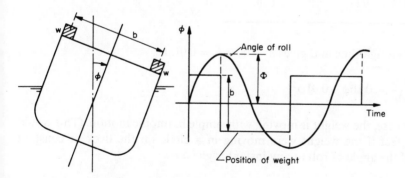

Fig. 12.28 Instantaneous weight transfer

The change in potential energy of the weight at each transfer is $wb\sin\phi$. Hence, approximately

$$wb\phi = \Delta\overline{GM}\phi\left(-\frac{d\phi}{dn}\right)$$

or

$$-\frac{d\phi}{dn} = \frac{w}{\Delta}\frac{b}{\overline{GM}}$$

It follows that the moving weight can increase the roll amplitude up to the value appropriate to this value of $d\phi/dn$.

EXAMPLE. Assuming that for a rolling ship, the slope of the curve of declining angles is $-d\phi/dn = a\phi + b\phi^2$, find the values of a and b given the following corresponding values of $-d\phi/dn$ and ϕ in degree units:

ϕ	5	10	15	20
$-\dfrac{d\phi}{dn}$	0·75	2·00	3·75	6·00

The above figures apply to a 3000 tonne frigate with a metacentric height of 1 m. A mass of 15 tonnes is made to move across the deck in simple harmonic motion with an amplitude of 6 m. Find the steady rolling angle which can be set up by the weight.

Solution: To find the values of a and b the values of $-(1/\phi)\,d\phi/dn$ must be plotted against ϕ

ϕ	5	10	15	20
$-\dfrac{1}{\phi}\dfrac{d\phi}{dn}$	0·15	0·20	0·25	0·30

This is a straight line and gives $a = 0·10$, $b = 0·01$, i.e.

$$-\frac{d\phi}{dn} = 0·10\phi + 0·01\phi^2$$

In this case, the weight is moving with simple harmonic motion. (This would be the effect if the weight were moving in a circle on the deck at constant speed.) If the angle of roll at any instant is given by

$$\phi = \Phi \sin\frac{2\pi t}{T_0}$$

then the distance of the weight from the centre line is

$$\frac{b}{2}\sin\left(\frac{2\pi t}{T_0} + \frac{\pi}{2}\right)$$

where b is the double amplitude of motion.

The movement of ship and weight must be 90 degrees out of phase for an efficient system.

The work done by the weight in moving out to out (i.e. per swing) is

$$\int_{-b/2}^{+b/2} w\phi \, d\left\{ \frac{b}{2}\sin\left(\frac{2\pi t}{T_0}+\frac{\pi}{2}\right)\right\}$$

$$= w\,\Phi.\frac{b}{2}\frac{2\pi}{T_0}\int_{-T_0/2}^{T_0/2} \sin\frac{2\pi t}{T_0}\cos\left(\frac{2\pi t}{T_0}+\frac{\pi}{2}\right)dt$$

$$= \frac{\pi}{T_0}wb\Phi\int_{0}^{T_0/2}\sin^2\frac{2\pi t}{T_0}\,dt$$

$$= \frac{\pi}{T_0}wb\Phi\frac{1}{2}\left[t-\frac{T_0}{4\pi}\sin\frac{4\pi t}{T_0}\right]_{0}^{T_0/2}$$

$$= \frac{\pi}{4}wb\Phi$$

i.e.

$$\frac{\pi}{4}wb\Phi = \Delta\overline{GM}\Phi\left(-\frac{d\phi}{dn}\right)$$

From which

$$-\frac{d\phi}{dn} = \frac{\pi}{4}\frac{wb}{\Delta\overline{GM}} = \frac{\pi}{4}\frac{m\;b}{\Sigma\;\overline{GM}}$$

Hence, if ϕ is the steady rolling angle produced

$$0{\cdot}1\phi+0{\cdot}01\phi^2 = \frac{\pi}{4}\times\frac{15}{3000}\times\frac{2(6)}{1}\times\frac{180}{\pi}$$

whence,

$$\phi = 12{\cdot}2 \text{ degrees}$$

Experiments and trials

MODEL EXPERIMENTS

Although considerable advances have been made recently in the theoretical prediction of ship motions, the theory is not adequate on its own and much reliance is placed on model experiments.

In principle, the following methods of testing are available:

(i) By representing an actual irregular wave pattern and running the model in that pattern to record motions, wetness, power, etc.

(ii) By running the model in regular waves and obtaining response amplitude operators to be used in the super-position theory to predict performance in actual sea conditions. To give accurate results such tests must be carried out in relatively mild waves, e.g. length to height ratios of about 40:1.

(iii) By running the model in an irregular but standard wave pattern and analysing the data to provide the response amplitude operators. A special case of this type of testing is the *transient wave testing* or impulse wave testing. For this type of testing, the wavemaker is started at one of its higher frequencies and progressively slowed down. Thus, it initially produces short waves which are gradually overtaken by the later, longer waves. It is usual to arrange for the waves nominally to coalesce at some point behind the wave-maker. The model starts in calm water, passes through a short length of waves and finishes its run in calm water. By analysing the complete wave and motion records a full picture of the model's responses is obtained. Reference 9 describes this method of testing.

Each procedure has its own advantages and disadvantages and each is used for specific purposes. The second method requires less complicated test facilities and can provide the basic data from which the ship behaviour in any spectrum can be deduced. The number of experiments required to cover adequate ranges of ship speed, direction and wave-length is very great. The time spent in the tank can be reduced by adopting the third method, provided the length of each run is adequate to render the subsequent statistical analysis accurate. For this, each run should provide at least 200 complete motion cycles. This limitation does not apply to transient wave testing. The first method is necessary for a thorough comparison of ship and model data, and for the realistic study of wetness and slamming which depend not only on the statistical properties of the wave and motions but also upon the phase relationships, i.e. upon the actual wave surface and motion at any time. The adequacy of the third method for this type of study depends upon the realism of the standard spectrum used. Various spectra have been advocated by different authorities in the past but the spectra agreed by the International Towing Tank Conference are now in common use.

As with wave records discussed in Chapter 9, it must be remembered that the results of a particular series of experiments can only be regarded as a sample of all possible experimental outcomes. To illustrate this, consider a single run in an irregular wave system. The actual surface shape repeats itself only after a very long period of time, if at all. The actual model data obtained from a particular run depends on when, during that period, the experiment is run. Tests for statistical significance can be applied

Test facilities

Until recent years, seakeeping experiments were carried out in the long narrow ship tanks used for resistance and propulsion work. In these tanks, it was only possible to study the response of the model when heading directly into or away from the waves which were generated by a wave-maker at one end of the tank. The principal wave generators used are (Fig. 12.29) an oscillating paddle, a vertically oscillating plunger or a pneumatic system in which the air pressure is varied over an area of the water surface. To ensure that the generated wave form is not unduly distorted by reflections from the end of the tank wave absorption devices, termed beaches, are provided.

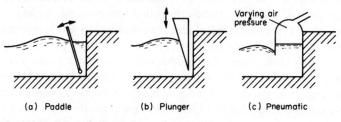

(a) Paddle   (b) Plunger   (c) Pneumatic

Fig. 12.29 Types of wave-maker

The early wave-makers were designed to generate regular waves of either trochoidal or sinusoidal form. The first advance was to vary the motion of the wave generator in a controlled manner so as to produce an irregular wave profile with the desired spectral properties. More recently special tanks, commonly termed seakeeping basins, have been constructed to permit models to be run at any heading relative to the wave system. These facilities are also capable of producing more complex waves including short-crested systems.

One of the earliest of these basins specially designed for sea-keeping experiments is that at Wageningen in Holland. This retains the ability to run the model below a carriage carrying much of the data recording equipment although with the minimum of restraint imposed on the model. The wave-maker installation consists of a large number of small flaps. By varying the motion of the flaps and the phase relationship between flaps, an irregular wave pattern can be created with the line of crests at the desired angle to the path of the model.

Other specialized facilities such as that at the Admiralty Experiment Works, Haslar, make use of a completely free radio-controlled model. The basin at AEW is 400 ft long by 200 ft wide with plunger type wave-makers disposed as shown diagrammatically in Fig. 12.30. Each 200 ft bank of wave-makers comprises five plungers each with its own control system. The large Seakeeping

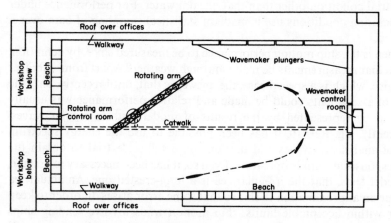

Fig. 12.30 Seakeeping basin at AEW, Haslar

Basin at the Naval Ship Research and Development Centre has a bridge carrying a carriage so that free or constrained models can be tested. The Mitaka Ship Experiment Basin in Japan is 80 m × 80 m with a channel 50 m long in which models can be accelerated. This uses radio-controlled free-running models.

At first sight, the use of a free model seems ideal as avoiding any guide systems interfering with the motion of the model. However, this technique presents the experimenter with many difficulties. The model must contain its own propulsion system, power supplies, radio-control devices as well as being able to record much of the experimental data. It must be ballasted so as to possess the correct stability characteristics and scaled inertias in order that its response as a dynamic system will accurately simulate that of the ship. Further, all this must be achieved within a relatively small model such as the 16 ft long model typically used at AEW. Too large a model restricts the effective length of each run which is very significant for experiments where data have to be analysed and presented in a statistical form.

As theoretical and technological advances are made the test facilities and techniques are gradually improved.

SHIP TRIALS

Ship trials are carried out for a variety of reasons, including:

(*a*) to confirm that the ship meets her design specification as regards performance;
(*b*) to predict performance during service;
(*c*) to prove that equipment can function properly in the shipboard environment;
(*d*) to provide data on which future ship designs can be based.

It was seen in Chapters 10 and 11 that as regards resistance and propulsion, performance trials are usually carried out in calm water to provide data for (*a*), (*b*) and (*d*) above. This is not because it is thought that the ship will generally operate under such conditions, but because of the difficulties of achieving a standard trial condition other than that of calm water. For performance under actual operating conditions use is made of statistical sampling of data over a long period.

How then is the ship motion performance to be measured since, by definition, it requires that measurements be made in rough weather? Apart from stabilizer performance, which is a special case, the answer is that, until recently, only the roughest of assessments could be made and relative performance was usually assumed to be represented by the results of model tests in regular waves. More recently, e.g. Ref. 10, it has been possible to use the energy spectrum method of analysis of waves and motions on a full-scale trial to obtain the motion response amplitude operators. Even so, it has been necessary to assume, as for model tests, that the irregular sea is a long-crested one. An actual sea can only be an approximation to this so that some error arises. In order to keep this error within acceptable limits, ship motion trials involve sending ships to areas in which approximately long-crested waves are likely to be encountered and often keeping them there for long periods until the right conditions are met. Alternatively, the trials party, with their recording equipment, are sent on the ship's normal voyage hoping to meet acceptable conditions on the way.

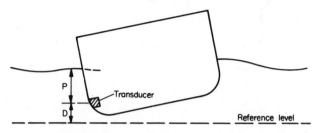

Fig. 12.31 N.I.O. shipborne wave recorder

One of the earliest recorders used for ship trials was the shipborne wave recorder developed by the Institute of Oceanographic Sciences (formerly NIO, Ref. 11). It is shown in principle in Fig. 12.31. It measures the height of the sea surface by measuring the water pressure at a transducer on the hull. To this is added the height of the transducer above an imaginary reference surface by double integration of the vertical acceleration of the point, measured by an accelerometer. An instrument in the ship itself has the advantage that phase relationships between the waves and motions can be deduced. It cannot, however, sense the direction of the waves relative to the ship unless an array of transducers is used. Its record is affected by the variation of pressure with depth below the wave surface and by the presence of the ship itself in the wave system. It is now more usual to use a freely floating buoy transmitting signals to the trials ship over a radio link. Vertical motions of the buoy are recorded by an accelerometer and movement of the wave surface relative to the buoy by resistive probes. Roll, pitch and azimuth sensors monitor the attitude of the buoy. For studying complex wave systems in detail several buoys may be used.

A typical sequence for a ship motion trial is to:

(*a*) carry out measured mile runs at the start of the voyage to establish the ship's smooth water performance and to calibrate the log;
(*b*) carry out service trials during passage to record sample ship motions and propulsive data under normal service conditions;
(*c*) launch the recording buoy, record conditions and recover buoy, when conditions are considered suitable, i.e. waves appear to be sufficiently long-crested;
(*d*) carry out a manoeuvre of the type shown in Fig. 12.32 recording motions and waves for each leg.

Figures denote time in minutes spent on each leg. The accuracy of the analysis depends upon the number of oscillations recorded. For this reason, the legs running with the seas are longer than those with ship running head into the waves. The overall time on the manoeuvre has to be balanced against the possibility of the sea state changing during the trial. The two sets of buoy records and a comparison of the results from the initial and final legs provides a

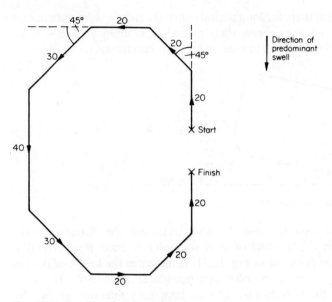

Fig. 12.32 Typical seakeeping manoeuvre

guide to the stability of the trial conditions. The remaining steps of the sequence are:

(*e*) launch buoy for second recording of waves;
(*f*) repeat (*c*), (*d*) and (*e*) as conditions permit;
(*g*) carry out service trials on way back to port;
(*h*) carry out measured mile runs on return.

On return to harbour, a very lengthy analysis is required even when high speed digital computers are used. Indeed, this type of trial would not be feasible without computer aid.

STABILIZER TRIALS

Stabilizers, fitted to reduce rolling in a seaway, can be specified directly in terms of roll under stated conditions but such performance can never be precisely proven on trial. As an alternative a designer may relate performance to the steady angle of heel that can be generated by holding the fins over in calm water at a given speed. Heel can be measured directly to establish whether or not such contractual requirements have been met. Forced rolling trials in calm water can be used to study the performance of shipborne equipment under controlled conditions. It is often difficult to distinguish the effects of the stabilizers from the cross-coupling effect of the rudders; indeed, it is possible to build up a considerable angle of roll in calm water by the judicious use of rudder alone.

Theory

Although theory cannot, as yet, replace model investigations, considerable advances have been made in recent years. That good results can be obtained by applying theory is demonstrated in Fig. 12.33 which is based on results produced at AEW, Haslar, for a frigate at Froude number 0·4.

The theory used is based on Ref. 12. In this type of approach—commonly called the *strip theory*—the hydrodynamic forces are calculated for various cross-sections of the ship using standard data on added mass, etc. Integrating along the length leads to the overall forces and moments acting on the hull. Refinements can be introduced to allow for the fact that there is a free surface on which waves are created, and for the fact that the problem is really one of three dimensions rather than two.

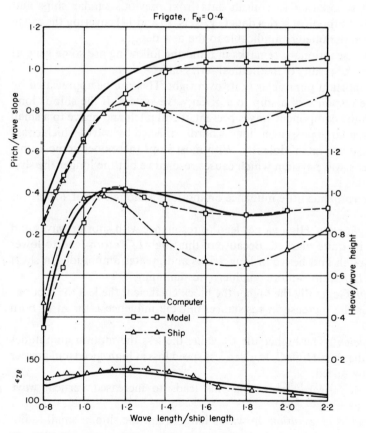

Fig. 12.33 *Comparison of ship, model and computed motions*

A computer is essential to the theoretical estimation of motions. However, once a programme is available, its value can be considerable. The number of possible form configurations is very large and to thoroughly test each, for a range of parent forms, is a formidable task. With the computer, a theoretical methodical series can be calculated and model tests can then be arranged to check a few spots on the curves. Model tests would still be needed for unusual hull forms.

Influence of form on seakeeping

It can be dangerous to generalize on the effect of varying form parameters on the seakeeping characteristics of a design. A change in one parameter often leads to a change in other parameters and a change may reduce motions but increase wetness. Again, the trend arising from a given variation in a full ship may not be the same as the trend from the same variation in a fine ship. This accounts for some apparently conflicting conclusions from different series of experiments. It is essential to consult data from previous similar ships and particularly any methodical series data (e.g. Refs. 13 and 14) covering the range of principal form parameters applicable to the new design.

With the above cautionary remarks in mind the following are some general trends based on the results of methodical series data:

Length is an important parameter in its own right. This can be appreciated by considering the response of a ship to a given wave system. If the ship is long compared with the component waves present, it will pitch and heave to a small extent only, e.g. a large passenger liner is hardly affected by waves which cause a 3000 tonf frigate to pitch violently. With most ships there does come a time when they meet a wave system which causes resonance but the longer the ship the less likely this is.

Length to beam ratio has little influence on motions although lower L/B ratios are preferable.

Length to draught ratio. High values lead to resonance with shorter waves and this effect can be quite marked. Because of this, high L/T ratios lead to lower amplitudes of pitch and heave in long waves and greater amplitudes in short waves. A high L/T ratio is more conducive to slamming.

Block coefficient. Generally the higher the block coefficient the less the motions and the greater the increase in resistance, but the influence is small in both cases.

Prismatic coefficient. The higher the C_P value the less the motion amplitudes but the wetter the ship. High C_P leads to less speed loss at high speed and greater speed loss at low speed.

Waterplane area forward. Increasing this leads to increased vertical wave bending moment.

Longitudinal radius of gyration. In waves longer than the ship, a small radius of gyration is beneficial in reducing motions.

A bulbous bow generally reduces motions in short waves but can lead to increased motions in very long waves.

Forward sections. U-shaped sections usually give less resistance in waves and a larger longitudinal inertia. V-shaped sections usually produce lower amplitudes of heave and pitch and less vertical bow movement. Above-water flare has little effect on motion amplitudes but can reduce wetness at the expense of increased resistance.

Freeboard. The greater the freeboard the drier the ship.

It will be noted that a given change in form often has one effect in short waves and the opposite effect in long waves. In actual ocean conditions, waves of all lengths are present and it would not be surprising, therefore, if the motions, etc., in an irregular wave system showed less variation with form changes. This is borne out by Ref. 2 which shows that, for conventional forms, the overall performance of a ship in waves is not materially influenced by variations in the main hull parameters. This suggests that for a marked reduction in motion amplitudes, unconventional forms must be adopted. Proposals for unorthodox forms are basically of two types:

(*a*) Concentration of most of the displacement in a hull remote from the water surface with only a small waterplane area. By this means, the exciting forces and moments are reduced.

(*b*) Use of large underwater appendages to damp the motion. The appendage may be purely passive or may use flaps to actively control the motion.

Concluding remarks

Necessarily, this chapter has been concerned with an elementary approach to seakeeping. It has assumed that linear theory is applicable, which is true only within limits. It has assumed also that each motion discussed is independent of the other; cross-coupling between heave and pitch and between roll and sway can be appreciable and for some cases, important. While the student must not try to run before he can walk, he must remain aware of the deficiencies of this elementary theory. The reference on page 468 to the cross-coupling between rudder and stabilizers for example should suggest that the design of control systems should not be pursued independently but as a single problem. Advances in theory are occurring rapidly. Random process theory and the introduction to the subject of seakeeping of such devices as impulse response functions and Fourier transforms are enabling fundamental advances to be made, although some may find the mathematics formidable. References 23 and 24 give an introduction and further references for the student to pursue.

Problems

1. The mast of a small floating raft, due to the passage of a train of deep water waves, is observed to oscillate with a period of 7 s and amplitude from the vertical of ± 8 degrees. Find the height, length and velocity of the waves in metric units. (RNC)

2. A box-shaped vessel has a length of 50 m, beam 12 m, draught 3 m, freeboard 6 m. The height of the c.g. above the bottom is 4·5 m. Assuming that the weight is uniformly distributed throughout the length and section of the vessel, and neglecting the effects of associated water, calculate the free periods of roll, pitch and heave in salt water. (RNC)

3. A vessel, length 200 m, whose periods of free roll and pitch are $12\frac{1}{2}$ and 10 s

respectively, is steaming at 20 knots in a sea of wave-length 250 m. Calculate the headings on which the greatest rolling and pitching are likely.

4. A ship is rolling with a constant amplitude, the rolling being maintained by moving a weight across the deck, i.e. the energy put into the ship by the moving weight just balances the energy dissipated by damping.

Show, by general arguments, that the ideal case is one in which the weight is transferred instantly from the depressed side to the elevated side at the end of each swing.

Compare the relative weights required to maintain a given small rolling amplitude assuming

(a) instantaneous transfer
(b) weight moving with constant velocity
(c) weight moving with s.h.m.

The amplitude of the movement is the same in each case.

[*Note:* Assume rolling motion is given by $\phi = \Phi \sin (2\pi t/T)$.]

5. Show that, neglecting damping forces, the rolling of a ship to small angles in still water, without ahead motion, is simple harmonic. Hence, derive an expression for the natural period of oscillation of the ship in terms of the radius of gyration (k) and the $\overline{\text{GM}}$ of the ship. What is the effect of entrained water? How do rolling considerations affect the choice of $\overline{\text{GM}}$ for a passenger ship?

During rolling trials on an aircraft carrier, a natural period of roll of 14 s was recorded. The displacement was 50,000 tonnef and the $\overline{\text{GM}}$ was 2·5 m. The inertia coefficient, allowing for the effect of entrained water is 20 per cent. Calculate the radius of gyration of the aircraft carrier.   (HMDTC)

6. A ship, 4000 tonne displacement, 150 m length, 15 m beam and 1 m metacentric height has a rolling period of 10·5 s and a decrement equation

$$-\frac{\mathrm{d}\phi}{\mathrm{d}n} = 0{\cdot}20\phi + 0{\cdot}15\phi^2 \quad (\phi \text{ in radians})$$

If the ship is to be rolled to an amplitude of 10° estimate the weight required to be moved instantaneously across the deck assuming that it can be moved through 12 m.

7. The differential equation for the rolling motion of a ship in regular waves can be expressed in the form:

$$\ddot{\phi} + 2k\omega_0\dot{\phi} + \omega_0^2\phi = \omega_0^2 F_0 \sin \omega_E t$$

Explain the significance of the terms in this equation.

The equation of the rolling motion of a particular ship in regular waves can be expressed in the form:

$$\ddot{\phi} + 0{\cdot}24\dot{\phi} + 0{\cdot}16\phi = 0{\cdot}48 \sin \omega_E t$$

where ϕ is the roll angle in degrees.

Calculate the amplitudes of roll when ω_E is equal to 0·2, 0·4 and 0·8, commenting upon their relative magnitudes. What would be the period of damped rolling motion in calm water?   (RNC)

8. A ship motion trial is carried out in a long-crested irregular wave system.

The spectrum of the wave system as measured at a stationary point is defined by the following table:

$S_\zeta(\omega)$, (wave height)$^2/\delta\omega$ (m²s)	1·2	7·6	12·9	11·4	8·4	5·6
ω, frequency (1/s)	0·3	0·4	0·5	0·6	0·7	0·8

The heave energy spectrum obtained from accelerometers in the ship, when moving at 12 knots on a course of 150 degrees relative to the waves, is defined as follows:

$S_Z(\omega_E)$, (heave)$^2/\delta\omega_E$ (m²s)	0·576	1·624	1·663	0·756	0·149	0·032
ω_E, frequency of encounter (1/s)	0·4	0·5	0·6	0·7	0·8	0·9

Derive the response curve, in the form of heave/wave height, for the ship at this speed and heading, over the range of frequencies of encounter from 0·4 to 0·9. (RNC)

9. The successive maximum angles in degrees recorded in a model rolling experiment are:

Port   15 (start)   10·4   7·7   5·9
Starboard   12·3   8·9   6·7

What are the 'a' and 'b' coefficients? What maximum angle would you expect to be attained at the end of the tenth swing? (RNC)

10. A vessel, unstable in the upright position, lolls to an angle α. Prove that, in the absence of resistance, she will roll between $\pm\phi$ or between ϕ and $\sqrt{(2\alpha^2 - \phi^2)}$ according as ϕ is greater or less than $\alpha\sqrt{2}$. All angles are measured from the vertical.

Explain how the angular velocity varies during the roll in each case. (RNC)

11. A rolling experiment is to be conducted on a ship which is expected to have 'a' and 'b' extinction coefficients of 0·08 and 0·012 (degree units).

The experiment is to be conducted with the displacement at 2100 tonf and a metacentric height of 2·75 ft. The period of roll is expected to be about 9 s.

A mechanism capable of moving a weight of 6 tonf in simple harmonic motion 30 ft horizontally across the vessel is available.

Estimate:

(a) the maximum angle of roll likely to be produced,
(b) the electrical horsepower of the motor with which the rolling mechanism should be fitted (assume an efficiency of 80 per cent). (RNC)

12. A vessel which may be regarded as a rectangular pontoon 100 m long and 25 m wide is moving at 10 knots into regular sinusoidal waves 200 m long and 10 m high. The direction of motion of the vessel is normal to the line of crests and its natural (undamped) period of heave is 8 s.

If it is assumed that waves of this length and height could be slowed down relative to the ship, so that the ship had the opportunity of balancing itself statically to the wave at every instant of its passage, the ship would heave in the effective period of the wave and a 'static' amplitude would result. With the wave at its correct velocity of advance relative to the ship a 'dynamic' amplitude will result which may be regarded as the product of the 'static' amplitude and the so-called 'magnification factor'.

Calculate the amplitude of heave of the ship under the conditions described in the first paragraph, making the assumption of the second paragraph and neglecting any Smith correction.

The linear damping coefficient k, is 0·3.   (RNC)

13. A ship, 4000 tonne displacement, 140 m long and 15 m beam has a transverse metacentric height of 1·5 m. Its rolling period is 10·0 s and during a rolling trial successive (unfaired) roll amplitudes, as the motion was allowed to die down, were:

11·3, 8·6, 6·8, 5·6, 4·5, 3·7 and 3·1 degrees

Deduce the 'a' and 'b' coefficients, assuming a decrement equation of the form

$$-\frac{\mathrm{d}\phi}{dn} = a\phi + b\phi^2$$ (RNC)

14. The spectrum of an irregular long-crested wave-system, as measured at a fixed point, is given by:

$S_\zeta(\omega)$, (wave amplitude)$^2/\delta\omega$ (m^2 s)	0·3	1·9	4·3	3·8
ω, (frequency) (1/s)	0·3	0·4	0·5	0·6

A ship heads into this wave system at 30 knots and in a direction such that the velocity vectors for ship and waves are inclined at 120 degrees. Calculate the wave spectrum as it would be measured by a probe moving forward with the speed of the ship.

Discuss how you would proceed to calculate the corresponding heave spectrum. Illustrate your answer by calculating the ordinate of the heave spectrum at a frequency of encounter of 0·7 s.

The relationship between amplitude of heave and wave amplitude at this frequency of encounter for various speeds into regular head seas of appropriate length should be taken as follows:

heavy amplitude / wave amplitude	0·71	0·86	0·92	0·95	0·96
speed (knots)	20	40	60	80	100

Assume that, to a first approximation, the heave amplitude of a ship moving at speed V obliquely into long-crested waves is the same as the heave amplitude in regular head seas of the same height and of the same 'effective length' (i.e. the length in the direction of motion) provided the speed V_1 is adjusted to give the same frequency of encounter.   (RNC)

15. In the main text, the second worked example deals with wetness. Verify that the results quoted for ship speeds of 22·1 knots and 26·6 knots are valid.

16. A ship 440 ft long has a freeboard of 23 ft. Assuming a natural pitching period of 3·64 s in air, calculate the percentage of the year for which it is anti-

cipated the ship will be very wet when travelling at a Froude number of 0·265.
17. A ship 430 ft long has a natural period of pitching in air of 3·45 s. Calculate
the ship speed corresponding to a Froude number of 0·265 and the percentage
of the year the ship will be wet and very wet at this speed with freeboards of
25 ft and 30 ft.
18. Assuming that a ship heaves in a wave as though the relative velocity of
wave and ship is very low, show that the 'static' heave is given by

$$\frac{\text{heave amplitude}}{\text{wave amplitude}} = -\frac{\sin n\pi}{\pi n} \sin \frac{2\pi t}{T_E}$$

for a rectangular waterplane, where

$$n = \frac{\text{length of ship}}{\text{length of wave}} = \frac{L}{\lambda}$$

and the wave is defined by

$$\zeta = \frac{H}{2} \sin\left(\frac{2\pi n x}{L} - \frac{2\pi t}{T_E}\right)$$

Show that there is zero 'static' response at $n = 1·0$.

References

1. Kato, H. On the approximate calculation of ship's rolling period. *JSNAJ*, Vol. 89, 1956.
2. Ewing, J. A. and Goodrich, G. J. The influence on ship motions of different wave spectra and of ship length. *TRINA*, 1967.
3. Lewis, E. V. Ship motions in oblique seas. *TSNAME*, 1960.
4. Aertssen, G. Service performance and seakeeping trials on *m.v. Jordaens. TRINA*, 1966.
5. Lewis, E. V. Increasing the speed of merchant ships. *TSNAME* (Metropolitan Section), 1959.
6. Swaan, W. A. and Rijken, H. Speed loss as a function of longitudinal weight distribution. *TNECI*, 1963.
7. Newton, R. N. Wetness related to freeboard and flare. *TRINA*, 1960.
8. Parker, M. N. Brief review of ship-stabilizing systems. *Shipping World and Shipbuilder*, 3 December, 1964.
9. Davis, M. C. Cdr. and Zarnick, E. E. Testing ship models in transient waves. *Fifth Symposium on Naval Hydrodynamics*, 10–12 September, 1964.
10. Canham, H. J. S., Cartwright, D. E., Goodrich, G. J. and Hogben, N. Seakeeping trials on OWS *Weather Reporter. TRINA*, 1962.
11. Tucker, M. J. A shipborne wave recorder. *TINA*, 1956.
12. Korvin-Kroukovsky, B. V. and Jacobs, W. R. Pitching and heaving motions of a ship in regular waves. *TSNAME*, 1957.
13. Swaan, W. A. and Vossers, G. The effect of forebody section shape on ship behaviour in waves. *TRINA*, 1961.
14. Vossers, G., Swaan, W. A. and Rijken, H. Experiments with series 60 models in waves. *TSNAME*, 1960.
15. Lewis, E. V. Ship speeds in irregular seas. *TSNAME*, 1955.
16. Conolly, J. E. *Standards of good seakeeping for destroyers and frigates in head seas.**
17. Conolly, J. E. Rolling and its stabilization by active fins. *TRINA*, 1969.
18. Conolly, J. E. and Goodrich, G. J. Sea trials of anti-pitching fins. *TRINA*, 1970.
19. Ewing, J. A. The effect of speed, forebody shape and weight distribution on ship motion. *TRINA*, 1967.
20. Lewison, G. R. G. On the reduction of slamming pressures. *TRINA*, 1970.
21. Murdey, D. C. An analysis of longitudinal bending moments measured on models in head waves. *TRINA*, 1972.
22. Ochi, M. K. and Motter, E. *Prediction of extreme ship responses in rough seas of the north Atlantic.**
23. *International symposium on the dynamics of marine vehicles and structures in waves*, University College London. Published by Inst. of Mech. Engs., 1974.*
24. Price, W. G. and Bishop, R. E. D. *Probabilistic theory of ship dynamics*. Chapman Hall, 1974.

13 Manoeuvrability

Theory

All ships require to be controllable in direction in the horizontal plane so that they can proceed on a straight path, turn or take other avoiding action as may be dictated by the operational situation. They must further be capable of doing this consistently and reliably not only in calm water but also in waves or in conditions of strong wind. In addition, submarines require to be controllable in the vertical plane, to enable them to maintain or change depth as required whilst retaining control of fore and aft pitch angle.

Considering control in the horizontal plane, a study of a ship's manoeuvrability must embrace the following:

(a) the ease with which it can be maintained on a given course. The term steering is commonly applied to this action and the prime factor affecting the ship's performance is her directional or dynamic stability. This should not be confused with the 'ship's stability as discussed in Chapter 4;
(b) the response of the ship to movements of her control surfaces, the rudders, either in initiating or terminating a rate of change of heading;
(c) the ability to turn completely round within a specified space.

For control in the vertical plane, it is necessary to study:

(a) ability to maintain constant depth;
(b) ability to change depth at a controlled pitch angle.

Submarine stability and control is dealt with in more detail in a later section.

It is clear from the above, that all ships must possess some means of directional control. In the great majority of cases, this control is exercised through surfaces called rudders fitted at the after end of the ship. In some cases, the rudders are augmented by other lateral force devices at the bow and, in a few special applications, they are replaced by other steering devices such as the vertical axis propeller. This chapter is devoted mainly to the conventional, rudder steered, ship but the later sections provide a brief introduction to some of the special devices used.

It is important to appreciate that it is not the rudder forces directly in themselves that cause the ship to turn. Rather, the rudder acts as a servo-system which causes the hull to take up an attitude in which the required forces and moments are generated hydrodynamically on the hull. Rudders are fitted aft in a ship because, in this position, they are most effective in causing the hull to take up the required attitude and because they benefit from the increased water

476

velocity induced by the propellers. At low speed, when the rudder forces due to the speed of the ship alone are very small, a burst of high shaft revolutions produces a useful side force if the propellers and rudders are in line.

In the early days of man's movements on" water, directional control was by paddle as in a canoe today. That is to say, he controlled his heading by applying a force either on the port or starboard side of his craft. As his vessels grew in size, course was changed by means of an oar over the after end which was used to produce a lateral force. Later again, this was replaced by a large bladed oar on each quarter of the ship and, in turn, this gave way to a single plate or rudder fitted to the transom. The form of this plate has gradually evolved into the modern rudder. This is streamlined in form to produce large lift forces with minimum drag and with the shape of the leading edge sections designed to reduce the variation of lift force with angle of attack. More recently again, the single rudder has given way to twin or multiple rudders.

DIRECTIONAL STABILITY OR DYNAMIC STABILITY OF COURSE

It was seen in Chapter 4, that when disturbed in yaw there are no hydrostatic forces tending either to increase or decrease the deviation in ship's head. In this mode, the ship is said to be in a state of neutral equilibrium. When under way, hydrodynamic forces act on the hull which can have either a stabilizing or destabilizing effect. However, in the absence of any external corrective forces being applied, the ship will not return to its initial line of advance when subject to a disturbance. Hence, *directional stability* cannot be defined in terms precisely similar to those used for transverse stability. A ship is said to be directionally stable when, having suffered a disturbance from an initial straight path, it tends to take up a new straight line path.

Figure 13.1 shows an arrow with a large tail area well aft of its centre of gravity. Consider a small disturbance which deflects the arrow through a small angle ψ relative to its initial trajectory. The velocity of the arrow is still substantially along the direction of the initial path and the tail surfaces, being now at an angle of attack ψ, develop a lift force F which is in the direction shown. This force is clearly acting in such a manner as to reduce ψ since it is equivalent to a side force F acting at, and a moment M acting about, the c.g. Provided the tail surfaces are large enough, the forces acting on the rest of the arrow

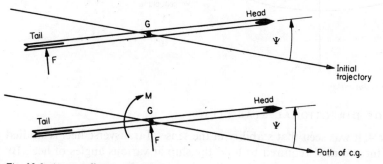

Fig. 13.1 Arrow suffering a disturbance

will be negligible compared with *F*. More precisely, *F* can be regarded as the resultant force acting on the arrow.

The sideways force acting at G will have the effect of changing the direction of movement of the c.g. but, as *M* causes ψ to decrease, *M* and *F* will decrease becoming zero and then negative as the axis of the arrow passes through the path of the c.g. Thus, the arrow will oscillate a little and then settle down on a new straight path. The deviation from the original path will depend upon the damping effect of the air and the relative magnitudes of *M* and *F*. It follows that to maintain a near constant path, the arrow should have large tail surfaces as far aft of G as possible. Directional stability of this very pronounced type is often referred to as 'weather-cock' stability by an obvious analogy.

Application to a ship

It is not possible to tell merely by looking at the lines of a ship whether it is directionally stable or not. Applying the principle enunciated above, it can be argued that for directional stability the moment acting on the hull and its appendages must be such that it tends to oppose any yaw caused by a disturbance, i.e. the resultant force must act aft of G. The point at which it acts is commonly called the *centre of lateral resistance*. As a general guide, therefore, it is to be expected that ships with large skegs aft and with well rounded forefoot will tend to be more directionally stable than a ship without these features but otherwise similar. Also, as a general guide, long slender ships are likely to be more directionally stable than short, tubby forms.

The sign convention used in this chapter is illustrated in Fig. 13.2.

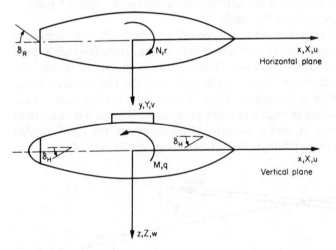

Fig. 13.2 Sign convention

THEORY OF DIRECTIONAL STABILITY

In Chapter 4, it was seen that stability in the sense of transverse heel is studied by noting the moment required to hold the ship at various angles of heel. By analogy, it might be supposed that directional stability can be studied by determining the moment required to hold the hull at various angles of yaw, i.e. to give it a lateral component of velocity. This is partly true but, in this case, a dynamic situation is involved and the lateral force induced by the yaw will cause the ship to start to turn. It is thus also necessary to consider the forces and moments induced by this rotation.

Consider a ship in a steady turn of large radius under the action of a small rudder angle, δ_R.

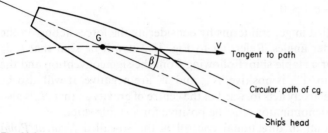

Fig. 13.3

In a steady turn, the resultant lateral force and yawing moment are zero. Hence

$$vY_v + rY_r + \delta_R Y_{\delta_R} - mVr\cos\beta = 0$$

and

$$vN_v + rN_r + \delta_R N_{\delta_R} = 0$$

where subscripts v, r and δ_R denote differentiation with respect to the lateral component of velocity (radial), rate of change of heading and rudder angle respectively, i.e. $Y_v = \partial Y/\partial v$, etc. Y denotes component of force on ship in y direction and N the moment of forces on ship about z-axis. m is the mass of the ship and the last term on the left-hand side of the force equation is the centrifugal force term.

Put into words, the moment equation expresses the fact that:

Moment = 0 = lateral velocity (rate of change of moment with lateral velocity)
  + angular velocity (rate of change of moment with angular velocity)
  + rudder angle (rate of change of moment with rudder angle)

We are concerned with small variations from a straight course, i.e. v, r and δ_R are small and $\cos\beta$ is approximately unity.

Putting $\cos\beta = 1$ and expressing the equations non-dimensionally we obtain

$$v'Y_v' + r'Y_r' + \delta_R Y_{\delta_R}' - m'r' = 0 \quad \text{where, for example,} \quad Y'_{\delta_R} = \frac{1}{\frac{1}{2}\rho V^2 l^2}\frac{\partial Y}{\partial \delta_R}$$

$$v'N_v' + r'N_r' + \delta_R N_{\delta_R}' = 0 \quad V \text{ being a typical velocity.}$$

Eliminating v'

$$\frac{r'}{\delta_R} = \frac{N'_v Y'_{\delta_R} - N'_{\delta_R} Y'_v}{N'_r Y'_v - N'_v (Y'_r - m')}$$

If the denominator is zero, r'/δ_R is infinite and the ship will turn without any rudder angle being applied. It can be shown that this is an unstable condition, and for stability the denominator, known as the stability index, must be positive, i.e.

$$N'_r Y'_v - N'_v (Y'_r - m') > 0$$

This can be justified in general terms by considering the forces acting on the ship for small rudder angles. Referring to Fig. 13.2 it will be seen that r'/δ_R must be negative for a stable ship. Following from the sign convention and the geometry of the ship, Y'_{δ_R} is positive, N'_{δ_R} and Y'_v are negative. It will also be seen later that Y effectively acts forward of the centre of gravity so that N'_v is also negative. Thus the denominator must be positive for a stable ship.

An important point in directional control is the so-called *Neutral Point* which is that point, along the length of the ship, at which an applied force, ignoring transient effects, does not cause the ship to deviate from a constant heading. This point is a distance ηL forward of the centre of gravity, where

$$\eta = \frac{N'_v}{Y'_v}$$

Typically, η is about one-third, so that the neutral point is about one-sixth of the length of the ship abaft the bow.

It can be readily checked (Fig. 13.4) that with a force applied at the neutral point the ship is in a state of steady motion with no change of heading but with a steady lateral velocity, i.e. a steady angle of attack.

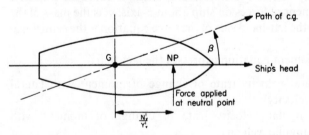
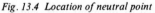

Fig. 13.4 Location of neutral point

When moving at an angle of attack β, lateral velocity $-v$, the non-dimensional hydrodynamic force and moment are vY'_v and vN'_v respectively, i.e. the hydrodynamic force effectively acts at a distance $(N'_v/Y'_v)L$ ahead of the c.g. directly opposing the applied force, so that there is no tendency for the ship's head to change. If the applied force is of magnitude F, then the resulting lateral velocity is

$$v = \frac{F}{Y_v}$$

Until the velocity has built up to this required value, there will be a state of imbalance and during this phase there can arise a change of heading from the initial heading.

It follows, that if the force is applied aft of the neutral point and acts towards port the ship will turn to starboard, and if applied in the same sense forward of the neutral point the ship turns to port. Clearly, the greater the distance of application of the force from the neutral point the greater the turning influence, other things being equal. This explains why rudders are more effective when placed aft. If $\eta = \frac{1}{3}$, then the 'leverage' of a stern rudder is five times that of a bow rudder. At the stern also, the rudders gain from the effect of the screw race.

If, in the equation above for r'/δ_R, $N'_{\delta_R} = x'Y'_{\delta_R}$ then

$$\frac{r'}{\delta_R} \text{ is proportional to } \frac{N'_v}{Y'_v} - x'$$

That is, for a given rudder angle, the rate of change of heading is greatest when the value of x' is large and negative. This again shows that a rudder is most effective when placed right aft.

THE ACTION OF A RUDDER IN TURNING A SHIP

The laws of dynamics demand that when a body is turning in a circle, it must be acted upon by a force acting towards the centre of the circle of sufficient magnitude to impart to the body the required radial acceleration. In the case of a ship, this force can only arise from the aerodynamic and hydrodynamic forces acting on the hull, superstructure and appendages. It is usual, in studying the turning and manoeuvring of ships, to ignore aerodynamic forces for standard manoeuvres and to consider them only as disturbing forces. That is not to say that aerodynamic forces are unimportant. On the contrary, they may prevent a ship turning into the wind if she has large windage areas forward.

To produce a radial force of the magnitude required, the hull itself must be held at an angle of attack to the flow of water past the ship. The rudder force must be capable of holding the ship at this angle of attack; that is, it must be able to overcome the hydrodynamic moments due to the angle of attack and the rotation of the ship. The forces acting on the ship during a steady turn are illustrated in Fig. 13.5 where F_H is the force on the hull and F_R the rudder force. F_H is the resultant of the hydrodynamic forces on the hull due to the angle of attack and the rotation of the ship as it moves around the circle.

If T is the thrust exerted by the propellers and F_H and F_R act at angles α and γ relative to the middle line plane then, for a steady turn with forces acting as shown in Fig. 13.5, these forces must lead to the radial force $\Delta V^2/R$, i.e.

$$T - \frac{\Delta V^2}{R}\sin\beta = F_H\cos\alpha + F_R\cos\gamma$$

$$-\frac{\Delta V^2}{R}\cos\beta + F_H\sin\alpha = F_R\sin\gamma$$

$$F_H\overline{GE} + F_R\overline{GJ} = 0$$

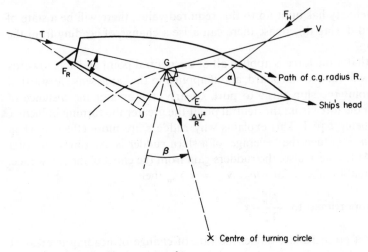

Fig. 13.5 Action of rudder in turning ship

The radial components of the forces on the rudder and the hull, F_R and F_H, must have a resultant causing the radial acceleration.

Consider a ship of 100 MN displacement turning in a circle of 500 m radius at a steady speed of 20 knots. The radial force required is given by

$$\overline{F} = \frac{V^2}{R}\Sigma = \frac{V^2}{R}\frac{\Delta}{g}$$

$$= \frac{100(20 \times \frac{1852}{3600})^2}{500 \times 9.807} = 2.16\,\text{MN}$$

Measurement of manoeuvrability

THE TURNING CIRCLE

Figure 13.6 shows diagrammatically the path of a ship when executing a starboard turn. When the rudder is put over initially, the force acting on the rudder tends to push the ship bodily to port of its original line of advance. As the moment due to the rudder force turns the ship's head, the lateral force on the hull builds up and the ship begins to turn. The parameters at any instant of the turn are defined as:

Drift angle. The drift angle at any point along the length of the ship is defined as the angle between the centre line of the ship and the tangent to the path of the point concerned. When a drift angle is given for the ship without any specific point being defined, the drift angle at the centre of gravity of the ship is usually intended. Note that the bow of the ship lies within the circle and that the drift angle increases with increasing distance aft of the pivoting point which is defined below.

Advance. The distance travelled by the centre of gravity in a direction parallel to the original course after the instant the rudder is put over. There is a value of advance for any point on the circle, but if a figure is quoted for advance with no other qualification the value corresponding to a 90 degree change of heading is usually intended.

Transfer. The distance travelled by the centre of gravity perpendicular to the original course. The transfer of the ship can be given for any point on the circle, but if a figure is quoted for transfer with no other qualification the value corresponding to a 90 degree change of heading is usually intended.

Tactical diameter. The value of the transfer when the ship's heading has changed by 180 degrees. It should be noted that the tactical diameter is not the maximum value of the transfer.

Diameter of steady turning circle. Following initial application of the rudder there is a period of transient motion, but finally the speed, drift angle and turning diameter reach steady values. This usually occurs after about 90 degrees change of heading but, in some cases, the steady state may not be achieved until after 180 degrees change of heading. The steady turning diameter is usually less than the tactical diameter.

Pivoting point. This point is defined as the foot of the perpendicular from the centre of the turn on to the middle line of the ship extended if necessary. This is not a fixed point, but one which varies with rudder angle and speed. It may be forward of the ship as it would be in Fig. 13.6, but is typically one-third to one-sixth of the length of the ship abaft the bow. It should be noted, that the drift angle is zero at the pivoting point and increases with increasing distance from that point.

The turning circle has been a standard manoeuvre carried out by all ships as an indication of the efficiency of the rudder. Apart from what might be termed the 'geometric parameters' of the turning circle defined above loss of speed on turn and angle of heel experienced are also studied.

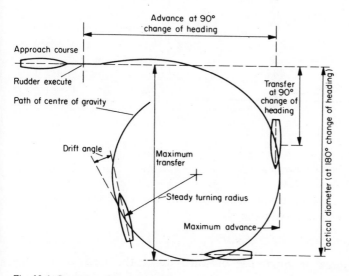

Fig. 13.6 Geometry of turning circle

Loss of speed on turn

As discussed above, the rudder holds the hull at an angle of attack, i.e. the drift angle, in order to develop the 'lift' necessary to cause the ship to accelerate towards the centre of the turn. As with any other streamlined form, hull lift can be produced only at the expense of increased drag. Unless the engine settings are changed, therefore, the ship will decelerate under the action of this increased drag. Most ships reach a new steady speed by the time the heading has changed 90 degrees but, in some cases, the slowing down process continues until about 180 degrees change of heading.

Angle of heel when turning

When turning steadily, the forces acting on the hull and rudder are F_H and F_R. Denoting the radial components of these forces by lower case subscripts (i.e. denoting these by F_h and F_r respectively) and referring to Fig. 13.7, it is seen that to produce the turn

$$F_h - F_r = \frac{\Delta V^2}{Rg}$$

where V = speed on the turn, R = radius of turn.

$$\begin{aligned}
\text{Moment causing heel} &= (F_h - F_r)\overline{KG} + F_r(\overline{KH}) - F_h(\overline{KE}) \\
&= (F_h - F_r)(\overline{KG} - \overline{KE}) + F_r(\overline{KH} - \overline{KE}) \\
&= (F_h - F_r)\overline{GE} - F_r\overline{EH}
\end{aligned}$$

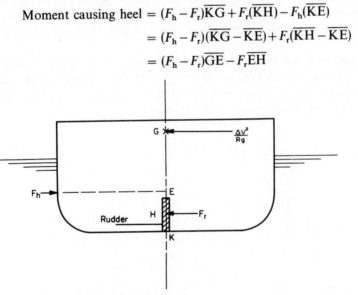

Fig. 13.7 Forces producing heel when turning

For most ships, E, the centre of lateral resistance, and H are very close and this expression is given approximately by

$$\text{Moment causing heel} = (F_h - F_r)\overline{GE}$$

This moment causes the ship to heel outwards during the steady turn. When the rudder is initially put over, however, F_r acts before F_h has built up to any significant value and during this transient phase the ship may heel inwards. It should also be noted that the effect of F_r during the steady turn is to reduce the angle of heel, so that if the rudder angle is suddenly taken off, the ship will heel to even larger angles. If the rudder angle were to be suddenly reversed even more serious angles of heel could occur.

It will be appreciated that F_h acts at the centre of lateral resistance only if the angle of heel is small. For large heel angles, the position of E is difficult to assess. For small angles of heel

$$\Delta \overline{GM} \sin \phi = (F_h - F_r)\overline{GE}$$

$$= \frac{\Delta V^2}{Rg}\overline{GE}$$

Hence

$$\frac{Rg \sin \phi}{V^2} = \frac{\overline{GE}}{\overline{GM}}$$

It must be emphasized, however, that the angle of heel obtained by this type of calculation should only be regarded as approximate. Apart from the difficulty of accurately locating E, some ships, particularly high speed vessels, suffer an apparent loss of stability when underway because of the other forces acting on the ship and appendages due to the flow around the ship when it is turning. Reference 1 refers to destroyers which 'take a more pronounced heel when making turns than would be expected from their transverse stability characteristics'. In Ref. 2, Coles mentions that British destroyers built in the 1930s experienced greater heel than the theoretical expression above indicates for speeds up to about 25 knots, but that above that speed the heel was rather less.

EXAMPLE 1. A vessel turns in a radius of 300 m at a speed of 20 knots under the action of a rudder force of 1·5 MN. If the draught of the ship is 5 m, $\overline{KG}$ is 6 m and $\overline{GM}$ is 2 m, find the approximate angle of heel during the steady turn.

Solution : Let displacement of ship be ΔMN

Radial force required to cause ship to turn

$$= \frac{\Delta(20 \times \frac{1852}{3600})^2}{300 \times 9·807}\text{ MN}$$

Assume that $\overline{KE}$ will be approximately $\frac{5}{2} = 2·5$ m. Then $\overline{GE} = 3·5$ m and

$$\Delta\text{MN}(2\text{ m}) \sin \phi = \frac{\Delta\left(\dfrac{20 \times 1852}{3600}\right)^2}{300 \times 9·807} \times 3·5$$

$$\therefore \quad \sin \phi = 0·063$$

$$\phi = 3\tfrac{1}{2}° \text{ approx.}$$

THE ZIG-ZAG MANOEUVRE

It can be argued that it is not often that a ship requires to execute more than say a 90 or 180 degree change of heading. On the other hand, it often has to turn through angles of 10, 20 or 30 degrees. It can also be argued that in an emergency, such as realization that a collision is imminent, it is the initial response of a ship to rudder movements that is the critical factor. Unfortunately, the standard circle manoeuvre does not adequately define this initial response and the standard values of transfer and advance for 90 degrees change of heading and tactical diameter are often affected but little by factors which have a significant influence on initial response to rudder. Such a factor is the rate at which the rudder angle is applied. This may be typically 3 degrees per second. Doubling this rate leads to only a marginally smaller tactical diameter but initial rates of turn will be increased significantly.

The zig-zag manoeuvre, sometimes called a Kempf manoeuvre after G. Kempf, is carried out to study more closely the initial response of a ship to rudder movements (see Fig. 13.8). A typical manoeuvre would be as follows. With the ship proceeding at a steady speed on a straight course the rudder is put over to 20 degrees and held until the ship's heading changes by 20 degrees. The rudder angle is then changed to 20 degrees in the opposite sense and so on.

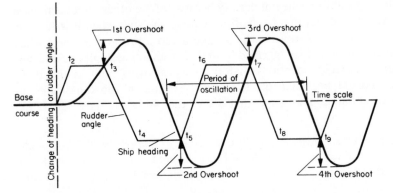

Fig. 13.8 The zig-zag manoeuvre

Important parameters of this manoeuvre are:

(a) the time between successive rudder movements;
(b) the *overshoot* angle which is the amount by which the ship's heading exceeds the 20 degree deviation before reducing.

The manoeuvre is repeated for a range of approach speeds and for different values of the rudder angle and heading deviation.

THE SPIRAL MANOEUVRE

This manoeuvre, sometimes referred to as the Dieudonné Spiral after J. Dieudonné who first suggested it, provides an indication of a ship's directional stability or instability.

To perform this manoeuvre, the rudder is put over to say 15 degrees star-board and the ship is allowed to turn until a steady rate of change of heading is achieved. This rate is noted and the rudder angle is reduced to 10 degrees and the new steady rate of change of heading is measured. Successive rudder angles of 5°S, 0°, 5°P, 10°P, 15°P, 10°P, 5°P, 0°, 5°S, 10°S and 15°S are then used. Thus, the steady rate of change of heading is recorded for each rudder angle when the rudder angle is approached both from above and from below. The results are plotted as in Fig. 13.9, in which case (*a*) represents a stable ship and case (*b*) an unstable ship.

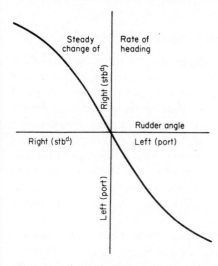

Fig. 13.9(a) Presentation of spiral manoeuvre results (stable ship)

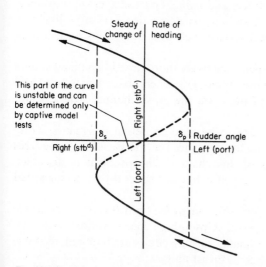

Fig. 13.9(b) Presentation of spiral manoeuvre results (unstable ship)

In the case of the stable ship, there is a unique rate of change of heading for each rudder angle but, in the case of an unstable ship, the plot exhibits a form of 'hysteresis' loop. That is to say that for small rudder angles the rate of change of heading depends upon whether the rudder angle is increasing or decreasing. That part of the curve shown dotted in the figure cannot be determined from ship trials or free model tests as it represents an unstable condition.

It is not possible to deduce the degree of instability from the spiral manoeuvre, but the size of the loop is a qualitative guide to this. Of direct practical significance, it should be noted that it cannot be said with certainty that the ship will turn to starboard or port unless the rudder angle applied exceeds δ_S or δ_P, respectively.

STANDARDS FOR MANOEUVRING AND DIRECTIONAL STABILITY

The standards required in any particular design depend upon the service for which the ship is intended but, in any case, they are not easy to define. The problem is made more difficult by the fact that good directional stability and good manoeuvrability are to some extent conflicting requirements, although they are not actually incompatible as has often been suggested. For instance, a large rudder can increase the directional stability and also improve turning performance. Also, in a long fine form increasing draught-to-length ratio can increase stability without detriment to the turning. On the other hand, increasing beam-to-length ratio improves turning but reduces the directional stability. Placing a large skeg aft will improve directional stability at the expense of poorer turning ability.

For a large ocean-going ship, it is usually possible to assume that tugs will be available to assist her when manoeuvring in the confined waters of a harbour. The emphasis in design is therefore usually placed on good directional stability for the long ocean transits. This leads to less wear on the rudder gear, especially if an automatic control system is fitted, and reduces overall average resistance. The highest degree of directional stability is demanded for ships likely to suffer disturbances in their normal service such as supply ships replenishing smaller naval units at sea.

For medium size ships which spend relatively more time in confined waters and which do not normally make use of tugs, greater emphasis has to be placed on response to rudder. Typical of these are the cross channel steamers and anti-submarine frigates.

What are the parameters that are to be used to define the manoeuvring capabilities? They are those parameters measured in the various manoeuvres described in the earlier sections of this chapter. The problem is discussed in Ref. 3 and the quantitative data given below are generally those suggested by these authors.

Tactical diameter-to-length ratio. For ships in which tight turning is desirable this may be, say, 3·25 for modern naval ships at high speed, with conventional rudders at 35 degrees. Where even smaller turning circles are required, recourse is usually made to some form of lateral thrust unit.

A *T.D./L* value of 4·5 is suggested as a practicable criterion for merchant types desiring good handling performance. Values of this ratio exceeding 7 are regarded as very poor.

Turning rate. For very manoeuvrable naval ships this may be as high as 3 degrees per second. For merchant types, rates of up to $1\frac{1}{2}$ degrees per second should be achieved in ships of about 100 m at 16 knots, but generally values of 0·5–1·0 degrees per second are more typical.

Speed on turn. This can be appreciably lower than the approach speed, and typically is only some 60 per cent of the latter. This in itself is a very good reason for not using large rudder angles unless the operational situation demands it. Particularly in ships with low shaft horsepower, the time to accelerate back to speed again can be appreciable.

Angle of heel. A very important factor in passenger ships and one which may influence the standard of transverse stability incorporated in the design.

Directional stability. Clearly, an important factor in a well balanced design. The inequality presented earlier as the criterion for directional stability can be used as a 'stability index'. Unfortunately, this is not, by itself, very informative. A reasonable design aim is that the spiral manoeuvre should exhibit no 'loop', i.e. the design should be stable even if only marginally so.

Time to turn through 20 degrees. This provides a measure of the initial response of the ship to the application of rudder. Ships with similar turning diameters can vary appreciably in their initial response. For instance, tactical diameter is not influenced very much by the rate at which rudder is applied but initial response generally is. It is suggested that the time to reach 20 degrees might typically vary from 80 to 30 seconds for speeds of 6–20 knots for a 150 m ship. The time will vary approximately linearly with ship length.

Overshoot. The overshoot depends on the rate of turn and a ship that turns well will overshoot more than one that does not turn well. If the overshoot is excessive, it will be difficult for a helmsman to judge when to start reducing rudder to check a turn with the possible danger of damage due to collision with other ships or a jetty. The overshoot angle does not depend upon the ship size and values suggested are 5·5 degrees for 8 knots and 8·5 degrees for 16 knots, the variation being approximately linear with speed.

Rudder forces and torques

RUDDER FORCE

The rudder, being of streamlined cross-section, will be acted upon by a lift and drag force when held at an angle of attack relative to the flow of water. The rudder must be designed to produce maximum lift for minimum drag assuming that the lift behaves in a consistent manner for all likely angles of attack. The lift developed depends upon:

(a) The cross-sectional shape;
(b) The area of the rudder, A_R;
(c) The profile shape of the rudder and, in particular, the aspect ratio of the rudder, i.e. the ratio of the depth of the rudder to its chord length;

(*d*) The square of the velocity of the water past the rudder;
(*e*) The density of the water, ρ;
(*f*) The angle of attack, α.

Hence, the rudder force F_R, can be represented by

$$F_R = \text{Constant} \times \rho A_R V^2 f(\alpha)$$

the value of the constant depending upon the cross-sectional and profile shapes of the rudder. A typical plot for $f(\alpha)$ is as shown in Fig. 13.10.

At first, $f(\alpha)$ increases approximately linearly with angle of attack but then the rate of growth decreases and further increase in α may produce an actual fall in the value of $f(\alpha)$. This phenomenon is known as *stalling*.

Typically, for ships' rudders, stalling occurs at an angle between 35 and 45 degrees. Most ship rudders are limited to 35 degrees to avoid stall, loss of speed and large heel on turn. Stall is related to the flow relative to the rudder; in turning the water flow is no longer aligned with the ship's hull but across the stern, thereby allowing larger rudder angles before stall occurs than are possible when the rudder is first put over. This cross-flow affects also wake and propeller performance.

Many formulae have been suggested for calculating the forces on rudders. One of the older formulae is

$$\text{Force} = 1{\cdot}12 \, A_R V^2 \sin(\delta_R) \text{ lbf}$$

where A_R is measured in ft^2 and V is measured in ft/s.

If A_R is measured in m^2 and V in m/s, the formula becomes:

$$\text{Force} = 577 \, A_R V^2 \sin(\delta_R) \text{ newtons}$$

V being the velocity of water past the rudder, allowance must be made for the propeller race in augmenting the ship's ahead speed. Typical values assumed are:

Rudder behind propeller, $V = 1{\cdot}3 \times$ (Ship speed)

Centre-line rudder behind twin screws, $V = 1{\cdot}2 \times$ (Ship speed).

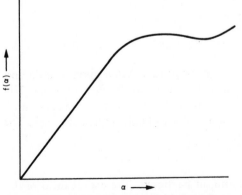

Fig. 13.10 Variation of $f(\alpha)$ with angle of attack

Reference 4 gave the following formulae for twin rudders behind wing propellers:

Ahead motion: Force $= 0.041\,A_R V^2\,\delta_R$ lbf

Astern motion: Force $= 0.037\,A_R V^2\,\delta_R$ lbf

where A_R is measured in ft^2, V is measured in ft/s, and δ_R is measured in degrees. In metric units, the formulae become:

Force $= 21.1\,A_R V^2\,\delta_R$ newtons, for ahead motion

Force $= 19.1\,A_R V^2\,\delta_R$ newtons, for astern motion

Using the same parameters, Baker and Bottomley have suggested that for middle line rudders behind single screws

Force $= 0.035\,A_R V^2\,\delta_R$ lbf

In metric units:

Force $= 18.0\,A_R V^2\,\delta_R$ newtons

In these formulae V is taken as the true speed of the ship, allowance having been made in the multiplying factors for the propeller race effects.

More comprehensive formulae are given in Ref. 5 based on extensive experimental and theoretical work. It is recommended that for naval applications all-movable control surfaces be used with square tips, NACA 0015 sections and a moderately swept quarter chord line. Figure 13.11 illustrates a typical control surface and gives the offsets for the NACA 0015 section, in terms of the chord c and distance x from the nose.

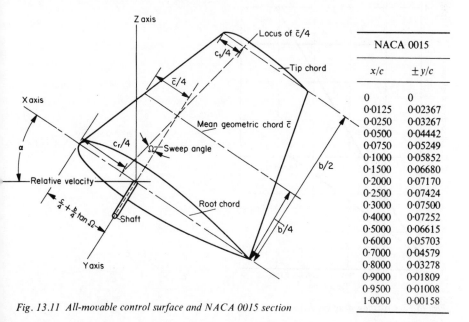

NACA 0015	
x/c	$\pm y/c$
0	0
0·0125	0·02367
0·0250	0·03267
0·0500	0·04442
0·0750	0·05249
0·1000	0·05852
0·1500	0·06680
0·2000	0·07170
0·2500	0·07424
0·3000	0·07500
0·4000	0·07252
0·5000	0·06615
0·6000	0·05703
0·7000	0·04579
0·8000	0·03278
0·9000	0·01809
0·9500	0·01008
1·0000	0·00158

Fig. 13.11 All-movable control surface and NACA 0015 section

The formulae recommended are:

$$C_L = \frac{\text{Lift}}{\frac{1}{2}\rho A V^2} = \left[\frac{a_0 a_e}{\cos \Omega \left(\dfrac{a_e^2}{\cos^4 \Omega} + 4 \right)^{\frac{1}{2}} + \dfrac{57 \cdot 3 a_0}{\pi}} \right] \alpha + \frac{C_{D_c}}{a_e} \left(\frac{\alpha}{57 \cdot 3} \right)^2$$

where

a_e = effective aspect ratio = (span)²/(planform area)
a_0 = section lift curve slope at $\alpha = 0$
   = 0·9 $(2\pi/57\cdot3)$ per degree for NACA 0015
C_{D_c} = crossflow drag coefficient (Fig. 13.12)
   = 0·80 for square tips and taper ratio = 0·45

and

$$C_D = \frac{\text{Drag}}{\frac{1}{2}\rho A V^2} = C_{d_0} + \frac{C_L^2}{0 \cdot 9 \pi a_e}$$

where

C_{d_0} = minimum section drag coefficient
   = 0·0065   for   NACA 0015.

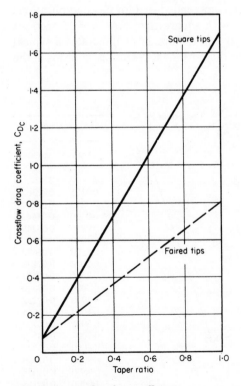

Fig. 13.12 *Crossflow drag coefficient*

CENTRE OF PRESSURE POSITION

It has been seen that it is the rudder force which is important in causing a ship to turn, as the lever of the rudder force from the neutral point is not significantly affected by the position of the centre of pressure on the rudder itself. However, it is necessary to know the torque acting on the rudder to ensure that the steering gear installed in the ship is capable of turning the rudder at all speeds.

For a flat plate, Joessel suggested an empirical formula for the proportion of the breadth of the plate that the centre of pressure is abaft the leading edge and expressed it as:

$$0 \cdot 195 + 0 \cdot 305 \sin(\alpha)$$

For rudders, the geometry of the cross-section will have an influence upon the centre of pressure position. Reference 4 considered that for a rectangular rudder behind a fin or skeg the centre of pressure is $0 \cdot 35$ times the chord length abaft the leading edge. For a rudder in open water this value is reduced to $0 \cdot 31$. For motion astern the rudder is always effectively in clear water and the figure of $0 \cdot 31$ is used in both cases and measured relative to the after edge of the rudder.

Reference 5 recommends a torque (pitching moment) coefficient

$$C_{\mathrm{T}} = \frac{\text{torque}}{\frac{1}{2}\rho A V^2 \bar{c}} = \left[0 \cdot 25 - \left(\frac{\partial C_{\mathrm{m}}}{\partial C_{\mathrm{L}}}\right)_{C_{\mathrm{L}}=0} \right] \left(\frac{\partial C_{\mathrm{L}}}{\partial \alpha}\right)_{C_{\mathrm{L}}=0} \alpha - \frac{1}{2}\frac{C_{\mathrm{D_e}}}{a_{\mathrm{e}}}\left(\frac{\alpha}{57 \cdot 3}\right)^2$$

where

$$\bar{c} = \text{mean geometric chord} = \frac{c_{\mathrm{t}} + c_{\mathrm{r}}}{2}$$

$$\left(\frac{\partial C_{\mathrm{m}}}{\partial C_{\mathrm{L}}}\right)_{C_{\mathrm{L}}=0} \quad \text{and} \quad \left(\frac{\partial C_{\mathrm{L}}}{\partial \alpha}\right)_{C_{\mathrm{L}}=0}$$

are defined in Fig. 13.13.

Torque is measured about the quarter-chord point of the mean geometric chord.

The centre of pressure is defined chordwise and spanwise by the following relationships:

Chordwise from leading edge at the mean geometric chord (as percentage of the mean geometric chord),

$$= 0 \cdot 25 - \frac{C_{\mathrm{T}}}{C_{\mathrm{L}} \cos \alpha + C_{\mathrm{D}} \sin \alpha}$$

Spanwise measured from the plane of the root section (as percentage of the semi-span):

$$= \frac{C_{\mathrm{L}}\left(\frac{4}{3\pi}\frac{b}{2}\right)\cos \alpha + C_{\mathrm{D}}\left(\frac{b}{2}\right)\sin \alpha}{\frac{b}{2}(C_{\mathrm{L}} \cos \alpha + C_{\mathrm{D}} \sin \alpha)}$$

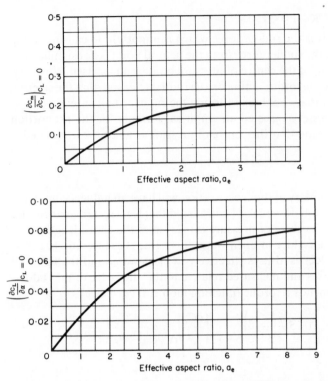

Fig. 13.13 Variation of chordwise centre of pressure and lift curve slope with aspect ratio

Typical curves for a NACA 0015 section control surface are reproduced in Fig. 13.14.

In the absence of any better guide, the figures quoted above should be used in estimating rudder forces and torques. However, because of the dependence of both force and centre of pressure on the rudder geometry it is recommended that actual data for a similar rudder be used whenever it is available. In many instances, rudders have sections based on standard aerofoil sections and, in this case, use should be made of the published curves for lift and centre of pressure positions making due allowance for the effect of propellers and the presence of the hull on the velocity of flow over the rudder.

In practice, the picture is complicated by the fact that the flow of water at the stern of a ship is not uniform and may be at an angle to the rudders when set nominally amidships. For this reason, it is quite common practice to carry out model experiments to determine the hydrodynamic force and torque acting on the rudder. As a result of such tests, it may be deemed prudent to set the rudders of a twin rudder ship at an angle to the middle line plane of the ship for their 'amidships' position.

CALCULATION OF FORCE AND TORQUE ON NON-RECTANGULAR RUDDER

It is seldom that a ship rudder is a simple rectangle. For other shapes the rudder profile is divided into a convenient number of strips. The force and centre of

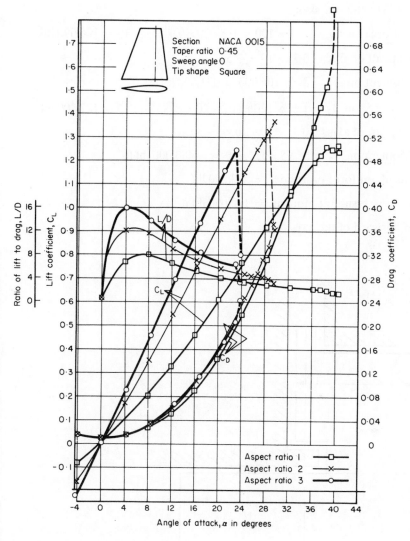

Fig. 13.14 Lift and drag for NACA 0015 sections

pressure are assessed for each strip and the overall force and torque obtained by summating the individual forces and torques.

EXAMPLE 2. Calculate the force and torque on the centre line gnomon rudder shown, Fig. 13.15, for 35 degrees and a ship speed of 20 knots. The ship is fitted with twin screws.

Solution: The rudder can conveniently be divided into two rectangular areas A_1 and A_2, A_1 being the smaller. Applying the older formula for force and Gawn's formulae for c.p. position (Ref. 4) (see page 493),

Area A_1 is behind a skeg

∴   Force on $A_1 = 1\cdot12 \times 100 \times (1\cdot2 \times 20 \times \frac{6080}{3600})^2 \sin 35 = 106{,}000$ lbf.

c.p. aft of axis $= 0\cdot35 \times 10 = 3\cdot5$ ft

Moment on $A_1 = 3\cdot5 \times 106{,}000 = 371{,}000$ lbf ft

Force on $A_2 = 1\cdot12 \times 120 \times (1\cdot2 \times 20 \times \frac{6080}{3600})^2 \sin 35 = 127{,}200$ lbf ft

c.p. aft of axis $= 0\cdot31 \times 20 - 10 = -3\cdot8$ ft

Moment on $A_2 = -3\cdot8 \times 127{,}200 = -483{,}000$ lbf ft

Hence resultant force on rudder $= 233{,}200$ lbf

resultant moment $= 112{,}000$ lbf ft

with c.p. forward of the axis.

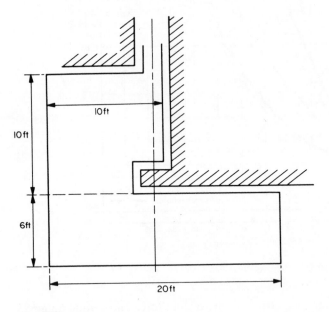

Fig. 13.15

EXAMPLE 3. Calculate the force and torque on the spade rudder shown in Fig. 13.16, which is one of two working behind twin propellers. Assume a rudder angle of 35 degrees and a ship speed of 20 knots ahead. If the stock is solid with a section modulus in bending of $0\cdot1$ m³, calculate the maximum stress due to the combined torque and bending moment.

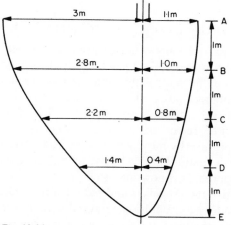

Fig. 13.16

Solution: Assuming that the force on the rudder is given by $21 \cdot 1 \ A_R V^2 \delta_R$ newtons, that the c.p. is $0 \cdot 31 \times$ the chord length aft of the leading edge and that the force acts at the same vertical position as the centroid of area of the rudder.

Level	Total chord length (m)	S.M.	F(area)	Lever below stock	F(moment)	c.p. aft of leading edge	c.p. aft of axis	F(torque)
A	4·1	1	4·1	0	0·0	1·27	0·17	0·70
B	3·8	4	15·2	1	15·2	1·18	0·18	2·74
C	3·0	2	6·0	2	12·0	0·93	0·13	0·78
D	1·8	4	7·2	3	21·6	0·56	0·16	1·15
E	0	1	0	4	0·0	0·00	0·00	0·00
			32·5		48·8			5·37

Area of rudder $= \frac{1}{3} \times 1 \times 32 \cdot 5 = 10 \cdot 83 \text{ m}^2$

c.p. aft of axis $5 \cdot 37/32 \cdot 5 = 0 \cdot 165$ m

c.p. below stock $= \dfrac{48 \cdot 8}{32 \cdot 5} = 1 \cdot 502$ m.

Force on rudder $= 21 \cdot 1 \times 10 \cdot 83 \times \left(\dfrac{20 \times 1852}{3600} \right)^2 \times 35 = 847{,}000$ newtons

Bending moment at stock $= 847{,}000 \times 1 \cdot 502 = 1 \cdot 272$ MN m.
Torque on rudder $= 0 \cdot 165 \times 847{,}000 = 140{,}000$ N m

The combined effect of the bending moment M and torque T is equivalent to a bending moment M' given by

$$M' = \tfrac{1}{2}(M + \sqrt{M^2 + T^2})$$

hence $M' = 1 \cdot 276$ MN m

Max stress $= M'/Z = 1 \cdot 276/0 \cdot 1 = 12 \cdot 76 \text{ MN/m}^2.$

Experiments and trials

MODEL EXPERIMENTS CONCERNED WITH TURNING AND MANOEUVRING

For accurate prediction of ship behaviour, the model must represent as closely as possible the ship and its operating condition. The model ideally then must be self-propelled, the rudder angle must be controllable and the model's behaviour must be recorded by either internal or external instruments. In some early experiments, a human operator was carried to operate the rudder. This made it difficult to achieve the correct degree of stability and, in any case, the operator tended to correct the heel on turn by movements of his body. Even if heel is not being studied, changing the natural heel will have an influence on the other parameters of the ship response. It is now the usual practice to use battery powered electric motors to drive the propellers and radio control links for rudder and motor control. The model self-propulsion point is different from that for the ship due to Reynolds' number effects, and the response characteristics of the model and ship propulsion systems differ but the errors arising from these causes are likely to be small. They do, however, underline the importance of obtaining reliable correlation with ship trials.

Both the National Physical Laboratory and the Admiralty Experiment Works (Ref. 6) in recent years have added to their facilities large tanks which have the ability to test the turning and manoeuvring performance of models. Other tanks are being set up throughout the world. The facilities offered at the various tanks differ but the following is a brief description of those provided by the Manoeuvring Tank at the Admiralty Experiment Works, Haslar. The basin is 400 ft long and 200 ft wide with overhead camera positions for recording photographically the path of the model. The models are typically 16 ft long, radio controlled and fitted with gyros for sensing heel. Lights are set up on the model at bow and stern so that when the model is underway they lie in a known datum plane. These lights are photographed using a multiple exposure technique so that the path of the model can be recorded on a single negative. When enlarged to a standard scale, the print has a grid superimposed upon it to enable the co-ordinates of the light positions to be read off and the drift angle deduced. As exposures are taken at fixed time intervals, the speed of the model during the turn can be deduced besides the turning path. The heel angle is recorded within the model. The process is illustrated diagrammatically in Fig. 13.17.

The same recording techniques can be used to record the behaviour of a model when carrying out zig-zag or spiral manoeuvres or any other special manoeuvres which require a knowledge of the path of the model. Two points have to be borne in mind, however, if a human operator is used as one element of the control system. One, is that being remote from the model the experimenter has to rely upon instruments to tell him how the model is reacting. He cannot sense the movements of the ship directly through his sense of balance and hence his reactions to a given situation may differ from those in a ship. The second point is that the time he has to react is less. Because Froude's law of comparison applies, the time factor is reduced in proportion to the square root of the scale factor, i.e. if the model is to a scale of $\frac{1}{36}$th full size, permissible reaction times

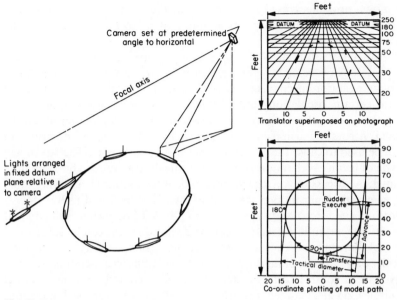

Fig. 13.17

will be reduced to $\frac{1}{6}$th of those applying to the helmsman on the ship. In the same way, the rate at which the rudder is applied must be increased to six times that full scale. It follows that, whenever possible, it is desirable to use an automatic control system or, failing this, a programmed sequence of rudder orders in order to ensure consistency of results.

By using suitable instrumentation, the rudder forces and torques can be measured during any of these manoeuvres. Typically, the rudder stock is strain gauged to record the force and its line of action.

MODEL EXPERIMENTS CONCERNED WITH DIRECTIONAL STABILITY

It has been seen that spiral manoeuvres can be used to determine whether a ship is directionally stable or not. The same applies to the model but, although the size of the 'loop' can provide some rough qualitative guide to the degree of instability, there is no way at all of determining the degree of stability of a directionally stable ship from this type of manoeuvre.

It is necessary, therefore, to carry out experiments in which the derivatives of force and moment described earlier can be measured. Consider first the derivatives of force and moment with respect to transverse velocity (or yaw angle). These can be measured in a conventional long ship tank by measuring the forces and moments required to hold the model at various yaw angles over a range of speeds. In this work, it is usually assumed that the forces and moments measured on the model can be scaled directly to full scale using the Froude law of comparison. It is possible that some part of these quantities is dependent on Reynolds' number but, at the present time, not enough is known to enable this refinement to be made. Such tests are usually carried out both with and without model propellers fitted and working, as the changed velocity distribution at the stern due to the propeller action is likely to be significant and its effect can be deduced in this way.

The so-called curvature derivatives, i.e. those of side force and yaw moment with respect to yaw velocity, can be measured in conventional ship tanks using a planar motion mechanism (Ref. 7). Basically, the model is constrained to execute certain oscillations and the forces and moments measured. By analysing these data, the derivatives and various cross-coupling terms can be determined. A rotating arm facility such as that at AEW, Haslar, described in Ref. 6 can be used to cause the model to move in a circular path. The advantage of this type of facility is that non-linearities in the derivatives can be more fully investigated. A discussion on constrained model testing using a towing tank, rotating arm and planar motion mechanism tests is to be found in Ref. 14.

By plotting side force and yaw moment to a base of transverse velocity and yaw velocity the required derivatives can be deduced. These can be substituted in the simple formulae already quoted to demonstrate stability and position of neutral point. More commonly, the data, including cross-coupling terms, derivatives from control surfaces, etc., are fed into computers which predict turning circles, zig-zag manoeuvres, etc. The validity of this approach is demonstrated in Fig. 13.18 which is taken from Ref. 8.

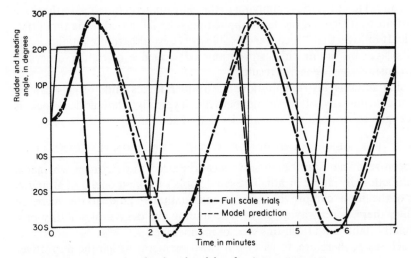

Fig. 13.18 Comparison of trial and predicted data for zig-zag manoeuvre

SHIP TRIALS

The credibility of theoretical or model experimental methods for predicting the manoeuvring characteristics of ships depends on establishing reliable correlation with the full-scale ship. Reference 14 states that although there is not an exact correspondence of trajectories, there is sufficient correlation between model and ship to believe that the behaviour of the model represents the behaviour of the ship. Several methods can be used for recording the path of a ship at sea including

(*a*) a log to measure ship speed and a compass to record the ship's head. It is approximate only as most logs are inaccurate when the ship turns;
(*b*) use of a theodolite or camera overlooking the trial area. Limited by the depth of water available close in shore;
(*c*) the use of a navigational aid such as the Decca system to record the ship's position at known intervals of time. For accurate results the trials area must be one which is covered by a close grid;
(*d*) the use of bearing recorders at each end of the ship to record the bearings of a buoy. This is the method generally used by the Admiralty Experiment Works, Haslar.

With a series of refinements it has been developed into a very reliable and accurate system. Among the refinements should be mentioned the use of a specially designed buoy which moves with the wind and tide in a manner representative of the ship, and the use of automatic recording of bearing angles with cameras to correct human errors in tracking the buoy. In addition to the bearings of the buoy, records are taken of ship's head, shaft r.p.m., rudder angle and heel angle all to a common time base which is synchronized with the bearing records.

The arrangement of the trials equipment in the ship is illustrated in Fig. 13.19.

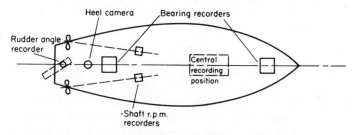

Fig. 13.19 Arrangement of turning trials equipment on board ship

Analysis of turning trials results

Having developed the film records, all of which have a common time base, the bearing of the buoy from each recorder is plotted to a base of ship heading. From this plot, the bearings at every 30 degrees (or any other desired angular spacing) can be obtained. These are then set out relative to a base line representing the distance apart of the two recorders as in Fig. 13.20, where α and β are the two bearings appropriate to 120 degrees change of heading. From the intersection of the two bearing lines a perpendicular $\overline{CD}$ is dropped on to the base line. Then $\overline{CD}$ and $\overline{DG}$ define the position of the buoy relative to the G of the ship and the ship's centre line. Turning now to the right hand plot in Fig. 13.20, radial lines are set out from a fixed point which represents the buoy and the position of the ship for 120 degrees change of heading is set out as indicated.

This process is repeated for each change of heading and the locus of the G position defines the turning path. The drift angle follows as the angle between the tangent to this path and the centre line of the ship. Information on rates of turn is obtained by reference to the time base.

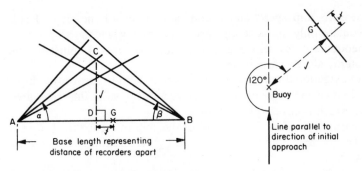

Fig. 13.20 Analysis of turning trial data

Angle of heel is recorded by photographing the ensign staff against the horizon or using a vertical seeking gyro.

Ship trials involving zig-zag and spiral manoeuvres do not require a knowledge of the path of the ship. Records are limited to rudder angle and ship's head to a common time base. The difficulty of recording the spiral manoeuvre for an unstable ship has already been mentioned. Only the two branches of the curve shown in full in Fig. 13.9(*b*) can be defined.

Rudder types and systems

TYPES OF RUDDER

There are many types of rudder fitted to ships throughout the world. Many are of limited application and the claims for a novel type of rudder should be critically examined against the operational use envisaged for the ship. For instance, some rudders are only of benefit in single screw ships of relatively low speed. It is not possible to cover all the types of rudder in a book such as this and discussion is limited to the four types illustrated in Fig. 13.21.

The choice of rudder type depends upon the shape of the stern, the size of rudder required and the capacity of the steering gear available.

The *balanced spade rudder* is adopted where the ship has a long cut up, the rudder size is not so great as to make the strength of the rudder stock too severe a problem and where it is desired to keep the steering gear as compact as possible.

The *gnomon rudder* is used where the size of rudder requires that it be supported at an additional point to the rudder bearing, but where it is still desired to partially balance the rudder to reduce the size of the steering gear.

Unbalanced rudders are used where the stern shape precludes the fitting of a balanced rudder. The number of pintles fitted is dictated by strength considerations.

BOW RUDDERS AND LATERAL THRUST UNITS

Why should it be necessary to consider bow rudders at all? It has been shown that if a lateral force is applied at the neutral point a ship follows a straight path at an angle of attack, the angle of attack depending on the magnitude of the

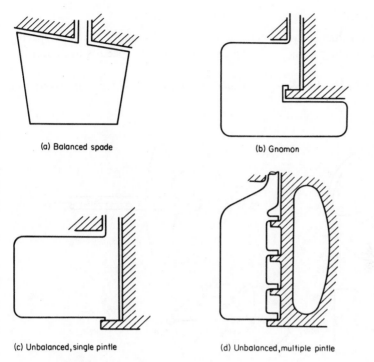

(a) Balanced spade

(b) Gnomon

(c) Unbalanced, single pintle

(d) Unbalanced, multiple pintle

Fig. 13.21 Rudder types

force. Thus, it would be of considerable use to a navigator if he could cause a force to be applied at any selected point along the ship's length, i.e. he could control ship's head and path independently. This could be achieved if control surfaces were fitted at both ends of the ship.

Also, if the only rudders fitted are those aft there is a greater danger that damage could render the ship uncontrollable. This is particularly important in wartime when ships are liable to be attacked by weapons homing on the propellers.

Against these considerations it must be remembered that because the neutral point is generally fairly well forward rudders at the bow are relatively much less effective. Neither can they benefit from the effects of the screw race. Unless they are well forward and therefore exposed to damage, the flow conditions over the bow rudder are unlikely to be good. These factors generally outweigh the possible advantages given above and only a few bow rudders as such are fitted to ships in service.

To some extent, these disadvantages can be overcome by fitting a lateral thrust unit at the bow. Typically, such a device is a propeller in a transverse tube. Reference 10 showed that, based on model data, the effect of these units may be seriously reduced when the ship has forward speed. The fall in side force amounted to nearly 50 per cent at 2 knots, 40 per cent occurring between 1 and 2 knots. Placing the unit further aft reduces the effect of forward speed. Contra-rotating propeller systems are recommended for lateral thrust units.

SPECIAL RUDDERS AND MANOEUVRING DEVICES

It has been seen that conventional rudders are of limited use at low speeds. One way of providing a manoeuvring capability at low speed is to deflect the propeller race.

This is achieved in the *Kitchen rudder*, the action of which is illustrated in Fig. 13.22.

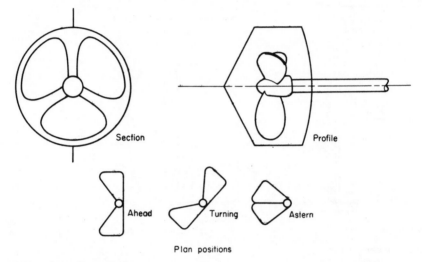

Section   Profile

Ahead   Turning   Astern

Plan positions

Fig. 13.22 Kitchen rudder action

The rudder consists essentially of two curved plates shrouding the propeller. For going ahead fast, the two plates are more or less parallel with the propeller race causing little interference. When both plates are turned in plan, they cause the propeller race to be deflected so producing a lateral thrust. When the two plates are turned so as to close in the space behind the propeller, they cause the ahead thrust to be progressively reduced in magnitude and finally to be transformed into an astern thrust albeit a somewhat inefficient one. The same principle is used for jet deflectors in modern high speed aircraft.

The Kitchen rudder is used mainly for small power boats. It will be appreciated from the above, that not only can it provide lateral thrust at low ahead speed but that it can also be used to vary the magnitude and/or sense of the propeller thrust. Thus in a boat so fitted the shafts can be left running at constant speed.

An alternative to using deflector plates to deflect the propeller race would be to turn the propeller disc itself. This is the principle of the Pleuger *active rudder* which is a streamlined body actually mounted on a rudder, the body containing an electric motor driving a small propeller. To gain full advantage of such a system, the rudder should be capable of turning through larger angles than the conventional 35 degrees.

The power of the unit varies, with the particular ship application, between about 50 and 300 h.p. With the ship at rest, the system can turn the ship in its own length.

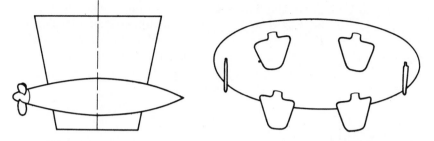

Fig. 13.23(a) Active rudder   Fig. 13.23(b) Voith-Schneider propeller

A different principle is applied in the *vertical axis propeller* such as the *Voith-Schneider propeller*, Fig. 13.23(b). This consists essentially of a horizontal disc carrying a number of vertical blades of aerofoil shape.

As the horizontal disc is rotated about a vertical axis, a special mechanism feathers the blades in such a way as to provide a thrust in any desired direction. The thrust is caused to act fore and aft for normal propulsion and athwartships for steering. The limitation of this type of propeller is the power which can be transmitted to the disc. In some cases, they are fitted specially for manoeuvring as in the case of the two units fitted to the German aircraft carrier *Graf Zeppelin* for negotiating the Kiel Canal. These units were placed well forward and each had an input of 450 hp and a diameter of 1600 mm.

Many special rudder forms have been developed over the years. Claims are made for each type of special advantages over more conventional rudder types. Such claims should be carefully examined to ensure that the advantages will be forthcoming for the particular application in mind as, in most cases, this is only so if certain special conditions of speed or ship form apply.

Amongst the special types mention can be made of the following:

(a) the *flap rudder*, Fig. 13.24, in which the after portion of the rudder is caused to move to a greater angle than the main portion. Typically, about one-third of the total rudder area is used as a flap and the angle of flap is twice that of the main rudder. The effect of the flap is to cause the camber of rudder section to change with angle giving better lift characteristics. The number of practical applications is not great, partly because of the complication of the linkage system required to actuate the flap;

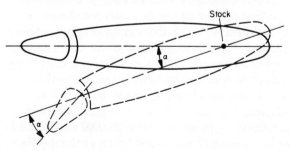

Fig. 13.24 Flap rudder

(b) as a special example of the flap rudder, flaps of quite small area at the trailing edge can be moved so as to induce hydrodynamic forces on the main rudder assisting in turning it. Such a rudder is the *Flettner rudder* Fig. 13.25. The flaps act as a servo system assisting the main steering gear;

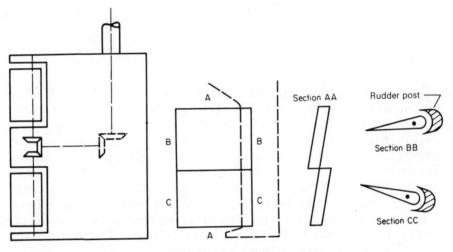

Fig. 13.25 Flettner rudder   Fig. 13.26 Balanced reaction rudder

(c) so-called *balanced reaction rudders*, Fig. 13.26, in which the angle of attack of the rudder sections varies over the depth of the rudder. It attempts to profit from the rotation of the propeller race, and behind propellers working at high slip and low efficiency is claimed to produce a forward thrust;

(d) streamlined rudders behind a fixed streamlined skeg. This is similar in principle to the flap rudder except that only one part moves. By maintaining a better aerofoil shape at all angles the required lift force is obtained at the expense of less drag and less rudder torque. Such a rudder is the *oertz rudder*.

(e) rotating cylinder rudder. The fact that a cylinder rotating in a fluid stream develops a lift normal to its axis and the stream flow, has been known for a very long time as the Magnus effect. Recently the principle has been applied by NPL to improve ship manoeuvring. Having studied several configurations NPL concluded that the use of a rotating cylinder at the leading edge of the rudder was the most practical. Normal course-keeping was unimpaired and for relatively low cylinder power, attached flow could be maintained for rudder angles up to 90 degrees i.e. stall which often occurs at 35 degrees could be inhibited. An installation proposed for a 250,000-tonne tanker had a cylinder one meter in diameter driven at 350 r.p.m. absorbing about 400 kW. It was predicted that the turning circle diameter would be reduced from about 800 m with 35 degrees of rudder to about 100 m at about 75 degrees of rudder with the cylinder in operation. Subsequently sea trials on a 200-tonne vessel were carried out to confirm the principle (Ref. 15) and the ship could turn indefinitely almost in its own length.

AUTOMATIC CONTROL SYSTEMS

Many ships, particularly those on long ocean voyages, travel for long periods of time on a fixed course, the only deviations in course angle being those necessitated by variations in tide, waves or wind. To use trained helmsmen for this type of work is uneconomical and boring for the men concerned. It is in these circumstances that the automatic control system or automatic 'pilot' is most valuable.

Imagine a system which can sense the difference, ψ_e, between the ordered course and the actual course and which can cause the rudder to move to an angle proportional to this error, and in such a way as to turn the ship back towards the desired course, i.e.:

$$\delta_R = \text{Const.} \times \psi_e = a\psi_e, \text{ say}$$

Then, as the ship responds to the rudder the course error will be reduced steadily and, in consequence, the rudder angle will also reduce. Having reached the desired course, the rudder angle will reduce to zero but the ship will still be swinging so that it is bound to 'overshoot'. Thus, by repetition of this process the ship will oscillate about the desired course, the amplitude of the oscillation depending upon the value of the constant of proportionality used in the control equation.

How can the oscillation be avoided or at least reduced? Consider what the helmsman does. He mentally makes provision for the rate of swing of the ship and applies opposite rudder before the desired course angle is reached to eliminate the swing. By introducing a rate gyro into the control system it also can sense the rate of swing and react accordingly in response to the following control equation

$$\delta_R = a\psi_e + b\left(\frac{d\psi_e}{dt}\right)$$

By careful selection of the values of a and b, the overshoot can be eliminated although, in general, a better compromise is to allow a small overshoot on the first swing but no further oscillation as this usually results in a smaller average error. It would be possible to continue to complicate the control equation by adding higher derivative terms. A ship, however, is rather slow in its response to rudder and the introduction of higher derivatives leads to excessive rudder movement with little effect on the ship. For most applications the control equation given above is perfectly adequate.

The system can be used for course changes. By setting a new course, an 'error' is sensed and the system reacts to bring the ship to a new heading. If desired, the system can be programmed to effect a planned manoeuvre or series of course changes. For an efficient system the designer must take into account the characteristics of the hull, the control surfaces and the actuating system. The general mathematics of control theory will apply as for any other dynamic system. In some cases it may be desirable to accept a directionally unstable hull and create course stability by providing an automatic control system with the appropriate characteristics. This device is not often adopted because of the danger to the ship, should the system fail. Simulators can be used to study the relative performances of manual and automatic controls. The consequences of various modes of failure can be studied in safety using a simulator, including the ability of a human operator to take over in the event of a failure. Simulators are also particularly valuable training and testing aids for seamen.

Ship handling

TURNING AT SLOW SPEED OR WHEN STOPPED

It has been seen that the rudder acts in effect as a servo-system in controlling the attitude of the ship's hull so that the hydrodynamic forces on the hull will cause the ship to turn. At low or zero speed, the magnitude of any hydrodynamic force, depending as it does to a first order on V^2, is necessarily small. Since under these conditions the propeller race effect is not large, even the forces on a rudder in the race are small.

The ship must therefore rely upon other means when attempting to manoeuvre under these conditions. A number of possibilities exist:

(a) A twin shaft ship can go ahead on one shaft and astern on the other so producing a couple on the ship causing her to turn. This is a common practice, but leverage of each shaft is relatively small and it can be difficult to match the thrust and pull on the two shafts. Fortunately, some latitude in fore and aft movement is usually permissible.

(b) If leaving a jetty the ship can swing about a stern or head rope. It can make use of such a device as a pivot while going ahead or astern on the propeller.

(c) When coming alongside a jetty at slow speed, use can be made of the so-called 'paddle-wheel' effect. This effect, which has yet to be adequately explained in physical terms, results from a lateral force acting on the stern/ propeller/rudder combination in such a way as to cause the stern to swing in the direction it would do if the propeller were running as a wheel on top of a hard surface. In a twin-screw ship the forces are generally in balance. Now, consider a twin-screw ship approaching a jetty as in Fig. 13.27. If both screws are outward turning (that is viewed from aft, the tip of the propellers move outboard at the top of the propeller disc), the port shaft can be set astern. This will have the effect of producing a lateral force at the stern acting towards the jetty, besides taking the way off the ship and producing a moment on the shafts tending to bring the ship parallel to the jetty.

(d) The screw race can be deflected by a special device such as the Kitchen rudder or, to some extent at least, by twin rudders behind a single propeller.

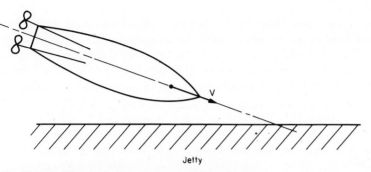

Fig. 13.27 Paddle-wheel effect when coming alongside a jetty

Clearly, unless the race can be deflected through about 90 degrees this system cannot be used without, at the same time, causing the ship to move fore and aft.

(*e*) Use one of the special manoeuvring devices described above.

INTERACTION BETWEEN SHIPS WHEN CLOSE ABOARD

Even in deep water, interaction effects can be significant as discussed in Ref. 11. The pressure field created by a ship moving ahead in open water is illustrated in Fig. 13.28, its actual form depending on the ship form.

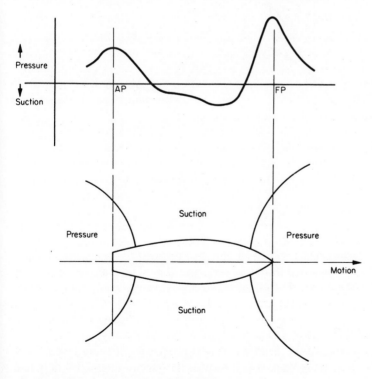

Fig. 13.28 Pressure field for ship in deep water

The pressure field extends for a considerable area around the ship, and any disturbance created in this field necessarily has its reaction on the forces acting on the ship. If the disturbance takes place to one side of the ship, it is to be expected that the ship will, in general, be subject to a lateral force and a yawing moment.

This is borne out by the results given in Ref. 11 for a ship A of 740 ft (226 m) and 36,890 tonf overtaking a ship B of 567 ft (173 m) and 23,570 tonf on a parallel course. The results are reproduced in Fig. 13.29. From these, it is seen that the ships are initially repelled, the force of repulsion reducing to zero when the bow of A is abreast the amidships of B. The ships are then attracted, the force becoming a maximum soon after the ships are abreast and then reducing and becoming a repulsion as the ships begin to part company.

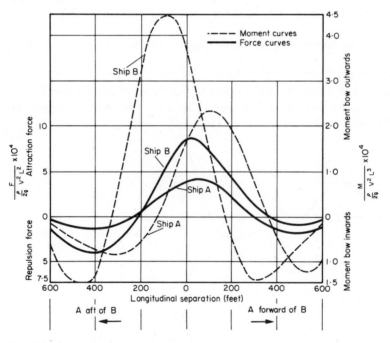

Fig. 13.29 Interaction forces and moments

The largest forces experienced were those of attraction when the two ships were abreast. They amounted to 26 tonf on A and 35 tonf on B at 10 knots speed and 50 ft (15 m) separation. The forces vary approximately as the square of the ship speed and inversely with the separation.

When running abreast, both ships are subject to a bow outward moment but to a bow inward moment when approaching or breaking away.

To be able to maintain the desired course it is necessary to counteract these variations in force and moment, which means that the ship must not only use its rudder but must also run generally at an angle of yaw.

Ship trials show that replenishment at sea operations are perfectly feasible at speeds of up to about 20 knots and such operations are quite commonplace nowadays.

In addition to, or in place of, the disturbance created by a ship in close company, the pressure field of a ship may be upset by a canal bank, pier or by the proximity of the sea bed. In the case of a vertical canal bank or pier, the result will be a lateral force and yawing moment as for the replenishment at sea operation. By analogy, the effect of shallow water is a vertical force and trimming moment resulting in bodily sinkage of the ship and trim by the stern. This effect can lead to grounding on a sandbank which may have been expected to be several feet below the keel.

While naval architects think of these attractions in terms of Bernouilli's equation, mariners recognize the canal effect as 'smelling the ground' and the bodily sinkage in shallow water as 'squat' (Ref. 20).

Stability and control of submarines

The increased underwater speed of submarines has necessitated a very much closer study of dynamic stability and control than formerly. The subject assumes great importance to both the commanding officer and the designer because of the very short time available in which to take corrective action in any emergency : many submarines are restricted to a layer of water which is of the order of at most two or three ship lengths deep. To the designer and research worker, this has meant directing attention to the change in the character of the forces governing the motion of the submarine which occurs as the speed is increased. For submarines of orthodox size and shape below about ten knots the hydrostatic forces predominate. In this case, the performance of the submarine in the vertical plane can be assessed from the buoyancy and mass distributions. Above 10 knots, however, the hydrodynamic forces and moments on the hull and control surfaces predominate.

To a certain degree, the treatment of this problem is similar to that of the directional stability of surface ships dealt with earlier. There are differences however between the two, viz. :

(a) the submarine is positively stable in that B lies above G so that having suffered a small disturbance in trim when at rest it will return to its original trim condition;

(b) the limitation in the depth of water available for vertical manoeuvres;

(c) the submarine is unstable for translations in the z direction (see Chapter 4);

(d) it is very difficult to obtain a precise equilibrium between weight and buoyancy, even on trial, and it is impossible during normal service with fuel and other stores being consumed all the while.

It follows, from (c) and (d) above, that the control surfaces or hydroplanes will have, in general, to exert an upward or downward force on the submarine. Also, if the submarine has to remain on a level keel or, for some reason, the submarine cannot be allowed to trim to enable the stability lever to take account of the trimming moment, the control surfaces must also exert a moment. To be able to exert a force and moment on the submarine which bear no fixed relationship one to another requires two separate sets of hydroplanes. Usually, these are mounted well foward and well aft on the submarine to provide maximum leverage.

Consider a submarine turning in the vertical plane (Fig. 13.30).

Fig. 13.30

Assume that the effective hydroplane angle is δ_H, i.e. the angle representing the combined effects of bow and stern hydroplanes.

In a steady state turn, with all velocities constant, the force in the z direction and the trimming moment are zero. Hence

$$wZ_w + qZ_q + mqV + \delta_H Z_{\delta_H} = 0$$

$$wM_w + qM_q + \delta_H M_{\delta_H} - mg\overline{BG}\theta = 0$$

where subscripts w, q and δ_H denote differentiation with respect to velocity normal to submarine axis, pitching velocity and hydroplane angle respectively. Compare the equations for directional stability of surface ships given on p. 479.

mqV is a centrifugal force term

$mg\overline{BG}\theta$ is a statical stability term.

In the moment equation M_w, M_q and M_{δ_H} are all proportional to V^2, whereas $mg\overline{BG}\theta$ is constant at all speeds. Hence, at high speeds, $mg\overline{BG}\theta$ becomes small and can be ignored. As mentioned above, for most submarines it can be ignored at speeds of about 10 knots. By eliminating w between the two equations so simplified

$$\frac{q}{\delta_H} = \frac{M_w Z_{\delta_H} - M_{\delta_H} Z_w}{M_q Z_w - M_w(Z_q + mV)}$$

As with the surface ship problem the necessary condition for stability is that the denominator should be positive, i.e.

$$M_q Z_w - M_w(Z_q + mV) > 0$$

This is commonly known as the *high speed stability criterion*.

If this condition is met and statically the submarine is stable, then it will be stable at all speeds. If it is statically stable, but the above condition is not satisfied, then the submarine will develop a diverging (i.e. unstable) oscillation in its motion at forward speeds above some critical value.

Now by definition $q = \mathrm{d}\theta/\mathrm{d}t = \dot\theta$, so that differentiating the moment equation with respect to time

$$\dot{w}M_w + \dot{q}M_q + \dot{\delta}_H M_{\delta_H} - mg\overline{BG}q = 0$$

But in a steady state condition as postulated $\dot{w} = \dot{q} = \dot\delta_H = 0$. Hence $q = 0$ if $\overline{BG}$ is positive as is the practical case. That is, a steady path in a circle is not possible unless $\overline{BG} = 0$. Putting $q = 0$, the equations become

$$wZ_w + \delta_H Z_{\delta_H} = 0$$

$$wM_w + \delta_H M_{\delta_H} - mg\overline{BG}\theta = 0$$

i.e.

$$w = -\delta_H \frac{Z_{\delta_H}}{Z_w}$$

and

$$\dot\theta = \delta_H\left(M_{\delta_H} - \frac{Z_{\delta_H}}{Z_w}M_w\right)\Big/ mg\overline{BG}$$

Now rate of change of depth $= V(\theta - w/V)$ if w is small $= V\theta - w$, i.e.

$$\frac{\text{depth rate}}{\delta_H} = \left(VM_{\delta_H} - VM_w\frac{Z_{\delta_H}}{Z_w} + mg\overline{BG}\frac{Z_{\delta_H}}{Z_w}\right)\Big/ mg\overline{BG}$$

The depth rate is zero if

$$V = -\left(mg\overline{BG}\frac{Z_{\delta_H}}{Z_w}\right)\Big/\left(M_{\delta_H} - M_w\frac{Z_{\delta_H}}{Z_w}\right)$$

$$= mg\overline{BG}\Big/\left(M_w - M_{\delta_H}\frac{Z_w}{Z_{\delta_H}}\right)$$

From the equation for θ, if the hydroplanes are so situated that

$$\frac{M_{\delta_H}}{Z_{\delta_H}} = \frac{M_w}{Z_w}$$

then θ is zero. The depth rate will be $\delta_H Z_{\delta_H}/Z_w$ which is not zero. The ratio M_w/Z_w defines the position of the *neutral point*. This corresponds to the similar point used in directional stability and is usually forward of the centre of gravity. A force at the neutral point causes a depth change but no change in the angle of pitch.

The equation for depth rate can be rewritten as

$$\text{depth rate}/\delta_H = \frac{Z_{\delta_H}}{Z_w}\left(1 - \frac{V}{V_c}\right)$$

where

$$V_c = mg\overline{BG} \Big/ \left(M_w - \frac{M_{\delta_H}}{Z_{\delta_H}} \cdot Z_w \right)$$

or

$$\text{depth rate}/\delta_H = \frac{Z_{\delta_H} V}{mg\overline{BG}} \left\{ \frac{M_{\delta_H}}{Z_{\delta_H}} - x_c \right\}$$

where

$$x_c = \frac{M_w}{Z_w} - \frac{mg\overline{BG}}{VZ_w}$$

The first of these two expressions shows that (depth rate)/δ_H is negative, zero or positive as V is greater than, equal to or less than V_c respectively. V_c is known as the *critical speed* or *reversal speed*, since at that speed the planes give zero depth change and cause reverse effects as the speed increases or decreases from this speed. Near the critical speed the value of $(1 - (V/V_c))$ is small—hence the hydroplanes' small effect in depth changing.

It will be seen that θ is not affected in this way since

$$\frac{\theta}{\delta_H} = -\frac{Z_{\delta_H}}{Z_w}\frac{1}{V_c} = -\frac{Z'_{\delta_H}}{Z'_w}\frac{V}{V_c}$$

The magnitude of θ/δ_H changes with V but not its sign. If stern hydroplanes are considered, a positive hydroplane angle produces a negative pitch angle (bow down), but depth change is downwards above the critical speed and upwards below the critical speed.

The second expression for depth change illustrates another aspect of the same phenomenon. x_c denotes a position $mg\overline{BG}/VZ_w$ abaft the neutral point,

$$\frac{mg\overline{BG}}{VZ_w} = \frac{mg\overline{BG}}{\frac{1}{2}\rho L^2 Z'_w V^2}$$

hence x_c is abaft the neutral point by a distance which is small at high speed and large at low speed. The critical situation is given by $x_c = M_{\delta_H}/Z_{\delta_H}$, i.e. centre of pressure of the hydroplanes. The position defined by x_c is termed the *critical point*. Figure 13.31 illustrates the neutral and critical point positions. Figure 13.32 shows a typical plot of x_c/L against Froude number. The critical speed can be obtained by noting the Froude number appropriate to the hydroplane position, e.g. in the figure

$$\frac{V_c}{\sqrt{gL}} = 0.05$$

i.e.

$$V_c = 3 \text{ knots if } L = 100 \text{ m}$$

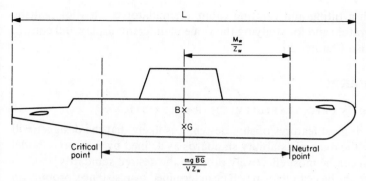

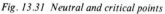

Fig. 13.31 Neutral and critical points

EXPERIMENTS AND TRIALS

As in the case of the directional stability of surface ships, the derivatives needed in studying submarine performance can be obtained in conventional ship tanks using planar motion mechanisms and in rotating arm facilities. The model is run with and without propellers, hydroplanes and stabilizer fins to enable the separate effects of these appendages to be studied. Data so obtained are used to predict stability and fed into digital or analogue computers. The computer can then predict the manoeuvres the submarine will perform in response to certain control surface movements. These can be used to compare with full-scale data obtained from trials. If an analogue computer is used, it can be

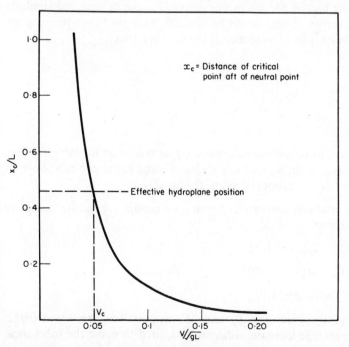

Fig. 13.32 Variation of critical point with speed

associated with a tilting and rotating cabin, a simulator created for realistic training of operators and for studying the value of different display and control systems. (See also Chapter 2.)

Design assessment

MODIFYING DYNAMIC STABILITY CHARACTERISTICS

In common with most features of ship design, it is likely that the designer will wish to modify the dynamic stability standards as defined by the initial model tests. How then can he most effectively produce the desired standards?

In most cases, the basic hull form will be determined by resistance, propulsion and seakeeping considerations. The designer can most conveniently modify the appendages to change the dynamic stability. The procedure is similar for submarines and surface ships but is illustrated below for the former.

Assuming that the hydroplanes are correctly sized, the designer concentrates on the stabilizer fins (skeg for the lateral plane). If the contributions of these fins to Z'_w and M'_w, as determined from the model results with and without fins, are $\delta Z'_w$ and $\delta M'_w$ the effective distance of the fins from the centre of gravity is X_s, say, where:

$$\frac{X_s}{L} = -\frac{\delta M'_w}{\delta Z'_w}, \quad \text{i.e. } \delta M'_w = -\frac{X_s}{L}\delta Z'_w$$

The negative sign arises because the fins are aft.

The effect of the fins on the curvature derivatives can be deduced similarly or, if not available from direct model tests, it can be argued that the rotation causes an effective change of incidence at the fin, such that:

$$\delta Z'_q = \frac{X_s}{L}\delta Z'_w$$

and

$$\delta M'_q = \left(\frac{X_s}{L}\right)^2 \delta Z'_w$$

If the derivatives, as originally determined, give rise to an unstable motion, the required increase in fin area can be deduced using the above relationships and assuming that $\delta Z'_w$ is proportional to the fin area.

EXAMPLE 4. The stability derivatives found for a certain submarine, complete with all appendages are:

$$Z'_w = -0.02, \quad Z'_q = -0.01$$

$$M'_w = 0.012, \quad M'_q = -0.005$$

$$m' = 0.024$$

The corresponding figures for Z'_w and M'_w without fins are 0 and 0.022. Calculate the percentage increase in fin area required to make the submarine just stable assuming m' is effectively unaltered.

Solution: The stability criterion in non-dimensional form is

$$M'_q Z'_w - M'_w(Z'_q + m') > 0$$

Substituting the original data gives $-0\!\cdot\!000068$ so that the submarine is unstable.

If the fin area is increased by p per cent then the derivatives become

$$Z'_w = -0\!\cdot\!02 + p(-0\!\cdot\!02)$$

$$M'_w = 0\!\cdot\!012 + p(-0\!\cdot\!01), \quad \text{in this case } X_s = -\tfrac{1}{2}L$$

$$Z'_q = -0\!\cdot\!01 + p(-0\!\cdot\!01)$$

$$M'_q = -0\!\cdot\!005 + p(-0\!\cdot\!005)$$

Substituting these values in the left-hand side of the stability criterion and equating to zero gives the value of p which will make the submarine just stable.

Carrying out this calculation gives $p = 14\!\cdot\!8$ per cent, and the modified derivatives become

$$Z'_w = -0\!\cdot\!023, \quad Z'_q = -0\!\cdot\!0115$$

$$M'_w = 0\!\cdot\!0105, \quad M'_q = -0\!\cdot\!00575$$

EFFICIENCY OF CONTROL SURFACES

Ideally, the operator of any ship should define the standard of manoeuvrability he requires in terms of the standard manoeuvres already discussed. The designer could then calculate, or measure by model tests, the various stability derivatives and the forces and moments generated by movements of the control surfaces, i.e. rudders and hydroplanes. By feeding this information to an analogue or digital computer he could predict the ship performance, compare with the stated requirements and then modify the design as necessary. He could modify stability by changing skeg or fin areas as already explained, and modify the areas of control surfaces to provide the desired response.

As a simpler method of comparing ships, the effectiveness of control surfaces can be gauged by comparing the forces and moments they can generate with the forces and moments produced on the hull by movements in the appropriate plane. Strictly, the force and moment on the hull should be the combination of those due to lateral velocity and rotation, but for most purposes they can be compared separately; for example the rudder force and moment can be compared with the force and moment due to lateral velocity to provide a measure of the ability of the rudder to hold the hull at a given angle of attack and thus cause the ship to turn. The ability of the rudder to start rotating the ship can be judged by comparing the moment due to rudder with the rotational inertia of the ship. The ability of hydroplanes to cope with a lack of balance between weight and buoyancy is demonstrated by comparing the force they can generate with the displacement of the submarine. It is important that all parameters be measured in a consistent fashion and that the suitability of the figures obtained be compared with previous designs.

Effect of design parameters on manoeuvring
The following remarks are of a general nature and based upon Ref. 14. Model tests are needed for studying the effects of specific changes to a design.

Speed. For surface vessels increased speed leads to increased turning diameter for a given rudder angle although the rate of turn normally increases. For submerged bodies, turning diameters are sensibly constant over the speed range.

Trim. Generally stern trim improves directional stability and increases turning diameter. The effect is roughly linear over practical speed ranges.

Draught. Somewhat surprisingly limited tests indicate that decrease in draught results in increased turning rate and stability. This suggests that the rudder becomes a more dominant factor both as a stabilizing fin and as a turning device.

Longitudinal moment of inertia. Changes in inertia leave the steady turning rate unchanged. A larger inertia increases angular momentum and leads to larger overshoot.

Metacentric height. Quite large changes in metacentric height show no significant effects on turning rate or stability.

Length/beam ratio. Generally speaking the greater this ratio the more stable the ship and the larger the turning circle.

Concluding remarks
This chapter has presented important basic theory but the student must again be aware of its limitations and how it is currently being developed. The theory presented has been a simple linear one and this provides a useful starting point. However, many problems are, or appear to be, highly non-linear. This has led to the introduction of higher degrees of derivative to obtain a better representation of the way forces and moments, whose deviations from a steady state condition are other than small, can vary. Such problems concern, for example, steering in a seaway (particularly in a following sea), high-speed large-angle submarine manoeuvring when the body shape may have important effects, athwartships positioning of big ships and drilling vessels. Unfortunately, such approaches are critically dependent upon the validity of the mathematical representation adopted for the fluid forces. One limitation of these analyses is that they assume the forces and moments acting on the model to be determined by the motion obtaining at that instant and are unaffected by its history. This is not true and Ref. 21 describes how, when two fins (like a ship and its rudder) are moving in tandem and the first is put to an angle of attack, there is a marked time delay before the second fin experiences a change of force. The reference uses a linear functional mathematical representation which includes a 'memory' effect and shows how the results in the frequency and time domains are related. The approach is limited to linear theory but the inclusion of memory effects provides an explanation for at least some of the non-linearities shown previously to arise in large amplitude motions. The theory of functionals would appear to be capable of development to embrace the whole range of ship hydrodynamic problems such as berthing, ship-to-ship interactions and even unsteady propulsion problems.

Problems

1. A rudder placed immediately behind a middle line propeller is rectangular in shape, 3 m wide and 2 m deep. It is pivoted at its leading edge. Estimate the torque on the rudder head when it is placed at 35 degrees, the ship's speed being 15 knots.
(AP & S)

2. A ship turns in a radius of 300 m at a speed of 20 knots under the action of a rudder force of 100 tonnef. If the draught of the vessel is 5 m $\overline{KG}$ is 6 m and $\overline{GM}$ is 2 m find the approximate angle of heel during the steady turn.

3. A rudder is shaped as shown. If it is on the middle line in a single screw ship, how far abaft the leading edge is the centre of pressure?
(AP & S)

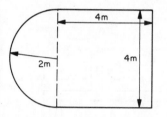

Fig. 13.33

4. A rudder has a profile as sketched in Fig. 13.34.

Calculate the force on this rudder when operating behind a single centre-line screw at a ship speed of 20 knots ahead with the rudder at 35 degrees. Use the formula due to Baker and Bottomley.

What is the value of *d* in order that the torque is zero in this condition assuming the rudder is effectively in open water.

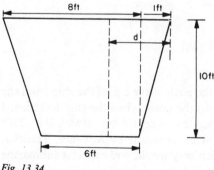

Fig. 13.34

5. Calculate the force and torque on the spade rudder shown, which is one of two working behind twin propellers. Assume a rudder angle of 35 degrees and a ship speed of 18 knots ahead.

6. The rudder sketched in Fig. 13.36 has sections similar to NACA 0015. Calculate the force and torque on the rudder for 20 knots ahead speed, with the rudder at 35 degrees, assuming no breakdown of flow occurs.

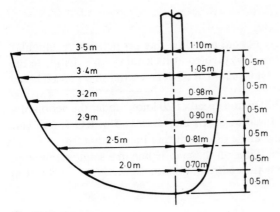

Fig. 13.35

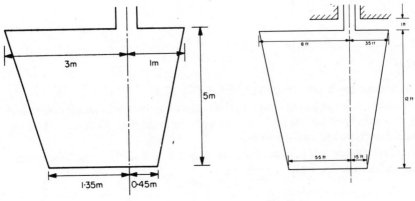

Fig. 13.36   *Fig. 13.37*

7. Describe the action of the rudder on a ship
   (a) when it is first put over,
   (b) when the ship is turning steadily.
   Sketch a typical turning circle, giving the path of the c.g. of the ship from the point when the helm is first put over up to the point when the ship has turned through 360°. Show the position of the ship (by its centre line) at 90°, 180°, 270° and 360° turn. Show on your diagram what is meant by Advance, Transfer, Tactical Diameter and Drift Angle. Which way would you expect a submarine to heel when turning? Give reasons.   (HMDTC)
8. The balanced rudder, shown in Fig. 13.37, has a maximum turning angle of 35° and is fitted directly behind a single propeller.
   What torque and bending moment are applied to the rudder stock at the lower end of the sleeve bearing, when the rudder is put over at a ship's speed of 26 knots?
   In the force equation, $P = KAV^2\delta_R$ (P in lbf, A in ft^2, V in knots), take the constant $K = 0.100$. Also, if the length of an elemental strip of the rudder surface,

drawn at right-angles to the centre line of the stock, is 1 then assume the centre of pressure of the strip to be 0·321 from the leading edge.

(HMDTC)

9. Using Fig. 13.11, plot an NACA 0015 section with a chord length of 5 m. Calculate the area of the section, the distancê of the centroid from the nose and the section modulus about each principal axis, assuming a solid section.
Take the x/c values at intervals of 0·1.

10. A twin-screw vessel has a rectangular spade rudder 1·5 m wide and 2 m deep. The axis is 0·5 m from the leading edge. If friction at the rudder stock bearings and in the stearing gear may be taken as 5000 N m, estimate the range of possible angles which the rudder can take up if the steering gear is damaged while the ship is underway at 30 knots. Distance of centre of pressure abaft leading edge may be taken as chord $(0·195 + 0·305 \sin \theta)$.

11. Details of two ship designs A and B are given below.

	Ship A	Ship B
Length on WL, L(m)	215	252·5
Beam, B(m)	24	26·75
Draught, T(m)	7·625	8·0
Area of rudder, A_R(m^2)		50

Design B achieved a tactical diameter of 4·3 ship lengths at 28 knots. Assuming that tactical diameter $=$ const. $\times L^3 T/BA_R$, calculate the rudder areas necessary to give tactical diameters of 3, 3·5 and 4·0 ship lengths in design A at the appropriate speed.

12. Calculate the approximate heeling moment acting on a ship of 60 MN displacement assuming

Force on rudder $= 21A_R V^2 \delta_R$ newtons, A_R in m^2, V in m/s, δ_R in degrees
Length of ship $= 150$ m
$A_R =$ rudder area $= 50$ m^2
$V =$ ship speed $= 18$ knots on turn
$\delta_R =$ rudder angle $= 35$ degrees
Draught $= 8$ m
$\overline{KG} = 10$ m

Height of centroid of rudder above keel $= 5$ m

$$\frac{TD}{L} = 3·6.$$

13. Two designs possess the following values of derivatives

	Y'_v	N'_v	Y'_r	N'_r	m'
Design A	−0·36	−0·07	0·06	−0·07	0·12
Design B	−0·26	−0·10	0·01	−0·03	0·10

Comment on the directional stability of the two designs.
Assuming both designs are 100 m long how far are the neutral points forward of the centres of gravity?

522 Basic ship theory

14. The directional stability derivatives for a surface ship 580 ft long are:

$$Y'_v = -0.0116, \qquad N'_r = -0.00166$$
$$N'_v = -0.00264, \qquad m' = 0.00798$$
$$Y'_r = -0.00298$$

Y'_v and N'_v without a 100 ft^2 skeg were -0.0050 and 0 respectively.

Show that the ship, with skeg, is stable and calculate the distance of the neutral point forward of the c.g. and the effective distance of the skeg aft of the c.g. What increase in skeg area is necessary to increase the stability index by 20 per cent?

15. A submarine 100 m long has the following non-dimensional derivatives:

$$Z'_w = -0.030, \qquad M'_q = -0.008$$
$$M'_w = 0.012, \qquad m' = 0.030$$
$$Z'_q = -0.015$$

Calculate the distance of the neutral point forward of the c.g. Is the submarine stable?

If $\overline{BG} = 0.5$ m and displacement is 4000 tonnef, calculate the critical speed for the after hydroplanes which are 45 m aft of the c.g.

References

1. Saunders, H. E. Hydrodynamics in ship design, Vol. 1. *SNAME*, 1965.
2. Cole, A. P. Destroyer turning circles. *TINA*, 1938.
3. Gertler Morton and Gover, S. C. Handling quality criteria for surface ships. *First symposium on ship manoeuvrability, David Taylor Model Basin*, 24 and 25 May, 1960. *DTMB Report*, 1461, October, 1960.
4. Gawn, R. W. L. Steering experiments, Part I. *TINA*, 1943.
5. Whicker, L. F. and Fehlner, L. F. Free-stream characteristics of a family of low-aspect-ratio, all-movable control surfaces for application to ship design. *DTMB Report*, 933, December, 1958.
6. Newton, R. N. New facilities at Admiralty Experiment Works, Haslar. *TRINA*, 1962.
7. Gertler, M. The DTMB planar-motion-mechanism system. *Proceedings of Symposium on towing tank facilities, instrumentation and measuring techniques*, Zagreb, Yugoslavia. September, 1959.
8. Chislett, M. S. and Strøm-Tejsen, J. Planar motion mechanism tests and full-scale steering and manoeuvring predictions for a *Mariner* class vessel. *International Shipbuilding Progress*, Vol. 12, May, 1965.
9. Newton, R. N. Turning and manoeuvring trials. *TNECI*, Vol. 76, 1959–60.
10. English, J. W. The design and performance of lateral thrust units for ships. *TRINA*, 1963.
11. Newton, R. N. Some notes on interaction effects between ships close aboard in deep water. *First symposium on ship manoeuvrability, David Taylor Model Basin*, 24 and 25 May, 1960.
12. Nonweiler, T. R. F. The stability and control of deeply submerged submarines. *TRINA*, 1961.
13. Rydill, L. J. A linear theory for the steered motion of ships in waves. *TRINA*, 1959.
14. Burcher, R. K. Developments in ship manoeuvrability. *TRINA*, 1972.
15. First sea trials of the rotating cylinder rudder. *Naval Architect*, Oct., 1972.
16. Hagen, G. R. A. Contribution to the hydrodynamic design of rudders.*
17. ter Horst, J. A. M. *Automatic track guidance of a minesweeper.*
18. Zuidweg, J. K. *Automatic track keeping as a control problem.*
19. Chislett, H. W. J. Replenishment at sea. *TRINA*, 1972.
20. Dand, I. W. and Ferguson, A. M. The squat of full ships in shallow water. *TRINA*, 1973.
21. Bishop, R. E. D., Burcher, R. K. and Price, W. G. Determination of ship manoeuvring characteristics from model tests. *TRINA*, 1975.
22. Eda, H. Directional control and stability of ships in restricted channels. *TSNAME*, 1971.
23. van Berlekom, W. B. and Goddard, T. Manoeuvring of large tankers. *TSNAME*, 1972.
*Ship Control Systems Symposium, Bath University, 1972.

14 Major ship design features

Few enterprises are as diverse as ship design. While the subjects of the preceding chapters are fundamental to the design and behaviour of a ship as a whole, there is yet a range of sciences which must be blended to create an acceptable whole—machinery and electrical distribution, piping systems, earning capacity, equipment, cargo handling, weapons installation, domestic arrangements and internal decoration are some. If the naval architect is to achieve the correct balance amongst all features, he must be familiar with them all, at least to the point of being able to judge for himself to what extent the claims of the individual specialist should be met.

This chapter discusses a number of individual features of the ship which contribute to the design. This list is not exhaustive. For many of the features, the naval architect will be personally responsible; for others, he must acquire sufficient knowledge to be in a position to discuss, to argue, to cajole. With the advance of science, this becomes more and more difficult, but the need for a single knowledgeable co-ordinating authority does not diminish and this task cannot be fulfilled better than by a competent naval architect who is responsible for the ship as a whole unit.

Machinery

The days of tailor made machinery for ships have passed. Even for warships, the choice is becoming one of selecting a combination of standard units rather than designing a new set of propulsive machinery for each new ship. The reason for this is that the high costs of setting up production equipment for a new machinery set is not justified unless a large production order is anticipated. In fact, tooling is set up for relatively few different units throughout the world, often under licence from another country.

Merchant ships, in general, do not need great flexibility in machinery performance because they operate for a large percentage of their lives at constant, economic speed. For this, they need economical, reliable machinery, selected on the grounds presently described for which proven, standard units are usually satisfactory. Choice is normally between steam and diesel machinery. Warships require a greater degree of flexibility, operating normally at cruising speed with occasional bursts of high speed. This can be achieved in a variety of ways, but modern surface warships tend towards a selection of the following:

(a) CODAG. This is a combination of diesel and gas turbine, the former for operation at maximum efficiency at cruising speed with the latter introduced for high speed.

(*b*) COSAG. This is a combination of steam turbine and gas turbine. As well as giving power for high speed bursts, the gas turbines also permit the ships to get under way with very short notice—the four hours' notice to steam is no longer required. This system was fitted to many RN frigates and destroyers in the 1960s but has been superseded by COGOG.
(*c*) COGOG. Machinery is all gas turbine, blended in size to give satisfactory performances at various speeds by the selection of different units.

A ship needs a compact, light, economical machinery installation having a long life, little maintenance and flexibility of operation to suit propulsion and auxiliary demands. Factors affecting the choice of machinery for a ship are as follows:

(*a*) Powers needed to propel the ship at the maximum speed and endurance speed;
(*b*) Weight and space demands. Weight is normally compared in terms of the weight of machinery per unit of power delivered.
(*c*) Availability of standard units in the powers required. Single diesel engines developing up to 50,000 s.h.p. are now available, (with direct drive);
(*d*) Fuel consumption. This is usually expressed in terms of weight of fuel per unit of power per hour. Weight of fuel to achieve the required endurance is often 10 per cent of a merchant ship's displacement and 20 per cent of a warship's and therefore an important influence on displacement and economics of operation of the ship;
(*e*) Vulnerability of installation. Unitized installation (i.e. separate self-contained units) in a warship may be required to reduce the risk of total immobilization of the ship by a single hit (see Fig. 14.1);

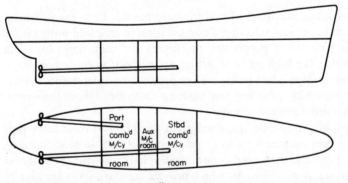

Fig. 14.1 Unitized machinery installation

(*f*) Operating crew. Numbers and skill of operators are important, particularly if the machinery is complex enough to demand new training facilities. This also encourages an owner to be consistent throughout his fleet;
(*g*) Ease of maintenance and reliability. Facilities on the intended route are relevant to the maintenance routine when this is carried out by replacement, as is common with small units;

(*h*) Noise and vibration generation. This is an important factor with submarines, anti-submarine frigates and passenger liners;

(*i*) Tonnage allowances;

(*j*) Business agreements. Business connections may affect choice of contractors;

(*k*) Overall economy. For merchant ships this is of extreme importance. Economic factors which affect the choice of machinery are divided into three groups:

  (i) Capital costs—buying price, taxation, borrowing rates;

  (ii) Operating costs—fuel, crew, insurance, port charges, maintenance and repair, shore overheads;

  (iii) Utilization—maintenance and survey time, port turn round time. Utilization for a tanker is often more than 80 per cent, 300 days a year being spent at sea, while for a trawler it may be as high as 90 per cent.

At present about 51 per cent of the UK's gross tonnage is steam driven, although nearly all tramps and most cargo liners are motor driven. The largest ships tend to favour steam turbines or direct drive diesels. Steam-driven tankers registered in the UK are nearly five times as common as motor-driven tankers. However, the diesel engine is self-contained and produced under the control of one manufacturer and so less liable to delay ship completion; it is easier to operate and has an easier spares position. Diesels also show advantages of fuel consumption and often of overall economy.

Table 14.1
Propulsion machinery for 10,000 *s.h.p.*

	Geared steam turbine	Geared steam turbine	Long life gas turbine, uncooled	Long life gas turbine, cooled	Heavy oil engine
Steam conditions, p.s.i.g	600	850	—	—	—
Superheater outlet °F (°C)	850 (454)	1050 (566)	—	—	—
Max. gas temp. °F (°C)	—	—	1250 (677)	2200 (1204)	—
Fuel consumption, propulsion only, lbf/s.h.p. hr	0·511	0·477	0·495	0·39	0·38
Tonf per day	54·75	51·0	53·0	41·75	40·75
Main machinery weight, wet tonf	268	212	140	103	425

Table 14.1 taken from Ref. 1 compares different 10,000 s.h.p. main propulsion units. Table 14.2 derived from Ref. 2 makes a similar comparison for larger powers. Despite a large main machinery weight, the fuel consumption is the lowest for the diesel; a better criterion for comparing machinery installations is the sum of machinery and fuel weights, the latter depending on endurance. Table 14.3 makes a comparison on this basis for the 10,000 s.h.p. installations showing that at the higher endurance only the long life cooled gas turbine shows an appreciable advantage.

Table 14.2
Propulsion machinery for higher s.h.p.

	Geared steam turbine	Steam turbo-electric	Heavy diesel	Aircraft type gas turbine
Shaft horsepower	25,000	25,000	20,000	20,000
Steam conditions, p.s.i.g.	600	600	—	—
Superheater outlet, °F (°C)	950 (510)	950 (510)	—	—
Max. gas temp., °F (°C)	—	—	—	1539 (835)
Fuel consumption, propulsion only, lbf/s.h.p. hr	0·475	0·492	0·360	0·546
Tonf per day	127·2	132·0	77·1	117·0
Main machinery weight, wet, tonf	448	625	765	75

Table 14.3
Machinery plus fuel weights

	Weights, tonf				
	Machinery	Fuel (a)	(b)	Total (a)	(b)
Geared steam turbine 600 p.s.i.g./850°F (454°C)	268	548	1095	816	1363
Geared steam turbine 850 p.s.i.g./1050°F (566°C)	212	510	1020	722	1232
Gas turbine, uncooled	140	530	1060	670	1200
Gas turbine, cooled	103	418	835	521	938
Heavy oil engine	425	408	815	833	1240

(a) 3600 miles endurance
(b) 7200 miles endurance

Auxiliary machinery must be added again to these figures before a judgement can be made. Diesel ships may require auxiliary boilers to produce steam for domestic purposes, electrical generation or evaporators. It is not, therefore, possible to make any generalizations concerning choice of machinery; it is common to carry out quite detailed design studies of alternative installations before a choice is made by consideration of all the factors described above.

Rises in fuel costs made nuclear propulsion increasingly attractive and by 1974 it was more economical. There remain operational problems and social opposition to such machinery arising from fear of a reactor accident. In nuclear submarines, pioneered in the USA, the reactor provides a source of heat which consumes no oxygen and needs only rare refuelling. This permits it to operate under the ice caps and totally submerged elsewhere for very long periods, often many weeks. The need for the icebreaker to return frequently to fuelling posts is removed by the nuclear reactors, fitted first in the USSR ship *Lenin*. The nuclear reactor is, of course, only a heat source to produce steam or gas for turbines, and the weight and space demands of the reactor, shielding and protection, so far much exceed the demands of boiler and fuel that they replace. At present too, the reactors produce steam in a condition which requires large heavy steam plant. Withdrawal space for the reactor core is needed, much where a funnel would have required space. Greater electrical generator capacity is needed for a reactor fitted ship to meet safety and auxiliary demands of the reactor. An integrated system in which the steam generation occurs within the main pressure vessel (Ref. 16) found favour and was fitted in the *Otto Hahn*. The choice of main propulsion plant can have a big influence upon the type of electrical generator plant adopted as is next discussed.

ELECTRICAL GENERATION

Depending upon the type of main propulsion machinery, one or more types of prime mover will be used for electrical generation, e.g. in a steam ship, steam turbo-alternators are fitted with back-up plant powered by diesels or gas turbines. The number of plants depends upon the total capacity required. This capacity for a ship might at first sight be thought to be the 'total connected load', i.e. the sum of all electrical demands. It is not so simple as this because, first, there are several conditions in which the ship requires different electrical equipment working and, secondly, in any one such condition there is a diversity of equipment in use at any moment. The diversity factor is largely a matter of experience. Conditions for which electrical demands are calculated vary with types of ship but may include the following:

(*a*) normal cruising, summer and winter (in a cargo ship, 40–50 per cent of the normal cruising load is due to machinery auxiliaries);
(*b*) harbour, loading or unloading;
(*c*) action, all weapons in use;
(*d*) salvage, ship damaged and auxiliaries working to save the ship;
(*e*) growth during the ship's life (typically 20 per cent is allowed in merchant ships and warships),

There has been a rapid growth in the generator capacity of ships since 1939—a destroyer design, for example, which might have needed 1 MW in 1950, needed 3 MW by 1960 and 6 MW by 1970. Generating capacity must be provided to meet suitably any of these loads. Machines should be loaded in these conditions near maximum efficiency. Other considerations enter into the problem too—the needs of maintenance, availability of steam in harbour, break down, growth during the ship's life, capacity when damaged.

From all of these considerations, the numbers, sizes and types of generators are decided. The greatest flexibility would be provided by a large number of small capacity machines, but this is not the most efficient way. Too many generators could be very heavy and involve complex control systems. In addition to the main generators usually a salvage generator is sited remote from the primary generators and above the likely damaged waterline if possible.

Systems

Apart from the electrical systems, over fifty different systems may be found in a major warship for conveying fluids of various sorts around the ship. Even simple ships may have a dozen systems for ventilation, fire fighting, drainage, sewage, domestic fresh water, fuel oil, compressed air, lubricating oil, etc. Because their proper blending into the ship affects very many spaces, it is desirable that the naval architect should have complete control of them, except those local systems forming part of a machinery or weapons installation, even if certain of them are provided by a subcontractor. The naval architect must be completely familiar with the design of all such fluid systems and be capable of performing the design himself.

ELECTRICAL DISTRIBUTION SYSTEM

The generation of electrical power has already been discussed briefly. Classification Societies allow considerable flexibility in the method of distribution of this power, but the basic design aims are maximum reliability, continuity of supply, ease of operation and maintenance and adaptability to load variation. All this must be achieved with minimum weight, size and cost. The actual system adopted, depends very much upon the powers involved. Prior to 1939, installations were small, e.g. 70 kW in a typical cargo ship. Few passenger liners had as much as 2 MW. Most installations were d.c. and it was not until after 1950 that shipowners began to require a change to a.c. generation and distribution. This change was influenced very much by the savings in weight and the reduction in maintenance effort accruing which became more important as powers increased. Typical figures for ships in 1973

10,000 tonf dwt. dry cargo ship	1 MW
Tankers	1·5–5 MW
Container ship (3·3 kV)	8 MW

Of ships classed with Lloyd's Register in 1972 over 90 per cent of the total electrical capacity was a.c.

Since 1948 all major warship installations in the Royal Navy have been a.c. Distribution is achieved by feeding from a small number of breakers grouped on the switchboard associated with each generator to electrical distribution centres throughout the ship.

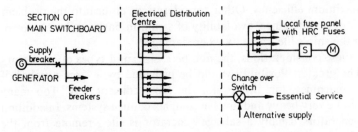

Fig. 14.2 Typical distribution system

Distribution from the EDC is by moulded case circuit breakers of 250 and 100 amp capacity. Finally power is supplied to small circuits of less than 30 A by high rupturing capacity fuses. Because of their relatively high starting currents, motors in excess of $4\frac{1}{2}$ kW are supplied through MCBs. Important services such as steering are provided with alternative independent supplies by well-separated cable routes from two generators feeding a change-over switch. In case of damage, a system of emergency cables is provided for rigging through the ship to connect important services to generators which are still running.

Typical voltages of distribution are:

Merchant ships: d.c. 220 V (power and lighting)
110 V for some small ships
a.c. 440 V at 60 Hz or 380 V at 50 Hz
3·3 kV at 50 or 60 Hz generation in few ships
115 V or 230 V at 60 Hz (lighting)

Warships: a.c. 440 V at 60 Hz 3-phase
115 V at 60 Hz for lighting and domestic single phase circuits.

Most warships and merchant ships adopt the insulated neutral system in order to preserve continuity of supplies even under fault conditions. Many shipowners have preferred a single solid bus bar system with all connected generators operating in parallel. This system gives maximum flexibility with minimum operating staff. The maximum installed capacities are limited by the circuit breaker designs, e.g. assuming breakers of 100 kA interrupting capacity, the system is limited to 1800 kW at 240 V d.c. and 3000 kW at 440 V a.c. Other disadvantages are that a fault at the main switchboard may cause total loss of power, and maintenance can be carried out only when the ship is shut down. The alternative is the split bus bar system which gives greater security of supply and enables maintenance to be carried out by closing down one bus bar section.

PIPING SYSTEMS

Design of any liquid piping system begins by plotting on ship plans the demands for the fluid and by joining the demand points by an economical piping layout compatible with the architecture of the ship. (A discussion of the type of piping network to be adopted occurs later but it needs to be chosen at this stage.) Pipe sizes are then allocated on a trial basis by permitting velocities generally about 1·5–2 m/s at which level experience has shown that erosion and noise are not excessive. It may later be found desirable to allow some stretches to run at speeds up to 3 m/s. From this network, must be estimated the pressure required from the pump to create this flow. Figure 14.3 shows in perspective a very simple open-ended network that might result. By working back from the presumed simultaneous demands, the flows in the different parts of the system can be found by simple addition and pipe sizes allocated. The pump must then be capable of drawing water from I and delivering it to the remotest point against (*a*) the resistance of the system and (*b*) against gravity. Resistance of the system is due to friction in the pipes and resistance (or losses) due to bends, junctions, valves, expansions, contractions, filters and nozzles. Fortunately, all of these fittings losses can be expressed in similar form

$$\text{fitting loss} = K\rho\frac{V^2}{2}$$

where K is a factor defined in Table 14.4, ρ is the mass density of the fluid, V is the velocity of flow.

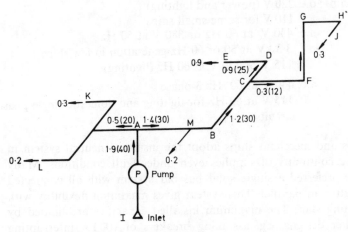

Fig. 14.3 Typical simple open ended network

Now, the frictional loss in a circular pipe is

$$\text{frictional loss} = f\frac{L}{D}\rho\frac{V^2}{2}$$

where f is a factor dependent on Reynolds' number and pipe roughness as given in Fig. 14.4, L is pipe length, and D is pipe bore.

If a pipe is assumed smooth, the fitting loss can conveniently be expressed in the same form as the frictional loss by calling it a number of diameters of equivalent length of pipe—a gate valve, for example, (Table 14.4) is equivalent to the frictional loss due to about eleven diameters of pipe length. Ship pipes are relatively smooth with the possible exception of small diameter steel pipes and this is a common and convenient artifice; while there are clearly approximations involved, it is accurate enough for most ship systems.

The total head, therefore, required of the pump is

$$H = \Sigma f\frac{L}{D}\rho\frac{V^2}{2} + \Sigma(K_1 + K_2 + \ldots)\rho\frac{V^2}{2} + \rho h$$

Table 14.4
Losses in fittings

Fitting	$K = \dfrac{\text{loss}}{\rho V^2/2g}$	Equiv. length $\dfrac{L}{D} = \dfrac{K}{f}$
Gate valve	0·2 for $D = 25$ mm	11
	0·1 for $D = 300$ mm	9
90° Angle valve or 60° oblique valve	3·0 for $D \geqslant 50$ mm	190
	4·5 for $D = 12$ mm	215
Globe valve	6·0 for $D \geqslant 50$ mm	375
	9·0 for $D = 12$ mm	430
Oblique valve 45°	2·5 for $D \geqslant 50$ mm	160
	3·5 for $D = 12$ mm	150
Diaphragm valve	1·5	70
Plug or straight through cock	0·4	20
Sudden contraction	On outlet velocity	
	0·4 for $A_1/A_2 = 10$	—
	0 for $A_1/A_2 = 1$	
Sudden expansion	On inlet velocity	
	0·8 for $A_1/A_2 = 0·1$	—
	0·2 for $A_1/A_2 = 0·5$	
Inlet, smoothed entry	0	0
90° bend, radius R	0·3 for $R > 2D$	15
Outlet	1·0	50
Equal tee,		
flow past	0·3	15
flow round	1·2	60
flow from branch	1·8	90
Elbow, 90°	0·6	30
45°	0·1	12
Strainer	0·8	40

Note: Interpolate linearly. Do not extrapolate

where h is the vertical separation of inlet and outlet. What is important to realize is that if the pump delivers along the most resistful path, all other paths will be satisfactory. This worst path, called the index path or circuit may not always be obvious from inspection and several paths will have to be examined to find the most resistful one. Having determined this, other paths may have to be made equally resistful by the insertion of obstructions such as orifice plates to avoid too high a delivery and pressure. Let us illustrate these points by an example.

EXAMPLE. Calculate the performance required of the salt water pump for the system shown in Fig. 14.3 which meets the demands shown in litres per second. Estimated lengths and fittings, not shown in Fig. 14.3, are given in the table below. The inlet to the pump, I, is at a pressure of 50 kN/m² and the vertical heights separating I and E and I and J are respectively 15 m and 20 m. Delivery is required at a pressure of 150 kN/m².

	Length, m	90° Elbows	45° Oblique valves
IA	10	0	0
AM	45	2	2
MB	6	1	1
BC	12	4	1
CD	20	2	2
DE	12	0	1
CF	3	1	0
FG	6	1	1
GH	6	2	0
HJ	6	0	1

Solution: It is not obvious from inspection whether IAE or IAJ is the index path, although IAK or L are clearly not. It will be assumed that the pipes are smooth. Tabular form is most convenient for this calculation to find $\Sigma[f(L/D) + K_1 + K_2 + \ldots]V^2$ which must then be multiplied by $\rho/2$. Take v to be $1\cdot05 \times 10^{-6}$ m²/s.

	Length (m)	L/D	Equiv. fitt. L/D	Total L/D	V (m/s)	$R_n = \dfrac{VD}{v}$	f	$f\dfrac{L}{D}V^2$
IA	10	250		310	1·5			14·3
Tee			60					
AM	45	1500	370	1885	2·0	$5\cdot7 \times 10^4$	0·0205	154·6
Branch			15					
MB	6	200	185	385	1·7	$4\cdot9 \times 10^4$	0·021	23·4
BC	12	400	275	675	1·7			41·0
Total (i)								**233·3**
Tee			15					
CD	20	800	370	1185	1·8	$4\cdot3 \times 10^4$	0·0215	82·5
DE	12	480	155	685	1·8			47·7
Outlet			50					
Total (ii)								**130·2**
Tee			60					
CF	3		30					
FG	6		180					
GH	6	1750	60	2280	2·7	$3\cdot1 \times 10^4$	0·024	398·9
HJ	6		150					
Outlet			50					
Total (iii)								**398·9**
(i)+(ii)								363·5
(i)+(iii)								632·2

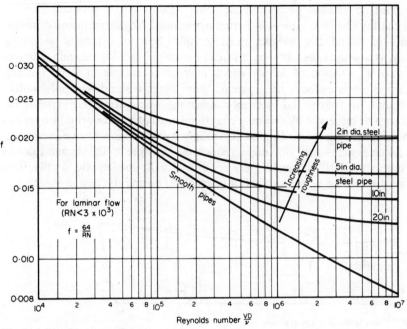

Fig. 14.4 Pipe friction coefficient

Even without gravity head, the index path is clearly IAJ. For this path the total losses are

$$\tfrac{1}{2} \times 632.2 \, \frac{m^2}{s^2} \times 1025 \, \frac{kg}{m^3} = 324{,}000 \ N/m^2$$

The pump must also deliver against gravity head which is

outlet pressure + gravity head − inlet pressure

$$150{,}000 \ N/m^2 + 20m \times 1025 \, \frac{kg}{m^3} \times 9{\cdot}807\frac{m}{s^2} - 50{,}000 \ N/m^2 = 301 \ kN/m^2$$

Therefore, total delivery required by the pump = 1·9 litres per second at a pressure differential of 625 kN/m².

This example illustrates the principles of pipe system design. For a given fluid, it is possible to devise charts showing frictional loss plotted against pipe velocity, diameter and quantity which speed up the calculation. The example shows also the relatively large effects of valve losses and the effects of pinching the pipe diameter. If the final 21 m of piping, for example, were to be of 18 mm diameter instead of 12 mm, the pressure required of the pump would be reduced by 138 kN/m² and this would be an obvious next step in designing this particular system (when IAL would become the critical path).

Several factors affect the choice of the type of system for a particular purpose. By the nature of the demand, some systems must be closed and, once the system is primed, gravity does not influence pump characteristics (except for impeller cavitation), so that the pump delivers solely against system resistance—a hot water heating system is typical. Whether open ended, like firemain and domestic systems, or closed, the designer must consider how important is system reliability. If a simple distribution, as in the example, is adopted, pump failure will cause a cessation of supply which may be acceptable in some systems. Such a system is called a tree system. More often, a standby supply will be needed and this is achieved by cross connecting two adjacent tree systems, the whole ship being served by several tree systems each of which normally operates independently. (Fig. 14.5.) Emergency supply by one pump to two cross connected tree systems will, of course, reduce the pressure at the demand points and, unless properly designed, may result in totally inadequate supply. This case must therefore be the subject of calculation during the design stage.

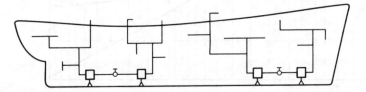

Fig. 14.5 Cross connected tree systems

Systems of importance where no interruption of supply can be tolerated are designed as ring mains with a number of pumps running in parallel. This type of system permits pumps to be rested or to break down or pipes to be damaged with a high chance of maintaining supply to equipment. Chilled water systems in warships, where deprivation of cooling water to some equipment for even a few seconds would damage performance, are typical. There are many different index paths in this case depending upon which pumps are operating or whether cross connections are opened to isolate a damaged section; moreover, the positions of null points where there is no flow in the system are not obvious. There will be a number of trial flow patterns to be tried and here again is a fruitful area for computer programming. A typical large ship chilled water ring main system is shown simplified in Fig. 14.6. There are many variations possible to this scheme and different safety and emergency devices can be incorporated; for example, automatic pressure actuated starting for alternative pumps. In a complex system, it is necessary to regulate the flow to each facility concerned by means of constant flow devices in order that the system may be balanced. Such devices meter the flow to the required amount for a wide range of pressure differential.

In this short description of the design of piping systems, it has not been possible to cover all design features, for which separate textbooks are available. The matching of the pump characteristic normally designed by a sub-contractor, to the system demands must be considered with care to ensure stable operation. Positioning of the pump in the ship is also important to avoid a high suction demand on the pump. System priming must be considered. The need for a

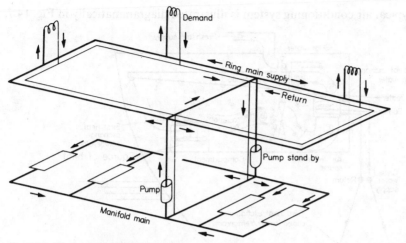

Fig. 14.6 Ring main chilled water system

reservoir or gravity tank to even out the fluctuations in demand is also important. Filtering and flushing of the system must be considered and bleed valves at local high points provided to remove trapped air.

AIR CONDITIONING AND VENTILATION

It is commonly believed that ventilation in a ship is required to enable people to breathe. In fact, an atmosphere fit for breathing can be achieved on very small quantities of fresh air—a small fraction of that needed for ventilation. The major purposes of ventilation are:

(a) to remove heat generated in the ship;
(b) to supply oxygen for supporting burning;
(c) to remove odours.

For most compartments outside machinery spaces, the need to remove heat predominates. Looked at from this point of view, it is clear why normal ventilation often fails to provide comfort. Air drawn in from outside must leave hotter than it entered; a hot, muggy day outside will produce hotter, muggier conditions inside. Heat created within a compartment will be collected by the ventilation air which will be exhausted, hotter, to the atmosphere—one of the two natural sinks for heat available to a ship.

Air conditioning uses the other major natural heat sink, the sea. Heat produced within the ship is ultimately exhausted to the sea and an air conditioning system must efficiently permit this transfer, as will presently be described (Fig. 14.7). While ventilation does remove heat and may create complete comfort for machinery, it cannot effect proper control of the three principal factors which affect human comfort, namely

(a) air temperature
(b) air humidity
(c) air purity.

It is these three factors which air conditioning controls, to varying degree.

A typical air conditioning system is illustrated diagrammatically in Fig. 14.7.

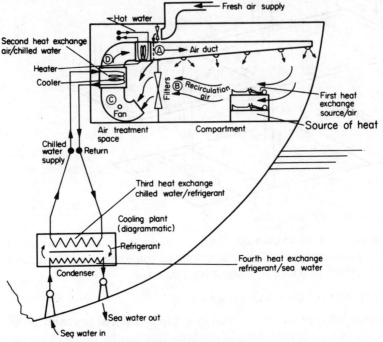

Fig. 14.7 Typical air conditioning system, diagrammatic

The source of heat in the compartment first loses some heat to the air blown over it; this air is passed through a fan, together with a modicum of fresh air and over the surfaces of a coil heat exchanger rendered cold by chilled water, before returning to the compartment. The chilled water carries this heat to refrigeration machinery which conveys it to the sea in its condenser. Heat produced by the source must therefore be efficiently transferred from one medium to another three or four times until it reaches the sea. There are three principal components of the process; in reverse order they are:

(a) Refrigeration machinery for cooling and calorifiers for heating. Design of this is a specialized task which can conveniently be isolated from the design of the whole system, provided that the tasks required of it are adequately defined by the system designer (i.e. pressure–quantity relationship, temperature ranges, etc.);

(b) Water systems, chilled water and hot water. These are designed in the manner already described previously for piping systems. There may well be requirements for dual chilled water supply for important equipment and devices providing a constant flow are often essential;

(c) Air system. This system, involving two heat exchanges, is the crux of air conditioning and is the subject of the calculations described presently. In so doing, it is necessary to assume on the part of the reader, a familiarity with some elementary physics; some definitions of air measurement are given in Chapter 9. Basically, the air system is a recirculatory one with a small quantity of fresh air make up, sufficient only to keep bacteria levels and odours down. Physiologists recommend between 5 and 10 ft³/min per occupant, (0·0025–0·005 m³/s), although less will limit bacteria.

All ambient air contains water. The amount carried can be measured by two thermometers, one of which is kept wet and the relationships between wet and dry bulb readings have been related by a chart known as the *psychrometric chart*. This chart relates wet and dry bulb temperatures, latent and total heats, percentage relative humidity and specific volume of air in any condition. Such a chart is shown in Fig. 14.8.

What condition of air is comfortable to personnel? Such is the accommodating nature of the human body that there is a good deal of latitude, but experiments have shown that the areas shaded in Fig. 14.8 for summer and winter are the most suitable. Any air conditioning system should therefore aim to produce communal compartment conditions in the middle of this shaded area and to enable individual cabin occupants to select conditions over such a range. ·

A further measure of human comfort is provided by the *effective temperature* (ET) *scale* (it is not a temperature), which is a variable ratio of wet/dry temperatures and also air velocity, found experimentally to accord a feeling of comfort. Reference 7 illustrates it. Above 78 ET, (25 ET in SI) discomfort increases and it is this limit, known also as the *threshold of comfort*, to which warship systems are designed to operate in extreme tropical ambients. This limit, shown in Fig. 14.8 for light air movement as 'design effective temperature', although the extreme design condition, is infrequently met in warships which operate, like merchant ships, within the comfort zones.

The first step in the process of air conditioning design is the determination of the sources of heat. A given compartment gains heat by conduction through deck and bulkheads, from electrical equipment, hot pipes, lighting, the ventilation fan itself and from personnel. Each of these is a source of sensible heat and personnel, in addition, are a source of latent heat of evaporation. Heat given off by personnel depends on how heavily they are working; average figures are given in Table 14.5.

Table 14.5
Personnel heat

	Sensible heat	Latent heat	Total
People seated, resting	150 (44)*	250 (73)*	400 (117)*
People walking, working	150 (44)*	450 (132)*	600 (176)*
	Btu/hr (Watts)*		

Gains through boundaries follow the law

Heat gain $= U \times$ surface area $\times$ temperature difference

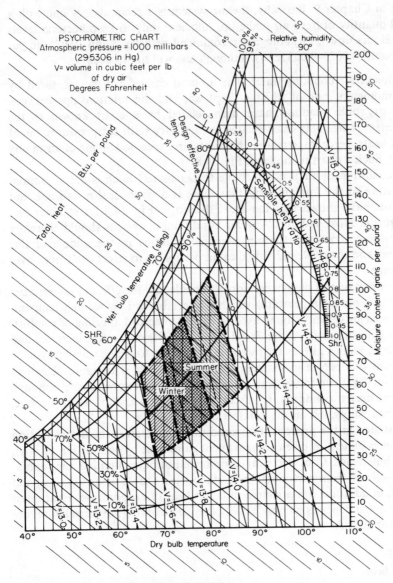

Fig. 14.8 Psychrometric chart (Imperial units)

U is the rate of heat transferred per unit area per degree and is derived from the thermal conductivity constant k for the material of the boundary. Values for some materials are given in Table 14.6.

To obtain U, the insulating effect of the still air next to the boundary, known as *surface film resistance* R, must be added in. For air outside the ship R is about 0·22 in British units (0·039 in metric), for air inside manned compartments it is 0·63 (0·110 metric) and for a closed air space 1·0 (0·18 metric) and for water is 0·005 (0·001 metric).

Table 14.6
Thermal conductivity constants

Material	k $\left(\dfrac{\text{Btu in.}}{\text{ft}^2 \text{ hr} \,°\text{F}}\right)$	k $\left(\dfrac{\text{W}}{\text{mK}}\right)$
Standard glass fibre marine board	0·30	0·043
Cork slab	0·29	0·042
Block asbestos	0·38	0·055
Plywood, fireproofed	1·05	0·152
Teak, across grain	0·96	0·139
Cork linoleum	0·50	0·072
Aluminium	830	120
Steel	320	46
Glass (in shadow)	7	1·01

$$U = \frac{1}{R + \Sigma(x/k)}$$

where x is the insulation thickness. Furthermore, due to imperfections in fitting, the k values for insulants given in Table 14.6 are, from experience, doubled. Thus for a surface of 25 mm steel + 25 mm glass fibre + 6 mm plywood inside manned compartments,

$$U = \frac{1}{0·110 + 0·5(0·0005 + 0·5814 + 0·0395)} = 2·376 \text{ W/m}^2\text{K}$$

Temperature difference is normally that of compartment temperatures but where surfaces are exposed to the sun, as in the tropics, they are assumed to acquire temperatures of 140°F (60°C) if horizontal and 120°F (49°C) if vertical. Machinery space deckheads are assumed to be at 180°F (82°C) and galleys and auxiliary machinery rooms at 120°F.

The whole heat gain calculation is performed on standard forms from which are derived

(*a*) total heat

(*b*) sensible heat ratio $= \dfrac{\text{sensible heat}}{\text{total heat}}$

A typical heat load calculation might appear as in Table 14.7. t_0, t_i and t_d are temperatures outside, inside and the difference.

Having performed the heat gain calculation, it is necessary to return to the psychrometric chart. The cycle of operation of the air in the compartment is: heat and moisture gained by recirculation air which is returned, augmented by some fresh air, to the cooling coil; at the coil it is cooled below its dew point to remove heat and moisture and, with possibly some after warming, returned to the compartment. This cycle must be constructed on the psychrometric chart so illustrated in Fig. 14.9 for the positions illustrated in Fig. 14.7.

Table 14.7
Heat gain calculation

Source	Dimensions (m)	Type	t_0 °C	t_i °C	t_d K	Area A, m²	U W/m²K	Heat gain UAK (W)
Port bulkhead	10×3 25 mm	MFMB	49	29	20	30	2·38	1428
Stbd. bulkhead	10×3 25 mm	MFMB	34	29	5	30	2·38	357
After bulkhead	8×3 25 mm	MFMB	29	29	0	24	2·49	0
Fwd. bulkhead	8×3 30 mm	MFMB	49	29	20	24	2·18	1046
Crown	10×8 6 mm	lino	29	29	0	80	6·58	0
Deck	10×8 50 mm	MFMB	49	29	20	80	1·45	2320
								5151
Body heat, sensible	28 men × 44							1232
Lights	2000 W							2000
Equipment	5·85 kW							5850
Space heaters	2 kW							2000
Fan	1·6 h.p. × 745·7							1193
TOTAL, SENSIBLE								17,426
Body heat, latent	28 men × 132							3696
TOTAL HEAT								21,122

$$\text{SENSIBLE HEAT RATIO} = \frac{17,426}{21,122} = 0{\cdot}825$$

After leaving the after warmer at A, the air picks up sensible and latent heat along AB, constructed to a slope representing the sensible heat ratio obtained from the heat gain calculation and of length given by the total heat gain. At B, the air leaves the room near the edge of the comfort zone along the 25 ET line. BC is obtained by proportioning BE in the ratio of recirculation/fresh air, E representing the condition of the intake air. (This will generally have been pre-treated at the point where it enters the ship in order to avoid excessively hot or cold trunks between that point and the compartment.) At C, the air mixture enters the cooler. CD represents the extraction by the coil to give a point D horizontally from A since the heat added by the after warm DA is all sensible. D needs to be compatible with the available chilled water temperature and, for an efficient cooler, on the 90 per cent relative humidity line. CD then represents the total heat and sensible heat ratio of the coil (or coil slope) which permits a suitable coil to be selected from a standard range. There is a certain amount of trial and error about this process, but it is not difficult to reach a satisfactory cycle with B at the edge of the comfort zone of Fig. 14.8 or at least below the 25 ET line. Often, this can be achieved without after warm. The quantity of air recirculated is now obtained from the sensible heat pick up in the room over the dry bulb temperatures represented by A and B. If this, as in the heat gain example, is 9°C, with the specific heat of air 1009J/kgK.

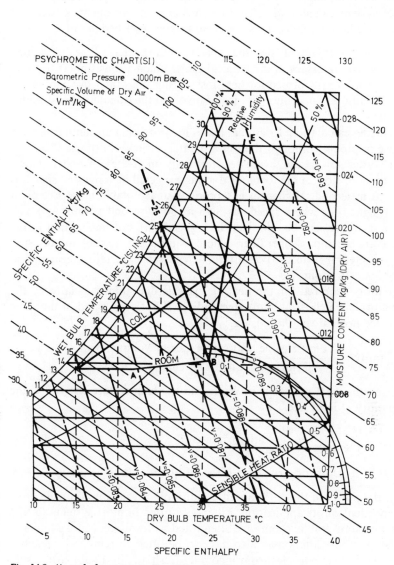

Fig. 14.9 Air cycle for system in Fig. 14.7, using SI psychrometric chart.

$$\text{recirculation air returned at B} = \frac{17{,}426}{9 \times 1009}$$

$$= 1\cdot92 \text{ kg of dry air per second.}$$

This must now be proportioned up with the fresh air to give the total air to be handled by fan and cooler. Alternatively, this may be obtained directly from the sensible heat and dry bulb readings of C and D. A fuller description of this process may be found from Refs. 4 and 6.

This process is fundamental to good air conditioning design and represents the nub of system calculation. There are, however, many other calculations which the space here available does not permit to be described in full:

(a) Heater sizing. It is unlikely that the capacity of the heater will be determined by after warm necessary in the tropical cycle. Calculations similar to those for heat gain are performed for heat loss during the winter cycle, often on the same form. Because humidity is not involved the calculation is straightforward;

(b) Trunk sizing calculation. Frictional losses in air ducting are similar in form to those in piping, although there is a greater variety of fittings. Pressures are an order lower and expressed normally in inches of water gauge. Velocity of air flow in the tortuous ducting expected in congested spaces is about 10 m/second. Higher speeds produce unacceptable noise except in long straight runs where speeds as high as 30 m/second permitting much smaller trunking, can be adopted. Such speeds are not uncommon in the space available in passenger liners where twin ducts, one cool and one hot, are also sometimes fitted, so permitting each passenger to adjust the temperature of his own cabin;

(c) Air quantity required for the heating cycle is determined usually by the cooling cycle which is the more demanding. If not, it is found in the same way as for normal ventilation, viz.:

$$\text{Air quantity} = \frac{\text{Total sensible heat rate} \times \text{specific volume of air}}{\text{Temperature rise} \times \text{specific heat of air}}$$

If the sensible heat gain H is in Watts and the temperature rise is 3°C the air quantity Q in m³/sec.

$$Q = \frac{H \times 0.88}{3 \times 1009} = \frac{H}{3500} \text{approximately}$$

With H in BTU/hr for a rise of 5°F the air quantity in ft³/min is $Q = H/5$.

Finally, the purity of the air in an air conditioning system is controlled to a degree dependent on its application. Filters are fitted in most systems to trap dust, fluff and soot. Public rooms are often fitted with tobacco smoke filters.

In warships, some filters may also have to be fitted to remove radioactive and other dangerous particles from incoming fresh air. In a submarine, submerged for long periods, the purity of the air must be controlled more closely by removing carbon dioxide and hydrogen and by generating oxygen.

Further information can be obtained from Refs. 5, 6 and 7.

FUEL SYSTEMS

There are several reasons why the type of fuelling system needs to be decided early in the design. Principally, the weight and disposition of fuel have an important effect on stability and trim of the ship and the demands on space need early consideration. Being low in the ship, a large quantity of fuel has a stabilizing effect. As is explained later, special consideration must be given to stability when fuel is used up. Delivery of a satisfactory quantity of fuel oil from service tank to boiler or engine, while important, is a simple matter, effected by a simple local system. An important influence on the ship design, the whole system is considerably more extensive in order to achieve some or all of the following:

(*a*) to store sufficient fuel to enable the ship to achieve its required range in rough weather;
(*b*) to accept high pressure re-fuelling without spillage or structural damage to the ship;
(*c*) to provide to the service tank fuel of sufficient quality;
(*d*) to ballast empty fuel tanks with sea water and to discharge such water overboard without polluting coastal waters;
(*e*) to accept fuel at positions consistent with the supply ship supply points.

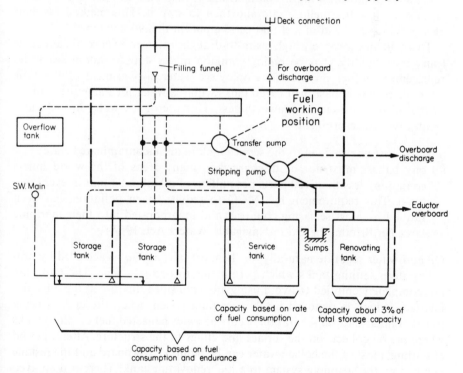

Fig. 14.10 Diagrammatic warship fuel system

Stowage of oil is usually effected in double bottoms and in deep tanks right forward and right aft in cargo ships. An adequate margin of quantity—often 20 per cent—should be provided over that needed for the planned route before refuelling in port or at sea, to allow for rough weather and emergencies. Warships in peacetime rarely operate below 50 per cent capacity and in wartime 20 per cent is uncomfortably low.

Warships alongside oilers provide easy targets and need therefore to accept fuel at high speed and pressure. Also, it is desirable that escorts should spend a minimum of time off the screen. Bunkering may be a critical part of the turn round time for a merchant ship. Some ingenious systems have been devised to provide fuel at high speed to the tank network without allowing the consequent high pressure to cause structural damage to the ship. Such pressures may be as high as 150 lbf/in^2 when delivering 400–600 tonf/hr through a 6 in. hose and this would certainly rupture most tanks. A typical system in a warship is shown diagrammatically in Fig. 14.10. All but one of the storage tanks are connected to a manifold on the bottom leg of an L- or inverted T-shaped tank. Three-quarters of the way up the vertical trunk is the inlet to the indicator storage tank which can be observed by the engineer controlling the operation. Clearly, all of the other storage tanks must be full before fuel rises in the trunk to this inlet, showing the engineer that he is approaching the end of the operation. Soundings or indicator alarms in the trunk or final tank can provide the check signals to slow the fuelling rate and then to stop it. This method of filling clearly limits the head of fuel that can be put on the storage tank.

To avoid an excessively high beam-to-draught ratio, and yet retain adequate transverse stability, it is becoming common in warships to adopt sea water replacement of fuel. Submarines employ sea water displacement of diesel oil. Oil tankers may ballast their cargo tanks with sea water for the return journey to the oil ports to ensure seaworthiness. This use of sea water in fuel tanks creates two basic problems:

(a) fuel must be provided to the service tank in an uncontaminated state;
(b) oily ballast must not be discharged in many areas of the world unless containing less than 100 parts per million of oil (about $\frac{1}{2}$ pint in every two tons). This requirement by IMCO to reduce beach pollution, has been ratified by most seafaring countries and incorporated into their maritime laws. (In Britain, the Oil in Navigable Waters Act, 1957.)

Oil and water separate naturally for the most part and (a) is achieved by providing deep settling tanks which permit this to occur in time. The tanks are not completely emptied to avoid using any emulsified mixture at the oil/water interface, which is removed by the stripping system when the tank is being rested. Similar natural separation occurs in water ballasted fuel or cargo tanks where the oil collects on the surface and clings to the structure. After a period of settling, most of the ballast water can be pumped overboard and the residue pumped by the stripping system to a fuel renovating tank. There it is sprayed by a chemical additive or de-mulsifier which assists separation and the water can again be discharged. Oil centrifuges can be fitted to speed separation.

There are four systems associated with fuelling and ballasting, some using common piping:

(a) Fuel filling. This delivers fuel from standard deck connections to the storage tanks usually using shore or supply ship's pumps. Air escapes and sounding tubes to every tank are needed;

(b) Fuel transfer. Suctions are placed low in the tanks and fitted with devices to reduce air drawing but not right at the bottom, where heavy sludge collects. This is used to control the ship's trim as well as supplying fuel to the service tanks and much piping may be common with (a);

(c) Sullage stripping. This is to remove residues, emulsified mixture and sludge;

(d) De-ballasting. Often, this employs salt water eductors instead of pumps. Some oil tankers employ a re-cycling system using fresh water to deal with residue after cargo tanks have been cleaned by steam hoses.

SEWAGE SYSTEMS AND WASTE DISPOSAL

Pollution of harbours by sewage is now actively discouraged in many parts of the world and in some places, forbidden. As a result, the fitting of sewage treatment systems is becoming common practice. Waste from heads, urinals and galleys is directed to a sewage treatment tank deep in the ship, passing first through a unit which reduces the solid material to particles. One common type of system utilizes a treatment tank divided by weirs into three sections, the first an aeration compartment supplied by air at the bottom from a compressor. This assists breakdown by bacteria and the resulting sludge weirs to the second, a settling compartment: here sludge settles at the bottom, for re-cycling to the first compartment and clear effluent weirs at the top into the third compartment. Laundry, bathroom and scupper waste goes directly to the third compartment which is pumped out via an underwater discharge. The treatment tank should be about 2 m deep with a plan area of about 0·1 m² per person served, and the planes of the weirs should be athwartships to minimize the ship motion effects.

A sewage system permits heads and bathrooms to be sited lower in the ship and to be used while the ship is in dry dock. This is helpful to a naval architect who is normally faced with excessive demands for space high in the ship, and should be known before any serious layout is attempted as compartments must be grouped to accommodate it. Chemical sewage treatment is also possible.

Garbage grinders in food preparing spaces discharge directly overboard below water. Can crushers ensure that this type of waste sinks or can be stowed more economically for discharge in port. Smoke from incinerators is offensive and should discharge into the main stack or be thrown well clear of the ship, although some modern incinerators are smokeless.

CATHODIC PROTECTION

Electrochemical corrosion occurs when two dissimilar metals are present in an electrolytic medium. Sea water is an efficient electrolyte. Different parts of the same metal made dissimilar, perhaps, by work, or a metal and its oxide are sufficiently dissimilar to create such corrosion as shown in Fig. 14.11. An anodic area, such as iron oxide, is eaten away creating more rust, while an electric current is created, leaving the metal at the anodic area and entering it at the cathodic area, where no corrosion occurs. Painting, if perfect, increases

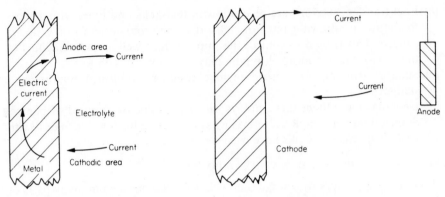

Fig. 14.11 *Electrolytic corrosion*   Fig. 14.12 *Sacrificial anode*

electrical resistance and retards the process but at any imperfection in the paint, deep pitting may be caused by concentrating the electrolytic effects.

Average values of the electrical potential for a number of different metals against the same standard in sea water at 25°C are given in the electro-chemical scale of Table 14.8. Where the difference between two potentials exceeds about 0·25 volts, appreciable corrosion of the metal with the higher potential (the anode) will occur, if the junction is moist.

Table 14.8
Electro-chemical table

Material	Potential, volts
Magnesium alloy sheet	1·58
Zinc base die casting	1·09
Galvanized iron	1·06
Aluminium alloy (14% Zn) casting	0·91
Aluminium alloy (5% Mg)	0·82
Cadmium plating	0·78
Aluminium alloy extrusion	0·72
Mild steel	0·70
Cast iron, grey	0·70
Duralumin (Al/Cu) alloy	0·60
Chromium plating on mild steel	0·53
Brass	0·30
Stainless steel, austenitic	0·25
Gunmetal	0·24
Aluminium bronze	0·23
Phosphor bronze	0·22
Copper	0·18
Millscale (Fe_3O_4)	0·18
Monel (nickel alloy)	0·16
Nickel plating	0·14
Silver plating	0·01

Another metal, higher up the electro-chemical scale, placed nearby in the electrolyte, transforms the whole of the first metal of Fig. 14.11 into a cathode if the effect is sufficient to overwhelm the local action and no corrosion occurs there (Fig. 14.12). All corrosion occurs at the new metal which is the sacrificial anode. Such protection is commonly applied to small static objects such as buoys, and individual piles and materials used for the anodes include very pure zinc, magnesium or aluminium. They are also used, often ineffectually, at sea inlets.

A more efficient form of cathodic protection is effected by opposing the natural effect by impressing a direct current in the circuit and adopting anodes which may or may not corrode. The whole immersed surface thus becomes cathodic. This is called impressed current cathodic protection, and is suitable for large areas such as liquid cargo tanks and the outside of the hull. The system can be used for ships building or laid up, as well as those in service. The current density required is about $1 \, mA/ft^2$ of surface area ($10 \, mA/m^2$) and the potential needed to create this varies with draught, speed, temperature and salinity; typically, it is about one volt. Automatic control units are needed to give this adjustment relative to a half cell datum fixed to the hull. A suitable permanent anode is provided by a plate of platinum-covered titanium fixed to an area of the hull covered with an epoxy resin insulant designed to spread the protective effects. Sacrificial impressed current anodes of trailing aluminium wire are not uncommon.

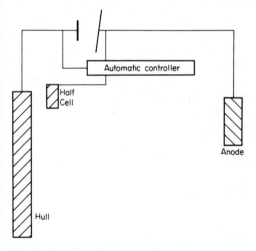

Fig. 14.13 Impressed current cathodic protection

There are several reasons why a decision on whether cathodic protection is to be adopted needs to be made before the design of the ship commences. Space and power demands need to be known but primarily, corrosion margins have to be decided. Classification societies permit a reduction of about 10 per cent in section structural modulus of ships protected by an approved process of cathodic protection. Certainly a substantial reduction in corrosion margin is justified.

As well as the external surfaces of the hull and the internal surfaces of liquid cargo tanks, cathodic protection is applicable to piping and machinery systems.

Equipment

One of the important processes in a ship design is the laying out of the weather deck. In aircraft carriers, the length of the flight deck and, thereby, the size of the ship, is largely determined by the equipment—pull out of arrester wires, lengths of catapults, spotting positions for aircraft. While in other ships, it is not of such prime importance, it does require early consideration. Anchors and cables, cargo handling equipment, boats and davits, helicopter landing, towing equipment, storing equipment, accommodation ladders, hatch cover gear, are some of the major items of equipment which profoundly affect weather deck layout and which must be fitted in with the demands of air intakes, exhausts, superstructure requirements, bridge layout, navigation and accommodation needs; many of these features, must of course be associated with compartments below.

CARGO HANDLING

Turn round time is an important economic factor in the operation of all ships, particularly short haul ships. The method of handling cargo is therefore of fundamental importance in the ship design process. Shapes and sizes of cargo, port facilities, effect of weather, working space and trading patterns all affect the question, while the various cycles of operation which interlock must be compatible if a pile up of cargo or an idle gang are to be avoided. Method study techniques are valuable in studying the operations and defining interfaces. At an early stage in the design of the ship, it is necessary to fix hold dimensions and weather deck layout and these are affected by the unit size of cargo, methods of transfer within and outside the ship, the number of hatches athwartships and other demands of cargo handling.

Specialized ships need specialized handling gear which is often installed ashore. In such cases, the same gear can deal with several similar ships. This is less costly and avoids penalizing each ship. Bulk carriers employ various ingenious forms of endless bucket hoist or dredge with conveyor belt transfer all built into the ship, or they may rely on complicated shore based excavator cranes. Roll-on roll-off ships can be devised for standard wheeled cargo. Among the more difficult problems, is the general cargo vessel which in the past has had to deal with a wide variety of packages stowed at the ingenuity of the first mate. The introduction of standard pallets, standard general cargo containers and bulk containers is progressing and these clearly make the job of stowage predictable, quicker and safer. So called 'container ships' are becoming common. How much cargo can make efficient use of such standard packages depends on the trade and routes envisaged for the ship, but there is certainly some scope for them. One problem is the creation of suitable distribution and collection centres in each country.

Handling in and out of the holds of a general cargo ship is most commonly performed by union purchase, illustrated in Fig. 14.14. Two derricks are guyed into fixed positions and their two hoist wires joined to a common hook. Manipulation of the speeds of the two winches driving the hoist wires achieves the required transfer. There are many variations of this and other schemes involving derricks, often with powered topping lifts. Fixed or travelling cranes or overhead gantry cranes are sometimes fitted. Combinations of lifts and athwartships travellers, called siporters are common in passenger liners for baggage. In the hold itself, transport to lift or plumbing position is effected by truck of some type.

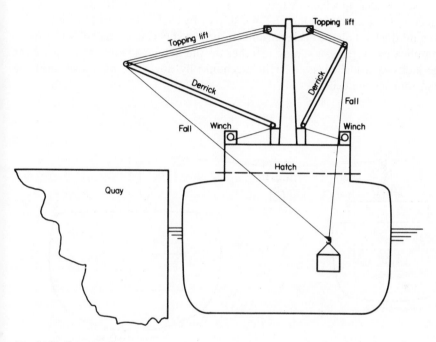

Fig. 14.14 Union purchase

There are many combinations of handling equipment available to the naval architect who must work out with the owners the most efficient scheme and design it into the ship from the beginning. Reference 10 gives some further information and references and illustrates certain of the economic considerations; these can lead to some surprising conclusions—for example, that some parts of a ship may best be left empty because they are uneconomic to fill with cargo!

REPLENISHMENT OF PROVISIONS

For a passenger liner or warship carrying 2000 people, the problem of transporting twenty tons of victuals a day is large. Ideally, the designer will group his storerooms and cold and cool rooms in a block, served by a lift or conveyor to the preparing spaces and to the weather deck, close to the point where, in port, the provisions are brought on board. Additional mechanical handling equipment may be provided for horizontal transfer of provisions.

In addition, the warship needs to replenish at sea since it may operate for prolonged periods in waters where there are no ports. A position for replenishment at sea must be worked into the weather deck layout, kingpost, winch, landing area and route as described in Ref. 15. For use with ammunitioning procedures, this may require special consideration. The rig for replenishment at sea comprises, basically, a kingpost or high point on each ship between which is stretched a jackstay or highwire which is kept at a constant tension by a self rendering winch. A traveller on pulleys is then run along the jackstay pulled either on a closed loop by one ship or by each ship in turn on an inhaul. To land the load on the deck, tension on the jackstay is slackened off or, in more complicated systems, a sliding member on the kingpost, with the eyeplate for the jackstay attached, is brought mechanically down the kingpost, until the load touches the deck.

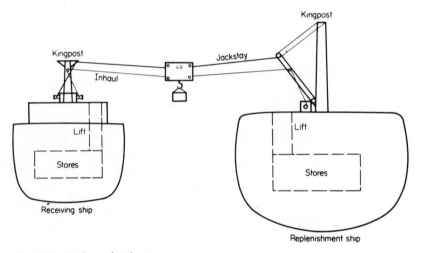

Fig. 14.15 Rig for replenishment at sea

BOATS AND DAVITS

Requirements for life saving apparatus have already been outlined in Chapter 5. In passenger liners, it is safe and convenient to allocate one complete superstructure deck—the boat deck—for access to boats and life rafts. Gravity davits make this possible in an efficient manner. In small warships, boats are generally grouped amidships to avoid interference with the weapons placed forward and aft. A 27 ft whaler is usually provided to act as a seaboat and this is usually stowed just aft of the bridge. Liferafts are provided for lifesaving.

Weapons

THE SHIP-WEAPON SYSTEM

Gone are the days when weapons could be developed in the knowledge that they would receive widespread fitting in the fleet. Such is the need for complete integration of a weapon system into a ship, that neither can be properly developed without being influenced by the other at all stages. The Naval Staff must regard the ship–weapon system as a unit, and it must be developed by the designers as a complete concept.

Whether the weapon be fired from the air, land, surface ship or submarine against targets in, on or under the sea or on land, any weapon system contains basically four elements:

(a) surveillance;
(b) guidance, tracking and illumination;
(c) data handling;
(d) mechanical handling.

Figure 14.16 illustrates these four elements and their integration into a ship.

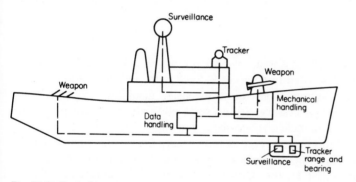

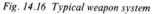
Fig. 14.16 Typical weapon system

The surveillance system awakens the ship to a potential threat. It may be a long range radar high in the ship, a long range search sonar below the keel or information from an aircraft or other external source. Pride of place must be reserved for this system, the eyes and ears of the ship. Information on the threat is passed to the tracking device which locks on to the echo and provides range and bearing information and guidance to the weapon, the target sometimes being illuminated by electromagnetic waves or pulses to assist the process. The tracking and guidance device may be narrow beam radar or sonar, visual or television sight.

Information thus received must be processed in various ways if the target is to be intercepted by a weapon at the right point. A digital or analogue computer effects this processing of the data in accordance with programs determined in advance by the mathematics of any situation. Such processed data is fed to the mechanical handling system, launcher and weapon continuously, the launcher following its directions until the weapon is fired. Further guidance is now required to direct the weapon on to the target; a guided missile may ride a radar beam or be commanded from the ship; a guided missile or underwater weapon may home on to its target by devices built into the weapon. There are many variations of this basic theme.

Even the simplest systems are very expensive to produce and make a big demand on the ship. It is necessary to combine elements of systems as far as is possible, for example, to use common radars and common data handling. How is the overall efficiency of the system to be judged? With a weapons payload in a ship often less than 5 per cent of its displacement, it must be guarded against inefficient use of weight and space and unnecessary duplication. The weight of the projectiles relative to the handling system must be as high as possible; in a simple manually handled missile system, the projectile weight may be 15 per cent or more of the overall system weight, while in a system involving automatic handling it may be less than 10 per cent. Space occupied by projectiles is often only 5 per cent of compartment volume. Silo launching increases these efficiencies. Ideally, the range of the surveillance radar should be just enough to establish the target in time to allow the guidance system to pick it up and fire a defensive weapon to intercept it at a minimum acceptable range.

SHIP FITTING PROBLEMS

The environments in which a weapon system must exist and operate in a ship have already been discussed in Chapter 9. Such is the delicacy of many parts of modern weapon systems, that quite extensive insulation from excessive shock and vibration is necessary. Stiffness too plays an important part, since several parts of a system must not become out of alignment due to the elasticity of the structure and this must be considered in siting the various elements of the system. Stiffness of seating, too, may be important in determining the characteristics of the servo loop for the stabilizing equipment. Prefabrication of some parts of a weapon system is sometimes desirable to enable them to be completed in controlled conditions remote from the hurly burly of a shipyard; sufficient stiffness may be more difficult to achieve in such cases, and there may be penalties in structure weight and electric wiring but it should be considered.

Disposition of the different elements of a weapon system must be considered relative to their vulnerability. Lengthy lines of communication are undesirable and, if possible, the sensors, control and weapons should be closely grouped in the ship. Facilities common to several weapon systems like a central computer need to be well protected.

From the first, the naval architect is faced with numerous conflicting demands for upper deck siting. Different weapon systems, command from the bridge, navigation arrangements, all demand minimum blind arcs while boats, anchors and cables, replenishment at sea, funnels, air intakes and exhausts all must be accommodated in demanding positions. At an early stage in design, a weather deck layout and sketch of rig must be attempted and blind arcs of each weapon system deduced. Arcs of tracking/guidance aerials must be compatible with those of the weapon they control.

Blind arcs for radars, sonars and visual sights are, generally, simply the physical blind areas although, spurious reflections and side lobe interference may complicate the problem. For projectiles, the blind arc is greater than that given by the physical obstruction due to wind, gravity drop, missile dispersion and ship motion. These may conveniently be deduced from the trigonometry of the situation, a computer easing the labour of calculation. In addition, there are frequently limitations to the separation of different parts of a system, to the lengths of waveguides and to the proximity of different apparatus. Modern communications require large parts of the ship's structure to be energized to act as aerials and to be of certain dimensions in consequence to give the desired frequency bands. Effects of recoil and of blast from guns and missiles on structure, equipment and personnel must be considered.

With all these and many more conflicting demands, compromise is necessary and is best achieved early in design. An influence diagram illustrating the influences governing the shipfitting of a weapon system, is shown in Fig. 14.17.

Accommodation

Demands on a warship for crew accommodation are so great that they comprise a major design feature of the ship and the size of the ship is profoundly affected by its complement. Part of the growth in size of warships since the second world war is traceable to:

(a) an increase in standards of accommodation;
(b) an increase in complements.

The first results from the social changes ashore while the second results from the greater complexity of modern ships and a higher maintenance load. Such is the total through cost of each man, that from a financial point of view, complements must be cut to the bone. Each man requires not only space and weight in a messdeck but a small proportion of galley, heads, provision room, stores, chapel and many other facilities which enlarge the ship, requiring bigger machinery, more fuel, higher maintenance, etc. Standard weight allowances in warships are fourteen men to the tonf alone and seven men to the tonf with

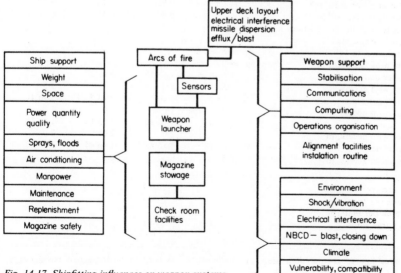

Fig. 14.17 Shipfitting influences on weapon systems

their immediate messdeck effects, but the overall effect of an addition to complement is much more than this for the reasons stated.

Spaces in a warship coming under the general heading of accommodation are cabins, sea cabins, wardroom, anteroom, messdecks, galleys, serveries, vegetable preparing spaces, beef screens, aircrew refreshment bar, bakery, pantries, drying rooms, dining halls, sculleries, incinerators, bathrooms, heads, laundries, cinema, sound reproduction room, television studio, chapel, schoolroom, library, recreation spaces, NAAFI canteen, bookstall, barber's shop, ice cream bar, tobacco kiosk, sick bay, dental clinics and prisons. Not all ships have all these spaces. Layout of the ship to effect a suitable juxtaposition of all of these and other spaces is a considerable task and requires a familiarity with all features of life on board ship. In general, men do not like noise or smell, they do not like sleeping where they eat, they are happier if they can see daylight, they like opportunities for privacy as well as communal activities, they need to be reasonably close to adequate bathrooms and toilets, their sleep should be uninterrupted by others changing watch and their food should be well served, diverse and dependable. If the naval constructor achieves all of these without compromising the ship's fighting ability, he has done well indeed.

In the early stages of design, space must be allocated to each feature of the ship, in order to estimate the ship's size. As a first guide for warships, the allowances of Table 14.9 are useful. All space allocation depends much on the

Table 14.9
Initial accommodation space estimates for warships

	Officers	Chief Petty Officers	Petty Officers	Junior Rates
Cabins, area, each, m²	4–8			
Sleeping area per man, m²		2·10	1·55	1·44
Recreation area per man, m²		0·75	0·75	0·50
Dining area per man, m²		0·40	0·35	0·28
Seating in recreation area, ratio of man		2/3	2/3	2/3
Wardroom sittings, max.	2			
Table space, m	0·6			
Anteroom area per man, m²	1·0			
Showers per man	1 to 8	1 to 15	1 to 20	1 to 25
Space with access	1·5	1·5	1·5	1·5
Washbasins per man	1 to 3	1 to 5	1 to 8	1 to 10
Space with access, m²	1·0	1·0	1·0	1·0
WCs per man	1 to 6	1 to 15	1 to 15	1 to 15
Space with access, m²	2·0	2·0	2·0	2·0
Urinals per man	1 to 18	1 to 45	1 to 45	1 to 45
Space with access, m²	0·5	0·5	0·5	0·5
Laundry area per man, m²		0·1		
Galley area per man, m²		0·2		
Sickbay area per man, m²				
Large ships		0·1		
Small ships		0·07		

Note: area figures are net deck areas after allowance has been made for access passageways, hatches, etc.

shape available, and rough layouts of selected spaces should be made to confirm the values used. In arranging the layout of compartments, dining halls must be arranged adjacent to serveries with a suitable flow of traffic for self service without cross flow or congestion; cold and dry store rooms should be readily accessible to the preparing spaces for daily supplies, lifts being provided where possible.

Because the tasks are quite different, the magnitude of the accommodation problem in a merchant ship (except passenger liners) is much smaller and it is doubtful whether the size of a cargo ship is appreciably affected by its complement. Large aircraft carriers may have complements of 3–4000, a 5000 tonf guided missile destroyer may carry 500 men while a 200,000 tonf deadweight oil tanker may carry less than 30. Accommodation standards in merchant ships, as a result, are relatively much higher, minimum standards being enforced by the laws of the country of registry.

For merchant ships, crew's accommodation is generally grouped as follows:

(a) Deck and engineer officers. In single or double cabins. Bathroom with one bath or shower and one washbasin for every six persons. Separate smoke room and dining saloon;
(b) Petty officers. Cabins and washing facilities as for officers. Separate messroom. Messrooms based on 1 m² per man;
(c) Engine room hands. Separate sleeping and dining accommodation. Bathrooms as for officers. The ILC recommended minimum floor area per person in sleeping rooms as:
 3·75 m² (40·36 ft²) in ships 1000–3000 tons
 4·25 m² (45·75 ft²) in ships of 3000–10,000 tons.
 4·75 m² (51·13 ft²) in ships 10,000 tons or over.
 Where two ratings share one room the figures are reduced by 1 m² per person.
(d) Deck hands. As for engine room hands. Bathrooms as for officers. Crew's smoke room shared with (c).

Clothes washing facilities are required with drying and ironing facilities. The whole accommodation should be sited above the summer loadline, be provided with natural light, ventilation, artificial light and heating. Passengers are to be totally segregated from the crew. The rules are variable depending on size and type of ship and reference should be made to the appropriate legislation.

Measurement

There are two measurements of a merchant ship's earning capacity which are of fundamental importance to its design and operation. These are *deadweight* and *tonnage*. Deadweight is related to the weight of cargo and tonnage is related to the volume of cargo. *Deadmass* is now increasingly used.

The deadweight of a ship is the difference between the load displacement up to the minimum permitted freeboard and the light displacement. The lightweight comprises hull weight and machinery. Deadweight is therefore the weight of all cargo, oil bunkers, fresh and feed water, stores, crew and effects. The weight of the cargo alone is called the *cargo deadweight*. A ready reckoner of deadweight against draught for a particular ship is often supplied to the ship's master in the form of a *deadweight scale*, shown in Fig. 14.18.

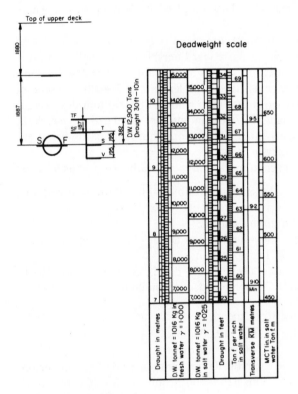

Fig. 14.18 Deadweight scale

A coefficient used in the early estimation of dimensions and the study of economics is the ratio of deadweight to deep displacement; this is called the deadweight ratio or *deadweight coefficient* and normally refers to summer load draught. The deadweight coefficient for the type ship will be a guide for the new design; typical values are given in Table 14.10 and in Chapter 15, although, since there is considerable variation in apparently similar ships, these should be treated with caution.

The volume of a ship is expressed in tons of 100 ft³ (2·83 m³) and is referred to as its *tonnage*. On its tonnage are based the charges for berthing the ship, docking, passage through canals and locks, and for many other facilities. It is often used as a coarse measure of a ship's size and is also confused, by the layman, with displacement.

Records of measurement of a ship's size in this manner can be traced back in the United Kingdom to the thirteenth century for the carriage of wine. A standard size of barrel, called a 'tun', was decreed in the fifteenth century for this purpose and taxes and harbour dues were based upon a ship's 'tunnage'. Over the centuries, various rules for assessing this tonnage, as it became, were devised, the most influential being the Moorson system of 1853.

Table 14.10
Typical values of deadweight coefficient

Ship	Deadweight coefficient $= \dfrac{\text{Deadweight}}{\text{Deep } \Delta}$
150 ft, Coaster	0·62
250 ft, Shelter deck and one deck	0·70
350 ft, Three island and two decks	0·74
450 ft, Refrig. shelter deck and two decks	0·58
550 ft, Container ship	0·60
700 ft, Bulk carrier	0·82
1000 ft, Oil tanker	0·86

Tonnage regulations have not always led to safe design. In 1773, the formula on which tonnage was assessed was $0\cdot515(L-0\cdot6B)B^2$, where L is the length and B the breadth of the ship. Because this did not include draught, owners required small beam and large draught to reduce tonnage; this, however, created poor stability and many ships were lost as a result. More recently, in order to exempt the 'tween decks and still permit them to carry cargo, the shelter deck was 'opened' by the provision of a tonnage hatch in the upper deck and openings in main transverse bulkheads resulting in minimal safety standards; the regulations were, in fact, formed to permit this exemption and are responsible for a huge number of shelter deck ships constructed in this artificial manner.

By the middle of the twentieth century, many different methods of assessment of tonnage existed; among the important tonnage regulations were the International, British, United States, Suez and Panama. Efforts by the Inter-Governmental Maritime Consultative Organization (IMCO) were directed in the 1960s towards producing an internationally agreed system of tonnage measurement, preferably by the application of simple formulae and this proved successful in 1969 when an international conference adopted the formulae given on page 560, which are being ratified by each country represented at IMCO.

There are two tonnages of primary interest no matter which authority is measuring or registering the ship. These are *gross tonnage* and *register tonnage* (*net*). The regulations governing their measurement are complicated but are summarized for the British Tonnage Regulations below. Other regulations differ only in detail.

The *tonnage deck* is the upper deck in vessels having one deck and the second deck in all other cases. Spaces above are 'tween decks and superstructures.

The *underdeck tonnage* is the total volume in tons of $100 \, \text{ft}^3$ of the ship below the tonnage deck to the inside of frames, underside of deck plating and above the inner bottom. This is obtained by detailed calculations, in a manner somewhat similar to that for displacement calculations and varies in detail for individual regulations; tonnage measured according to the tonnage regulations may, therefore, be slightly different from the actual volume of the spaces below the tonnage deck calculated for, say, cargo capacity.

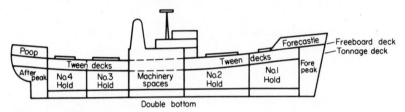

Fig. 14.19 General cargo ship

The *overdeck tonnage* is the volume to the inside of frames and deck plating of the 'tween decks, poop, bridge, forecastle, deckhouses and erections above the tonnage deck less the exempted spaces. Spaces *exempted* include dry cargo space (unless in a break in the deck) and certain closed-in spaces associated with machinery, safety equipment, navigation, galleys, washrooms, water ballast and workshops. *The gross tonnage* is the sum of the underdeck and overdeck tonnages plus volumes of hatchways (less one-half per cent of gross tonnage computed without hatchways), plus light and air spaces which are included at the owner's request in the measurement of the machinery spaces.

The register tonnage is the gross tonnage less the following deductions:

(i) Master's accommodation, crew's accommodation and provision store-rooms (limited to a maximum of 15 per cent of the total tonnage of Master's and crew's accommodation) but not fresh water;

(ii) Spaces below deck allocated exclusively to steering, navigation, safety equipment and sails (for ships propelled exclusively by sail, up to a maximum of $2\frac{1}{2}$ per cent of gross tonnage);

(iii) Spaces below deck allocated, with certain provisos, to workshops, pumps, donkey engine and boiler;

(iv) Spaces below deck used exclusively for water ballast up to a maximum of 19 per cent of the gross tonnage, including exempted spaces such as the double bottom and capacity below line of floors containing water ballast, oil fuel, etc.;

(v) Spaces below the upper deck occupied by propelling machinery. In ships propelled by screws, if the volume of this space is between 13 and 20 per cent of the gross tonnage, the deduction is 32 per cent of the gross tonnage; if the space occupied is less than 13 per cent of the gross tonnage, the deduction is in direct proportion to 32 per cent; if the volume of the propelling machinery is in excess of 20 per cent of the gross tonnage, the propelling power deduction is $1\frac{3}{4}$ times the tonnage of the propelling space.

The United Kingdom has incorporated the 1964 IMCO recommendations on the treatment of shelter deck and other 'open' spaces in the Merchant Shipping (Tonnage) Regulations 1967, made under the Merchant Shipping Act 1965; the recommendations permit the closing of all tonnage hatches and openings whilst retaining the exemption from measurement of the spaces they were fitted to. Under these regulations, which introduced the tonnage mark, dry cargo spaces in the upper 'tween decks may now be exempted from the gross tonnage (as given above in the definition of overdeck tonnage) provided

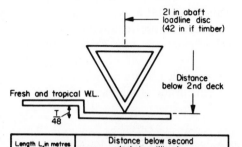

Length L, in metres	Distance below second deck in millimetres				
L_t L_t/D_s	12	14	16	18	20
67 and under	51	51	51	51	51
73	118	51	51	51	51
79	201	51	51	51	51
85	294	120	51	51	51
91	398	199	51	51	51
97	515	288	119	51	51
103	643	388	196	51	51
109	785	499	285	118	51
115	943	624	386	200	52
121	1111	758	494	288	124
127	1279	900	617	397	220
133	1450	1054	757	527	342
139	1636	1222	912	671	478
145	1829	1397	1074	823	621
151	2020	1570	1233	971	761

	12	14	16	18	20
157	2203	1735	1384	1112	894
163	2374	1888	1525	1241	1015
169	2537	2033	1656	1363	1128
175	2694	2173	1783	1479	1236
181	2850	2312	1907	1593	1342
187	2999	2441	2024	1700	1440
193	3144	2569	2139	1804	1536
199	3286	2694	2250	1905	1628
205	3425	2814	2357	2001	1716
211	3561	2933	2462	2096	1803
217	3694	3048	2562	2187	1886
223	3825	3161	2662	2276	1966
229	3951	3270	2758	2361	2043
235	4075	3376	2851	2443	2117
241	4197	3479	2941	2523	2188

Fig. 14.20 The tonnage mark

that the ship has placed on its side a tonnage mark and that this tonnage mark is not submerged. If it is submerged, the space is to be included in the tonnage. As a result, many ships now have two sets of tonnages and the Certificate of British Tonnage is available in three versions:

(a) for ships not assigned a tonnage mark;
(b) for ships assigned a tonnage mark and two sets of tonnages;
(c) for ships assigned a tonnage mark at the loadline and only one set of tonnages.

(c) results from the requirement that when the statutory loadline is assigned on the assumption that the second deck is the freeboard deck, the tonnage mark is placed in line with the deepest loading permitted by the assigned load line marks and only one set of tonnages assigned.

The distance of the tonnage mark below the moulded line of the second deck amidships, depends only upon the length of the second deck, L_t, and the height of the second deck at side above the top of keel, D_s. Extracts from the statutory table and the shape of the tonnage mark are given in Fig. 14.20. Full definitions are available in the Merchant Shipping (Tonnage) Regulations, 1967 published by HMSO.

The measurements of ships described above are statutory, i.e. required by the law of the country of registry. Two measurements not required by law but of use, where pertinent, to the owner, and designer are *grain capacity* and *bale capacity*. Grain capacity is the cargo volume in cubic metres or cubic feet out to the bottom and deck plating, excluding space filled by frames and other structure. Bale capacity is the cargo volume to the inside of the frames or sparrings on frames and beams.

New Tonnage Regulations

Two years after 25 countries registering at least 65 per cent of the gross tonnage of the world have formally ratified it, the 1969 IMCO proposals come into force. They are applicable to the gross and net tonnages of all new and converted ships and, at the Owner's request, to existing ships. The tonnage mark will disappear and, after a further 12 years, the old measurement system will be abandoned also for ships existing today. The formulae are as follows:

Gross tonnage, $GT = K_1 V$

Net tonnage, $NT = K_2 V_c \left(\dfrac{4d}{3D} \right)^2 + K_3 (N_1 + \dfrac{N_2}{10})$

where $K_1 = 0\cdot2 + 0\cdot02 \log_{10} V$

V = total volume of all enclosed spaces, m^3.

$K_2 = 0\cdot2 + 0\cdot02 \log_{10} V_c$

V_c = total volume of all cargo spaces, m^3.

d = moulded draught amidships, m.

D = moulded depth amidships, m.

$K_3 = 1\cdot25 \left(1 + \dfrac{GT}{10,000} \right)$

N_1 = number of passengers (in cabins $\geqslant$ 8 berths).

N_2 = number of passengers not included in N_1.

note that: $\left(\dfrac{4d}{3D} \right)^2$ must not be taken as greater than unity.

$K_2 V_c \left(\dfrac{4d}{3D} \right)^2$ must not be taken as greater than 0·25 GT.

NT must not be taken as less than 0·30 GT

if $N_1 + N_2$ is less than 13, N_1 and N_2 shall be taken to be zero.

d is the assigned summer loadline draught or, for passenger ships, the deepest subdivision loadline draught

V and V_c are calculated for metal ships to the inside of shell plating and are to include appendages.

While these new regulations are considerably simpler than the old ones, they still require a great deal of precise definition of geometry and phrases such as 'enclosed spaces' and 'excluded spaces'. National regulations should be consulted for the definitions.

Problems

1. Discuss the bases on which machinery may be chosen for a merchant ship. How do the arguments differ for a warship? What types of main propulsion machinery are available? Discuss the main properties of each.
2. Write a short description of the problems of

(a) nuclear main propulsion;
(b) all gas turbine propulsion;
(c) diesel-electric propulsion.

3. What factors affect the size and type of electrical generation in a warship? Describe briefly how electrical distribution may be achieved in merchant ships and warships.
4. Compare the properties of tree systems and ring main systems for fluid distribution in a ship. How are the calculations performed for each?
5. What does air conditioning seek to achieve that normal ventilation does not? Describe the series of heat exchanges in a ship's air conditioning system and how each is efficiently secured.
6. How does the choice of fuel system affect a ship design? Describe a system for rapid fuelling.
7. How do the laws on oil and sewage pollution affect the design of a ship?
8. Describe the principles of cathodic protection and how they are put into effect.
9. What is a container ship? Discuss the various ways of mechanical handling of cargo into and out of general cargo carriers.
10. Describe the various elements of a ship–weapon system and how they interact. What problems face the naval architect in siting these elements and what effects has the ship on the design of the weapon system?
11. A pump is required to deliver 400 tonnes of fresh water an hour at a pressure of 150 kN/m² along 50 m of straight horizontal steel piping containing two diaphragm valves and a strainer. Estimate the pump delivery pressure required for (a) 15 cm diam. and (b) 20 cm diam. piping. Ambient temperature is 20°C.
12. A lubricating pump is sited in one side of a square network of 12 mm bore smooth piping circulating 0·25 m³ of oil per minute in closed circuit. Each side of the square is 6 m long and there are two 45 degree oblique valves and two strainers in the complete circuit. If the loss in the equipment being supplied is negligible, calculate the pressure differential at the pump and the corresponding horsepower required. The kinematic viscosity and specific gravity of the oil are respectively 5·1 × 10⁻⁴ m²/s and 0·90. What would be the figures if the piping were increased to 36 mm.?
13. The following table represents an open ended main salt water service in a merchant ship. If a delivery at a pressure of 80 lbf/in² is required at the remote end of the system and there is positive pressure of 15 lbf/in² at the drowned pump suction, estimate the performance required of the pump. If the overall efficiency of the pump is 0·72, what steady power is required of the electrical supply to the pump motor?

Leg	Length (ft)	Bore (in.)	Fittings	Delivery (gal/min)
PA	48	4	1 strainer 3 easy bends 1 globe valve	40 at A
AB	60	3	1 90° angle valve 5 easy bends	30 at B
BC	40	2	2 90° angle valves 4 easy bends	40 at C
CD	160	2	1 globe valve 7 easy bends 1 plug cock	120 at D

14. A package protecting a guided weapon is 16 ft long and 4 ft × 4 ft in section and is constructed of $\frac{1}{16}$ in. thick aluminium. It is taken from an air conditioned magazine where the dry bulb temperature is 85°F to the upper deck where it is 110°F in the shade. What is the rate of heat gain through the box? What would it be with $\frac{3}{4}$ in. glass fibre all round?

15. The refrigerated hold of a cargo ship is 15 m × 15 m in plan and 8 m high above the tank top which is 1 m above the keel. The draught of the ship is 5 m in the Red Sea. On the after side of the hold there is a machinery space whose temperature is 50°C and on the forward side a hold at 30°C. Sea temperature is 25°C, the deck head is at 35°C and the sides 30°C on the cold side and 45°C on the sunny side.

All surfaces are lined with 1 cm of plywood and 15 cm of cork slab. All steel-work is 1 cm thick.

Calculate the capacity required for refrigeration machinery to maintain a temperature of −10°C in the hold.

16. The package of question 14 is loaded on deck off Singapore in an ambient of 88/78°F before being sealed. How much can the package be cooled before condensation occurs inside? If taken into a magazine at 68°F, how much moisture will collect in the package? The missile occupies 20 per cent of the space.

17. Recirculation air is required to leave a room at 80/68°F and be mixed with an equal quantity of fresh air at 90/84°F before being passed to a coil having a slope of 0·42. The sensible heat ratio of the room is 0·65. If the air leaves the cooler at 90 per cent relative humidity, estimate how much heat per pound of air must be supplied by the after warmer.

18. Heat gain calculations for a messdeck for sixty men show the total heat to be 44,000 Watts of which 40 per cent is latent. Fresh air is drawn in at the rate of 0·005 m³/sec per man and is at 34/31°C. Conditions in the room should not exceed 25 ET. Avoiding the need for after warm, construct a suitable psychrometric cycle, stating the performance required of the coil and the air quantity needed. Air should leave the coil at 90 per cent relative humidity.

19. A frigate design is to have a complement of fourteen officers, fifty chief petty officers, fifty-four petty officers and 206 junior ratings. Make a first

estimate of the space which would be needed for living spaces, toilet facilities, laundry, galley and sick bay.

20. A warship has a length of 360 ft and a beam of 43 ft. The only decks suitable for accommodation are No. 2 deck and the forward half of No. 3 deck, each of which is expected to have a waterplane coefficient of 0·70. Estimate what proportion of these spaces should be given over to the accommodation of the previous question, assuming that the laundry is sited on No. 4 deck and that sewage is discharged directly overboard. What would be this proportion if a sewage system enabled all heads and bathrooms to be sited on No. 4 deck?

21. Distinguish between deadweight and tonnage. Distinguish between exemptions and deductions and state what sort of spaces you expect each to include.

Define tonnage deck, underdeck tonnage, gross tonnage, register tonnage. What allowances are made for propelling machinery spaces?

22. Explain the purpose of the tonnage mark and how it came into being. What is the relationship between tonnage mark and loadline mark? Sketch each.

23. What did the 1969 International Conference on Tonnage Measurement achieve?

24. A cargo ship has a moulded depth and assigned freeboard of 20 m and 4m respectively. Its gross volume is 10^5 m³ and cargo volume is 78 per cent of this.

Calculate the formulae gross and net tonnages. What would the net tonnage become (*a*) if freeboard could be reduced to 3 m or (*b*) if 15 cabin passengers were carried?

References

1. Brown, T. W. F. A marine engineering review, past, present and future. *TRINA*, 1960.
2. Norton, E. Modern trends in marine propulsion machinery. *TRINA*, 1962.
3. Gray, D. Marine electrical systems. *Technical symposium on ships gear international*, 1966.
4. Fitzer, H. C. *Electrical power installations in warships*. Published Inst Marine Engs, 1969.
5. *A guide to current practice*. Institution of Heating and Ventilating Engineers, London, 1970
6. Handbook American Society of Heating, Refrigerating and Ventilating Engineers, 1974.
7. Jones, S. J. and MacVicar, J. K. W. The development of air conditioning in ships. *TINA*, 1959.
8. Newton, R. N. *Practical construction of warships*. Longmans, 1970.
9. Carter, L. T. and Crennell, J. T. The cathodic protection of ships against sea water corrosion. *TINA*, 1955.
10. Hopper, A. G., Judd, P. H. and Williams, G. Cargo handling and its effect on dry cargo ship design. *TRINA*, 1964.
11. *Manual of Seamanship*, HMSO, 1967.
12. *Crew accommodation in merchant ships*. Dept of Trade, HMSO, 1953 and *Dept of Trade handbook*, HMSO, 1971.
13. *Merchant shipping (tonnage) regulations 1967*,Dept of Trade, HMSO, 1967, and *Tonnage measurement of ships*. HMSO, 1972.
14. Palmer, S. J. The impact of gas turbines on the design of major surface warships. *TRINA*, 1974.
15. Chislett, H. W. J. Replenishment at sea. *TRINA*, 1972.
16. Edwards, J. Prospects for nuclear propulsion of merchant ships. *TNEC*, 1974.
17. Crombie, R. and Acock, G. P. *Corrosion in the marine environment*. Publ Inst Marine Engs., 1974.
18. Wilson, E. The 1969 international conference on tonnage measurement of ships. *TRINA*, 1970.
19. Clark, R. Cargo handling in modern unit load pallet ships. *The Naval Architect*, July, 1973.
20. Meek, M. and Ward, N. Accommodation in ships. *TRINA*, 1973.
21. Tonnage measurement of ships. *Instructions to surveyors (DTI)*. HMSO, 1972.
22. Oil in Navigable Waters Act 1955 and *Dept of Trade manual on the avoidance of pollution of the sea by oil, 1967*. HMSO.
23. International Labour Conference. Convention concerning crew accommodation on board ship. *Convention 133*, HMSO, 1972.

15 Ship design

The *raison d'être* for the naval architect is the design of ships. This chapter, therefore, represents the culmination of the work of this book. While many of the individual aspects of naval architecture, e.g. ship motion, can be fascinating studies in themselves it is the welding together of all these aspects into an integrated design that presents the real challenge. In general, there is no unique solution in ship design. Rather, the ship is a compromise between many requirements which have to be correctly evaluated by the naval architect and the finished product reflects much of his personality.

A new ship is born when an actual or forecast situation shows that a new ship is, or will be, required. Ships are expensive to design, build and operate so that their development cannot be embarked upon lightly. Several years must elapse between the design inception and the reality of the ship, making forward planning essential. This planning must be done by the ship operator. In the case of merchant ships, charterer or the owner and for warships it is the defence staff of the Ministry of Defence.

The basic need is for a ship to transport a payload, be it passengers, cargo or weapons, under certain specified conditions of speed, distance and environment. The ship operator must state his requirements in such a way as to ensure that the resulting ship is able to carry out his planned policy. This may mean, for a liner, carrying passengers in certain standards of luxury or, for a warship, supporting the Government's foreign policy. In both the military and commercial spheres, requirements peculiar to certain payloads lead to specialist ship types, e.g. oil tankers, submarines, and some of these are discussed in the next chapter. The differences between military and commercial ships arise not only from the different payloads but also from the conditions of service. The warship designer must take prime account of the fact that his ship has to be able to withstand enemy action. The merchant ship designer must meet regulations of classification societies and the country's laws. In both cases, the result is the introduction of certain special design features.

Whilst making every endeavour to meet the operator's demands, the naval architect must apply his specialist knowledge to ensure that the ship is a sound engineering product. In this, he is assisted by many research and development groups. By studying their work, and often actively collaborating with them, the naval architect ensures that his general knowledge of the engineering and physical sciences is kept up to date. Of more direct application to his work are projects concerned with the hydrodynamic and structural design of ships. Some of these groups were mentioned in Chapter 1. All collaborate on a national and international scale to avoid unnecessary duplication of work and to ensure the rapid communication of ideas and knowledge. Before proceeding to consider the actual design processes let us consider the nature of the 'customer'.

The Ministry of Defence (MOD) acts as the customer for warships on behalf of the nation. It is within the Navy Department of that ministry that the detailed requirements are drawn up for the design and the design itself is carried out. It is the responsibility of the MOD to ensure that adequate military support can be given to enable the foreign policy of the country to be implemented. The central staffs watch that the correct balance is maintained between the three services and guide the naval staff in the interpretation of the broad policies. The naval staff draw up the requirements for specific ships and weapon systems for the approval of the Admiralty Board. The Board is also advised by operational research departments.

The shipping company is the customer for merchant ships on behalf of the shareholders. Depending upon the size and formation of the company, more or less work is farmed out to agencies or consultants who can operate more efficiently in serving the needs of several small companies. The company may negotiate directly with a shipbuilder or may act through a shipbroker. The shipbroker can provide information on the products of several shipbuilders enabling a more selective purchase to be made. It is common practice for owners to charter their ships to operators on the basis of total responsibility (bareboat) or for a voyage or for a specified time.

Major policy decisions are taken by the Board of Directors, e.g. they would decide whether to operate cargo-liners or pure passenger liners on a given route. Assisting them in their deliberations is a market research organization which analyses market trends to highlight profitable lines of development, e.g. the exploitation of natural gas supplies in North Africa led to a specialized gas carrier.

In the case of both military and commercial ships, the naval architect has his part to play as the principal technical adviser to the Board keeping them informed as to the general feasibility of new concepts from the initial stages.

Having seen briefly how a requirement is conceived, the requirement itself can be considered in more detail.

Requirements

WARSHIPS

It has been seen that requirements for warships are drawn up by the naval staff. They are known as *Staff Requirements* and cover the following aspects of the ship:

Function. A frigate may be required to act as part of the air defence and/or anti-submarine defence of a task force.

General characteristics such as speed, endurance, operating areas. These may contain special requirements for operating at speed in waves or for manoeuvrability.

Weapons including missiles, guns, radars, sonars, etc.

Communications including numbers of links between ship and shore, ship and ship or ship and aircraft.

Accommodation. Numbers of officers and men and the general standards of accommodation.

Stores and logistics. Scale of provisioning for victualling and naval stores. Requirements for replenishing at sea or in harbour with solids and liquids.

Aviation arrangements. Numbers and types of aircraft to be carried and the scale of support facilities.

Operating characteristics. The intended intervals between dockings and refits and the period for which the ship is to be able to operate continuously at sea.

The staff requirements specify only those things of direct concern to the operator, e.g. although they lay down speed and endurance the selection of type of machinery and number of shafts is left to the designer to select to give the best ship to meet the other requirements. Again, no mention would be made of standards of stability or strength. These are professional matters left to the discretion of the naval constructors.

In formulating the requirements, the naval staff are assisted by the technical departments concerned, principally by the Director General, Ships, (DG Ships) to ensure that what is asked for is realistic in terms of the existing state of technology. Supported by a series of design studies of increasingly greater detail, the requirements for a new ship are progressively developed from an outline statement to a detailed statement of the equipment to be carried in, and the operational characteristics of, the ship. Throughout these deliberations a careful watch is kept on the cost of the ship, number of men required to man it and the general effectiveness of the design. Design economics are discussed more fully in the next section. The naval constructor must assess the cost of his ship to build and operate and balance this against its value. It is impossible to define the value to the nation of a warship in monetary terms. The assessment has to be rather one of comparison of the costs of various alternative methods of meeting the overall requirement. When the detailed designs have been agreed between the naval staff and DG Ships they are submitted to the Admiralty Board for approval. Having satisfied themselves that the requirements define the ship they need the Board directs DG Ships to develop the design to a yet more detailed state.

MERCHANT SHIPS

The actual process of developing the *Owner's Requirements* varies from company to company but is broadly similar in principle to the above. The technical staff must collaborate closely with the market research teams to ensure that the requirements can satisfy the needs of the market concerned while remaining feasible. Progressively more detailed studies are produced for the approval of those responsible for the overall operation of the company. The amount of time and effort involved in this development process depends very much on the differences between previous ships and the new design.

During times of empty order books, some shipbuilders have produced a standard design of ship as a speculative venture. Such schemes have generally not been successful financially. This is a reflection of the variation which can exist in ships of superficially the same type.

One aspect of ship operation which is fundamental to the formulation of the requirements is that of *design economics*. If it were necessary to select a single factor which, more than any other, influenced the design of merchant ships it would be economics. This influence is illustrated by the growth of the super-tanker. It has been estimated that, at 1966 prices, the cost of carrying crude oil from North Africa to Britain was reduced to about a third by using 100,000 tonf deadweight tankers instead of 20,000 tonf ships. In addition, the building cost of the larger ship was only some £30 per tonf compared with £75 to £100 for the smaller ship. High fuel costs have not today markedly changed these relativities.

A broad view of economics must be taken and the shipowner must attempt to assess the cost of the ship over its whole life and set this against the money he estimates it can earn for him. Included in his calculations must be the fact that a new ship may reduce the earnings of other ships of his fleet.

For the entire planned life of the ship the annual *cash flows* must be estimated. The following are the major sources:

(*a*) ship design and production costs in instalments;
(*b*) owner's down payment and loan acquired;
(*c*) owner's extras;
(*d*) investment grant (if any);
(*e*) loan interest and capital repayment;
(*f*) running costs for fuel, crew, port charges, fees, etc.;
(*g*) maintenance and repair costs;
(*h*) profit;
(*i*) corporation and other taxes.

Note that the *depreciation* is not a cash flow, although it will probably be required to assess the tax payable. All of these cash flows must be brought to a common basis by referring to them as if they happened simultaneously. This is necessary because cash has a time value or an opportunity value in that it might, perhaps, be used more profitably in some other way. The basis for comparison is the profitability of an investment earning compound interest at a rate *r*.

Arguments concerning the correct rate *r* to use are difficult but are based either upon alternative opportunities, leading to an *opportunity cost rate* or upon a personal preference for speedy profit leading to a *time preference rate*. P_o after *i* years becomes:

$$P_i = P_0(1+r)^i$$

where P_0 = present sum, and P_i = sum produced after *i* years. That is,

$$P_o = P_i(1+r)^{-i}$$

Thus for every £1 accruing in *i* years' time the equivalent present value is $£(1+r)^{-i}$. If A_i is the nett cash flow calculated for *i* years' time then the nett present value of the project is given by

$$\text{NPV} = \sum_{i=0}^{i=n} A_i(1+r)^{-i}$$

where the summation is made over the life of the ship ($= n$ years).

The NPV can be used to compare a number of designs, different ways of financing a given design and different dates for commencement of construction. Any project with a positive NPV is a reasonable investment but that with the highest NPV would be chosen. Although general changes in prices may occur over the years, the NPV approach remains valid in terms of real purchasing power. There is an increasing emphasis upon the economic commitment of resources by warships but Ref. 15 warns of the limitations of applying discounting techniques to ships of the Navy.

Several variations of this process are common. For example, *required freight rate* (RFR) or *shadow price* is the charge that would have to be made to carry the freight to give zero NPV. *Yield* and *permissible price* are other measures of investment profitability. (Ref. 16).

EXAMPLE 1. A ship is estimated to have a capital cost of £1 m. A useful life of 20 years is predicted with a scrap value of £50,000. It is expected that the ship will earn £0·5 m for each full year's operations but that due to special survey requirements this will be reduced by £60,000 and £100,000 in the 12th and 16th years. The running costs in each year, after allowance for tax, are estimated to be as in column 3 of the table below. Calculate the nett present value assuming a discount rate of 7 per cent.

Solution

Year (i)	Cash flows after tax			Discount factor $(1+0.07)^{-i}$	Discounted cash flows $A_i(1+0.07)^{-i}$
	(+)ve	(−)ve	Nett = A_i		
1	500,000	300,000	200,000	0·93458	187,000
2	500,000	50,000	450,000	0·87344	393,000
3	500,000	305,000	195,000	0·81630	159,000
4	500,000	310,000	190,000	0·76290	145,000
5	500,000	320,000	180,000	0·71299	128,000
6	500,000	315,000	185,000	0·66634	123,000
7	500,000	320,000	180,000	0·62275	112,000
8	500,000	325,000	175,000	0·58201	102,000
9	500,000	330,000	170,000	0·54393	92,000
10	500,000	320,000	180,000	0·50835	92,000
11	500,000	330,000	170,000	0·47509	81,000
12	440,000	335,000	105,000	0·44401	47,000
13	500,000	315,000	185,000	0·41496	77,000
14	500,000	330,000	170,000	0·38782	66,000
15	500,000	335,000	165,000	0·36245	60,000
16	400,000	350,000	50,000	0·33874	17,000
17	500,000	320,000	180,000	0·31657	57,000
18	500,000	345,000	155,000	0·29586	46,000
19	500,000	360,000	140,000	0·27651	39,000
20	550,000	370,000	130,000	0·25842	34,000

Total £2,057,000
Less initial cost £1,000,000

NPV £1,057,000

Note: Variations in negative cash flows reflect costs of surveys, varying earnings and allowances on capital cost. This latter leads to the very low figure for year 2, it being assumed that tax allowances suffer an effective delay of 1 year.

Other important features of the requirements for a ship are the intended *trade* and *trade route*. The trade defines the general type of ship required which may be either special service (e.g. tanker, trawler) or general purpose (e.g. tramp steamer). The size of ship follows from the quantity of the specified cargo to be carried as determined from economic considerations.

The trade route defines the ocean areas, harbours, etc., in, or from which, the ship will operate. The ocean areas indicate the waves and wind conditions and depth of water. A ship designed for coastal work can be expected to shelter in severe storms, a transatlantic liner cannot. Standards of strength, stability and freeboard must be adjusted accordingly and the optimum hull form will be different. The climate experienced determines the need for air conditioning, anti-icing or ice breaking facilities. The length of route influences the standards of insulation, speed and endurance. The old tea clippers are an example of the influence of trade and trade route on the design of the ship.

Some routes involve passage of canals or similar waterways, e.g. Suez Canal, Panama Canal, St. Lawrence Seaway. This may place restrictions on overall dimensions or demand special equipment such as towing fairleads, sewage treatment plants, etc. Special design features may arise from the rules laid down for assessing transit fees. Such features would aim to reduce the fee paid while retaining high cargo carrying capacity.

The ports, and particularly the terminal ports, may influence the overall dimensions and the cargo handling facilities required. It would be illogical to build into the ship facilities for discharging cargo rapidly if the port cannot accept them at that rate. The development of specialized port facilities for handling containers is a good example of the blend of ship and port design.

Design studies

PRELIMINARY STUDIES

It has been seen that some preliminary design work is a necessary adjunct to the proper development of the requirements. In particular, it is necessary to assist in calculating the economics of the proposed new ship and for this purpose an accuracy of about 5 per cent is desirable.

During this phase, several designs are developed in parallel covering a range of the main parameters and enabling a sounder choice to be made. At this stage, the parameters on which the naval architect concentrates are:

space allocation;
main dimensions—length, beam, depth, draught;
displacement and deadweight;
form parameters—block and prismatic coefficients;
weather deck layout;
machinery type and layout.

INTERNAL VOLUME

Before proceeding to consider the principal dimensions, it is necessary to obtain some idea of the volume required. This is generally a more significant parameter for modern warships than weight; the same is true for cargo ships carrying low density cargoes. Figure 15.1 shows the approximate variation of deck space with displacement of modern warships and Fig. 15.2 shows the broad allocations of space within a guided missile destroyer. The naval architect would analyse his existing ships in some detail, and then assess the space demanded by each item of the new requirements adding margins to cover items not specified and to allow for design development.

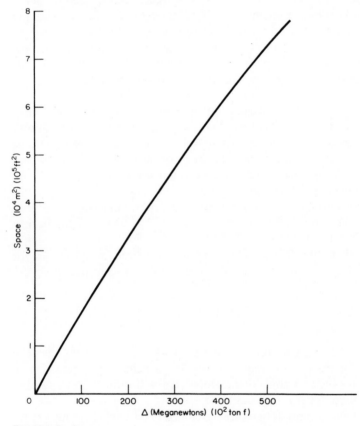

Fig. 15.1 Deck space

Having assessed the volume required, the principal dimensions must be arranged so as to provide this as a usable volume in the new ship.

PRINCIPAL DIMENSIONS

The naval architect makes considerable use of data from previous ships and will endeavour to find one which closely meets the needs of the new requirements. This is referred to as a *type ship* or *basis ship* and good approximations to the

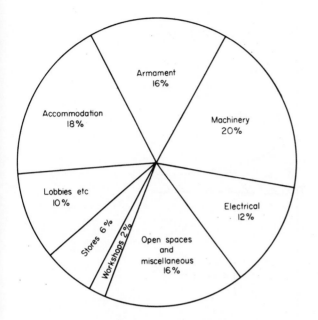

Fig. 15.2 Typical space allocations in a guided missile destroyer

size of the new design can be obtained by considering the changes from the type ship.

The broad bands within which the main dimensions of ships of various types lie are given in Figs. 15.3 and 15.4 in terms of ratios. These enable a start to be made in selecting main dimensions. More specific guidance can be obtained by analysing previous designs to show how the various dimensions are related as in Ref. 3 on which Table 15.1 is based. Each designer should produce his own data in a consistent fashion and emphasis should be placed upon the most recent designs. The relationship between beam and length can also be expressed as

$$B = L^n$$

and in the discussion in Ref. 3 it was suggested that, with B and L in ft:

$n = 0.685 – 0.690$ for passenger-cargo liners
$n = 0.680 – 0.685$ for cargo liners carrying large deck loads
$n = 0.675 – 0.680$ for more general cargo liners
$n = 0.665 – 0.670$ for coasters
$n = 0.650 – 0.655$ for dumb lighters and tugs.

By considering the products of the main dimensions, an approximation to the internal volume can be obtained. Not all this volume is available for cargo even after making allowance for machinery, accommodation, etc. Within tanks or holds themselves, allowance must be made for structural members when carrying oil or other bulk cargoes. When the cargo is in boxes or bales the spaces between

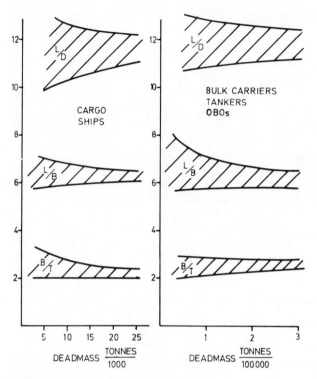

Fig. 15.3 General ranges of principal dimensions.

stiffeners is unlikely to be filled so that the usable volume is reduced. The reduction is greater still in refrigerated cargo ships because of the space devoted to insulation. Typical capacities expressed as a percentage of the moulded capacity are:

Tank or grain capacity,   98
Bale capacity,   88
Insulated capacity,   72

For dense cargoes the limitation may be on weight rather than internal volume. In such a case, the dimensions can be obtained by assuming that the length is related to the trial speed V_T, and displacement by a relationship of the type

$$L = \text{Constant}[V_T/(2 + V_T)]^2 \Delta^{\frac{1}{3}}, \text{ ft}$$

Reference 3 proposes that V_T be taken as $\frac{1}{2}$–1 knot above the service speed and that the following constants be used:

Single screw ships,   23·5 ⎫ ⎧ L in ft
Twin screw ships, moderate speed,   24   ⎬ ⎨ V_T in knots
Twin screw ships, high speed,   26   ⎭ ⎩ Δ in tonf

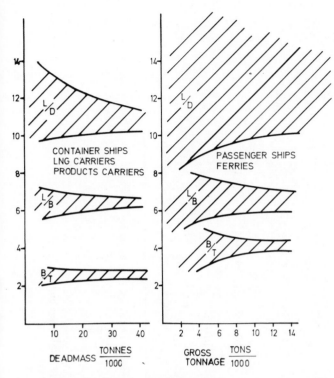

Fig. 15.4 General ranges of principal dimensions.

If the displacement is in MN and L is in metres, the approximate values of the three constants are 33, 34 and 37 respectively. If the displacement is in tonnef and L in metres they become 7·1, 7·3 and 7·9 approximately.

Having thus established the dimensions within, perhaps, 5 per cent, we can proceed to an examination of displacement.

DISPLACEMENT AND DEADWEIGHT

Even when space is more critical than weight, an early assessment of displacement is necessary. The deadweight is given in the requirements and, as a first approximation, the displacement may be obtained by multiplying this by a factor based on previous similar ships. Typical values of the deadweight/displacement ratio, (or deadmass/Σ) are:

Passenger liner,	0·35	Container ship,	0·60
Cargo ship,	0·67	Large tanker,	0·86
Ore carrier,	0·82	Liquid gas carrier	0·62

In the case of warships, a first approximation to the displacement can be obtained by calculating the armament weight to be carried and multiplying by a factor deduced from previous similar ships. Typically, the factor is between 10 and 20.

Table 15.1
Relationships between principal form parameters

Item	Passenger liner British units	Passenger liner Metric units	Cargo ship British units	Cargo ship Metric units	Tanker British units	Tanker Metric units
	Type of ship					
Beam, B	$\dfrac{L}{9} + 20$	$\dfrac{L}{9} + 6{\cdot}10$	$\dfrac{L}{9} + 14$	$\dfrac{L}{9} + 4{\cdot}27$	$\dfrac{L}{7{\cdot}5} + 6{\cdot}5$	$\dfrac{L}{7{\cdot}5} + 1{\cdot}98$
Depth, D (see notes 2 and 3)	$\dfrac{B+1}{1{\cdot}5}$	$\dfrac{B+0{\cdot}3}{1{\cdot}5}$	$\dfrac{B-K}{1{\cdot}4}$	$\dfrac{B-0{\cdot}3K}{1{\cdot}4}$	$\dfrac{L}{13{\cdot}5}$	$\dfrac{L}{13{\cdot}5}$
Draught, T (see note 4)			$\tfrac{2}{9}D + 4$	$\tfrac{2}{9}D + 1{\cdot}22$	$\tfrac{2}{9}D + 4$	$\tfrac{2}{9}D + 1{\cdot}22$
(see note 5)			$\tfrac{2}{9}(D-h) + 6{\cdot}33$	$\tfrac{2}{9}(D-h) + 1{\cdot}93$		
Block coefficient (see note 6)	$1{\cdot}03 - \dfrac{V}{2\sqrt{L}}$	$1{\cdot}03 - \dfrac{V}{3{\cdot}6\sqrt{L}}$	$1{\cdot}06 - \dfrac{V}{2\sqrt{L}}$	$1{\cdot}06 - \dfrac{V}{3{\cdot}6\sqrt{L}}$	$1{\cdot}12 - \dfrac{V}{2\sqrt{L}}$	$1{\cdot}12 - \dfrac{V}{3{\cdot}6\sqrt{L}}$

Notes:
1. L = length BP.
2. Depth, D, will require adjustment to suit the depth of tanks plus a multiple of the deck head height.
3. $K = 6$ for moderate stability; $K = 9$ for good stability.
4. Applies to closed shelter deck type.
5. Applies to open shelter deck type; h is the 'tween deck height.
6. Assuming $V/\sqrt{L}$ ranges (V in knots):

	British units		Metric units
Passenger liners	>0·80	Passenger liners	>1·45
Cargo ship	0·65–0·80	Cargo ship	1·18–1·45
Tanker	<0·65	Tanker	<1·18

If some other factor such as endurance is to be significantly changed, then due allowance must be made for this using data from a type ship. When a number of small adjustments is made to the type ship, it is possible to deduce how each will vary in relation to displacement and apply what is commonly known as the *weight equation* to estimate the displacement of the proposed new design. For example, approximately half the hull group weight contributes to the longitudinal strength and this part varies roughly as $\Delta^{1\cdot1}$. The other half of the hull group weight varies approximately as $\Delta^{\frac{2}{3}}$. It can be shown also that

Machinery group weight varies as $\Delta^m V^n$

Fuel group weight varies as $\Delta^m V^{n-1} \times$ endurance, where for the speed considered $6m+n = 7$ and $n = 3+(\textcircled{C}/\textcircled{K}) \, \text{d}\textcircled{K}/\text{d}\textcircled{C}$

The use of the weight equation is best illustrated by the use of an example.

EXAMPLE 2. A guided missile destroyer of 6000 tonf, speed 30 knots and s.h.p. 60,000 at full power, has an endurance of 5000 miles at 18 knots. The group weights are: hull 2300 tonf, machinery 1500 tonf, armament 600 tonf, fuel 1200 tonf and equipment 400 tonf.

Estimate the displacement and group weights of a similar ship with an additional 50 tonf of armament and a full power speed of 28 knots. The endurance is to be 5500 miles at 20 knots. The following assumptions are to be made:

(*a*) S.h.p. varies as $V^{2\cdot8}$ at full power and as V^3 at 18–20 knots;
(*b*) Savings of 5 per cent are expected on both hull and machinery groups due to advances in design and materials;
(*c*) Fuel consumption rate is reduced by 2 per cent.

Solution: S.h.p. varies as $\Delta^m V^n$ where $6m+n = 7$. 'Hence, when $n = 3$, $m = \frac{2}{3}$ and when $n = 2\cdot8$, $m = 0\cdot7$.

Applying the weight equation approach, the type ship is first of all modified to reflect the stated changes except that in armament. This produces a revised armament weight which the modified type ship could carry if displacement remained constant. The displacement must now be changed to reflect the actual armament weight needed.

All the group weights, with the exception of the load, are regarded as functions of the displacement. Thus

$\Delta - \text{load}$ = hull plus machinery plus fuel plus equipment plus ...

i.e.

$$\Delta - \text{load} = a\Delta + b\Delta^m + c\Delta^{\frac{2}{3}} + d\Delta + \cdots$$

or

$$\Delta - L = \sum a\Delta^p$$

Hence,

$$\delta\Delta - \delta L = \sum pa\Delta^{p-1} \, \delta\Delta$$

$$= \frac{1}{\Delta} \sum pa\Delta^p \, \delta\Delta$$

Therefore

$$\delta\Delta\left(1 - \frac{1}{\Delta}\sum pa\Delta^{p}\right) = \delta L$$

or

$$\delta\Delta = \frac{\delta L}{1-k}$$

where

$$k = \frac{1}{\Delta}\sum (\text{index of weight group}) \times (\text{weight group})$$

A table can now be constructed as below:

Group	Type ship	Modification to type ship	Modified type ship	Index for change in Δ	Product of index and weight
Hull	2300	$\times 0.95$	2185	1	2185
Machinery	1500	$\times 0.95\left(\dfrac{28}{30}\right)^{2.8}$	1175	0.7	823
Armament	600	—	642	—	—
Fuel	1200	$\times 0.98\left(\dfrac{5500}{5000}\right)\left(\dfrac{20}{18}\right)^{2}$	1598	$\frac{2}{3}$	1066
Equipment	400	$\times 1$	400	1	400
	6000		6000		4474

In this case, then,

$$k = \frac{4474}{6000} = 0.746.$$

The armament to be carried is 650 tonf, i.e. it must be increased by 8 tonf. That is, $\delta L = 8$ tonf and

$$\delta\Delta = \frac{8}{1 - 0.746} = \frac{8}{0.254} = 31.5 \text{ tonf}$$

Hence the new displacement = 6030 tonf, say, i.e. displacement has increased by 0.5 per cent. The new group weights are

Hull $= 2185\,(1 + 0.5\%) = 2196$ tonf
Machinery $= 1175\,(1 + 0.7 \times 0.5\%) = 1179$ tonf
Armament $= 650$ tonf
Fuel $= 1598\,(1 + \frac{2}{3} \times 0.5\%) = 1603$ tonf
Equipment $= 400\,(1 + 0.5\%) = 402$ tonf

The weight equation is not used much nowadays as the conditions required to be fulfilled, if it is to be accurate, seldom apply. It is more common to use approximate formulae in the initial stages such as those proposed in Ref. 3.

Outfit weight for cargo ships $= \dfrac{3\cdot3LB}{100}$ tonf with L, B in feet

$$= \dfrac{35\cdot5LB}{10,000}\text{ MN with } L, B \text{ in metres}$$

Weight of diesel machinery $= \left(\dfrac{\text{s.h.p.}}{10}+200\right)$ tonf

$$= \left(\dfrac{MW}{0\cdot75}+2\right)\text{MN}$$

Weight of steam turbine machinery $= \dfrac{\text{s.h.p.}}{17}+280$ tonf

$$= \left(\dfrac{MW}{1\cdot27}+2\cdot8\right)\text{MN}$$

The net steelweight can be obtained from approximate formulae such as the following for bulk carriers (Ref. 4) for which a standard deviation of 5 per cent is claimed.

Net steelweight $= 1\cdot125 \times 10^{-3}L^{1\cdot65}(B+D+T/2)(0\cdot5C_{\mathrm{B}}+0\cdot4)/0\cdot8$ tonf
(British units)

$$= 2\cdot62 \times 10^{-4}L^{1\cdot65}(B+D+T/2)(0\cdot5C_{\mathrm{B}}+0\cdot4)/0\cdot8 \text{ MN}$$
(SI units)

At a later stage, the detailed group weights for a similar ship can be scaled according to known differences, e.g. deck weights can be scaled as deck areas, electrical generator weights can be scaled in proportion to their capacity, and so on. It is important that a consistent grouping of weights be adhered to and that adequate margins be allowed at each stage. It is also wise, in these early stages, to allow a disposable additional margin to compensate for possible changes in the requirements. In the case of warships, this is known as the *Board Margin of Weight* and is typically 2 per cent of the deep displacement. Some typical group weights expressed as percentages of the deep displacement are given in Table 15.2.

MACHINERY POWER

During the preliminary studies, the shaft horsepower required to propel the ship at its intended speed V, in knots, can be obtained from an approximate formula. Many exist and the following is taken from Ref. 3.

$$\text{s.h.p.} = H\dfrac{\Delta^{\frac{2}{3}}V^3[40-(L/200)+400(k-1)^2-12C_{\mathrm{B}}]}{15,000-n(L)^{\frac{1}{2}}}$$

with Δ in tonf and L in feet

$$\text{Power in kW} = 16\cdot07H\Delta^{\frac{2}{3}}V^3\dfrac{[40-(L/61)+400(k-1)^2-12C_{\mathrm{B}}]}{15,000-1\cdot81n(L)^{\frac{1}{2}}}$$

with Δ in MN and L in metres where H = hull correlation factor = 0·90 for all-welded hull, = 1·00 for welded butts, riveted seams, = 1·10 for all-riveted hull; k = 1·03 for passenger liner, = 1·06 for cargo ship, = 1·12 for tanker; and n = propeller r.p.m.

Such estimates should be replaced by more accurate assessments as soon as possible.

Table 15.2
Typical group weight percentages

Group	16 kt Cargo ship $L = 150$ m	22 kt Passenger ship $L = 240$ m	16 kt Tanker $L = 200$ m
Net steel	21	36	17·0
Wood and outfit	5	16·5	1·6
Hull systems	1·5	6	1·6
Machinery	5	5·9	2·3
Total light ship	32·5	64·4	22·5
Crew and passengers	0·2	0·6	1·6
Fuel	11	14	2·6
Fresh water	0·3	13	1·3
Dry cargo	35	8·0	—
Liquid cargo	21	—	72
Deadweight total	67·5	35·6	77·5
Deep displacement	100·0	100·0	100·0
Deadweight/displacement	0·675	0·⁻	0·775

CHOICE OF FORM

Having estimated the main dimensions there remains the choice of hull form. The initial choice is usually made on the basis of the powering characteristics. The naval architect, from experience, can usually define broad bands within which the value of certain form parameters should lie, e.g. fast passenger liners usually have block coefficients of between 0·55 and 0·63 and operate at Froude numbers which lie within the range 0·14 to 0·18. It is convenient, then, to plot data in ship terms covering these ranges as is done for resistance in Fig. 15.5 for a passenger liner 400 ft (122 m) LBP × 55 ft (16·8 m) moulded beam × 18 ft (5·5 m) moulded draught (from Ref. 5). Such plots take account of the scaling from the model to the actual size of ship, but must be taken in conjunction with propulsive coefficients to provide estimates of actual shaft horsepower.

Having selected the form coefficients, a curve of areas can be plotted and critical sections, e.g. those in way of machinery or magazines, checked to ensure adequacy. Quite small changes in the curve of areas can have significant effects on wave-making resistance as was discussed in Chapter 10. This emphasizes the importance of selecting a good curve initially and of being careful in modifying it. The beam is largely governed by stability and standards to be aimed at are discussed in Chapter 4. Changes in beam necessitated by stability

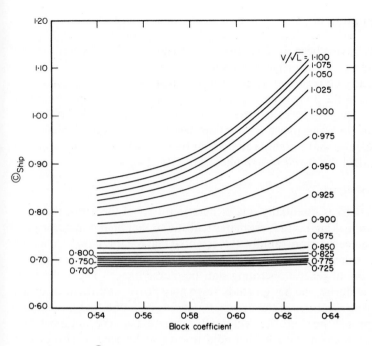

Fig. 15.5 Average© 1952–1962. Twin screw ships

must be reflected back into the powering calculations using methodical series data. The sections used at the ends of the ship are influenced by the desire to improve seakeeping and to be able to fit propellers and rudders of the desired size. Amidships, rise of floor assists with fairing but excessive amounts associated with well-rounded bilges may lead to large angles of heel when turning and poor large angle stability. If dock block loading is high, side blocks may be necessary making a flat bottom desirable. Dock block loading will certainly influence the keel half siding. A very square section makes the fitting of stabilizers more difficult.

WEATHER DECK LAYOUT AND PROFILE

These drawings effectively unite all the main features of the ship both internal and external. The cargo hatches match the hold locations; the funnel matches the position of the machinery; gun mountings are related to magazine positions. They also provide a means of illustrating the effectiveness of the deck equipment, e.g. that cranes or derricks can plumb deck hatches and over the ship's side; that guns have adequate arcs of fire. Not least, they provide the ship operator with a visual picture of his ship and to assist in this an artist's impression is usually prepared.

Based on these drawings, and other data supplied to them by the designer, the shipowners can decide which of the various design studies they prefer. This, then, provides the starting point for the development of the design.

Design development

A design study having been selected, the naval architect embarks upon a steady process of development which leads eventually to the finished ship. The process may conveniently be regarded as being in two phases. In the first phase, the design is taken to the point where it can be used as the basis for a contract to build the ship. This will be called the *Contract Design* phase and corresponds to the *Building Drawing* phase in warship design. In the second phase, the design is detailed so that the ship can be built by the craftsmen in the shipyard. This will be called the *Detail Design* phase.

CONTRACT DESIGN

The design process is essentially one of iteration. Part of the art of the naval architect lies in making his first estimates realistic so that final dimensions and layout can be achieved more rapidly. It is essential that reliable data be available from previous ships. This feedback of information applies to technical aspects of the design and to general operating statistics and criticism. The preliminary estimates made during the design study stage may prove inadequate and each will react on other features of the design, e.g. it may be found that more power is needed to propel the ship; this will involve more machinery and more fuel; the ship will grow again and a further adjustment may be needed. This process has been likened to a spiral (Ref. 6).

The design spiral (Fig. 15.6)

The development of the design may be likened to the tracing out of a spiral, each coil being smaller than the previous one as the final design configuration is approached. The spiral is entered with the statement of requirements, and the work already discussed above represents the first part of the spiral although for clarity it is repeated here. The designer selects his type or basis ship and obtains his first estimates of the principal dimensions, displacement and deadweight. These are checked for compatibility with the docks, harbours, canals and rivers the ship may have to use.

The next step is to select a curve of areas for the below water portion of the hull. This may be based on that for the type ship or based on methodical series data to provide the required powering characteristics. The curve of areas must be translated into a body plan, the shaping of individual sections being determined from previous successful practice or methodical series data, the same data being used to make an estimate of the shaft horsepower needed to drive the ship at its maximum and endurance speeds.

The type of machinery can now be selected considering all the points discussed in Chapter 14, i.e. power range, economy at operating speeds, manning, space and weight.

Each of the other items in the statement of requirements can be assessed for space based on the space analyses available for previous similar ships: for example, in a destroyer each man in the complement accounts for about 50 ft^2 of overall space for living, food, hygiene, etc. If detailed space analyses are

1. Assessment
2. Model experiment
3. Empirical formulae
4. Calculation

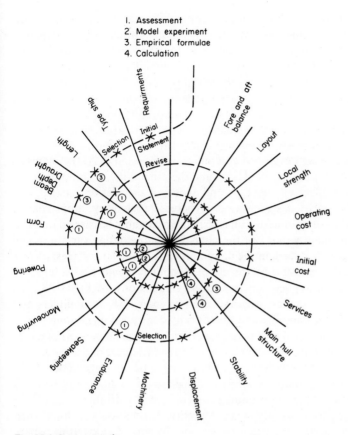

Fig. 15.6 Design spiral

available, it may be possible to allocate this space between various deck levels to check the validity of the original selection of dimensions, e.g. mess decks are rarely placed below the waterline in warships. These assessments are checked by producing a general arrangement plan for the ship. At this stage, it is not possible to show detail, but margins should be provided for the mass of minor items required around the ship such as stowages for fire-fighting equipments and electrical junction boxes.

Having achieved a satisfactory layout, weights must be estimated to check displacement and the longitudinal and vertical moments of weights. Hydrostatic data can be obtained from the body plan of the ship as discussed in Chapter 3. In most designs, this is now done by computer. The hydrostatic data enable the draught, trim and metacentre to be assessed for each condition of interest. If trim is by the bow, or excessive by the stern, weights have to be adjusted in the fore and aft direction. Usually, this adjustment can be achieved by varying the fore and aft distribution of fuel, but sometimes it is necessary to move the machinery block or other large weight blocks such as those associated with missile launchers and magazines to effect a longitudinal balance.

582   *Basic ship theory*

By calculating the value of $\overline{KG}$ from the vertical distribution of weights, and obtaining cross curves of stability from the body plan as discussed in Chapter 4, the curves of statical stability can be deduced together with the value of the metacentric height. From the stability curves so obtained the stability criteria given in Chapter 4 can be assessed. If the stability differs from that considered desirable, it can be changed either by varying the vertical distribution of weights or, more commonly, by changing the beam. The other principal dimensions may be kept constant or varied to maintain constant ratios related to the draught. The effect of such variations was discussed in Chapter 4.

Several authorities have developed computer-aided design (CAD) systems as explained in Chapter 2 and Ref. 14. These, and the general use of computers, are having a significant effect on the type and scope of calculation carried out, particularly in the early design stages. Whereas, previously, approximate relationships might have been used, full calculations can now be carried out, e.g. for hydrostatic and stability data. At the same time, more design variations can be considered up to a later stage in the design process. In the later stages, a more complete study is made possible by the use of computers as more advanced and complex theories can be applied, e.g. in strength calculations. BRITSHIPS is an example of a suite of computer programs used by many UK shipbuilders and covering design, lofting, planning and numerically controlled machining.

The designer has developed at this stage a good idea of arrangement of decks and bulkheads and so is able to specify a first order structural midship section. The moment of inertia of this section can be calculated by the method described in Chapter 6 and an approximate formula or rule used to assess the bending moment acting. The stresses so obtained are compared with those calculated for previous designs to assess their acceptability. If they are too high, then additions can be made to the structural section. Means of calculating where additions should be made to reduce stresses in the deck and/or the keel were fully described in Chapter 6.

A first estimate can be made of the ship services required to support the equipment and men specified in the ship requirements, e.g. the total electrical connected load can be calculated and diversity factors applied to give the installed generator power needed as discussed in Chapter 14. Outlines of chilled water and other services can similarly be made. Weights can be re-assessed to reflect changes in structure consequent to changes to improve stability and strength and to take account of the ship services.

By this time, the cost estimators can be provided with enough information to enable them to obtain an order of cost for the ship, including contingency factors to allow for those design features which are as yet not fully defined, e.g. at this stage the cost of the hull would be based upon average construction costs making due allowance for high grade steels and light alloys which are more expensive to fabricate. Based on previous experience, the fitting-out costs for various ship types can be estimated.

At this stage, all the main characteristics of the ship are defined and the requirements can be reviewed in order that the best value for money is obtained. If the cost is too high, then the requirements must be reduced in some way and the designer will be asked for suggestions as to which economies are likely to have the greatest cost effectiveness. On the other hand, the designer may, at this stage, be able to propose changes which although increasing cost a little will greatly improve the design.

Now the second coil of the main spiral is begun, although it will be appreciated that already the design process has been using feedback, e.g. modifications to the beam perhaps as a result of the stability calculations. On this second coil, the designer probes more deeply into each aspect of the design knowing that his basic design is sound. In returning to the form, critical sections can be checked to ensure that machinery, hold and magazines will fit into the ship. The modified form is sent to a ship tank for model tests covering resistance and propulsion (Chapters 10 and 11), manoeuvrability and directional stability (Chapter 13) and seaworthiness (Chapter 12). The results of experiments may lead to further changes of form, changes in the sheer line, etc., and also they will guide the designer on the positioning and shaping of various appendages such as bilge keels. If a bulbous bow was not part of the original design, it might be recommended at this stage. Usually, the ship tank authorities will not carry out all tests immediately but will recommend certain design features based on their expert knowledge and then carry out tests when the designer has incorporated as many features in the design as he can. They would recommend, perhaps, a rudder shape and size to achieve a specified turning performance. Upon further study the designer may find it impossible to provide the associated steering gear and have to settle for smaller rudders and reduced turning capability. The model tests would then be carried out with this reduced rudder area.

With a more accurate knowledge of the ship's powering and with a fuller knowledge of the machinery, which will have been developing in parallel with the ship design, a closer estimate can be made of the fuel needed to achieve the stated endurance.

The designer has already ensured that his ship is safe when operating normally. He now studies the hazard conditions as discussed in Chapter 5. He produces floodable length curves and studies damaged stability. Both may involve changes to the internal compartmentation and thus reflect upon the general arrangement. Also, at this stage, more accurate calculations are possible for the various tonnage measurements.

Structural design proceeds in accord with society rules or calculation as appropriate. First will come the main structural elements such as shell plating, decks, bulkheads and superstructure. These will be gradually refined to allow for local loads due to heavy weights, slamming in waves, etc. The methods employed in design are discussed in Chapters 6 and 7. These calculations use the main bending and shear stresses already defined by approximate methods. As the calculations proceed, better weight estimates become available and a longitudinal distribution can be found. By applying the methods of Chapter 6, an accurate assessment of the nominal bending moment amidships can be made to replace that previously obtained by approximate formula.

The revised weight estimates and their moments must be fed back into the stability calculations to check that the stability criteria are still satisfactory.

In this type of calculation, as in all others, an experienced designer will have allowed certain margins in the earlier calculations so that at this stage no radical changes should be necessary to the ship.

The process of iteration continues until the designer is satisfied that his design is sound. The final detailing of all aspects of the design can then proceed.

APPEARANCE AND LAYOUT

While developing the more technical aspects of the design, the naval architect must constantly have in mind the ultimate appearance and layout. A designer will always aim at producing a design pleasing to the eye; he will have difficulty with the funnel design where what is aesthetically most pleasing may lead to funnel gases trailing down over the after regions. In passenger liners, good appearance can attract passengers. In any ship, clean, graceful lines can add to a ship's prestige. Modern warships are often used as deterrents to prevent a cold war situation escalating into a conflict. To fulfil this role they must look as though they can hit hard should the need arise, i.e. they must possess a military aspect.

Layout concerns the internal distribution of spaces and facilities and the external disposition of superstructure and equipments or armaments. Internally, compartments, passageways, doors and hatches must be arranged to facilitate the flow of material and men in the normal running of the ship. Living spaces must provide ready access to bathrooms, dining halls and watch-keeping positions. At the same time, they should be kept clear of sources of excessive noise, vibration and smell. Compartments which are functionally related must be grouped together in a logical sequence.

Consider the catering facilities in a modern destroyer. These are typically as shown in Fig. 15.7.

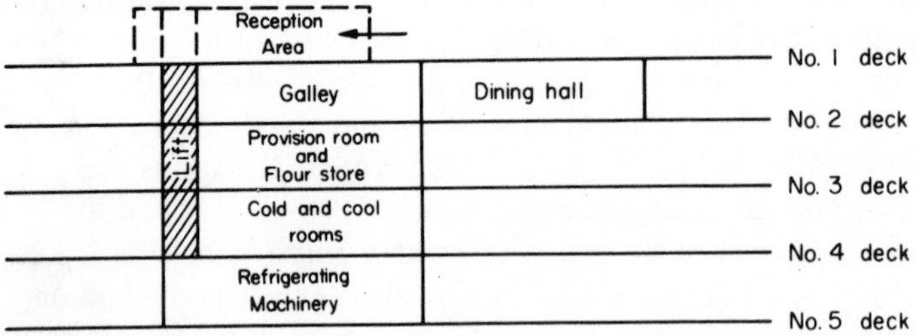

Fig. 15.7 Catering arrangements in destroyer

The victualling stores are received on the upper deck (No. 1 deck) at a position close to the top of a lift which can strike them down rapidly to the provision room, flour store or cold and cool rooms. The same lift can bring up stores each day to the preparation space at one end of the galley. After preparation, the food passes to the cooking area a.id then to the serving area which adjoins the dining hall. Such an arrangement requires the minimum of handling of the stores.

In other words, the layout must reflect the way the ship is used and the needs of the crew. In achieving this, the naval architect makes use of work study techniques as discussed later.

It is particularly important that the designer studies the routing of cables and pipes throughout the ship. These services are, in effect, the ship's arteries and their arrangement must ensure that all equipments are adequately served under normal and breakdown conditions. They must also be arranged economically, e.g. if several spaces require supplies of steam it is undesirable that all but one be grouped aft and the remaining one well forward.

Having decided on the correct relative positioning of compartments and the main service runs, the naval architect must apply similar principles to the layout within each space. He must ensure that flow of men and material is unimpeded and that operation and maintenance of equipments are as easy as possible. Again, it is clear that he must have a working knowledge of how his ship will be used.

By this stage, then, the designer has established:

(*a*) principal dimensions, displacement and deadweight;
(*b*) the stability and strength standards and hydrostatic data;
(*c*) power, speed, endurance, fuel stowages;
(*d*) the standards of protection and safety;
(*e*) a general arrangement of the ship and layouts of the more important spaces;
(*f*) runs of principal services;
(*g*) main structure.

This is adequate to define the ship for tendering purposes and the information is provided to possible shipbuilders in the form of drawings and specifications. Having negotiated a price with a shipbuilder the order for the ship can be placed and the detailing of the design can commence. The basic steps in warship design up to this stage are shown in Fig. 15.8.

Detailed design

After the ship has been ordered, there remains the task of detailing the design to enable the ship to be built by the craftsmen in the shipyard. Computers are already in use to control cutting machines using punched tape and that tape may itself be the output of another computer as the answer to a series of calculations. However, for the time being, the drawing remains the primary method of communicating the designer's ideas to the shipyard, amplified where necessary by installation specifications.

The designer issues more detailed guidance information to the Shipbuilder and the latter develops the detailed drawings. The drawings are of the following main types:

(*a*) structural drawings defining the scantlings (i.e. dimensions and weights) of all structural material and how it is to be disposed in bulkheads, decks, etc.;

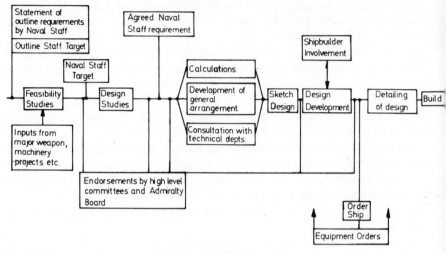

Fig. 15.8 Diagrammatic representation of warship design process

(b) layout drawings defining the layout of each space in the ship including passageways;

(c) service drawings defining the general runs of pipes and cables throughout the ship. These will be shown in detail in each drawing of individual compartments but overall drawings are needed to ensure that the services are distributed correctly. In warships, the services can be particularly complicated and composite services drawings are often used to ensure that one system does not foul another;

(d) equipment and machinery drawings defining individual equipments and machines.

During this phase of the design, the services of many specialist contractors and consultants are called upon. In developing the layouts of the public rooms in a passenger liner, experts in interior decoration and lighting are consulted. The details of the air conditioning system would probably be developed by a firm specializing in this work who would later be responsible for its installation in the ship. Specialists in cargo-handling equipment would advise on the type and arrangement of this type of equipment. In this way, the final design benefits from the latest developments in each branch of industry.

DRAWING SCHEDULES AND PROCEDURE CHARTS

If the ship is to be built to programme, a drawing schedule must be prepared and agreed with the shipyard, to ensure that drawings are completed in a steady flow, and in the correct order. In the case of a modern guided missile destroyer, some 25,000 drawings are involved of which the naval architect is responsible for about half. These are produced in the shipyard drawing office following guidance drawings issued by the MOD. For important spaces, the guidance drawings are sufficiently detailed to enable compartments to be lined out directly as discussed later. Besides the schedule it is necessary to agree on the procedure by which drawings are to be submitted to the designer by the ship-yard drawing office and commented upon by all those concerned.

When the shipbuilder receives the structural guidance drawings, he develops drawings showing the weldments from which the ship is to be built. The size and arrangement of weldments depend upon the shop, slip and cranage facilities available. When the ship is substantially complete as regards structure the layout drawings are used to *line-out* each space, i.e. lines are marked on decks and bulkheads to show where equipment is to be sited. In some cases, a three-dimensional line-out is used in which equipment and fittings are represented in three dimensions by laths of wood and wires. In the more complex spaces, such as the Operations Room in warships, a complete mock-up may be used to develop the drawing, the mock-up being in wood in a suitable position ashore. Following a line-out inspection, the drawing is finally modified and the compartment is fitted out to accord with it. The final inspection of the compartment may show that minor amendments are desirable. If these are agreed to be carried out the drawing must again be modified. The importance of a set of accurate drawings cannot be too strongly emphasized if a class of ships is to be built. During the later stages of building, the ship's systems and equipments are tested to ensure proper functioning. Since these trials are essentially to show that the design intent is fulfilled, the designer must play his part in defining the parameters to be measured and the values of those parameters which will be acceptable.

To ensure a consistent drawing standard, Ref. 7 is required to be worked to by the MOD, and to reduce the bulk of drawings needed to be stowed, all drawings have to be suitable for microfilming.

Support functions

There are a number of supporting functions or techniques which are used by the naval architect to help him arrive at an efficient design. Many have been developed in other industries and some are discussed briefly in the following paragraphs. Most involve a precise statement of the object and a critical analysis of various means of achieving this object.

DESIGN INFLUENCE DIAGRAMS

It has been seen that very few problems facing the naval architect can be treated in isolation. Most react upon, and are influenced by, many others and if the designer is to achieve the correct compromise between possibly conflicting demands it is important that he appreciates and studies all these inter-dependencies. One way of representing them diagrammatically is by the Design *Influence Diagram*, examples of which are given in Figs. 15.9 and 15.10. Each diagram could be extended almost indefinitely but it is convenient to limit each to the factors having a direct influence upon the central problem. Finally, all such diagrams could be interlocked into the overall design picture rather like the pieces of a huge jig-saw puzzle. It cannot be emphasized too strongly that ship design is far from being a process of simply selecting a few basic bricks and assembling them in orderly blocks, although where some of the smaller elements can be standardized for a number of ships, logistic support is simplified.

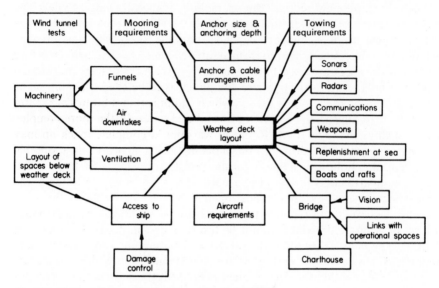

Fig. 15.9 Design influence diagram for weather deck (GMD)

NETWORK PLANNING

A design or construction process consists of a number of individual operations. As stated above, many of these are inter-related, and although it may be possible to carry out a number at the same time, others must follow in a definite sequence. A network is a means of showing diagrammatically the individual operations,

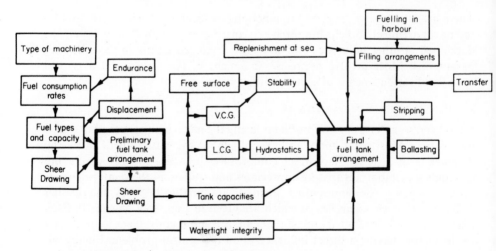

Fig. 15.10 Design influence diagram for fuel tanks

their sequence and inter-dependencies. A number of different techniques is available but all are similar in principle. Applied to the ship as a whole, network planning can show when materials should be ordered, can help with labour allocation and indicate the significance of delays on other dependent operations and on the overall programme. The network analysis is usually carried out by a computer and can provide the close control of progress so necessary in modern complex ships.

DEPENDENCY DIAGRAMS

As already discussed, the owner of a ship should state his requirements in terms of the capabilities he wishes his ship to possess. It is then for the designer to decide how best to provide those capabilities. During discussions between owner and designer it would be reasonable for the former to ask, in relation to each capability, the capital and running costs, manpower required on board and ashore, together with any special skills that may be needed from them. He would also expect to question the probability that the capability would be available when he needed it (availability) and that it would remain available for the time it was needed (reliability). For example, cargo-handling equipment must be available on arrival in port and remain serviceable for the unloading and loading operations.

To answer such questions the designer has to establish which elements of the design, such as structure and equipment, contribute to each capability. This can be shown on a dependency diagram (Fig. 15.11). The diagram can be used to show the effect on level of capability of failure or partial failure of an equipment. Overall availability and reliability can be calculated if individual figures for the components of the diagram are known. Both can be increased by either improving individual components or by duplication of equipment and/or supplies.

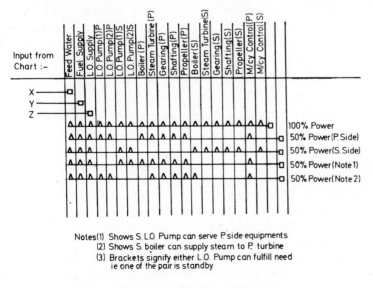

Notes(1) Shows S. L.O. Pump can serve P. side equipments
(2) Shows S. boiler can supply steam to P. turbine
(3) Brackets signify either L.O. Pump can fulfill need
ie one of the pair is standby

Fig. 15.11 Part of speed characteristic dependency diagram

The cost to acquire is the sum of the costs of the components and installation costs. Upkeep and manning requirements can be assessed by the same summation process.

Although this process sounds relatively simple, it can become quite complicated as will be appreciated when it is realized that some equipments may support more than one capability. The generation and distribution of electrical power is vital to almost every capability. Loss of part of the generator capacity may mean that not all capabilities can be met at once but the available power can be used for those most needed by the command. The representation of this type of complication needs careful thought and the interpretation of answers obtained from the use of dependency diagrams requires care.

WORK STUDY

In principle, a work study practitioner considers a certain process, perhaps design, fabrication, installation or maintenance, and asks himself:

What is achieved?	*Why* is it necessary?
Where is it done?	*Why* there?
When is it done?	*Why* then?
By whom is it done?	*Why* by that person?
How is it done?	*Why* in that way?

In asking 'Why?' the practitioner also seeks alternatives. He then assesses the advantages and disadvantages of the various solutions to decide which is the best. This critical examination of the facts often reveals that jobs are unnecessary or are carried out in a certain way by certain people for purely historical reasons. The end product should be a better way of achieving the desired aim. Better may mean that the process is cheaper, quicker, requires less men or is in some other way superior depending upon the terms of reference under which the study was conducted. Work study does not need a highly specialized practitioner; all engineers and technologists should use the tool when it is likely to be profitable. It is often an expensive tool and it should itself be the subject of cost-effectiveness enquiry before being employed.

DESIGN METHOD

Work study techniques are not usually directly applicable to abstract design, but the underlying principles, i.e. a logical sequence of questioning and a critical examination of the facts revealed by that questioning, apply. In design method applied to the design of a piece of machinery, say, the questioning must reveal the primary function of the equipment and this is not always as obvious as might be imagined. It must then be expanded to cover related functions and supporting services. The series of questions must then be asked of each phase in the life of the equipment from initial design, through manufacture, installation to usage and maintenance.

Clearly, the value of the questioning process is directly related to the accuracy and completeness of the answers. This demands an adequate level of knowledge on the part of the designer and highlights a need for a feedback of user experience with similar pieces of equipment. In the structural design of ships, for example, a designer must have a steady flow of data from ships at sea of any failures of structural elements. With this he can improve his design methods and choose realistic factors of safety.

VALUE ENGINEERING

This is a related technique in which, by a critical examination of the purpose and design of a piece of equipment and each of its elements, its 'value for money' can be assessed. In particular, economical production is a prime aim. This does not always mean the cheapest product, e.g. a pump costing £10 less to manufacture may cost an extra £50 for maintenance during its life. Value engineering studies often reveal that equipments are capable of doing much more than is required and can be simplified considerably and yet still be able to perform their prime function.

Assessment of 'value for money' is often made in terms of 'cost effectiveness' or 'cost benefit'. Effectiveness is a function of capability, availability for use and the correctness of the concept (utility). Related to total cost, this provides a measure by which to compare various solutions to a problem. The words '*cost effective*' are solely comparative and suggest the best of several possibilities. When effectiveness can be contrived into financial terms to show the overall benefit of a solution, the process by which comparison is made is called '*cost benefit analysis*'. Often, it may be necessary to allot a financial value to human life. environment or time in assessing benefits and dis-benefits.

In service

RELIABILITY

Reliability is defined as the ability of a product to function successfully, when required, for the period required, in the specified environment. It is therefore, also, one measure of the success of a designer. Individual units may possess a high degree of reliability but, in most cases, a system is involved with a large number of components, failure in any one of which can lead to failure of the overall system. The reliability of the system depends on the number of components and the reliability of each. Overall reliability is the product of individual reliabilities if in series. This is illustrated in Table 15.3.

Table 15.3
Reliability

Individual component reliability (%)	System reliability (%)				
	Number of components				
	10	60	100	250	500
99·99	99·9	99·4	99·1	97·5	95·1
99·90	99·0	94·2	90·5	77·9	60·7
99·00	90·4	54·8	36·6	8·1	0·7
98·00	81·7	29·8	13·3	0·6	0·0

How is ship design influenced by the need for reliability? It is only possible to answer this question in very broad terms. It leads to a steady development in design and techniques rather than revolutionary changes. Major changes, e.g. the introduction of novel propulsion machinery, will usually be studied initially ashore and in a special trials ship until it has proved its reliability. A new design of pump may be fitted with a proven design as a stand-by or as one of a group of pumps.

It is now possible to predict numerically the likelihood of surviving a particular period in service by a study of the characteristics of past failures. For many equipments and systems, for example, the probability of survival for a time t is given by $e^{-\lambda t}$ where λ is a constant called the failure rate (the reciprocal of which is the mean time between failures, MTBF).

MAINTAINABILITY

Clearly, reliability and maintainability are related. Both are influenced by the competence of the user but the greatest opportunity to reduce the time and effort needed for maintenance arises during design. Good access is vital if effective maintenance is to be possible. In laying out a compartment, the naval architect must have a working knowledge of how the compartment and the equipments in it will be used. Mock-ups and line-outs of compartments can assist in achieving an efficient layout but, in the end, success depends upon adequate attention to detail.

Looking at the literature for new motor cars, the steps taken to reduce the time and cost of regular maintenance usually figure high amongst the features quoted to help sell the car. So it is with ships. Too much maintenance can mean larger crews with higher wage bills or longer periods in harbour. At the same time, the risk of breakdown must be kept to a minimum.

References 8 to 12 discuss maintenance problems associated with various ship types. All emphasize the need for adequate protection of structure and the need to provide a good base for paint schemes by grit blasting and shop-priming the plating used. Additional protection is provided by impressed current cathodic protection systems and these are fitted to most new ships. Underwater surfaces must be treated to reduce fouling and so reduce the associated increase in resistance. The aim is to achieve an interval between dockings which is consistent with other requirements. In warships, the aim is two years to link up with the normal refit cycle; in passenger ships, it may be between 6 and 12 months depending on the service schedule; in cargo ships and tankers it is generally 12 months; it is also 12 months for cross-channel ships enabling work to be done during the winter months when trade is quiet. Twelve months also accords with the annual survey required by classification societies.

In the proper sense of the word, the material and equipment of a ship needs to be managed. Its reliability and maintainability can be predicted from the statistics of previous ships and their equipments so that the most economical material can be selected in design. In service, the best way to deal with failure can be judged from a knowledge of the dis-benefits of failure and the costs of the various ways of increasing availability for use—whether, for example, to replace a suspect equipment, duplicate it, supply it with more spares, effect some modification or to live with it. This requires information about the pattern of failures and the effort devoted to maintenance, and about the usage and availability of the functions of the ship. Data can be collected from an array of equipments and ships and fed into a computer which will collate it and print out information needed by managers. Such management information systems are playing an important part in material management and help designers select equipment which is sufficiently reliable without being unduly expensive.

Planned maintenance is best managed by a schedule of every item required, how often it is to be performed and the spares, tools and skills required. Most large shipping lines and navies run their planned maintenance in this way.

Generally, ship's staff carry cut routine maintenance at sea and larger jobs are tackled in port, during the normal turn round period, if possible. Repair or overhaul by replacement can reduce the time spent in harbour, particularly if the designer arranges that equipments can be readily removed. Complete machines are then removed and replaced by new or reconditioned machines. Apart from reducing the time spent by the ship in shipyard hands, the machinery can be refitted in the more favourable conditions of the factory and the refit work can be spread more evenly over the full year rather than being conditional on the presence of the ship. It does, however, require more spare units to be avail-

Table 15.4
Comparative repair costs. Passenger ship

Itemized repair costs per £100 total repair cost		
Hull: Structure	0·7	
Dry-docking	2·7	
Painting, external	2·4	
internal	3·9	
		9·7
Auxiliary machinery: Deck machinery	0·4	
Stabilizers	0·7	
Lifts	0·6	
		1·7
Electrical	1·1	
Pipe services	8·1	
Cargo gear and rigging	0·2	
Air conditioning and ventilation	2·9	
Refrigeration	2·0	
Decks and covering	1·5	
Life saving	5·1	
Fire prevention	0·6	
Navigational aids and radio	0·9	
Furnishings	8·8	
Galleys	4·0	
Laundries	0·9	
Hull fittings	0·6	
Other expenditure not itemized: e.g. boilers, main engines and auxiliaries, purser's department, crockery, etc.	51·9	
Total	100·0	

able at shipyards where the work is to be carried out. Standardization and rationalization of equipments and machinery can help a great deal besides easing the problem of supply of spare parts.

Comparative repair costs are given in Table 15.4 for a passenger ship of 28,000 gross tons when it was 10 years old.

SURVEYS

When it is intended to build a merchant ship or fleet auxiliary for classification by a classification society such as Lloyd's Register of Shipping, constructional plans and particulars of the hull, equipment and machinery have to be submitted through the local surveyors for approval before work is commenced. In cases involving novel design features or material, special tests may be demanded to ensure that the proposals will lead to a sound ship. Having approved the design proposals, the society must be satisfied that the ship is built in accordance with the proposals and throughout building the surveyors examine materials and workmanship. Such ships are said to be built under the society's *Special Survey during Construction* and carry a special symbol in front of their classification. The date of completion of this Special Survey is taken as the *Date of Build*. It is on this date that the sequence of surveys during service is based to ensure that the ships remain fit for classification.

In order that a ship should remain an acceptable insurance risk, it is necessary to prove by periodic surveys, carried out to the satisfaction of the classification society, that it is fit to retain its class. The periodic surveys to which the ship is subjected during its life are the *Annual Surveys* and *Special Surveys*. In addition to the annual surveys, all ships are examined in dry dock at intervals of about 12 months, the maximum permitted interval being 2 years. The special surveys become due at 4-yearly intervals, the first at 4 years from the date of build. The work required under these surveys can, by agreement, be carried out in rotation, i.e. *Continuous Survey*, provided any given compartment or piece of equipment is surveyed at intervals not exceeding 5 years and that extra spaces are opened up if defects are found.

Surveys are laid down for both the hull and its fittings and machinery. The scope and severity of the survey varies with the age of the ship, with regulations for ships under 5 years old, between 5 and 10 years old, and over 10 years old. Special requirements arise when a ship is 24 years old and at 12 yearly intervals thereafter.

In addition to the surveys required by the classification society, British ships have to undergo statutory surveys controlled by the Board of Trade. In the case of passenger ships carrying more than twelve passengers, a *Passenger Certificate* can only be issued if the ship meets the requirements of the Merchant Shipping Acts. In addition, the provisions of the International Convention for the Safety of Life at Sea require that the ship has a valid *Safety Certificate* before it puts to sea. Both certificates are valid for only one year and surveys are required for their renewal. Before they are issued initially, plans have to be submitted to the chief ship surveyor including hull structural plans, subdivision arrangements and calculations, fire protection arrangements and stability data in the damaged condition.

During *Annual Surveys* the surveyors must ensure that hulls are in good condition, that the principal structural scantlings are maintained and that arrangements are generally in accordance with the Board's requirements. A thorough examination is made of the outside of the hull in dry dock. The interior structure is examined and linings, etc., are removed as necessary. The surveyor also ensures that load line markings are correct and that stability data is available to the Master of the ship.

Special regulations apply to the survey of life-saving appliances and these have to be complied with before a Passenger Certificate is issued.

The regulations covering surveys are significant to the designer, not only because they determine the time equipment is to last and function, but because they also help determine the operational cycle for the ship.

In the case of warships, specifications and guidance drawings are prepared within the Navy Department of the MOD. Overseers are attached to each major shipyard to ensure that this guidance is correctly followed and that materials and methods of construction are satisfactory. The ship is finally accepted for the Royal Navy following a period of trials and inspections. During construction, the shipbuilder is required to meet fairly stringent requirements as regards cleanliness, quality of workmanship and material to ensure that the ship is as sound as possible when accepted into service. The shipbuilder must complete all grit blasting before machinery is installed and he must flush and clean all piping systems thoroughly. In this way, the maintenance load on the ship in later life is much reduced.

When in service, the ship is kept in an efficient fighting condition by the ship's own complement during self-maintenance periods. More extensive work is carried out during refits at 18–24 month intervals and long refits at intervals of about 5–6 years. Many warships also undergo a large-scale modernization after about 10 or 12 years to take advantage of developments in weapon systems. This is about half way through the normal useful life of a warship which is some 20 years. Refit work is usually carried out in one of H.M. Dockyards but, on occasion, is contracted out to private shipyards.

Problems

1. An aircraft carrier has a deep displacement of 29,600 tonf made up as follows: hull 10,000 tonf, equipment 1000 tonf, machinery 2500 tonf, fuel 3500 tonf, side protection 3700 tonf, deck protection 2800 tonf, aircraft and armament, 5500 tonf, margin 600 tonf.

A new design is to be similar but is required to carry 1000 tonf extra in the form of payload. Calculate the new displacement and group weights assuming s.h.p. varies as displacement to the power 0·6 at full speed and to the power $\frac{2}{3}$ at endurance speed. (RNC)

Note: It should be assumed that the weight of side protection varies as the linear dimension of the ship and deck protection as the square of the linear dimension.

2. A frigate of displacement 3200 tonf, speed 32 knots and s.h.p. of 50,000 at full

power, has an endurance of 5000 miles at 18 knots. The group weights are; hull 1200 tonf, machinery 800 tonf, fuel 700 tonf and equipment 200 tonf. The remaining 300 tonf is devoted to armament.

Estimate the displacement and group weights of a similar frigate with an additional 30 tonf of armament and a full speed of 31 knots. The endurance is to be 4500 miles at 20 knots. There will be a saving of 5 per cent in hull weight due to the use of light alloys and a saving of 4 per cent in machinery weight due to improved machinery design. A margin of 2 per cent of the displacement is required.

It should be assumed that the s.h.p. is proportional to $V^{2.8}$ at full power and V^3 at 18–20 knots. The fuel consumption rate does not change.   (RNC)

3. A design study for an all-welded cargo ship is estimated to have a displacement of 80 MN, a speed of 15 knots, a length of 144 m.

The ship is to be powered by diesels turning the propeller at 100 r.p.m.

Estimate a suitable block coefficient, deduce the power in kW required to propel the ship and hence obtain the approximate machinery weight.

4. A new design of passenger liner is to have a displacement of 20,000 tonnef and service speed of 23 kts. Estimate suitable values of length, beam, depth and block coefficient, assuming that the trial speed is to be 24 knots and that twin screws are to be fitted.

References

1. Goss, R. O. Economic criteria for optimal ship designs. *TRINA*. 1965.
2. *Lloyd's Register of Shipping*. Statistical Tables, 1965.
3. Watson, D. G. M. Estimating preliminary dimensions in ship design. *TIESS*, Vol. 105, 1961–2.
4. Murray, J. M. Large bulk carriers. *TIESS*, Vol. 108, 1964–5.
5. Turner, R. V., Harper, M. and Moor, D. I. Some aspects of passenger liner design. *TRINA*, 1963.
6. Miller, R. T. A ship design process. *Marine Technology*, October, 1965.
7. *Defence specification* 33A. HMSO, London, 1963.
8. Fulthorpe, H. J. and Coates, J. F. *The Royal Navy.**
9. Campbell, D. *Passenger ships.**
10. Church, J. E. *Cargo liners and cargo tramps.**
11. Campbell, J. P. *Cross-channel ships.**
12. Robinson, J. G. *Oil tankers.**
13. *Lloyd's Register of Shipping*. Rules and regulations for the construction and classification of steel ships, 1974.
14. Yuille, I. M. A. system for on-line computer aided design of ships—prototype system and future possibilities. *TRINA*, 1970.
15. Rawson, K. J. Towards economic warship acquisition and ownership. *TRINA*, 1973.
16. Buxton, I. Engineering economics applied to ship design. *TRINA*, 1972.
17. O'Loughlin, C. *The economics of sea transport*. Pergamon, 1967.
18. Leopold, R. and Reuter, W. Three winning designs FDL, LHA, DD–963. Method and selected features. *TSNAME*, 1971.
19. Purvis, M. K. Postwar design of frigates and guided missile destroyers, 1944–1969. *TRINA*, 1974.
20. Green, A. E. and Bourne, A. J. *Reliability Technology*. Wiley-Interscience, 1972.
21. Carter, A. D. *Mechanical Reliability*. MacMillan, 1972.

*References 8–12 presented at discussion on ship maintenance and associated design problems. *TRINA*, 1965.

16 Special ship types

Passenger ships

This type of ship is probably the most difficult for which to fix the requirements and design. The cargo is the public who can be quite fickle and safety regulations are severe. It is also in this field that the ship owner faces the greatest challenge from the air. The owner must decide how many passengers to carry, the standard of accommodation and service, the provision of public rooms, as well as the passage, speed and endurance. To arrive at a good specification, considerable research is required into traffic volume, passenger types, schedules, etc. It is not enough to measure these at the time of the design inception. The owner must predict public tastes and habits in 10 years' time and later. One recent trend has been towards cruise liners.

Some interesting facts and figures on the design of passenger liners are given in Ref. 1 and the following quotation is apt:

... it is the primary responsibility of the builder of a passenger liner to ensure that his design embodies those principles which lead to the minimum hull weight combined with optimum efficiency in propulsive performance and in fuel consumption, and at the same time to ensure that these features are obtained without detriment to the owner's requirements and that their achievement is linked with a minimum first cost.

Some of the economic aspects of passenger liner operation are illustrated in Table 16.1 and are based on a fuel cost of £65 per tonf and the assumption that the machinery is operated at 85 per cent of service power for 240 days per year. The table illustrates the importance of keeping weight to a minimum, even in space limited design, using model tests to achieve a good hull form. In spite of restrictions placed on the ship dimensions by owner's requirements, stability and berthing, it is claimed in Ref. 1 that a reduction in resistance of the order of 10 per cent has been achieved over a 20 year period.

Several modern designs of passenger ship have adopted layouts in which the main propulsion machinery is sited in the after quarter of the length. This provides for large areas of passenger accommodation free from machinery uptakes. This can be particularly significant in ships in which all passengers are of one class, although most of this advantage can be gained with machinery amidships with sided uptakes and downtakes. Another advantage of siting machinery aft is that large deck areas are kept free of funnel gases, and vibration levels in passenger areas are lower. On the debit side, however, the maximum longitudinal bending moments and shearing forces may be increased by as much as 25 per cent.

Table 16.1
Economics of passenger liner design for three typical ships (based on Ref. 1)

Length (ft/m)	Gross tonnage	Service speed (knots)	Load displace- ment (tonf)	Service s.h.p.	Fuel rate (tonf/day)	Annual fuel cost (£m)	Additional annual fuel cost associated with carriage of additional tonf of fixed weight (£)
600/183	25,000	21	27,000	25,000	142	2·2	42
740/226	42,000	27·5	39,000	65,000	332	5·2	100
940/287	75,000	30	60,000	150,000	725	11·3	134

The modern passenger liner poses many problems of interior decoration in the broadest sense. The height and dimensions of public rooms are important besides colour, lighting, furnishings and floor coverings. Usually, passengers will be drawn from many nations and public taste in each country must be considered. The spaces may be used for many functions, e.g. the lounge may be used for afternoon tea and dances besides being a comfortable sitting out area for much of the day. The shipowner often calls in a firm of consultants, who specialize in this work.

One of the more important recent developments in passenger ship design is the emergence of the drive-on/drive-off passenger and vehicle ferries. A significant increase in container lorry traffic and the seasonal nature of tourism creates a demand for these ships to be readily convertible. The designs are dominated by the need to segregate vehicles and passengers by substantial fire boundaries and to provide adequate subdivision without inhibiting through passage of vehicles. Often, this is achieved by a central through deck with end closure bulkheads and ramps for vehicles, with all passenger accommodation in the wings, outboard of longitudinal bulkheads. The outboard parts of the ships provide the necessary subdivision against flooding. As with cruise liners, the ships are space designed and their dimensions, as shown by Fig. 15.4 are more variable than with other ship types.

Submarines

Submarines are vehicles designed principally to operate at considerable depth. Most applications to date have been to warships. More recently, oceanographic research vessels and small vehicles for laying pipes and servicing well-heads on the sea bed have been produced. Submarines are uneconomic for general commercial work.

The fact that the vessel has to be able to operate either on the surface or while submerged means that all the usual naval architecture problems of buoyancy, stability, strength, powering, manoeuvrability, etc., have to be studied for both conditions. In addition, some of these problems have to be studied during the transition phase from one condition to another.

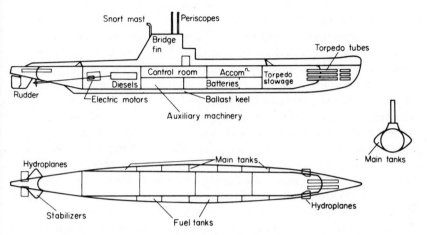

Fig. 16.1 Diagrammatic arrangement of conventional submarine

The general design of a conventional submarine is illustrated in Fig. 16.1. Major differences compared with a surface ship are:

(a) the shape, which is conditioned by the need to have efficient propulsion submerged;
(b) the enclosure of the main portion of the vessel in a pressure hull which is usually circular in cross-section to enable it to withstand high hydrostatic pressure at deep diving depths. The circular section means greater draught generally than a surface ship of the same displacement. It also requires that a docking keel be provided, unless special cradles are available, and a top casing for men to move around on in harbour;
(c) two additional sets of control surfaces, the hydroplanes, for controlling depth and trim angle;
(d) tanks, usually external to the pressure hull, which can be flooded to cause the vessel to submerge;
(e) a dual propulsion system. The submerged propulsion system is usually electric drive supplied by batteries and surface propulsion is usually by diesels. The batteries need frequent recharging, which means that a conventional submarine has to operate on the surface or at periscope depth for considerable periods. These disadvantages are overcome in nuclear submarines or in vessels with closed cycle engines;
(f) periscopes to enable the vessel to operate close to the surface;
(g) a special air intake, the schnorkel mast, to enable air to be taken in when operating at periscope depth;
(h) special means of controlling the atmosphere inside the submarine. Apart from the normal conditioning equipment, carbon dioxide absorbers and oxygen generators are provided.

It has already been pointed out that most of the naval architectural investigations have to be carried out twice. Special problems are:

(a) *Hydrostatics*. Although the hydroplanes can take care of small out-of-balance forces and moments, the vessel when submerged must have a buoyancy almost exactly equal to its weight and B must be vertically above G. For reasons of safety, in practice the buoyancy is usually maintained slightly in excess of the weight. The capacity of tanks within the pressure hull for adjusting weight and longitudinal moment is limited, so that initial design calculations must be accurate and weight and moment control are more critical than for a surface ship. In the latter case, errors involve change of draught and trim from the design condition. If a submarine is too heavy she will sink and if too light she will not submerge. If B and G are not in the same vertical line, very large trim angles will result as B cannot move due to movements of 'wedges' of buoyancy. The term trim here is used in the conventional sense. In submarines, fore and aft angles are usually termed pitch and the term trim is used to denote correct balance between buoyancy and weight. This critical balance between weight and displacement means that if weights are ejected, e.g. a torpedo, then a carefully metered quantity of water must be taken on board immediately to compensate;

(b) *Stability*. The stability of the submarine for heel and depth when submerged were discussed in Chapter 4. In the submerged state, longitudinal and transverse stability are the same. On the surface, the usual calculations can be applied but as the submarine dives the waterplane reduces considerably as the bridge fin passes through the surface. In this condition, B may still be relatively low and a critical stability condition can result.

Submarines are subject to special tests, the *trimming and inclining experiments*, to prove that the hydrostatic and stability characteristics are satisfactory in all conditions. The correct standard condition is then achieved by adjustments to the ballast keel;

(c) *Strength*. The usual methods of calculating the longitudinal strength can be applied, but a completely new set of calculations is needed to study the strength of the pressure hull against the crushing pressures at deep diving depth. Strengthwise, the optimum cross-section is circular but the problem of elastic instability are often the controlling factor in determining the scantlings of the pressure hull. Because of these requirements the pressure hull accounts for a relatively high percentage of the displacement of the submarine.

To assist in maintaining the circular cross-section of the vessel, the pressure hull is divided longitudinally by a few transverse bulkheads and a large number of transverse frames. Pressure hull thickness is obtained by the boiler formula, limiting the hoop stress to below the yield. There are two areas of particular concern which require investigation by some advanced mathematics:

(i) inter-frame collapse, i.e. collapse of the short cylinder of plating between frames under radial compression. Such a failure is likely to occur in a large number of nodes (see Chapter 7);

(ii) inter-bulkhead collapse, i.e. collapse of the pressure hull plating with the frames between bulkheads. This is sensitive particularly to the degree of out-of-circularity in construction;

An approximation to the effect of depth of operation on the weight of hull is obtained by considering the simple case illustrated in Fig. 16.2.

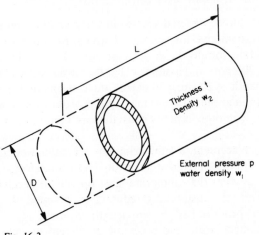

Fig. 16.2

A circular cylinder is chosen as being a good shape for withstanding external pressure. A sphere is better, but this form is used only for certain research vehicles. Stiffening is ignored and the hoop stress is used as the design criterion.

The force on half the cylinder due to an external pressure p is pDL. The hoop stress in the plating is then

$$\frac{pDL}{2tL} = \frac{pD}{2t}$$

For a given material, the permissible stress will be constant so that

$$t \propto pD$$

Now the buoyancy force acting on the cylinder is

$$w_1 \frac{\pi D^2}{4} L$$

and the weight of the cylinder itself, ignoring the end plates, is

$$w_2 \pi D L t$$

Hence, the proportion of buoyancy force devoted to supporting the weight of the structure is

$$\frac{w_2 \pi D L t}{w_1 \dfrac{\pi D^2}{4} L} = \frac{4w_2}{w_1} \frac{t}{D}$$

Since *t* is proportional to *pD*, it is seen that the ratio of structual weight to buoyancy increases linearly with increasing pressure, i.e. depth. There will be a depth when there will be nothing available for payload. For a given depth of submergence, in other words, for a given *p*, the ratio remains constant. Since other weights, e.g. machinery, crew, etc., are relatively less for a larger ship the large ship should have a higher deadweight/displacement ratio.

(*d*) *Dynamic stability*. This has already been discussed in Chapter 13 in some detail. The limited diving depth available for reasons of strength reduces the time available for corrective action should the vessel suddenly take on a bow down attitude. For example, at 20 knots and assuming that the vessel is already at 50 m depth with a collapse depth of 200 m, a 30 degree angle means that the vessel reaches her collapse depth in about 30 sec. If the depth of water available is less than collapse depth, as it would be in many coastal areas, then the time available is even less;

(*e*) *Powering*. For a given displacement, a submarine has a greater wetted surface area than a surface ship. This means a greater frictional resistance, which, for comparable conditions, means that the submarine must operate at depths where the wavemaking resistance is substantially reduced. In practice, this means operating at depths of the order of half the ship length or more.

The importance of length/diameter ratio and prismatic coefficient on submerged resistance is shown in Fig. 16.3 which is taken from Ref. 3. The USS *Albacore* provided much useful data on submerged performance at high speed. It had a length/beam ratio of about 7·4 compared with the ratio of about 10 in second world war submarines (Ref. 4). It also had a single screw which gave high propulsive efficiency.

A possible commercial application of the submarine is discussed in Ref. 5. A special feature affecting the economics of the situation is the ability of a submarine, if nuclear powered, to operate underneath ice and, therefore, to follow a route barred to surface ships without the expensive assistance of an icebreaker. To operate submerged in the ballast condition, it must be possible to introduce ballast water equal in weight to the cargo carried. This leads to a desire for a high density cargo. It would not be economic to cut large hatch openings in the hull, so the cargo should be capable of being loaded and unloaded rapidly through small openings.

In Ref. 5, a typical ore carrier was compared with a study of a submarine ore carrier with results as in Table 16.2.

Table 16.2
Comparison of surface ship and submarine

	Surface ship	Submarine
Displacement, tonf	41,000	50,000
Deadweight, tonf	30,000	28,000
Draught, m	10·4	17·9

The very large draught made it necessary to assume that the submarine would travel on the surface when over the Continental Shelf, besides posing special

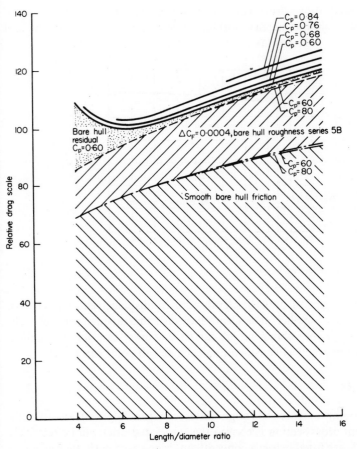

Fig. 16.3 Variation in total resistance with length/diameter ratio and prismatic coefficient

docking problems and making special transhipment bases necessary. Capital costs were high relative to the conventional ship, although they fell with increasing deadweight as illustrated in Table 16.3. At 28,000 tonf deadweight, the direct operating cost per tonf was about 30 per cent higher for the submarine.

Table 16.3

Comparative costs

Item	Proportional cost in conventional vessel	Proportional cost of submarine relative to surface vessel vs. deadweight		
		15,000 tonf dwt	28,000 tonf dwt	60,500 tonf dwt
Hull	0·40	0·93	0·83	0·77
Outfit	0·32	0·86	0·77	0·61
Machinery	0·28	1·24	0·90	0·65
Total	1·00	3·03	2·50	2·03

It was suggested above, from general considerations, that the deadweight/ displacement ratio should increase with increasing size. This was confirmed in Ref. 5 from which Fig. 16.4 is taken.

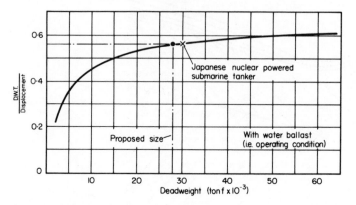

Fig. 16.4 Deadweight/displacement ratios

Taking the problems of draught, depth control, displacement, capital cost and operating costs together, it is clear that with the existing state of technological knowledge the submarine ore carrier or tanker can only be justified by some overriding practical consideration such as sub polar cap travel.

Hydrofoil craft

A hydrofoil moving at speed through water can generate considerable lift, and if an efficient cross-section is chosen the associated drag will be relatively low. If hydrofoils are fitted below a conventional high speed craft, they generate increasing lift as the speed increases, the lift being proportional to the square of the velocity. If the craft has sufficient power available, there will come a time when the lift on the foils is sufficient to lift the hull completely clear of the water. Having lost the resistance of the main hull, the craft can accelerate until the resistance of the foils and air resistance absorb the power available. A typical curve of R/Δ against $V/\sqrt{L}$ is shown in Fig. 16.5 which is taken from Ref. 6. The hump in the curve is associated with the very high wave resistance experienced just before the hull lifts clear of the water.

After the hull has lifted clear of the water, the lift required from the foils is constant. Thus, as the speed increases further, either the angle of incidence of the foil must reduce or the immersed area of the foil must decrease. This leads to two basic types of foil system, viz:

(a) *Surface piercing foils* in which, as the craft rises higher, the area of foil immersed reduces as it passes through the water surface;
(b) *Completely submerged, incidence controlled foils* in which the foils remain always submerged and the lift generated is varied by controlling the angle of attack of the foils.

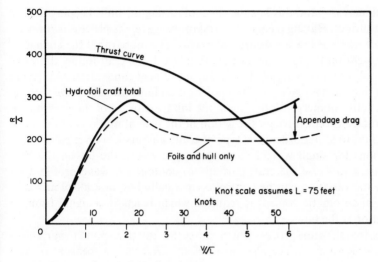

Fig. 16.5 *Resistance curve for hydrofoil craft*

These two systems are illustrated in Fig. 16.6.

Longitudinal balance must also be maintained, and it is usual to have a large foil area just forward or just aft of the longitudinal centre of gravity with a small foil at the stern or bow respectively. Any ratio of areas is feasible provided the resultant hydrodynamic force acts in a line through the c.g. The planform geometries are also illustrated in Fig. 16.6.

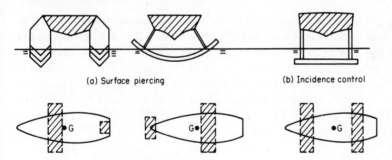

Fig. 16.6 *Basic foil geometries*

So far a calm water surface has been assumed. To understand what happens in waves, consider a surface piercing system as in Fig. 16.7. As the craft runs into the wave surface, the water level rises on the forward foil. The lift on the

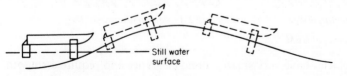

Fig. 16.7 *Surface piercing system in waves*

forward foil increases and this has the effect of raising the bow, keeping it clear of the wave surface. Having passed the crest of the wave, the process is reversed and the craft more or less 'contours' the waves. The more rapid the change of lift with draught on the foils the more faithfully will the craft follow the wave surface. By adjusting the rate of change, the movement can be lessened, giving a smoother ride but a greater possibility of the craft impacting the wave surface.

With the fully submerged foil system, the foil is unaware of the presence of the wave surface except through the action of the orbital motions of the wave particles. Thus, to a first order, this type of craft can pursue a level path which has attractions for small wave heights. In larger waves, the lift on the foils must be varied to cause the craft partially to contour the wave profile. In a small craft, the variation can be controlled manually but, in craft of any size, some form of automatic control is required which reacts to a signal from an altitude sensor at the bow.

It follows, that the same process which causes the craft to respond to variations in height of the water surface also provides the craft with a measure of trim stability. Roll stability will be present in a surface piercing system if the lift force which acts as the craft rolls, intersects the middle line plane of the craft above the vertical c.g. With a fully submerged foil system, roll stability is provided by means of flaps or ailerons which act differentially on the two sides of the craft in such a way as to provide a moment opposing the roll angle. This, again, is controlled by signals produced by a stable element in the craft.

Ground effect machines (GEMs)

The basic principle underlying all GEMs is the generation of a cushion of air between their undersurface and the surface over which they are moving, so that relatively low powers can be used to propel the vehicle forward at high speed. The air pressure in the cushion is higher than the ambient pressure so that an upward lift is generated which counterbalances the vehicle's weight, except that part which may be balanced by aerodynamic lift generated by the forward speed of the craft. It is possible to classify most GEMs as either depending on viscous flow or not, as in Fig. 16.8.

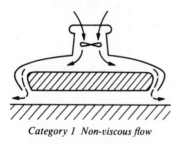
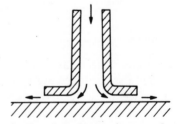

Category 1 *Non-viscous flow*   Category 2 *Predominantly viscous flow*

Fig. 16.8 Two categories of GEM

Category 2 vehicles have very small ground clearance and require a smooth surface over which to operate. This category is of less interest to the naval architect than category 1 vehicles of which the *hovercraft* is an example. The following notes are restricted to the simplified theory of the hovercraft.

A simplified hovercraft arrangement is shown in Fig. 16.9. Using the notation shown on this figure and assuming an air density ρ and a peripheral length of *l*, the following relationships can be deduced:

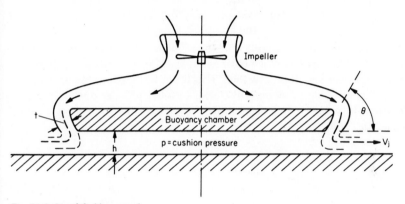

Fig. 16.9 Simplified hovercraft

Rate of change of momentum in the jet in a horizontal plane over an element δl of the periphery total length *l*.

$$= \rho V_j^2 t(1 + \cos \theta)\, \delta l$$

This may be equated to the force due to the cushion pressure over the same element as

$$\rho V_j^2 t(1 + \cos \theta)\delta l = ph\, \delta l$$

If the weight of the craft is Δ and the area of the cushion is S,

$$\Delta = pS + \text{jet reaction component } (\rho t l V_j^2 \text{Sin}\theta)$$

Hence

$$\Delta = \frac{\rho V_j^2 St(1 + \cos \theta)}{h} + \rho V_j^2 lt \text{Sin}\theta = \rho V_j^2 lt(\frac{1 + \text{Cos } \theta}{hl \,/\, S} + \text{Sin } \theta)$$

If only a vertical jet were used to produce the lift L_j (e.g. the down draught from a helicopter's rotor disc),

$$L_j = \rho V_j^2 \, lt$$

Hence

$$\frac{\Delta}{L_j} = \frac{S}{hl}(1 + \cos \theta) + \text{Sin } \theta$$

This may be regarded as the 'efficiency' of the hovercraft principle in augmenting lift.

Since h is a measure of the vehicle's ability to negotiate obstacles, it is likely to be fixed by the operator's requirements. Assuming that θ is also fixed, Δ/L_j depends upon the ratio S/l. This is greatest for a circle. This suggests that a circular planform is optimal for a hovercraft.

For a circle of diameter D

$$\frac{\Delta}{L_j} = \frac{\pi D^2}{4h\pi D}(1+\cos\theta) + \mathrm{Sin}\ \theta = \frac{D}{4h}(1+\cos\theta) + \mathrm{Sin}\ \theta$$

From this relationship, it is seen that for a given hover height the craft becomes more efficient the larger it becomes or, that for a given size craft, it can lift more as the hover height is decreased. This latter fact leads to the question as to whether it is possible to increase the craft's ability to clear obstacles whilst keeping h low in value. It has been shown to be possible by using a flexible 'skirt' as in Fig. 16.10.

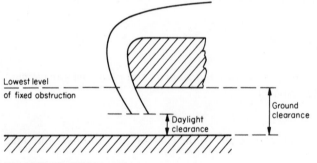

Fig. 16.10 Flexible skirt arrangement

So far, consideration has been directed only at lifting the vehicle off the surface. It is still required to propel it forwards. The total resistance to movement over water can be divided into three components.

(a) aerodynamic resistance which varies as (velocity)^2 and includes components for both the vehicle and the cushion itself;

(b) wave-making resistance which has a peak at low speeds and then falls away to a negligible value;

(c) momentum resistance which varies linearly with speed. This resistance arises from the fact that the air drawn into the craft leaves it at zero velocity relative to the craft and has therefore experienced an overall change of momentum which is proportional to the craft's velocity.

It is interesting to compare the GEM with the hydrofoil craft as they appear as competitors for a number of applications. Such a comparison was made in Ref. 9 which included also semi-displacement planing forms. Each must be considered in the context of the intended service. It may be that a particular property of one craft, such as the amphibious nature of some GEMs, overrides all other needs.

The relative performance in terms of speed for a given power is much affected by the waves likely to be met on the route. High running costs for the craft itself may be justified if it provides that short passage time for which passengers are prepared to pay. The reference suggests, and presents pertinent data, performance parameters such as:

Specific power = (Power)/(All-up weight) (Sustained speed)

Speed coefficient = (Sustained speed)/(All-up weight)$^{\frac{1}{3}}$

Effective lift/drag ratio = (Overall propulsive efficiency) (Lift)/(Drag)

When power (P) is in h.p. weight (W) in tonf and speed (V) is in knots

$$\text{Specific power} = \frac{P}{WV} = 6 \cdot 88/\eta\left(\frac{\text{lift}}{\text{drag}}\right)$$

In wave conditions represented by a significant wave height given by $\frac{1}{2}$(All-up weight)$^{\frac{1}{3}}$, specific powers for a speed coefficient of 20 are approximately:

Submerged foils	1·1
Surface piercing foils	1·7
Amphibious hovercraft	2·1

Some particulars taken from the reference are reproduced in Table 16.4. The technology of these craft is changing rapidly and this may cause changes in relative advantages and disadvantages of the various craft.

Table 16.4

	Foilcraft Surface-piercing			Hovercraft Submerged/Amphibious			Non-Amphibious	
	PT20	PT50	PT150	Dolphin	SRN6	SRN4	HM2	VT1
All-up weight (Tonf)	27	63	165	67	7·8	175	18·5	(76)
Disposable load (Tonf), L	7	14	33	17	2·7	64	5·7	(27)
Passenger seats	75	100–140	250	116	38	600	60	324
Cruise speed (knots)	35	34	(35)	48	56	70	35	(48)
Service speed (knots), V_s	33·5	32·5	(33·5)	47·5	35	45	31	(42)
Installed power (hp)	1000	2200	6800	3600	900	13600	820	3700
First cost (£1,000)	125	250	667	585	110	1600	90	(390)
Cost/Disp. ton-knot $£/V_s L$	536	530	622	725	1165	560	510	(360)

Note: Figures in parenthesis indicate estimates.

Catamarans

In recent years, the catamaran sailing vessel has become increasingly popular and the size of the largest has been steadily increasing. It is intriguing to enquire whether large ocean-going ships of this type are technically feasible and economically attractive.

That medium-sized ships based on the catamaran principle are feasible is undeniable. Two twin-hull paddle steamers of about 90 m length were built in 1874 and 1877 for the cross channel service. Details of these ships, which are described in some detail in Ref. 11, are given in Table 16.5.

Table 16.5
Twin-hull paddle steamers

	Castalia	*Calais–Douvres*
Length, extreme	290 ft	300 ft
	(88·4 m)	(91·4 m)
Breadth of each hull	17 ft	18·25 ft
	(5·18 m)	(5·56 m)
Distance between hulls	26 ft	25·5 ft
	(7·92 m)	(7·77 m)
Draught, as designed	6·5 ft	6·63 ft
	(1·98 m)	(2·02 m)
Total area of section of both hulls	209·5 ft^2	230 ft^2
	(19·5 m^2)	(21·4 m^2)
Speed, knots	10·96	14·75
I.h.p.	1516	4300

The main reason for using a twin-hull design was apparently to improve seakeeping. Quoting from Ref. 11, they were built '...for the purpose of reducing the horrors of the middle passage to a minimum'. The *Castalia* was in the form of two half-hulls connected by a system of cross girders and driven by two paddle wheels placed in the parallel sided tunnel between the hulls. The *Calais–Douvres* had two complete hulls and this was a more resistful arrangement, although Ref. 12 suggests that the planform arrangement is not important provided the speed–length ratio is not too high.

Both ships had a good reputation for seakeeping; thus, roll did not exceed 5 degrees when other ships rolled to 15 degrees. The *Castalia* was only operated for a limited period, apparently because the service really needed a 14 knot ship. The *Calais–Douvres* was a success economically and operated successfully for many years including occasions when bad weather prevented conventional ships putting to sea.

Refs. 13 and 26 deal with more recent work. The first paper describes a preliminary design of a 141 ft (43 m) oceanographic vessel. As a result of this work, it is concluded (Fig. 16.11) that in the high speed/displacement range, the relatively fine hulls of the catamaran leads to reduced wave-making resistance which more than compensates for the increased frictional resistance associated with their extra wetted surface. A reasonable separation of the two hulls is about 1·25 times the beam of each. The comparison between conventional and catamaran forms is based on results for hulls of the same length and draught, the beam of the conventional hull being twice that of each hull of the catamaran. This is unfair on the conventional hull, in which it would normally be possible to obtain the required displacement by increasing both length and beam. This work supports the experience with the earlier ships that manoeuvrability is good.

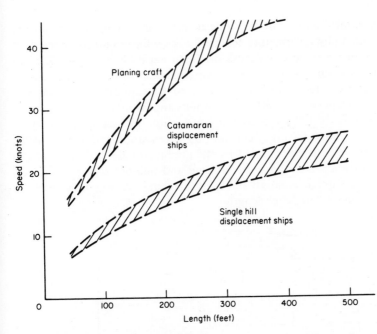

Fig. 16.11 Areas of favourable operation

A big advantage of the catamaran is a much enhanced deck area. Reference 13 claims that for the oceanographic vessel the cost would be 25 per cent more than for a conventional ship of the same displacement but 25 per cent less than one with the same deck area. At first sight, it would appear that the joining of the two hulls would present serious structural design problems but this is not so. Normal ship scantlings are adequate for the 'bridge' between the two hulls. For a given displacement, a larger dock is required than for a conventional form.

In summary, these ships are feasible but pose certain problems. Reference 26 discusses twin hull versions of a river cargo vessel, river waterbus, car ferry and container ship in comparison with conventional versions.

Aircraft carriers

The characteristics of an aircraft carrier are profoundly affected by the type of aircraft that it is required to operate, which may be fixed wing, deflected jet, vertical take off or helicopter. Unless the types and numbers of aircraft are known with some precision, the aircraft carrier will be larger and more expensive than it need be; there is a high price to pay for flexibility.

Fixed wing carriers are highly complex ships, often of 2000 compartments and carrying 4000 men. As well as all the domestic, navigational and machinery requirements associated with all surface ships, the aircraft carrier must operate, direct and maintain perhaps fifty complex aircraft. Fixed wing aircraft are catapulted by one of several catapults up to 100 m long at the fore end of the flight deck while the ship is steaming head to wind. Because they normally require a length for landing not available to them on a ship, the aircraft are retarded on landing by an arresting gear; a hook on the aircraft is directed on to a wire stretched transversely across the flight deck which is connected to a damping mechanism below. For both physiological and practical reasons, accelerations and decelerations higher than 5 or 6 g cannot be achieved and this gives minimum possible lengths for catapults and for arrester wire pull-out. To give flying speed of 120 knots to a 30 ton aircraft, for example, a catapult would need about 110 ft (30 m) of constant 6 g acceleration and 40,000 horse-power, some of which is contributed by the aircraft. Angle of descent of the aircraft and clearance over the stern, spacing and pull-out of arrester wires, centring gear and length of catapult and bridle catching gear thus all contribute in dictating minimum flight deck length.

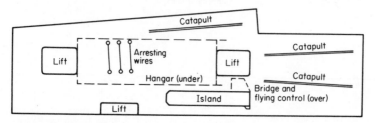

Fig. 16.12 Flight deck

Also accommodated by the flight deck are aircraft deck parks, fuelling positions, weapons areas, servicing positions, helicopter operating areas, landing aids and six or more aircraft and weapons lifts. The island itself, tradi-tionally on the starboard side, houses the bridge, flying control, action infor-mation centre, flight deck personnel and the long range radars and com-munications equipment for detecting and controlling aircraft many hundreds of miles away. Layout of the flight deck, in fact, determines the length of the ship (and thence displacement) fairly closely and the naval architect usually struggles to keep island size and flight deck length to a minimum. With an aircraft specified, however, his scope is limited.

The hangar below decks needs to be as wide and as long as possible and at least two decks high, even to accommodate aircraft with folded wings. Not only does this cause difficult access and layout problems for the rest of the ship, but it gives rise to some formidable structural problems, particularly if the hangar is immediately below the flight deck when the wide span grillages must support 30 ton aircraft landing on at high vertical deceleration.

At least thirty different piping systems are required, including flight deck fire main, fuelling, defuelling, air, hydraulics and liquid oxygen. Widespread maintenance facilities are required near the hangar for both aircraft and weapons. Underwater, a side protection system is fitted against mine and tor-pedo attack and armour is disposed around the vitals. The flight deck itself normally constitutes armour, although in some older carriers, this was relatively thin and the hangar was left open below it, armour being provided at hangar deck level.

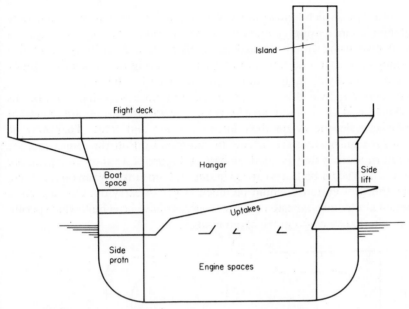

Fig. 16.13 Aircraft carrier section

Vertical take off aircraft provide somewhat similar problems except that catapults and arresting gear are not needed. Because these means of achieving take off and landing are then incorporated into the aircraft, smaller aircraft payloads are to be expected. While some noise insulation is needed in all carriers, deflected jet take off and landing create noise problems of much higher magnitude; these require special consideration and may mean that accommodation immediately below the flight deck is not possible. A problem associated with helicopters and VTOL aircraft arises with their vulnerability to gusts on landing and take off. They require smooth airflow and plenty of room.

Boats are stowed in pockets in the ship's side in order to keep the flight deck clear, together with items of ship's equipment, fairleads, capstans, etc. Accommodation arrangements in the ship are conventional except that additional spaces for aircrew such as briefing rooms, flying clothing cloakrooms and air intelligence spaces are needed.

Such is the power needed—over 200,000 s.h.p. for large carriers—that steam machinery plant is usual; a nuclear reactor avoids the need for frequent refuelling. A fleet train is needed for regular provisioning, of course, but an oiler is vulnerable.

Reference 14 gives some further information and an interesting history of development.

Bulk cargo carriers

The principal types of bulk cargo carrier are the oil tanker and the ore carrier, both single deck ships carrying the same predictable, homogeneous cargo throughout their length. Economics of trade has dictated a steady growth in size of both types which follow similar design patterns. Machinery is generally right aft and it is increasingly common to site all accommodation and navigation spaces aft, dispensing with the amidships superstructure. A walkway is provided in oil tankers to give safe fore and aft passage during heavy weather. Block coefficient is usually about 0·80 and economic speed 16–20 knots.

Oil tankers are divided by two longitudinal bulkheads in ships with beams up to 35 m (Lloyd's Rules) and three for greater beam. Ore carriers are somewhat more variable depending on their intended route and trade. They may be required for transporting ore in one direction and oil on the return journey or the return journey may be made in ballast. Figure 16.15 shows a typical ore carrier in which water ballast is carried in side and top tanks. When oil is carried, the side and bottom tanks would be much larger to carry oil. Ore and oil is not carried at the same time. Recently, ore carriers have been built which permit oil as an alternative cargo in the cargo holds.

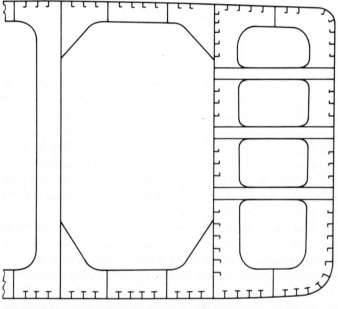

Fig. 16.14 Oil tanker midship section

Both transverse and longitudinal strength are of dominating importance in the design of bulk carriers especially large ones. This is discussed in Chapter 6 and in several of the references (e.g. 15, 16). Loading must be arranged to keep still water bending stress within the limits permitted by the classification societies. Often it is found economical to incorporate tanks or holds permanently empty in the length since the buoyancy they provide enables more cargo to be carried elsewhere, without exceeding permissible still water bending moment. Further-more, in the case of ore carriers, the metacentric height can become uncomfortably high without empty holds. Such empty holds introduce high shear forces. Plate longitudinals in the double bottom are consequently required for ore

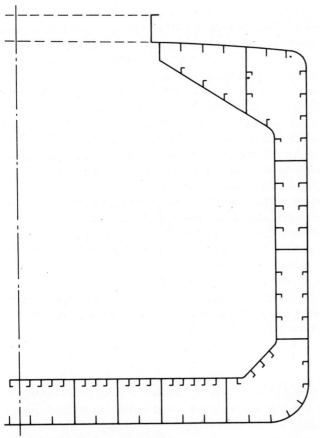

Fig. 16.15 Bulk carrier midship section

carriers, and empty tanks in oil tankers are staggered longitudinally from side to centre tanks.

With so many possibilities of creating strength and stability difficulties, the patterns of loading and unloading of these ships must be carefully controlled.

There are many other types of bulk carriers. Ships designed specifically for the bulk carriage of cars exist. Grain carriers, often affected by the need to sail the Great Lakes of North America are common. Grain carriers introduce special problems of stability due to the free surface effects of the grain. While shifting boards reduce the effects, large holds make these difficult to fit; covering the surface with bagged grain damps the free surface but does not remove the problem. Masters are required to take the ullages (i.e. height above the free surface) of the grain and to apply these to diagrams supplied by the Board of Trade for determining revised stability data. Expected angles of heel of the ship should not exceed 5 degrees when the grain has shifted to give a 12 degree surface after a 2 per cent settlement (see also Chapter 5). The bulk carriage of chemicals, molasses, vegetable oils and many other products, each brings its own problems.

A type of bulk carrier becoming of increasing importance is the liquefied natural gas carrier. Natural gas, predominantly methane, is given off in vast quantities in a few areas of the world, particularly at oilfields. For use in other countries, it needs to be transported economically. The gas is first liquefied by compressing it and cooling it to temperatures around minus 100°C in which condition it is pumped into transit tanks. Such tanks are isolated from the ship's structure by very thick insulation and the ship is fitted with double bottom and side protection. During its passage across the sea, certain of the gas boils off naturally either to waste or it may, economically, be used to help drive the ship, perhaps by gas turbine. To minimize this loss and avoid carrying refrigeration machinery, the ship needs to be fast and the characteristics of the ship are, again, determined by the economics of operation.

Material for the liquefield gas tanks must not be brittle at these very low temperatures—which render even rubber brittle. Suitable materials are certain aluminium alloys and some nickel steel alloys. It is very important, of course, to prevent the mild steel of the ship from being reduced in temperature by leakage of thc liquid, whereby it may become brittle (see Chapter 5 on brittle fracture). Reference 17 and later papers give more details of these ships.

Reference 18 discusses some other problems related to special liquid cargoes such as molasses, sulphuric acid and sulphur, including thermal stresses, explosive vapours and corrosive materials.

Fishing vessels

Fishing vessels are designed the world over to accord with the art of the fisher-man and the habits of the fish. Tradition and local marketing methods play a part in design too. There are perhaps three general classes of interest here, factory ships, drifters and trawlers.

Whaling boats are stout, stable boats which pursue and harpoon whales. Their catch is towed back to their parent factory ships, hauled up a shallow ramp or beach in the ship and disected. Glands secreting the valuable oils are taken to treatment rooms where the oils are removed, purified and pumped to storage tanks. Other treatment rooms deal with the meat and with further processes. Similar headquarters or factory ships exist for long range trawler fleets to remove oil from cod and halibut and also to store and treat the catches, manufacture ice and even to can some catches.

Drifters are, generally, small fishing vessels which catch those fish which live near the surface of the sea. They spread their nets between ships or from buoys and corks to derricks on the ships; with their engines cut they may drift with the tides or lie at anchor to make their catch. The herring and mackerel fleets of Europe and North America are typical.

Of particular interest to the naval architect is the commonest fishing vessel, the trawler. These ships drag behind them at a few knots, trawls which are long stocking-shaped nets open at one end. The trawl is let out on wires to the sea bottom where most of the fish around Europe and North America live. Heavy winches are needed to handle the huge trawls either from a gantry above a transom stern or from derricks over one side. The fish are landed on a sheltered area of deck, gutted and stowed below in the fish room, of which there is usually one, insulated, lined with aluminium, shelved and provided with ice trays. Trawlers suffer the worst of weather and are the subject of special provision in the freeboard regulations. They must be equipped with machinery of the utmost reliability since failure at a critical moment could endanger the ship. Both diesel and diesel-electric propulsion are now common. Ice accretion in the upperworks is a danger in certain weather, and a minimum value of $\overline{GM}$ of about 2·5 ft (0·75 m) is usually required by the owner. Good range of stability is also important and broaching to is an especial hazard.

To give adequate directional stability when trawling, experience has shown that considerable stern trim is needed, often as much as 5 degrees. Assistance in finding shoals of fish is given by sonar or echo sounding gear installed in the keel. No modern trawler is properly equipped without adequate radar, communication equipment and navigation aids. A typical stern fishing trawler is shown in Fig. 16.16.

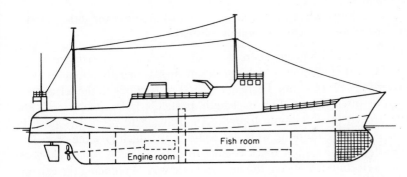

Fig. 16.16 Stern trawler

The trawler is the first type of ship for which a special analysis of resistance data has been produced. Reference 19 describes the production of this data by the regressional analysis of trawler forms for which tank tests have been made. A total resistance coefficient $C_R = RL/\Delta V^2$ is found to be a function of six geometrical parameters of the ship's form, L/B, B/T, C_m, C_P, longitudinal position of LCB and half angle of entrance of waterplane. From these, the e.h.p.$-V/\sqrt{L}$ curve can be produced to within an accuracy of a few per cent without the expense of tank tests. While the limited range of $V/\sqrt{L}$, displacement and form applicable to trawlers assisted the accuracy of the analysis, this represents an important breakthrough for the naval architect which may, with time, be applied to other forms, enabling optimum forms to be chosen with accuracy. Selection of the NPL standard range of propellers in conjunction with the trawler forms is also possible from the same data. As with tugs, this involves examination at two particular speeds for which ship conditions are different, viz. trawling speed and free running speed.

Tugs

Tugs are needed to pull dumb barges or cargo drones in inland waterways; they are needed to pull or push large ships in confined waters and docks, and they are needed to tow large ships on long ocean voyages. Tugs are broadly classified as inland, coastal or ocean, the largest of the ocean tugs approaching 1000 tonf (10 MN) in displacement. They often are capable of firefighting and salvage duties and may carry large capacity pumps for these purposes.

Apart from the requirements arising from the above, the main characteristics of tugs are:

(a) hull form and means of propulsion designed both for a given freerunning speed and a high thrust at zero speed (or bollard pull) or economical towing speed;
(b) upper deck layout to permit close access to ships with large overhang;
(c) a towing point above the longitudinal centre of lateral pressure, usually just aft of amidships on the centre line: the towing wire is often required to have a 180 degree clear sweep;
(d) good manoeuvrability;
(e) adequate stability when the towing wire is athwartships and either veering from a self rendering winch or about to break.

Hull form is based on normal considerations of minimum resistance for the maximum free running speed which, for ocean tugs, is usually about 20 knots and for river tugs 12–16 knots. There are several restrictions to the selection of form; there is often a restriction on length, particularly for inland craft and frequently a need for minimum draught. Air drawing to propellers must be prevented, usually by adopting wide flat sections aft which give the propellers physical protection as well. A block coefficient of 0·55–0·65 is usual. The form tends to be well rounded in consequence and one way of reducing the expense of such fabrication is to adopt a form composed of developable surfaces known as a *hydroconic form*. Reference 20 describes such a form and claims substantial reduction in fabrication costs. Resistance, despite several knuckle lines in the form, is not much higher than for a conventional form. The choice of propulsion unit is of fundamental importance because, like the trawler, there are two quite different conditions to meet, each at high efficiency—required free running speed and required bollard pull at zero speed or pull at towing speed. Choice of propulsion unit lies generally among the following:

(a) Paddle wheels. Paddle tugs are not uncommon. Feathering of the paddle blades to suit different wake conditions gives a high efficiency over a wide range of speeds and pulls although, because of the low immersion of the blades, air drawing and cavitation prevent really high performance: Manoeuvrability is good;
(b) Fixed propeller. Because of the different wake conditions (or slip) the efficiency of the propeller is poor at one of the two conditions. A Kort nozzle (see Chapter 10) flattens out the efficiency curve and can give an acceptable degree of efficiency at both conditions. If it pivots about a vertical

spindle a Kort nozzle also increases manoeuvrability. Twin propellers also increase manoeuvrability;

(c) Controllable pitch propeller. This meets all the range of wake conditions at efficiencies little below the maxima for the fixed propeller. First cost and maintenance are high but can well be justified in many cases;

(d) Vertical axis propeller. This is generally superior to the paddle wheel because of its increased immersion. It is directional and so increases manoeuvrability.

Upper deck layout is dictated by the need to get close in to a variety of vessels and by the need to keep the towing point above the longitudinal centre of lateral pressure so that a lateral pull has a minimum effect on manoeuvrability. The entire after half of the weather deck has only low obstructions and low bulwarks with tumble home and large freeing ports. Special towing hooks and slips are fitted. Superstructures are kept small and away from the sides where they might otherwise foul the attended ships. Hard wood fendering is fitted around the pushing areas and the structure inboard of these areas is reinforced.

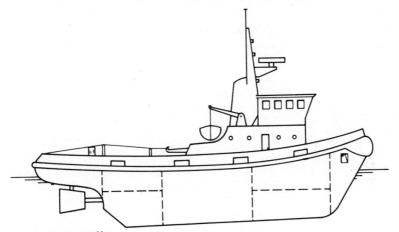

Fig. 16.17 Tug profile

A dangerous condition arises when the towing wire is horizontal and athwart-ships tending to capsize the tug. A self-rendering winch or a wire of known breaking strain limits the amount of the pull the tug must be capable of withstanding without undue heel. $\overline{GM}$s of 2 ft (0·6 m) are not unusual. Integral tug/barge systems can give good economy by creating higher utilisation of the propulsion section in association with several barges. The concept has been applied to combinations up to 35,000 tonne dead mass.

Offshore drilling rigs

Among the more unusual demands made upon the naval architect, is that for a mobile platform which can be held steady at any place in waters of up to 50–80 m depth in order to drill for oil or gas or for geological survey, pipe laying or other works. The need for these rigs is increasing with the world demand for increased power sources.

There is a wide variety of such craft, designed to the particular needs of an owner. The general trend is to operation in deeper and more exposed water. Although the rigs can cost several millions of pounds each they are more economical than, attempting to set up a series of fixed rigs. Two types are becoming common:

(a) platforms carried on submersible pontoons;
(b) platforms elevated on legs.

In the former type, the working platform may be at a fixed height above a pontoon which is sunk to the sea bottom into which locating piles are driven.

A large rig of this type designed for a depth of water of about 45 m would be about 60 m tall with 9 m diameter columns and a top deck with an area of some 4000 m². Alternatively, the rig may not touch the bottom. These submerged floating platforms become more economic in depths of 80 m or more. In the STAFLO drilling unit (Ref. 21) four large buoyancy chambers are submerged about 20 m in the operating conditions. These buoyancy chambers are connected by vertical stabilizing columns to the upper hull which is about 7 m above the water level. Such a rig displaces about 12,000 tonf (120 MN), carries a load of some 2500 tonf (25 MN) of equipment and has accommodation for sixty men. Model tests are carried out to study methods of anchoring and the stability of the platform in waves. Horizontal movements, pitch and heave cause bending moments in the drill pipe and have to be restricted to values depending on the depth of water.

The elevating deck type of rig is carried on legs which are driven downwards to the sea bottom where they are located by piles, enabling the platform to climb up the legs to the required height; often the lower ends of the mechanically operated legs are braced together by floodable pontoons. (Fig. 16.18).

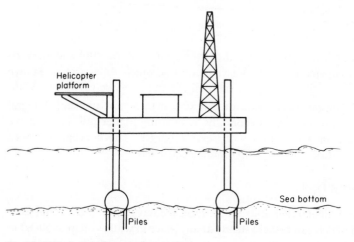

Fig. 16.18 Typical drilling platform, raised

Although some rigs are self-propelled propulsion is not a major consideration in design, although manoeuvrability under tow is very important. In addition to the mechanical design for drilling and elevating, the prime considerations of design are:

(a) stability under all conditions of operation and tow. A typical towing speed is $2\frac{1}{2}$ knots;
(b) strength and elastic stability of columns subject to the platform deadweight, tide forces, windage on the upperworks, wave action and drilling forces;
(c) strength of the platform subject to similar forces;
(d) launching arrangements;
(e) corrosion protection.

As the number of offshore rigs increases, so does the demand for vessels to service them; anchors have to be laid out; pipes, cement and other supplies have to be delivered in all weather conditions. The large multi-purpose support vessel is generally favoured because of its versatility. They need to be very manoeuvrable at low speed, for which bow thrust units are commonly fitted.

Yachts

For many years, the design, construction and sailing of yachts has been a fascinating art about which whole books are regularly published. This is because the science is too complex for precise solution—and indeed, few yachtsmen would wish it otherwise. Some tenable theories have, in fact, been evolved to help in explaining certain of the performance characteristics of sailing boats; Ref. 24 is the result of considerable investigation and gives further references.

A yacht, of course, obeys the fundamental theory described generally in this book for all surface ships. In addition, a yacht is subject to air forces acting on the sails and to water forces due to its peculiar underwater shape—forces which are negligible for ordinary surface ships. Sailing before the wind, a yacht is propelled by:

(a) the vector change of momentum of the wind, deflected by the sails;
(b) lift generated by the sails acting as aerofoils; because an aerofoil requires an angle of incidence, yachtsmen prefer sailing with wind on the quarter rather than dead astern, particularly when flying a spinnaker, to give them more thrust.

When sailing into the wind, the yacht is propelled only by a component of the lift due to the sails, acting as aerofoils. Lift and associated drag depend upon the set of the sails, their sizes, shapes, stretch and material, the angle of heel of the boat, the relative wind velocity and the presentation of the sails to the wind and to each other. Because the yacht does not quite point in the direction in which it is going and is also heeled, the hull too acts as an aerofoil, experiencing hydrodynamic lift and drag. These forces are shown in Fig. 16.19.

The transverse couple produced by air and water forces is reacted to by the hydrostatic righting moment to keep the boat in stable equilibrium. Large angle stability and dynamical stability are clearly of great importance.

Longitudinally, the relative position of hydrodynamic lift, the centre of lateral resistance and the lateral component of air lift determine whether the rudder carries weather helm, as shown in Fig. 16.19, or lee helm. Lee helm is dangerous because, if the tiller is dropped or the rudder goes free by accident, the boat

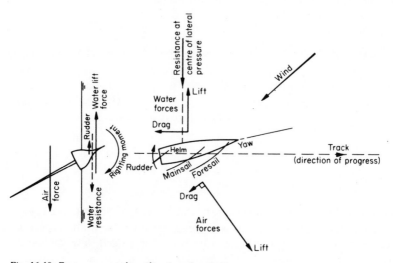

Fig. 16.19 Forces on a yacht sailing into the wind

will not come up into the wind but veer away and increase heel. Ideally, to minimize rudder drag, a yacht should carry slight weather helm in all attitudes and it is towards this 'balance' that yacht designers aim.

The resistance of a yacht calculated or measured in the manner conventional for surface ships, is not a very helpful guide to the yacht designer. Minimum resistance is required at small angles of yaw and small angles of heel, and these are different from the conventional figures. Resistance in waves is also of considerable importance and varies, of course, with the response of the boat to a particular sea—because of augment of resistance due to pitching, a yacht may well sail faster in Force 4 conditions than it does in Force 5, or better in the Portland Reaches than off Rhode Island.

A yacht designer must therefore achieve minimum resistance yawed, heeled and in waves, good longitudinal balance in all conditions and satisfactory stability. He must produce a rig which does not upset the longitudinal balance and which gives maximum performance for sail area permitted, in all conditions and direction of wind, particularly close to the wind. While some theory helps, the process overall remains much an art.

References

1. Turner, R. V., Harper, M. and Moor, D. I. Some aspects of passenger liner design. *TRINA*, 1963.
2. De Vito, Eugenio. Six recent atlantic liners. *TINA*, 1953.
3. Arentzen, E. S. and Mandel, P. Naval architectural aspects of submarine design. *TSNAME*, 1960.
4. Sims, A. J. British submarine design during the war (1939–45). *TINA*, 1947.
5. Crewe, P. R. and Hardy, D. J. The submarine ore carrier. *TRINA*, 1962.
6. Crewe, P. R. The hydrofoil boat: its history and future prospects. *TINA*, 1958.
7. Stanton Jones, R. *Some design problems of hovercraft*. Presented at the I.A.S. Annual Meeting in New York, Jan. 1961.
8. Crewe, P. R. and Eggington, W. J. The hovercraft—A new concept in maritime transport. *TRINA*, 1960.
9. Silverleaf, A. and Cook, F. A comparison of some features of high speed marine craft. *TRINA*, 1970.
10. Crago, W. A. Some notes on Hovercraft. *Transactions of the Society of Engineers (Incorporated)*. October, 1960.
11. Mackrow, G. C. On twin ship propulsion. *TINA*, 1879.
12. Saunders, H. E. *Hydrodynamics in ship design*, Vol. 2, 1965.
13. Michel, W. H. The sea-going catamaran ship—Its features and its feasibility, *International Shipbuilding Progress*, Vol. 8, No. 85, September, 1961.
14. Chapman, J. H. B. Development of the aircraft carrier. *TRINA*, 1960.
15. Kendrick, S. B. Structural design of supertankers. *TRINA*, 1970.
16. Murray, J. M. Large bulk carriers. *TIESS*, 1964–5.
17. Thomas, W. and Schwendner, A. LNG carriers: the state of the art. *TSNAME*, 1971.
18. Abrahamsen, E. Carriage of special liquid cargoes. *European Shipbuilding*, 1964 and 1965.
19. Doust, D. J. and O'Brien, T. P. Resistance and propulsion of trawlers. *TNECI*, 1958–9.
20. Corlett, E. C. B., Venus, J. and Gibson, C. H. The design, construction and operation of a class of twin screw tugs. *TINA*, 1958.
21. Pratt, W. and Roy, W. A. Offshore drilling barges. *TNECI*, 1959–60.
22. West, F. G. Practices and developments in off-shore oil exploration and production. *TIESS*, Vol. 108, 1964–5.
23. Field, A. J. and Thornburg, R. B. Development and operation of drilling vessels. *TIESS*, Vol. 107, 1963–4.
24. Crewe, P. R. Estimation of effect of sail performance on yacht close hauled behaviour. *TRINA*, 1964.
25. Marchaj, C. A. *Sailing theory and practice*. Adlard Coles, 1964.
26. Corlett, E. C. B. Twin-hulled ships. *TRINA*, 1969.
27. Aguirre, J. E. and Boyce, T. R. Estimation of wind forces on offshore drilling platforms. *TRINA*, 1974.
28. Hogben, N. Fluid loading on offshore structures. A state of the art appraisal: wave loads. *RINA Maritime Technology Monograph No. 1*, 1974.
29. Smith, C. S. Load prediction and stress analysis in relation to fatigue of ships and offshore structures. *The Naval Architect*, July, 1972.
30. Supply ships to meet the growing demands of the offshore industry. *The Naval Architect*, July 1974.
31. Hadler, J. and Hubble, E. Prediction of the power performance of series 62 planing forms. *TSNAME*, 1971.
32. Eames, M. C. and Jones, E. A. HMCS *Bras d'Or*—A 200-ton open-ocean hydrofoil ship, *TRINA*, 1971.
33. Eames, M. C. and Drummond, T. G. HMCS *Bras d'Or*—Sea trials and future prospects. *TRINA*, 1973.
34. Eddie, G. C. Technical developments in the fishing industry—work of the White Fish Authority. *TRINA*, 1971.
35. Meek, M. The first OCL container ships. *TRINA*, 1969.

Answers to Problems

Chapter 10

1. 781 N, 1·63 m/s, 4·05 × 10⁵.
2. 24·25, 27·64, 15·96, 12·37, 10·45 knots.
3. 34·2 knots, 19·7 knots.
4. 36 knots.
5. 0·524, 0·582, 13·4 MW.
6. 10·29 MW, 26·8 MW.
7. 28·14 knots.
8. 10·00, 12·11, 14·07 knots.
9. 28·257, 28·381, 28·370, 28·418, 28·319 knots.
10. 28·381 knots; 0·789, −0·453. 0·098, 0·034, −0·008.
11. 9·68 tonnef (94910 N).
12. 3465 hp, 0·97, 0·14.

Chapter 11

1. 12·54 knots.
2. $L = 233$ m, $B = 21·7$ m, $T = 7·2$ m, $\Delta = 200$ MN, 22·9 MW at 30 knots.
3. —.
4. 14 knots, 3·16 MW.
5. 35 per cent, 32·4 per cent.
6. 10,430 hp, 12,630 hp, $L = 493$ ft, $B = 80$ ft, $T = 29·5$ ft.
7. 28 knots.
8. 20,000 hp, 59,000 hp.
9. 14·3 ft, 24,000 s.h.p., 0·56, 16 ft, 229 r.p.m.
10. 9·09 ft, 0·716, 11·82 ft.
11. 21700 N/m², 769 r.p.m.
12. 550 r.p.m., 7·58 lbf, 9·12 lbf in.
13. 0·60, 0·961.
14. 11·95 tonf.
15. 21·45 lbf.
16. 448 r.p.m., 0·12, 0·110, 1·009.
17. 0·70, 2·45 m/sec.
18. 0·04, 0·0458, 0·66, 38,600 s.h.p.
19. 27·8 knots, 26·5 knots

Chapter 12

1. 3·39 m, 76·5 m, 10·93 m/s.
2. 8·69, 3·61, 3·47 secs.
3. 91½ degrees, 120½ degrees.
4. $a : b : c$ as $1 : \pi/2 : 4/\pi$.
5. 10·07 m.
6. 13·16 tonnef.
7. 3·71°, 5·00°, 0·93°, 16·5 s.
8. Heave = 0·41 (wave height) at $\omega_E = 0·60$.
9. $a = 0·083$, $b = 0·0079$; 3·62°.
10. —.

11. 8 degrees approx., 45 s.h.p.
12. 5·56.
13. $a = 0·12, b = 0·015.$
14. 2·03 m^2 s.
15. —.
16. 16 per cent.
17. 18·5 knots; 9·0 per cent, 41 per cent for $F = 25$ ft; 3·5 per cent, 25 per cent for $F = 30$ ft.
18. —.

Chapter 13

1. 0·222 MN m.
2. 3½ degrees.
3. 1·96 m.
4. 46·8 tonf, 2·82 ft.
5. 0·67 MN, 0·184 MN m.
6. 1·19 MN, 1·05 MN m.
7. —.
8. 51·6 tonf ft, 764 tonf ft.
9. 2·540 m^2, 2·127 m, 3·403 m^4, 0·0833 m^4.
10. $\pm 29°$ 20'.
11. 55·2, 47·3, 41·4 m^2.
12. 14·8 MN m.
13. A stable, B unstable; 19·4 m, 38·5 m.
14. 132 ft, 232 ft, 38 per cent.
15. 40 m, stable, 2·38 knots.

Chapter 14

11. 328 kN/m^2, 196 kN/m^2.
12. 112·7 MN/m^2 and 470 kW, 1·97 MN/m^2 and 8·2 kW.
13. 230 gal/min at 143 lbf/in^2; 23·2 kW for smooth pipes, 230 gall/min at 154 lbf/in^2; 25·6 kW for rough pipes.
14. 7200 Btu/hr, 3200 Btu/hr.
15. 10,700 J/s.
16. Approx. 13°F, about 1½ in^3.
17. About 2 Btu per lbf from 62/60 to 70/62·8.
18. Slope 0·49, off Coil 14/13, mix 30/23·6; 1·54 m^3/sec. (including fresh air) is one solution.
19. Approx. 11,000 ft^2.
20. (a) 64 per cent, (b) 57 per cent approx.
24. 30000 GT, 23232 NT, (a) the same, (b) 23307.

Chapter 15

1. 32,280; 10,905; 1092; 2636; 3711; 3812; 2969; 6500; 655 tonf.
2. 3257 tonf; 1160, 709, 789, 204, 330, 65 tonf.
3. 0·71, 2158 kW, 4·88 MN.
4. 601 ft, 87 ft, 59 ft, 0·56.

Index

Accommodation 553, 566
Active 377
Active fins 455
Active rudder 504
Active stabilizer systems 454
Active tank system 456
Active weights 455
Admiralty Experiment Works 371, 384
Advance 482
Advance coefficient 343
Ahead resistance coefficient 404
Air conditioning 535
Air drawing 618
Air, internal condition 325
Air purity 542
Aircraft carrier 611
Amplitude response operator 440
Analogue computer 515
Analysis pitch 355
Annual survey 594, 595
Appearance and layout 584
Appendage coefficient 344, 368, 370
Appendage resistance 352
Approximate formulae,
　centre of pressure 493
　group weights 577
　machinery power 577
　powering 361, 387, 394, 405
　principal dimensions 570
　roll period 430
　rudder force 490
Areas, curve of 415
Aspect ratio 492
Augment of resistance 367
Automatic control systems 507
Automatic pilot 507
Availability 589, 592
Axial inflow factor 362

Bacteria 537
Balanced reaction rudder 506
Bale capacity 560, 572
Bareboat charter 565
Basis ship 570
Beaches 465
Bernouilli, D 345
Bilge keels 457
Blade area ratio 355
Blade element theory 362
Block coefficient 470
Board margin of weight 577
Boats 550
Bollard pull 618
Boundary layer 349, 419
Boundary layer control 419

Bow rudder 502
BRITSHIPS 582
Brittle fracture 616
Broaching to 617
Bubble cavitation 365
Building drawings 580
Bulbous bow 470
Bulk carriers 613
Bunkering 544

Calais-Douvres 610
Camber, propeller 357
Canal effect 511
Cargo deadweight 556
Cargo drones 618
Cargo handling 548
Cargo ships 573
Cash flow 567
Castalia 610
Catamarans 609
Cathodic protection 545
Cavitation 364
Cavitation number 343
Cavitation tunnel 374, 392
Centre of lateral resistance 478, 484, 618, 619, 622
Centre of pressure 493
Certificates 594, 595
Characteristics 589
Charter 565
Circular notation 369
Circulation 363
Circulating water channel 380
Classification societies 528
Codag, Cosag, etc 523
Coil slope 540
Comparison, law of 370
Complements 553
Components of friction 345
Components of resistance, propulsion 343
Computers 469, 500, 515, 582, 585 589
Computer-aided design 582
Constant flow device 534
Container ships 548
Continuous survey 594
Contract design 580
Control surfaces 517
Control systems, automatic 507
Controllable pitch propeller 354, 357, 619
Correlation correction CA 397
Correlation of ship/model powers 344, 369, 395
Corresponding speed 370
Corrosion 545
Corrosion allowance 547

Cost benefit analysis 591
Cost effectiveness 591
Costs, repair 593
Critical path 589
Critical point 514
Critical speed 514
Cross coupling 468, 471
Cross section, effect on resistance 415
Crossflow drag coefficient 492
Curvature derivatives 500
Curve of areas 414

Damped motions 429
Dangerous cargoes 616
Davits 550
Deadmass 555, 573
Deadweight 555, 573
Deadweight/displacement ratio 573, 604
Deadweight scale, ratio, coefficient 556
De-ballasting 545
Decrement of roll 459
Delivered horsepower 367
Density 341
Dependency diagrams 589
Depreciation 567
Derricks 549
Design development 580, 586
Design economics 567
Design influence diagrams 587
Design method 590
Design, propeller 406
Design spiral 580
Design studies 569
Detail design 585
Developed blade area 354
Diesel machinery 523
Dieudonné spiral 486
Dimensional analysis 341
Dimensions, choice of principal 570
Directional stability 477, 488, 499, 617
Directional stability standards 488
Disc area 354
Discounted cash flow 567
Displacement 573
Drawing schedules 586
Drawings 586
Drift angle 482
Drifters 616
Drilling rigs 619
Ducted propellers 358
Ducting, air 542
Dynamic stability 477, 511, 602
Dynamic stability, design assessment 516

Economics 525, 567
Eddy making resistance 352
Eductors 545
Effective horsepower 344
Effective temperature 537
Electrical distribution 528
Electrical generation 527
Electro-chemical table 546
Elements of form diagram 384
Encounter frequency 437
Encounter spectrum 437
Endurance 416
Erosion 529
Exempted spaces 558
Expanded area ratio 355

Face cavitation 365
Face pitch 355
Factory ships 616
Failure rate 592
Ferries 598
Fins, active 455
Fins, fixed 457
Fishing vessels 616
Flap rudder 505
Flettner rudder 506
Fluid dynamics 341
Flyco 612
Following seas 442
Force on a rudder 494
From, choice of 578, 618
Form drag 352
Form, influence on seakeeping 470
Form resistance 352
Freeboard 449, 471
Friction in pipes 530
Frictional form resistance 351
Frictional resistance 349, 395
Froude constant notation 383
Froude number 342, 346, 348
Froude's law of comparison 370, 392
Fuel consumption 416, 524
Fuel systems, filling 542, 544
Functionals 518

Garbage grinders 545
Gas turbines 523
Gnomon rudder 502
Graf Zeppelin 505
Grain 615
Grain capacity 560, 572
Greyhound trials 377
Gross tonnage 557
Ground effect machine 606
Group weights 576, 578
Guided missile destroyer 571, 584

Haslar formula 399
Heat transfer 538
Heave 426, 428
Heeling during turn 484, 489
Helicopters 613
High speed stability 512
Horsepower 344, 367, 369
Horsepower, effective 344
Hotel load 416
Hovercraft 606
Hull efficiency 367, 368
Hull efficiency elements 367
Hull roughness measure 379
Hydraulic propulsion 359
Hydroconic form 618
Hydrofoil craft 604

Ice accretion 617
Icebreakers 526
IMCO (Inter-Governmental Maritime Consultative Organization) 557
Impressed current protection 547
Impulse response functions 472
Impulse wave testing 464
Incidence controlled foils 604
Inclining experiment 600
Index path, circuit 531
Influence diagrams 553

Information systems 593
Initial response to rudder 486
Inst of Oceanographic Sciences 467
Insulated capacity 572
Insulation 539
Interaction between ships 509
Interaction, ship and propeller 366
Internal volume 570
Iris correction 372
Isochronous rolling 428
ITTC correlation line 395, 397
ITTC spectra 464, 443

Jackstay 550
Jet propulsion 359
Joessel formula 493

Kelvin 346
Kempf manoeuvre 486
Kinematic viscosity 342
Kitchen rudder 504
Kort nozzle 618

Laminar flow 350
Latent heat 537
Lateral thrust units 502
Law of comparison 370, 392
Layout, design 584
Lee helm 622
Lenin 527
Lifting surface theory 419
Line out 587
Liquefied gas carriers 616
Load factor 368
Longitudinal strength 471, 614
Losses in pipes 530
Lucy Ashton trials 377, 395

Mach number 342
Machinery 523
Machinery, compatability with propeller 416
Machinery power 577
Magnification factor 432
Magnus effect 506
Main hump 348
Maintainability 592
Manoeuvrability 476
Manoeuvre, zig-zag, spiral 468, 498
Manoeuvring standards 488
Manoeuvring tank 465, 498
Manoeuvring trials 500
Material management 592
Measured mile 375
Measurement 555
Memory effect 518
Methodical series 390, 407, 414, 470, 579
Model self-propulsion point 373
Model testing 370, 463, 498
Model testing,
    cavitation tunnel 374
    directional stability 499
    hull efficiency elements 372
    propellers, open water 373
    resistance 371
    seakeeping 464
    submarines 515
    turning, manoeuvring 498
Momentum resistance 608
Momentum theory, propeller 360

Moorson system 557
Motion in waves 431, 436
MTBF 592

NACA 0015 section 491
Natural gas carriers 616
Net tonnage 557, 560
Net present value 567
Networks 588
Neutral point 480, 513
Noise 613
Nomenclature xiii
NSRDC 466
Nuclear power 526

Oblique seas, motion in 442
Oertz rudder 506
Offshore drilling rigs 619
Oil pollution 543, 544
Oil tankers 613
Operating characteristics 566
Operator, response amplitude 440
Opportunity cost 567
Ore carriers 613
Ore carriers, submarine 602
Orifice plates 531
Otto Hahn 527
Overdeck tonnage 558
Overload fraction 368
Overshoot 486, 489, 507

Paddle wheel 360, 618
Paddle wheel effect 508
Painting 545
Passenger certificate 594
Passenger ships 573, 579, 593, 597
Passive stabilizer systems 454
Penelope 377, 378
Performance, stabilizers 458
Personnel heat 537
Phase angle 432
Pi theorem 342
Pipe erosion 529
Piping systems 529
Pitching 426, 428
Pivoting point 483
Planar motion mechanism 500
Planned maintenance 593
Pleuger active rudder 504, 515
Polyox 419
Power estimation 392
Power estimation, Froude 393
Power in waves 424, 446
Powering 383, 602
Powering of ships 340, 383
Pressure field 509
Prismatic coefficient 414, 470
Prismatic hump 348
Procedure charts 586
Propeller, compatability 416
Propeller, controllable pitch 354
Propeller data 389
Propeller design 406
Propeller design diagram 410
Propeller, dimensions 407
Propeller efficiency 362, 368, 389
Propeller strength 416
Propulsion components 343
Propulsion device 353

Propulsive coefficient   344, 367, 386
Psychrometric chart   537

Quasi-propulsive coefficient   368
QPC factor   368

Radius of gyration   470
Rake, propeller   356
Random process theory   471
Refrigeration machinery   536
Refuelling   543
Register tonnage   557
Regressional analysis   387, 617
Relative rotative efficiency   366
Reliability   589, 591
Replenishment   549
Required freight rate   568
Requirements, ship   565
Residuary resistance   353, 387
Resistance   342
Resistance,
    air   352, 402
    appendage   352
    eddy making   352
    form   352
    frictional   349
    frictional form   351
    residuary   353
    wavemaking   345
Resistance coefficients   342, 343, 383
Resistance data presentation   383
Resistance, dimension changes   397
Resistance, effect of form   413
Resistance in pipes   530
Resistance prediction   392
Resistance tests   370
Resistance test facilities   371
Resistance, time out of dock   399
Response curves, ship motions   436
Response operators   440
Reversal speed   514
Revolutions, propeller   342
Reynolds' number   342, 350, 530
Ring mains   534
Rise of floor   579
Roll, approximate period   430
Roll on, roll off   548
Rolling in still water   426, 427
Rolling in waves   431
Rotating arm   465, 500, 515
Rotating cylinder rudder   506
Roughness, effect on resistance   351
Rudder   481
Rudder force   489
Rudder torque   494
Rudders, special types   504

Safety certificate   594
Sailing boats   621
Seakeeping   424
Seakeeping basins   465
Sensible heat ratio   539
Service requirements   591
Sewage systems   545
Shadow price   568
Shaft transmission efficiency   368
Shallow water effects   511
Sheet cavitation   365
Shelter deck ships   557

Shipborne wave recorder   467
Ship design   564
Ship handling   508
Ship-model correlation   369, 498
Ship motion   424, 426
Ship motion trials   466
Ship routing   425
Ship tank   370, 499
Ship trials   375, 466, 500
Shipborne wave recorder   467
Shrouded propeller   358, 619
Similarity   341
Simulator   508, 516
Singing propeller   365
Siporters   549
Skew back   356
Skin friction correction   394
Slamming   425, 453
Slip   355
Slip ratio   355
Smelling the ground   511
Smith correction, effect   467
Space estimates   510, 554
Spade rudder   502
Special surveys   594
Spectra, wave   437
Spectrum, encounter   439
Spectrum, motion   440
Speed coefficient   386
Speed in waves   424, 446
Speed, loss on turn   484, 489
Speed trials   375
Spiral, design   580
Spiral manoeuvre   486, 498
Squat   511
Stability and control, submarines   511
Stability derivatives   479, 499, 514, 517
Stability index   480, 489, 512
Stability standards   617
Stabilizers   425, 454
Stabilizer trials   468
Staff requirements   565
Stalling, rudder   490
Statistical analysis, resistance   387, 617
Steam machinery   523
Streamline rudders   506
Strength, propellers   416
Strip theory   469
Submarine ore carrier   602
Submarine trials   515
Submarines, stability and control   511, 599
Supercavitating propellers   365
Support functions, design   587
Surface film resistance   538
Surface piercing foils   604
Surface tension   341
Surge   426, 445
Surveys   594
Sway   426, 446
Systems   528

Tactical diameter   483, 488
Tank capacity   572
Tankers   572
Taylor, resistance data   385
Theory, seakeeping   469
Thermal conductivity   538
Threshold of comfort   537
Through costing   567

Thrust 342
Thrust coefficient 343, 389
Thrust deduction factor 367
Thrust horsepower 367
Time preference 567
Tip vortex cavitation 365
Tonnage 542, 560
Tonnage formulae 560
Tonnage mark 559
Torque 342
Torque coefficient 343, 389
Torque, rudder 494
Towing tanks 371
Transfer 483
Transfer of weights 461
Transient wave testing 464
Transition 350
Trawlers 616
Trial, manoeuvring 500
Trial, speed 375
Trials, ship motion 463
Trials, submarine 515
Trimming and inclining experiment 600
Triplets 416
Trunk sizing 542
Tugs 618
Tug/barge systems 619
Tun 556
Tuning factor 432
Turbulent flow 350
Turning at slow speed 508
Turning circle 482, 498, 501
Turning rate 489
Turning trial 500
Twin hull ships 609
Type ship 570
Types of rudder 502

Ullages 615
Unbalanced rudder 502
Undamped motions 427
Underdeck tonnage 557
Union purchase 548
Unitized machinery 524
Utility 591

Value engineering 591
Value for money 591
Vapour pressure 341
Velocity of sound 341
Ventilation 535
Vertical axis propeller 357 505, 619,
Viscosity 341
Viscosity, kinematic 342
Viscous pressure resistance 345,352
Voith-Schneider propeller 357, 505
Vortex 363
VTOL aircraft 613
Vulnerability 524

Wake 366
Wake, Froude, Taylor 366
Wake adapted propeller 380
Waste disposal 545
Water systems 536
Wave breaking resistance 352
Wave patterns 346
Wave recorder 467
Wavemakers 465
Wavemaking resistance 345, 415
Wave resistance calculation 419
Weapons 550
Weather deck layout 579
Weather helm 622
Weber number 342
Weight equation 575
Wetness 425, 449
Wetted length 414
Wetted surface coefficient 388, 394
Whaling boats 616
Wind propulsion, 360
Wind resistance 352, 402
Work study 590

Yachts 621
Yaw 426, 446
Yield 568

Ziz-zag manoeuvre 486, 498